_____Stanley Gibb

CW00585114

NEW ZEAL
CONCISE
STAMP CATALOGUE

First edition, 1990

Stanley Gibbons Publications Ltd
London and Ringwood

By Appointment to Her Majesty The Queen
Stanley Gibbons Ltd., London
Philatelists

Published by **Stanley Gibbons Publications Ltd.**
Editorial, Sales Offices and Distribution Centre:
5 Parkside, Christchurch Road, Ringwood,
Hants BH24 3SH

First Edition – March 1990

© Stanley Gibbons Publications Ltd., 1990

ISBN: 0–85259–238–8

Item No. 2893 (90)

Made and printed in Great Britain by Black Bear Press Limited, Cambridge, England

THE NEW ZEALAND CONCISE CATALOGUE

First Edition

The stamps of New Zealand have always been popular as they provide something for everyone. The specialist is attracted to the beauty of the Chalon Heads, the researcher to the complexities of the later Queen Victoria issues and the King George V papers, and the ordinary collector to the array of modern stamps. New Zealand has used a wide range of designers and stamp printers with the result that the contrasting styles provide additional interest to the most straightforward collection of its stamps.

To cater for the many existing collectors, and to encourage more interest in these issues, we are pleased to publish the *New Zealand Concise Catalogue*. This is the third volume in this new series which provides "one country" listings enhanced beyond the scope of our standard *Part 1 (British Commonwealth)* volume. In addition to New Zealand this volume in the *Concise* range also covers issues from Cook Islands with Aitutaki and Penhryn, Niue, Ross Dependency, Tokelau and Western Samoa (to 1961).

The listings are based on those from the *Part 1 (British Commonwealth)* catalogue using the same internationally-recognised SG catalogue numbers. Additional features in the *New Zealand Concise* include:

Inverted watermarks and similar varieties from 1874 with many listed for the first time.

1882–1900 issue revised to include the popular "Adson" stamps.

Commemorative and Health Stamp First Day Cover prices from 1924 onwards and for definitive stamps from 1970.

Counter Coil Pairs listed for King George VI (for the first time) and Queen Elizabeth II definitives.

Presentation Packs, Souvenir Packs and Post Office Yearbooks.

P.O. Postcards.

Stamp Booklets from 1901 onwards.

We continue to provide both unmounted and mounted mint prices for the King George VI period and the helpful Design Index for stamps issued from 1946 onwards is also included.

Prices have been revised with a special effort being made to quote them for the many new listings. We are most grateful for the assistance of Campbell Paterson Ltd. in providing this information.

Other volumes in the *Concise* range have been warmly welcomed and we hope that New Zealand collectors will also appreciate the many advantages provided by this new catalogue.

David J. Aggersberg

Stanley Gibbons International Ltd.

HEAD OFFICE, 399 STRAND, LONDON WC2R 0LX

Auction Room and Specialist Departments. Open Monday–Friday, 9.30 a.m. to 5 p.m.

Shop: Open Monday–Friday 9.30 a.m. to 6 p.m. and Saturday 10 a.m. to 4.00 p.m.
Telephone 01 (071 from May 1990) 836 8444 and Telex 28883 for all departments.

RINGWOOD OFFICE

Stanley Gibbons Publications, Parkside, Christchurch Road, Ringwood, Hants BH24 3SH.
Telephone 0425 472363. Telex 41271.

OVERSEAS BRANCHES

Stanley Gibbons (Australia) Pty. Ltd., P.O. Box 863J, Melbourne 3001, Australia.
Telephone (01 0613) 670-3332 and Telex AA 37223.

Stanley Gibbons (Singapore) Pte Ltd., Marina Square, P.O. Box 0001, Singapore, Republic of Singapore.
Telephone 336 1998 and Telex RS 38398 SINGSG.

Contents

Specialist Philatelic Societies

New Zealand Society of Great Britain. General Secretary—Mrs. M. Frankcom, Queens House, 34a Tarrant Street, Arundel, West Sussex BN18 9DJ.

Pacific Islands Study Circle of Great Britain. Secretary—Mr. J. D. Ray, 21 Woodvale Avenue, London SE25 4AE.

STANLEY GIBBONS PUBLICATIONS LIMITED
OVERSEAS REPRESENTATION

Stanley Gibbons Publications Ltd. are represented overseas by the following sole distributors (*) and main agents (**)

Australia*
Lighthouse Philatelic (Aust.) Pty Ltd
Box 62
Chippendale 2008
New South Wales
Australia

Belgium and Luxembourg*
Philac
Rue du Midi 48
Bruxelles
Belgium 1000

Canada*
Lighthouse Publications (Canada)
  Ltd.
255 Duke Street
Montreal
Quebec
Canada H3C 2M2

Denmark*
Nordfrim
DK 5450
Otterup
Denmark

Finland*
Suomen Poskimerkkeily OY
Ludvigin Katu 5
SF-00130 Helsinki
Finland

France*
Davo France SARL
30 Rue de Gren Elle
75007 Paris
France

West Germany (incl. West Berlin and
  Austria)*
Ka-Be Briefmarkenalben-Verlag
Volkhardt GMBH
Daimlerstrasse 15
Goppingen
West Germany

Hong Kong*
Po-on Stamp Service
GPO Box 2498
Hong Kong

Israel*
Capital Stamps
PO Box 3749
Jerusalem 91036
Israel

Italy
Secrian Srl
Via Pantellaria 2
I–20156 Milano
Italy

Japan*
Japan Philatelic Co Ltd
PO Box 2
Suginami-Minami
Tokyo
Japan

Netherlands*
Davo Publications
PO Box 411
7400 AK Deventer
Netherlands

New Zealand*
Philatelic Distributors Ltd
PO Box 863
New Plymouth
New Zealand

Norway*
Wennergren-Cappelen AS
Nedre Vollgate 4
PO Box 738
Sentrum N-0105
Oslo 1
Norway

South Africa*
Stanley Gibbons (Pty) Ltd
PO Box 930
Parklands
RSA 2121

Republic Coin and Stamp
  Accessories (Pty) Ltd
PO Box 260325
Excom 2023
Johannesburg
RSA

Sweden*
Chr Winther Soerensen AB
Box 43
S-310 Knaered
Sweden

Switzerland*
Dove of Basle
Birsigstrasse 111
4011 Basle
Switzerland

USA*
Lighthouse Publications Inc
274 Washington Avenue
Hackensack
New Jersey 07601
USA

West Indies/Caribbean*
Hugh Dunphy
PO Box 413
Kingston 10
Jamaica
West Indies

Prices

The prices quoted in this catalogue are the estimated selling prices of Stanley Gibbons Ltd at the time of publication. They are, *unless it is specifically stated otherwise*, for examples in fine condition for the issue concerned. Superb examples are worth more; those of a lower quality considerably less.

All prices are subject to change without prior notice and Stanley Gibbons Ltd may from time to time offer stamps below catalogue price in consequence of special purchases or particular promotions.

No guarantee is given to supply all stamps priced, since it is not possible to keep every catalogued item in stock.

Quotation of prices. The prices in the left-hand column are for unused stamps and those in the right-hand column are for used.

A dagger (†) denotes that the item listed does not exist in that condition and a blank, or dash, that it exists, or may exist, but no market price is known.

Prices are expressed in pounds and pence sterling. One pound comprises 100 pence (£1 = 100p).

The method of notation is as follows: pence in numerals (e.g. 5 denotes five pence); pounds and pence up to £100, in numerals (e.g. 4·25 denotes four pounds and twenty-five pence); prices above £100 expressed in whole pounds with the "£" sign shown.

Unused and Used stamps. The prices for unused stamps of Queen Victoria to King George V are for lightly hinged examples. King George VI mint stamps (1937–52) are priced in both unmounted (left-hand column) and mounted (centre column) condition. Mint stamps of the present reign are priced in unmounted condition only (though when not available, mounted mint stamps are often supplied at a lower price). The used prices are normally for stamps postally used, but may be for stamps cancelled-to-order where this practice exists.

Prices quoted for bisects on cover or on large piece are for those dated during the period officially authorised.

Minimum price. The minimum price quoted is five pence. This represents a handling charge rather than a basis for valuing common stamps, for which the 5p price should not be reckoned automatically, since it covers a variation in real scarcity.

Set prices. Set prices are generally for one of each value, excluding shades and varieties, but including major colour changes. Where there are alternative shades, etc., the cheapest is usually included. The number of stamps in the set is always stated for clarity.

The mint prices for sets containing *se-tenant* pieces are based on the prices quoted for such combinations, and not on those for the individual stamps. The used set price is for single stamps.

Used on Cover prices. To assist collectors, cover prices are quoted for issues up to 1945 at the beginning of each country.

The system gives a general guide in the form of a factor by which the corresponding used price of the loose stamp should be multiplied when found in fine average condition on cover.

Care is needed in applying the factors and they relate to a cover which bears a single of the denomination listed; strips and blocks would need individual valuation outside the scope. If more than one denomination is present the most highly priced attracts the multiplier and the remainder are priced at the simple figure for used singles in arriving at a total.

The cover should be of non-philatelic origin, bearing the correct postal rate for the period and distance involved and cancelled with the markings normal to the offices concerned. Purely philatelic items have a cover value only slightly greater than the catalogue value for the corresponding used stamps. This applies generally to those high-value stamps used philatelically rather than in the normal course of commerce.

Oversized covers, difficult to accommodate on an album page, should be reckoned as worth little more than the corresponding value of the used stamps. The condition of a cover affects its value. Except for "wreck covers", serious damage or soiling reduce the value where the postal markings and stamps are ordinary ones. Conversely, visual appeal adds to the value and this can include freshness of appearance, important addresses, old-fashioned but legible handwriting, historic town-names, etc. The prices quoted are a base on which further value would be added to take account of the cover's postal historical importance in demonstrating such things as unusual, scarce or emergency cancels, interesting routes, significant postal markings, combination usage, the development of postal rates, and so on.

First Day Cover prices. Prices are quoted for commemorative first day covers from 1929 onwards. These prices are for special covers (from 1945) franked with complete sets and cancelled by ordinary operational postmarks or the various standard "First Day of Issue" markings.

The New Zealand Post Office introduced its own Bureau first day covers from October 1969 and from that date prices are for such covers *except* for the Health miniature sheets which only exist on private or charity covers.

Prices for constant varieties. Prices are for unmounted mint single stamps, unless otherwise stated. Prices are not quoted for used stamps, since varieties tend not to be collected in this condition.

When ordered in pairs or positional blocks the extra stamps are charged at the prices of normals.

Guarantee

All stamps are guaranteed genuine originals in the following terms:

If not as described, and returned by the purchaser, we undertake to refund the price paid to us in the original transaction. If any stamp is certified as genuine by the Expert Committee of the Royal Philatelic Society, London, or by B.P.A. Expertising Ltd, the purchaser shall not be entitled to make any claim against us for any error, omission or mistake in such certificate.

Consumers' statutory rights are not affected by the above guarantee.

The recognised Expert Committees in this country are those of the Royal Philatelic Society, 41 Devonshire Place, London W1N 1PE, and B.P.A. Expertising Ltd, P.O. Box 163, Carshalton Beeches, Surrey SM5 4QR. They do not undertake valuations under any circumstances and fees are payable for their services.

Printers

B.D.T.	B.D.T. International Security Printing Ltd, Dublin, Ireland.
B.W.	Bradbury Wilkinson & Co, Ltd.
Courvoisier	Imprimerie Courvoisier S.A., La-Chaux-de-Fonds, Switzerland
D.L.R.	De La Rue & Co, Ltd, London, and (from 1961) Bogota, Colombia.
Enschedé	Joh. Enschedé en Zonen, Haarlem, Netherlands.
Format	Format International Security Printers, Ltd, London.
Harrison	Harrison & Sons, Ltd, High Wycombe.
J.W.	John Waddington Security Print, Ltd, Leeds
Questa	Questa Colour Security Printers, Ltd, London.
Walsall	Walsall Security Printers, Ltd.
Waterlow	Waterlow & Sons, Ltd, London.

General Abbreviations

Alph	Alphabet
Anniv	Anniversary
Brt	Bright (colour)
C, c	Chalky paper
C.	Overprinted in carmine
Des	Designer; designed
Dp	Deep (colour)
Eng	Engraver; engraved
Horiz	Horizontal; horizontally
Imp, Imperf	Imperforate
Inscr	Inscribed
L	Left
Litho	Lithographed
Lt	Light (colour)
mm	Millimetres
MS	Miniature sheet
O, o	Ordinary paper
Opt(d)	Overprint(ed)
P, Pf or Perf	Perforated
Photo	Photogravure
Pl	Plate
Pr	Pair
Ptd	Printed
Ptg	Printing
PVA	Polyvinyl alcohol (gum)
R	Right
R.	Row
Recess	Recess-printed
T	Type
Typo	Typographed
Un	Unused
Us	Used
Vert	Vertical; vertically
W or wmk	Watermark
Wmk s	Watermark sideways

(†) = Does not exist.

(—) (or blank price column) = Exists, or may exist, but no market price is known.

/ between colours means "on" and the colour following is that of the paper on which the stamp is printed.

Contacting the Catalogue Editor

The Editor is always interested in hearing from people who have new information which will improve or correct the Catalogue. As a general rule he must see and examine the actual stamps before they can be considered for listing; photographs or photocopies are insufficient evidence.

Submissions should be made in writing to the Catalogue Editor, Stanley Gibbons Publications Ltd. The cost of return postage for items submitted is appreciated, and this should include the registration fee if required.

Where information is solicited purely for the benefit of the enquirer, the Editor cannot undertake to reply if the answer is already contained in these published notes or if return postage is omitted. Written communications are greatly preferred to enquiries by telephone and the Editor regrets that he or his staff cannot see personal callers without a prior appointment being made. Correspondence may be subject to delay during the production period of each new edition.

Please note that the following classes or material are outside the scope of this Catalogue:

(a) Non-postal revenue or fiscal stamps.
(b) Postage stamps used fiscally.
(c) Local carriage labels and private local issues.
(d) Punctured postage stamps (perfins).
(e) Telegraph stamps.
(f) Bogus or phantom stamps.
(g) Railway or airline letter fee stamps, bus or road transport company labels.
(h) Postal stationery cut-outs.
(i) All types of non-postal labels and souvenirs.
(j) Documentary labels for the postal service, e.g. registration, recorded delivery, airmail etiquettes, etc.
(k) Privately applied embellishments to official issues and privately commissioned items generally.
(l) Stamps for training postal staff.

We regret we do not give opinions as to the genuineness of stamps, nor do we identify stamps or number them by our Catalogue.

Philatelic Information

CATALOGUE NUMBERS

The catalogue number appears in the extreme left column. The boldface Type numbers in the next column are merely cross-reference to illustrations. Catalogue numbers in the Gibbons *Stamp Monthly* Supplement are provisional only and may need to be altered when the lists are consolidated.

Our catalogue numbers are universally recognised in specifying stamps and as a hallmark of status.

Subsidiary classes of stamps are placed at the end of each country as separate lists, with a distinguishing prefix letter, for example D for postage due or O for official, in the catalogue number. Stamp booklets are also at the end of the country and have B numbers.

Inverted and other watermark varieties incorporate "Wi" within the number. Other items which only appear in the *New Zealand Concise* incorporate "Ea", etc.

CATALOGUE ILLUSTRATIONS

Stamps are illustrated at three-quarters linear size. Stamps not illustrated are the same size and format as the value shown, unless otherwise indicated. Overprints, surcharges and watermarks are normally actual size. Illustrations of varieties are often enlarged to show the detail.

BOOKLET STAMPS

Single stamps from booklets are listed if they are distinguishable in some way (such as design or watermark) from similar sheet stamps.

Se-tenant pane

Booklet panes are listed where they contain stamps of different denominations *se-tenant*, where stamp-size labels are included, or where such panes are otherwise identifiable. Booklet panes are placed in the listing under the lowest denomination present.

COIL STAMPS

Stamps only issued in coil form are given full listing. If stamps are issued in both sheets and coils, the coil stamps are listed separately only where there is some feature (e.g. watermark or perforation) by which single stamps can be distinguished.

Examples of the numbered gutter pairs from counter coils introduced in 1945 are listed in this catalogue.

COLOUR IDENTIFICATION

The 100 colours most used for stamp identification are given in the Stanley Gibbons Colour Guide; these, plus a further 100 variations for more specialised use, are included in the Stanley Gibbons Stamp Colour Key. The Catalogue has used the Guide and Key as standards for describing new issues for some years. The names are also introduced as lists are rewritten, though exceptions are made for those early issues where traditional names have become universally established.

In compound colour names the second is the predominant one, thus:

orange-red = a red tending towards orange;

red-orange = an orange containing more red than usual.

When comparing actual stamps with colour samples in the Guide or Key, view in a good north daylight (or its best substitute: fluorescent "colour-matching" light). Sunshine is not recommended. Choose a solid portion of the stamp design; if available, marginal markings such as solid bars of colour or colour check dots are helpful. Shading lines in the design can be misleading as they appear lighter than solid colour. Furthermore, the listings refer to colours as issued: they may deteriorate into something different through the passage of time.

Shades are particularly significant when they can be linked to specific printings, in general, shades need to be quite marked to fall within the scope of this Catalogue.

Modern colour printing by lithography is prone to marked differences of shade, even within a single run, and variations can occur within the same sheet. Such shades are not listed.

The listings use the following abbreviations for stamp colours: bl (blue); blk (black); brn (brown); car, carm (carmine); choc (chocolate); clar (claret); emer (emerald); grn (green); ind (indigo); mag (magenta); mar (maroon); mult (multicoloured); mve (mauve); ol (olive); orge (orange); pk (pink); pur (purple); scar (scarlet); sep (sepia); turq (turquoise); ultram (ultramarine); verm (vermilion); vio (violet); yell (yellow).

Overprints and surcharges are in black unless otherwise stated. The following abbreviations may be used to describe overprint or surcharge colours: (B.) = blue, (Blk.) = black, (Br.) = brown, (C.) = carmine, (G.) = green, (Mag.) = magenta, (Mve.) = mauve, (Ol.) = olive, (O.) = orange, (P.) = purple, (Pk.) = pink, (R.) = red, (Sil.) = silver, (V.) = violet, (Vm.) or (Verm.) = vermilion, (W.) = white, (Y.) = yellow.

ERRORS OF COLOUR

Major colour errors in stamps or overprints which qualify for listing are: wrong colours; albinos (colourless impressions), where these have Expert Committee certificates; colours completely omitted, but only on unused stamps (if found on used stamps the information is usually footnoted) and with good credentials, missing colours being frequently faked.

Colours only partially omitted are not recognised. Colour shifts, however spectacular, are not listed.

DATES OF ISSUE

Where local issue dates differ from dates of release by agencies, "date of issue" is the local date. Fortuitous stray usage before the officially intended date is disregarded in listing.

DESIGNERS

Designers' names are quoted where known, though space precludes naming every individual concerned in the production of a set. In particular, photographers supplying material are usually named only when they also make an active contribution in the design stage; posed photographs of reigning monarchs are, however, an exception to this rule.

FIRST DAY COVERS

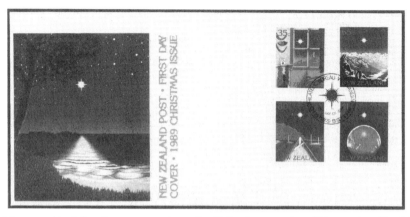

This catalogue provides listings for commemorative and health first day covers from 1929 onwards and for definitives from the introduction of the full New Zealand Philatelic Bureau Service in 1969.

For further details see under "Prices" on page vii.

GUM

All stamps listed are assumed to have gum of some kind and original gum (o.g.) means that which was present on the stamp as issued to the public. Deleterious climates and the presence of certain chemicals can cause gum to crack and, with early stamps, even make the paper deteriorate. Unscrupulous fakers are adept in removing it and regumming the stamp to meet the unreasoning demand often made for "full o.g." in cases where such a thing is virtually impossible.

MINIATURE SHEETS AND SHEETLETS

A miniature sheet contains a single stamp or set with wide inscribed or decorated margins. The stamps usually also exist in normal sheet format. This Catalogue lists, with **MS** prefix, complete miniature sheets which have been sold by the Post Office as indivisible entities and which are valid for postal purposes.

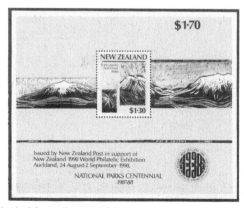

New Zealand miniature sheet containing a single stamp and sold at a premium
for the 1990 World Philatelic Exhibition, Auckland

A sheetlet or small sheet differs in that the individual stamps are intended to be purchased separately for postal purposes. For sheetlets, all the component postage stamps are numbered individually and the composition explained in a footnote. Note that the definitions refer to post office sale—not how items may be subsequently offered by stamp dealers.

Production as sheetlets is a modern marketing development chosen by postal administrations to interest collectors in purchasing the item complete; if he has done so he should, as with all *se-tenant* arrangements, keep the sheetlet intact in his collection.

OVERPRINTS AND SURCHARGES

Overprints of different types qualify for separate listing. These include overprints in different colours; overprints from different printing processes such as litho and typo; overprints in totally different typefaces, etc.

Major errors in machine-printed overprints are important and listable. They include: overprint inverted or omitted; overprint double (treble, etc.); overprint diagonal; overprint double, one inverted; pairs with one overprint omitted, e.g. from a radical shift to an adjoining stamp; error of colour; error of type fount; letters inverted or omitted, etc. If the overprint is handstamped, few of these would qualify and a distinction is drawn. We continue, however, to list pairs of stamps where one has a handstamped overprint and the other has not.

Varieties occurring in overprints will often take the form of broken letters, slight differences in spacing, rising spaces, etc.

PAPER TYPES

All stamps listed are deemed to be on "ordinary" paper of the wove type and white in colour; only departures from this are normally mentioned.

A coloured paper is one that is coloured right through (front and back of the stamp). In the Catalogue the colour of the paper is given in *italics*, thus:

purple/*yellow* = purple design on yellow paper.

Papers have been made specially white in recent years by, for example, a very heavy coating of chalk. We do not classify shades of whiteness of paper as distinct varieties.

The availability of many postage stamps for revenue purposes made necessary some safeguard against the illegitimate re-use of stamps with removable cancellations. This was at first secured by using fugitive inks and later by printing on chalky (chalk-surfaced) paper, both of which made it difficult to remove any form of obliteration without also damaging the stamp design. We have indicated the existence of the papers by the letters "**O**" (ordinary) and "**C**" (chalky) after the description of all stamps where the chalky paper may be found. Where no indication is given the paper is "ordinary".

Our chalky paper is specifically one which shows a black mark when touched with a silver wire. Stamps on chalk-surfaced paper can easily lose this coating through immersion in water.

PERFORATION MEASUREMENT

The gauge of a perforation is the number of holes in a length of 2 cm.

The Gibbons *Instanta* gauge is the standard for measuring perforations. The stamp is viewed against a dark background with the transparent gauge put on top of it. Though the gauge measures to decimal accuracy, perforations read from it are generally quoted in the Catalogue to the nearest half. For example:

Just over perf $12\frac{3}{4}$ to just under $13\frac{1}{4}$	= perf 13
Perf $13\frac{1}{4}$ exactly, rounded up	= perf $13\frac{1}{2}$
Just over perf $13\frac{1}{4}$ to just under $13\frac{3}{4}$	= perf $13\frac{1}{2}$
Perf $13\frac{3}{4}$ exactly, rounded up	= perf 14

However, where classification depends on it, actual quarter-perforations are quoted. Perforations are usually abbreviated (and spoken) as follows, though sometimes they may be spelled out for clarity.

P 14: perforated alike on all sides (read: "perf 14").

P 14 × 15: the first figure refers to top and bottom, the second to left and right sides (read: "perf 14 by 15"). This is a compound perforation.

Such headings as "*P* 13 × 14 (*vert*) and *P* 14 × 13 (*horiz*)" indicate which perforations apply to which stamp format—vertical or horizontal.

In rouletting, an early form of separation, the paper is cut, usually in a series of short lines parallel to the edge of the stamp, but none of it is removed.

PERFORATION ERRORS

Authenticated errors, where a stamp normally perforated is accidentally issued imperforate, are listed provided no traces of perforation (blind holes or indentations) remain. They must be provided as pairs, both stamps wholly imperforate, and are only priced in that form.

Pairs described as "imperforate between" have the line of perforations between the two stamps omitted.

Imperf between (*horiz pair*): a horizontal pair of stamps with perfs all around the edges but none between the stamps.

Imperf between (*vert pair*): a vertical pair of stamps with perfs all around the edges but none between the stamps.

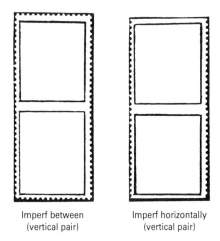

Imperf between   Imperf horizontally
(vertical pair)   (vertical pair)

Where several of the rows have escaped perforation the resulting varieties are listable. Thus:

Imperf vert (*horiz pair*): a horizontal pair of stamps perforated at top and bottom; all three vertical directions are imperf—the two outer edges and between the stamps.

Imperf horiz (*vert pair*): a vertical pair perforated at left and right edges; all three horizontal directions are imperf—the top, bottom and between the stamps.

Varieties of double, misplaced or partial perforation caused by error or machine malfunction are not listable, neither are freaks such as perforations placed diagonally from paper folds, nor missing holes caused by broken pins.

Items imperforate between stamp and margin are outside the scope of this catalogue.

POSTCARDS

From 1972 the Post Office produced sets of picture cards to accompany some commemorative issues. Each card shows an enlarged colour reproduction of one stamp.

Cards are priced in fine used condition for complete sets as issued, each franked with the appropriate stamp depicted and cancelled with an official postmark for first day of issue.

PRESENTATION AND SOUVENIR PACKS

Special packs comprising slip-in cards with printed commemorative inscriptions and notes on the back and with protective covering, were introduced in 1982 for some issues.

New Zealand 1989 Wildflowers Presentation Pack

Yearly Souvenir Packs, containing commemoratives, were introduced in 1970.

Special Post Office Yearbooks were first available in 1984. They contain all the issues for one year in a hardbound book, illustrated in colour complete with slip case. These are listed and priced.

PRINTING ERRORS

Errors in printing are of major interest to the Catalogue. Authenticated items meriting consideration would include: background, centre or frame inverted or omitted; centre or subject transposed; error of colour; error or omission of value; double prints and impressions; printed both sides; and so on. Designs *tête-bêche*, whether intentionally or by accident, are listable. Colours only partially omitted are not listed. However, stamps with embossing, phosphor or both omitted and stamps printed on the gummed side are included.

Printing technology has radically improved over the years, during which time photogravure and lithography have become predominant. Varieties nowadays are more in the nature of flaws which are almost always outside the scope of this book.

In no catalogue, however, do we list such items as: dry prints, kiss prints, doctor-blade flaws, colour shifts or registration flaws (unless they lead to the complete omission of a colour from an individual stamp), lithographic ring flaws, and so on. Neither do we recognise fortuitous happenings like paper creases or confetti flaws.

PUNCTURED STAMPS

Perforation holes can be punched into the face of the stamp. Patterns of small holes, often in the shape of initial letters, were applied as devices against pilferage. "Perfins" are outside the scope of the listings.

SE-TENANT COMBINATIONS

Se-tenant means "joined together". Some sets include stamps of different design arranged *se-tenant* as blocks or strips and, in mint condition, these are usually collected unsevered as issued. Such *se-tenant* combinations can often be supplied in used condition at a premium over the used prices of the individual stamps. See also the note on Set Prices.

Tokelau 1989 Food Gathering
se-tenant strip

SHEET SIZES

In describing the sheet arrangement we always give the number of stamps across the sheet first. For example, "50 (5 × 10)" indicates a sheet of fifty stamps in ten horizontal rows of five stamps each.

From 1971 most Crown Agents stocks were in sheets of 25, the stocks sent direct to the territories being often in double, uncut sheets of 50 (i.e. two panes of 25).

To qualify for listing any variety or flaw must be *constant* and so occur throughout the entire printing run, although instances can happen where the flaw gradually corrects itself or—having been noticed—it is corrected by the printer. Before constant varieties and flaws can be listed their sheet position must be known.

The notation for position is based on counting the rows downwards and the stamps across the row. Hence in this Catalogue R. 10/1 = row 10, stamp 1 (the first stamp in the tenth row down); the alternative designation for this position as used in "Through the Magnifying Glass" (Gibbons *Stamp Monthly*) is R. 10, S1 = row 10, stamp 1.

WATERMARK TYPES

Stamps are on unwatermarked paper except where the heading to the set states otherwise.

Watermarks are detected for Catalogue description by one of four methods: (1) holding stamps to the light; (2) laying stamps face down on a dark background; (3) by use of the Morley-Bright Detector, which works by revealing the thinning of the paper at the watermark; or (4) by the more complex electric watermark detectors such as the Signoscope.

The diagram below shows how watermark position is described in the Catalogue. Watermarks are usually impressed so that they read normally when looked through from the printed side. However, since philatelists customarily detect watermarks by looking at the back of the stamp, the watermark diagram also makes clear what is actually seen. Note that "G v R" is only an example and illustrations of the different watermarks employed are shown in the listings. These illustrations are actual size and shown in normal positions (from the front of the stamps).

	AS DESCRIBED (Read through front of stamp)		AS SEEN DURING WATERMARK DETECTION (Stamp face down and back examined)
	GvR	Normal	ᴚvＤ
	ᴚ∧Ｇ	Inverted	Ｃ∧ᴚ
	ᴚvＤ	Reversed	GvR
	Ｃ∧ᴚ	Reversed and inverted	Ｇ∧ᴚ
	GvR (sideways)	Sideways	Ｃ∧ᴚ (sideways)
	GvR (sideways)	Sideways inverted	ᴚvＤ (sideways)

New Zealand Watermark Types as seen through the front of the stamp.

1a

2

F 5

4

12a 6 mm

12b 7 mm

12c 4 mm

38

43 "Single" Wmk   **98** "Multiple Wmk"

WATERMARK ERRORS AND VARIETIES

Watermark errors are recognised as of major importance. They comprise stamps showing the wrong watermark devices or stamps printed on paper with the wrong watermark. Stamps printed on paper showing broken or deformed bits on the dandy roll, are not listable.

This Catalogue includes watermark inverted and sideways inverted varieties on the stamps of New Zealand and the dependent territories.

CATALOGUE NEW ISSUE SUPPPLEMENTS

The first Supplement recording new stamps not in this Catalogue appeared in the February 1990 number of *Gibbons Stamp Monthly*. See page ix for a FREE copy and subscription details.

NEW ZEALAND ALBUMS
from Stanley Gibbons
ONE COUNTRY ALBUM

This elegant 4-ring album provides an ideal setting for any straightforward New Zealand collection. Housed in a rich burgundy leather-effect binder with gold tooling on the cover and spine, the high quality cartridge leaves are laid out and written up to ensure that your collection is attractively displayed whatever its stage of development. Every stamp is illustrated and identified by its SG Catalogue number for ease of use and supplements are produced each spring to keep the collection up to date.
Item 5262 New Zealand One Country Album.

LUXURY HINGELESS ALBUMS

These impressive albums present the very ultimate in luxury, convenience and style. Their deeply padded binders are covered in navy blue leatherette rexine and decorated with the country's crest in traditional heraldic colours. The leaves are of the highest quality, tastefully laid out to give a superbly attractive display. Dates of issue, face value, colour and selected illustrations are provided for ease of use and a crystal clear protective mount already affixed in each space for the immediate insertion of your stamps.

Each album is presented in its own matching slip case for added protection.

Item 5288 Stanley Gibbons New Zealand Luxury Hingeless Album Volume 1 (1855–1967).
Item 5289 Stanley Gibbons New Zealand Luxury Hingeless Album Volume 2 (1967–date).

DAVO STANDARD ALBUM

A superior album attractively emblazoned with the country's crest on the cover and spine and incorporating solid brass screw peg fittings for exceptional convenience and security. It is covered in fine navy canvas and contains high quality cartridge leaves attractively laid out with a printed space for each stamp. The high capacity and large page size of this album enables all New Zealand issues to be accommodated in a single volume – it therefore represents excellent value for money.
Item 5288ST Davo New Zealand Standard Album.

DAVO LUXE REGULAR ALBUMS

The same format as the standard albums but produced in two separate volumes with binders and leaves of even more luxurious quality. The binder is covered in deeply padded navy blue leatherette rexine and provided with its own matching slip case. New supplements for all Davo albums are published annually in the spring.
Item 5288RG Davo Luxe Regular New Zealand Album Volume 1 (1855–1967).
Item 5289RG Davo Luxe Regular New Zealand Album Volume 2 (1967–date).

An illustrated colour brochure giving details and prices of these and all other Stanley Gibbons Publications products is available by post from:

Stanley Gibbons Publications Ltd.,
5 Parkside, Christchurch Road,
Ringwood, Hampshire BH24 3SH
Telephone 0425 472363

New Zealand

1855   12 Pence   = 1 Shilling
       20 Shillings = 1 Pound
1967   100 Cents   = 1 New Zealand Dollar

During the years of the early settlement of New Zealand mail for Sydney, New South Wales, was routed through an unofficial postmaster at Kororareka. The first official post offices did not open until 1841 when the New South Wales authorities relinquished supervision of the postal service. The British G.P.O. was responsible for the operation of the overseas mails from 11 October 1841 until the postal service once again passed under colonial control in 1848.

CC 1   CC 2

AUCKLAND

CROWNED-CIRCLE HANDSTAMPS

CC1 CC **1** AUCKLAND NEW ZEALAND (R.) (31.10.1846)
Price on cover   £300

NELSON

CROWNED-CIRCLE HANDSTAMPS

CC2 CC **1** NELSON NEW ZEALAND (R.) (31.10.1846)
Price on cover   £1100

NEW PLYMOUTH

CROWNED-CIRCLE HANDSTAMPS

CC3 CC **1** NEW PLYMOUTH NEW ZEALAND (R. *or* Black)
(31.10.1846) . . . . *Price on cover*   £1500

OTAGO

CROWNED-CIRCLE HANDSTAMPS

CC4 CC **2** OTAGO NEW ZEALAND (R.) (10.46) . . *Price on cover*   £1500

PETRE

CROWNED-CIRCLE HANDSTAMPS

CC5 CC **1** PETRE NEW ZEALAND (R.) (31.10.1846)
Price on cover   £1500

PORT VICTORIA

CROWNED-CIRCLE HANDSTAMPS

CC6 CC **2** PORT VICTORIA NEW ZEALAND (R.) (8.49)
Price on cover   £1000

RUSSELL

CROWNED-CIRCLE HANDSTAMPS

CC7 CC **1** RUSSELL NEW ZEALAND (R.) (30.10.1846)
Price on cover   £1400

WELLINGTON

CROWNED-CIRCLE HANDSTAMPS

CC8 CC **1** WELLINGTON NEW ZEALAND (R.) (31.10.1846)
Price on cover   £500

A similar mark for Christchurch is only known struck, in black, as a cancellation after the introduction of adhesive stamps.

PRICES FOR STAMPS ON COVER TO 1945	
Nos. 1/125	*from* ×2
Nos. 126/36	*from* ×3
Nos. 137/9	*from* ×2
No. 140	—
No. 141	*from* ×2
No. 142	—
Nos. 143/8	*from* ×2
Nos. 149/51	*from* ×10
Nos. 152/84	*from* ×2
Nos. 185/6	—
Nos. 187/203	*from* ×3
Nos. 205/7e	—
Nos. 208/13	*from* ×2
Nos. 214/16j	—
Nos. 217/58	*from* ×3
No. 259	—
Nos. 260/9	*from* ×3
No. 270	—
Nos. 271/6	*from* ×3
Nos. 277/307	*from* ×2
Nos. 308/16	*from* ×3
No. 317	—
Nos. 318/28	*from* ×3
Nos. 329/48	—
No. 349	*from* ×5
Nos. 350/1	—
No. 352	*from* ×5
Nos. 353/69	—
Nos. 370/86	*from* ×2
No. 387	*from* ×4
Nos. 388/99	*from* ×3
Nos. 400/666	*from* ×2
Nos. E1/5	*from* ×5
No. E6	*from* ×10
Nos. D1/8	*from* ×3
Nos. D9/16	*from* ×5
Nos. D17/20	*from* ×3
Nos. D21/47	*from* ×6
Nos. O1/24	*from* ×12
Nos. O59/66	*from* ×4
Nos. O67/8	—
Nos. O69/81	*from* ×5
Nos. O82/7	—
Nos. O88/93	*from* ×20
Nos. O94/9	*from* ×12
Nos. O100/11	*from* ×5
Nos. O112/13	—
Nos. O115/19	*from* ×15
Nos. O120/33	*from* ×10
Nos. O134/51	*from* ×4
Nos. P1/7	*from* ×8
Nos. L1/9	*from* ×6
Nos. L9a/12	—
Nos. L13/20	*from* ×10
Nos. L21/3	—
Nos. L24/41	*from* ×10
No. F1	—
No. F2	*from* ×5
Nos. F3/144	—
Nos. F145/58	*from* ×3
Nos. F159/68	—
Nos. F169/79	*from* ×3
Nos. F180/6	—
Nos. F187/90	*from* ×2
Nos. F191/203	*from* ×3
Nos. F204/11	—
Nos. F212/18	*from* ×2
Nos. A1/3	*from* ×2

CROWN COLONY

1   1*a*   2

(Eng by Humphreys. Recess P.B.)

1855 (18 July). *Wmk Large Star, W* **1***a. Imperf.*

1	**1**	1d. dull carmine (*white paper*)	£25000	£8000
2		2d. dull blue (*blued paper*)	£10000	£550
3		1s. pale yellow-green (*blued paper*)	£25000	£5250
		a. Bisected (6d.) (on cover)	†	£20000

The 2d. and 1s. on white paper formerly listed are now known to be stamps printed on blued paper which have had the blueing washed out.

Nos. 3a and 6a were used at Dunedin from March 1857 when the rate for ½ oz letters to Great Britain was reduced to 6d. All known examples are bisected vertically.

(Printed by J. Richardson, Auckland, N.Z.)

1855 (Dec). *First printing. Wmk Large Star, W* **1***a. White paper. Imperf.*

3*b*	**1**	1d. orange	£15000

1855 (Dec)–**57**. *No wmk. Blue paper. Imperf.*

4	**1**	1d. red	£6500	£1400
5		2d. blue (3.56)	£2250	£300
		a. Without value		
6		1s. green (9.57)	£10000	£3500
		a. Bisected (6d.) (on cover)	†	£15000

These stamps on blue paper may occasionally be found wmkd double-lined letters, being portions of the paper-maker's name.

1857 (Jan). *Wmk Large Star, W* **1***a. White paper similar to the issue of July* 1855.

7	**1**	1d. dull orange	—	£12000

This stamp is in the precise shade of the 1d. of the 1858 printing by Richardson on *no wmk* white paper. An unsevered pair is known with Dunedin cancellation on a cover bearing arrival postmark of Auckland dated "19.1.1857".

1858–63. *Hard or soft white paper. No wmk.* (*a*) *Imperf.*

8	**1**	1d. dull orange (1858)	£1300	£300
8*a*		2d. deep ultramarine (1858)	£1500	£750
9		2d. pale blue	£700	£175
10		2d. blue	£700	£175
11		2d. dull deep blue	—	£175
12		6d. bistre-brown (Aug 1859)	£2250	£500
13		6d. brown	£950	£300
14		6d. pale brown	£950	£300
15		6d. chestnut	£2000	£500
16		1s. dull emerald-green	£6500	£1000
17		1s. blue-green	£6500	£1200

(*b*) *Pin-roulette, about* 10 *at Nelson* (1862)

18	**1**	1d. dull orange	—	£4500
19		2d. blue	—	£4500
20		6d. brown	—	£4500
21		1s. blue-green	—	£6500

(*c*) *Serrated perf about* 16 *or* 18 *at Nelson* (1862)

22	**1**	1d. dull orange	—	£3250
23		2d. blue	—	£2750
24		6d. brown	—	£2750
25		6d. chestnut	—	£4750
26		1s. blue-green	—	£4750

(*d*) *Rouletted* 7 *at Auckland* (April 1859)

27	**1**	1d. dull orange	£4250	£3000
28		2d. blue	£5250	£2750
29		6d. brown	£3500	£2750
		a. Imperf between (pair)	£10000	£9000
30		1s. dull emerald-green	£5250	£3500
31		1s. blue-green	£6500	£3500

(*e*) *P* 13 *at Dunedin* (1863)

31*a*	**1**	1d. dull orange	—	£2000
31*b*		2d. pale blue	£2750	£1750
32		6d. pale brown	—	£5000

Other forms of separation, in addition to those shown above, are known, both on the stamps of this issue and on those of 1862. Some of the varieties are extremely rare, only single copies being known.

The 2d. in a distinctive deep bright blue on white paper wmkd. Large Star is believed by experts to have been printed by Richardson in 1861 or 1862. This also exists doubly printed and with serrated perf.

(Printed by John Davies at the G.P.O., Auckland, N.Z.)

1862 (Feb–Dec). *Wmk Large Star, W* **1***a.* (*a*) *Imperf.*

33	**1**	1d. orange-vermilion	£350	£110
34		1d. vermilion	£350	£110
35		1d. carmine-vermilion	£350	£140
36		2d. deep blue (Plate I)	£300	55·00
		a. Double print	—	£2000
37		2d. slate-blue (Plate I)	£1500	£160
37*a*		2d. milky blue (Plate I, worn)	—	£200
38		2d. pale blue (Plate I, worn)	£225	65·00
39		2d. blue (*to deep*) (Plate I, very worn)	£225	65·00
40		3d. brown-lilac (Dec 1862)	£275	£100
41		6d. black-brown	£600	70·00
42		6d. brown	£600	70·00
43		6d. red-brown	£500	60·00
44		1s. green	£750	£150
45		1s. yellow-green	£700	£140
46		1s. deep green	£850	£175

Nos. 37*a*/38 show some signs of wear on right of Queen's head and shades of No. 39 show moderate to advanced states of wear.

(*b*) *Rouletted* 7 *at Auckland* (6.62)

47	**1**	1d. orange-vermilion	£3000	£600
48		1d. vermilion	£1800	£600
48*a*		1d. carmine-vermilion	£2500	£700
49		2d. deep blue	£1700	£400
50		2d. slate-blue	£2750	£600
51		2d. pale blue	£1500	£500
52		3d. brown-lilac	£1700	£600
53		6d. black-brown	£2000	£400
54		6d. brown	£1700	£450
55		6d. red-brown	£1700	£400
56		1s. green	£2000	£500
57		1s. yellow-green	£3000	£500
58		1s. deep green	£3000	£600

(*c*) *Serrated perf* 16 *or* 18 *at Nelson* (8.62)

59	**1**	1d. orange-vermilion	—	£850
60		2d. deep blue	—	£700
		a. Imperf between (pair)	£4500	£2250
61		2d. slate-blue		
62		3d. brown-lilac	£2500	£1400
63		6d. black-brown	—	£1500
64		6d. brown	—	£1500
65		1s. yellow-green	—	£2000

(*d*) *Pin-perf* 10 *at Nelson* (8.62)

66	**1**	2d. deep blue	—	£1700
67		6d. black-brown	—	£2750

The dates put to above varieties are the earliest that have been met with.

1862. *Wmk Large Star, W* **1***a. P* 13 (*at Dunedin*).

68	**1**	1d. orange-vermilion	£550	£150
69		1d. carmine-vermilion	£550	£150
70		2d. deep blue (Plate I)	£250	30·00
71		2d. slate-blue (Plate I)	—	£700
72		2d. blue (Plate I)	£175	30·00
72*a*		2d. milky blue (Plate I)	—	£500
73		2d. pale blue (Plate I)	£175	30·00
74		3d. brown-lilac	£475	£110
75		6d. black-brown	£475	£110
		a. Imperf between (horiz pair)		
76		6d. brown	£425	48·00
77		6d. red-brown	£325	30·00
78		1s. dull green	£400	£180
79		1s. deep green	£450	£180
80		1s. yellow-green	£450	£160

See also Nos. 110/125 and the note that follows these.

1862. *Pelure paper. No wmk. (a) Imperf.*
81 **1** 1d. orange-vermilion £5500 £1700
82 2d. ultramarine £3250 £750
83 2d. pale ultramarine £3250 £750
84 3d. lilac . . . . £25000 †
85 6d. black-brown £1200 £210
86 1s. deep green £5500 £800

The 3d. is known only unused.

(b) Rouletted 7 at Auckland
87 **1** 1d. orange-vermilion . . . . — £4000
88 6d. black-brown £2000 £450
89 1s. deep green £3500 £950

(c) P 13 at Dunedin
90 **1** 1d. orange-vermilion £9500 £3000
91 2d. ultramarine £4500 £550
92 2d. pale ultramarine £4500 £550
93 6d. black-brown £3500 £300
94 1s. deep green £7000 £850

(d) Serrated perf 15 at Nelson
95 **1** 6d. black-brown . . . . — £3500

1863 (early). *Hard or soft white paper. No wmk. (a) Imperf.*
96 **1** 2d. dull deep blue (*shades*) £2250 £800

(b) P 13
96*a* **1** 2d. dull deep blue (*shades*) £1600 £475

These stamps show slight beginnings of wear of the printing plate in the background to right of the Queen's ear, as one looks at the stamps. By the early part of 1864, the wear of the plate had spread, more or less all over the background of the circle containing the head. The major portion of the stamps of this printing appears to have been consigned to Dunedin and to have been there perforated 13.

1864. *Wmk "N Z", W* **2**. *(a) Imperf.*
97 **1** 1d. carmine-vermilion £700 £200
98 2d. pale blue (Plate I worn) £750 £200
99 6d. red-brown £2000 £475
100 1s. green £850 £250

(b) Rouletted 7 at Auckland
101 **1** 1d. carmine-vermilion £4500 £2750
102 2d. pale blue (Plate I worn) £1400 £700
103 6d. red-brown £4250 £2750
104 1s. green £2750 £900

(c) P 13 at Dunedin
104*a* **1** 1d. carmine-vermilion £5000 £3500
105 2d. pale blue (Plate I worn) £550 £160
106 1s. green £1100 £550
a. Imperf between (horiz pair) £7500

(d) P 12½ at Auckland
106*b* **1** 1d. carmine-vermilion £3750 £2000
107 2d. pale blue (Plate I worn) . . . . £200 50·00
108 6d. red-brown . . . . £200 30·00
109 1s. yellow-green £4000 £2000

1864–67. *Wmk Large Star, W* **1***a. P 12½ (at Auckland).*
110 **1** 1d. carmine-vermilion (1864) . . . . 70·00 17·00
111 1d. pale orange-vermilion . . . . 80·00 17·00
a. Imperf (pair) £1400 £900
112 1d. orange . . . . £200 38·00
113 2d. pale blue (Plate I worn) (1864) . . . . 75·00 14·00
114 2d. deep blue (Plate II) (1866) . . . . 75·00 14·00
a. Imperf between (pair) . . . . — £2000
115 2d. blue (Plate II) . . . . 75·00 17·00
a. Retouched (Plate II) (1867) . . . . £130 19·00
c. Imperf (pair) (Plate II) £1100 £1100
d. Retouched. Imperf (pair) £1400 £1600
116 3d. brown-lilac (1864) £700 £500
117 3d. lilac . . . . 60·00 17·00
a. Imperf (pair) £1200 £900
118 3d. deep mauve . . . . £275 45·00
a. Imperf (pair) £1400 £900
119 4d. deep rose (1865) £1500 £250
120 4d. yellow (1865) . . . . 75·00 38·00
121 4d. orange £1000 £800
122 6d. red-brown (1864) . . . . 75·00 15·00
122*a* 6d. brown . . . . 75·00 15·00
b. Imperf (pair) £850 £850
123 1s. deep green (1864) £425 £150
124 1s. green . . . . £275 48·00
125 1s. yellow-green . . . . £100 45·00

The above issue is sometimes difficult to distinguish from Nos. 68/80 because the vertical perforations usually gauge 12¾ and sometimes a full 13. However stamps of this issue invariably gauge 12½ horizontally, whereas the 1862 stamps measure a full 13.

The 1d., 2d. and 6d. were officially reprinted imperforate, without gum, in 1884 for presentation purposes. They can be distinguished from the errors listed by their shades which are pale orange, dull blue and dull chocolate-brown respectively, and by the worn state of the plates from which they were printed.

1871. *Wmk Large Star, W* **1***a. (a) P 10.*
126 **1** 1d. brown . . . . £375 50·00

(b) P 12½ × 10
127 **1** 1d. deep brown . . . . — £750

(c) P 10 × 12½
128 **1** 1d. brown . . . . 90·00 14·00
a. Perf 12½ comp 10 (1 side) . . . . — 50·00
129 2d. deep blue (Plate II) . . . . — £4250
a. Perf 10* . . . . † £7500
130 2d. vermilion . . . . 95·00 15·00
a. Retouched . . . . £150 19·00
b. Perf 12½ comp 10 (1 side) £600 £250
c. Perf 10* . . . . † £7500
131 6d. deep blue £900 £425
a. Blue £700 £250
b. Imperf between (vert pair) . . . . — £3750
c. Perf 12½ comp 10 (1 side) £475 £175
ca. Imperf vert (horiz pair) . . . .

(d) P 12½
132 **1** 1d. red-brown . . . . 90·00 14·00
a. Brown (shades, worn plate) . . . . 90·00 14·00
b. Imperf horiz (vert pair) . . . . — £2250
133 2d. orange . . . . 45·00 15·00
a. Retouched . . . . £110 40·00
134 2d. vermilion . . . . 85·00 15·00
a. Retouched . . . . £150 50·00
135 6d. blue . . . . 85·00 17·00
136 6d. pale blue . . . . 45·00 17·00

In or about 1872 both 1d. and 2d. stamps were printed on some paper having a wmk of script letters "W. T. & Co." (=Wiggins Teape & Co) in the sheet, and other paper with the name "T. H. Saunders" in double-lined capitals in the sheet; portions of these letters are occasionally found on stamps.

*Only one used copy each of Nos. 129a and 130c have been reported.

1872. *No wmk. P 12½.*
137 **1** 1d. brown . . . . £250 40·00
138 2d. vermilion . . . . 45·00 18·00
a. Retouched . . . . £150 25·00
139 4d. orange-yellow £120 £350

1872. *Wmk "N Z", W* **2**. *P 12½.*
140 **1** 1d. brown . . . . — £2500
141 2d. vermilion . . . . £300 65·00
a. Retouched £600 £150

1872. *Wmk Lozenges, with* "INVICTA" *in double-lined capitals four times in the sheet. P 12½.*
142 **1** 2d. vermilion £2500 £550
a. Retouched £3750 £800

3

4

(Des John Davies. Die eng on wood in Melbourne. Printed from electrotypes at Govt Ptg Office, Wellington)

1873 (1 Jan). *(a) Wmk* "NZ", *W* **2**.
143 **3** ½d. pale dull rose (*p* 10) . . . . 60·00 14·00
144 ½d. pale dull rose (*p* 12½) . . . . £180 55·00
145 ½d. pale dull rose (*p* 12½ × 10) . . . . £110 42·00

(b) No wmk
146 **3** ½d. pale dull rose (*p* 10) . . . . 60·00 20·00
147 ½d. pale dull rose (*p* 12½) . . . . £180 60·00
148 ½d. pale dull rose (*p* 12½ × 10) . . . . £150 55·00

As the paper used for Nos. 143/5 was originally intended for fiscal stamps which were more than twice as large, about one-third of the impressions fall on portions of the sheet showing no watermark, giving rise to varieties Nos. 146/8. In later printings of No. 151 a few stamps in each sheet are without watermark. These can be distinguished from No. 147 by the shade.

1875 (Jan). *Wmk Star, W* **4**.

149	**3**	½d. pale dull rose (*p* 12½)	11·00	90
		a. Imperf between (pair)	£450	£275
150		½d. dull pale rose (*p nearly* 12)	60·00	5·50

1892 (May). *Wmk "NZ and Star", W* **12**b. *P* 12½.

151	**3**	½d. bright rose (*shades*)	5·00	25
		a. No wmk	7·00	2·25

5

6

7

8

9

10

11

12

12*a* 6 mm

12*b* 7 mm

12*c* 4 mm

(T **5**/**10** eng De La Rue. T **11** and **12** des, eng & plates by W. R. Bock. Typo
Govt Ptg Office, Wellington)

1874 (2 Jan)–**78**. *W* **12**a. A. *White paper*. (a) *P* 12½.

152	**5**	1d. lilac	60·00	3·25
		a. Imperf	£400	
		Wi. Wmk inverted	—	50·00
153	**6**	2d. rose	60·00	1·60
154	**7**	3d. brown	75·00	48·00
155	**8**	4d. maroon	£250	48·00
		Wi. Wmk inverted	£400	75·00
156	**9**	6d. blue	£180	10·00
		Wi. Wmk inverted	—	60·00
157	**10**	1s. green	£1000	25·00
		Wi. Wmk inverted	£1500	£150

(b) *Perf nearly* 12

158	**6**	2d. rose (1878)	£550	£180

(c) *Perf compound of* 12½ *and* 10

159	**5**	1d. lilac	£150	40·00
		Wi. Wmk inverted	—	60·00
160	**6**	2d. rose	£350	60·00
		Wi. Wmk inverted	—	90·00

161	**7**	3d. brown	£150	50·00
162	**8**	4d. maroon	£325	90·00
163	**9**	6d. blue	£190	40·00
		Wi. Wmk inverted	—	75·00
164	**10**	1s. green	£1000	95·00
		aa. Imperf between (vert pair)	†	—
		Wi. Wmk inverted		

(d) *Perf nearly* 12 × 12½

164*a*	**5**	1d. lilac (1875)	£650	£250
165	**6**	2d. rose (1878)	£650	£190

B. *Blued paper*. (a) *P* 12½

166	**5**	1d. lilac	65·00	29·00
167	**6**	2d. rose	90·00	29·00
		Wi. Wmk inverted	—	50·00
168	**7**	3d. brown	£200	65·00
169	**8**	4d. maroon	£425	£100
170	**9**	6d. blue	£300	48·00
171	**10**	1s. green	£1000	£190

(b) *Perf compound of* 12½ *and* 10

172	**5**	1d. lilac	£180	50·00
173	**6**	2d. rose	£500	80·00
174	**7**	3d. brown	£130	55·00
175	**8**	4d. maroon	£450	£110
176	**9**	6d. blue	£300	90·00
177	**10**	1s. green	£1000	£200

1875. *Wmk Large Star, W* **1**a. *P* 12½.

178	**5**	1d. deep lilac	£450	75·00
179	**6**	2d. rose	£300	15·00

1878. *W* **12**a. *P* 12 × 11½ (*comb*).

180	**5**	1d. mauve-lilac	40·00	2·00
181	**6**	2d. rose	40·00	1·40
182	**8**	4d. maroon	£120	38·00
183	**9**	6d. blue	80·00	10·00
184	**10**	1s. green	£110	27·00
185	**11**	2s. deep rose (1 July)	£350	£275
186	**12**	5s. grey (1 July)	£375	£275

This perforation is made by a horizontal "comb" machine, giving a
gauge of 12 horizontally and about 11¾ vertically. Single specimens can be
found apparently gauging 11½ all round or 12 all round, but these are all
from the same machine. The perforation described above as "nearly 12"
was from a single-line machine.

13

14

15

16

17

18

19

20

21

22

Description of Watermarks

*W*12*a*. 6 mm between "N Z" and star; broad irregular star; comparatively wide "N"; "N Z" 11½ mm wide.

*W*12*b*. 7 mm between "N Z" and star; narrower star; narrow "N"; "N Z" 10 mm wide.

*W*12*c*. 4 mm between "N Z" and star; narrow star; wide "N"; "N Z" 11½ mm wide.

Description of Papers

1882–88. Smooth paper with horizontal mesh. W **12***a*.
1888–98. Smooth paper with vertical mesh. *W* **12***b*.
1890–91. Smooth paper with vertical mesh. *W* **12***c*.
1898.   Thin yellowish toned, coarse paper with clear vertical mesh. *W* 12*b*. Perf 11 only.

In 1899–1900 stamps appeared on medium to thick white coarse paper but we do not differentiate these (except where identifiable by shade) as they are more difficult to distinguish.

PAPER MESH. This shows on the back of the stamps as a series of parallel grooves, either vertical or horizontal. It is caused by the use of a wire gauze conveyor-belt during paper-making.

Description of Dies

1d.

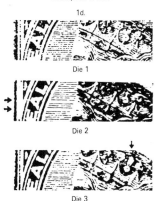

Die 1

Die 2

Die 3

1882. Die 1. Background shading complete and heavy.

1886. Die 2. Background lines thinner. Two lines of shading weak or missing left of Queen's forehead.

1889. Die 3. Shading on head reduced; ornament in crown left of chignon clearer, with unshaded "arrow" more prominent.

2d.

Die 1

Die 2

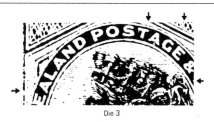

Die 3

1882. Die 1. Background shading complete and heavy.

1886. Die 2. Weak line of shading left of forehead and missing shading lines below "TA".

1889. Die 3. As Die 2 but with comma-like white notch in hair below "&".

6d.

Die 1

Die 2

1882. Die 1. Shading heavy. Top of head merges into shading.

1892. Die 2. Background lines thinner. Shading on head more regular with clear line of demarcation between head and background shading.

STAMPS WITH ADVERTISEMENTS. During November 1891 the New Zealand Post Office invited tenders for the printing of advertisements on the reverse of the current 1d. to 1s. stamps. The contract was awarded to Messrs Miller, Truebridge & Reich and the first sheets with advertisements on the reverse appeared in February 1893.

Different advertisements were applied to the backs of the individual stamps within the sheets of 240 (four panes of 60).

On the first setting those in a vertical format were inverted in relation to the stamps and each of the horizontal advertisements had its base at the left-hand side of the stamps when seen from the back. For the second and third settings the vertical advertisements were the same way up as the stamps and the bases of those in the horizontal format were at the right as seen from the back. The third setting only differs from the second in the order of the individual advertisements.

The experiment was not, however, a success and the contract was cancelled at the end of 1893.

(Des F. W. Sears (½d.), A. E. Cousins (2½d.), A. W. Jones (5d.); others adapted from 1874 issue by W. H. Norris. Dies eng A. E. Cousins (½d., 2½d., 5d.), W. R. Bock (others). Typo Govt Ptg Office)

1882–1900. *Inscr* "POSTAGE & REVENUE".

A. *W* **12***a*. *Paper with horiz mesh* (1.4.82–86). (*a*) *P* 12 × 11½

187	**14**	1d. rose to rose-red (Die 1)	35·00	4·00
		a. Imperf (pair)	£250	
		b. Imperf between (vert pair)		
		c. Die 2. *Pale rose to carmine-rose* (1886) .	30·00	4·00
188	**15**	2d. lilac to lilac-purple (Die 1)	40·00	4·00
		a. Imperf (pair)	£275	
		b. Imperf between (vert pair)	£275	
		Wi. Wmk inverted	70·00	8·00
		c. Die 2. *Lilac* (1886)	45·00	5·00
189	**17**	3d. yellow (1884)	45·00	4·50
190	**18**	4d. blue-green	55·00	4·50
191	**20**	6d. brown (Die 1)	60·00	3·75
		Wi. Wmk inverted	£125	25·00
192	**21**	8d. blue (1885)	65·00	45·00
193	**22**	1s. red-brown	75·00	11·00

(b) P 12½ (1884?)

193a	**14**	1d. rose *to* rose-red (Die 1)	£170	70·00

B. W **12**b. Paper with vert mesh (1888–95)

(a) P 12 × 11½ (1888–95)

194	**13**	½d. black (1.4.95).	25·00	48·00
195	**14**	1d. rose *to* rosine (Die 2)	35·00	3·50
		Wi. Wmk inverted	—	12·00
		a. Die 3. *Rose to carmine* (1889)	35·00	3·50
		ab. Red-brown advert (1st setting) (2.93) . . .		
		ac. Red advert (1st setting) (3.93)	45·00	10·00
		ad. Blue advert (2nd setting) (4.93)	55·00	25·00
		ae. Mauve advert (2nd setting) (5.93)	35·00	6·00
		af. Green advert (2nd setting) (6.93)		
		ag. Brown-red advert (3rd setting) (9.93) . .	35·00	6·00
		aWi. Wmk inverted	45·00	12·00
196	**15**	2d. lilac (Die 2)	40·00	3·50
		a. Die 3. *Lilac to purple* (1889)	40·00	3·50
		ab. Red advert (1st setting) (3.93)	60·00	15·00
		ac. Mauve advert (2nd setting) (5.93)	50·00	
		ad. Sepia advert (2nd setting) (5.93)	50·00	20·00
		ae. Green advert (2nd setting) (6.93)	—	75·00
		af. Brown-red advert (3rd setting) (9.93) . .		
		aWi. Wmk inverted	70·00	7·00
197	**16**	2½d. pale blue (1891)	38·00	5·50
		a. Brown-red advert (2nd setting) (4.93) . . .	38·00	10·00
		b. *Ultramarine* (green advert. 2nd setting)		
		(6.93)	48·00	12·00
198	**17**	3d. yellow	40·00	6·00
		a. Brown-red advert (2nd setting) (4.93) . . .	60·00	10·00
		b. Sepia advert (2nd setting) (5.93)		
199	**18**	4d. green *to* bluish green	48·00	2·75
		a. Sepia advert (2nd setting) (5.93)	60·00	10·00
200	**19**	5d. olive-black (1.2.91)	40·00	9·00
		a. Imperf (pair)	£275	
		b. Brown-purple advert (3rd setting) (9.93) .	60·00	25·00
201	**20**	6d. brown (Die 1)	60·00	2·25
		a. Die 2 (1892)	£110	50·00
		ab. Sepia advert (2nd setting) (5.93)		
		ac. Brown-red advert (3rd setting) (9.93) . .	£140	60·00
202	**21**	8d. blue	65·00	38·00
203	**22**	1s. red-brown	75·00	6·00
		a. Black advert (2nd setting) (5.93)	£300	£150
		b. Brown-purple advert (3rd setting) (9.93) .	£100	15·00
		Wi. Wmk inverted	£120	15·00

(b) Perf compound of 12 and 12½ (1888–91)

204	**14**	1d. rose (Die 2)	£190	75·00
		a. Die 3 (1889)		

(c) P 12½ (1888–89)

205	**14**	1d. rose (Die 3) (1889)	£160	90·00
		a. Mauve advert (2nd setting) (5.93)	£160	80·00
206	**15**	2d. lilac (Die 2)	£120	65·00
		a. Die 3. *Deep lilac* (1889)	£120	75·00
		ab. Brown-red advert (3rd setting) (9.93) . .	£120	75·00
207	**16**	2½d. blue (1891)	£170	90·00

(d) Mixed perfs 12 × 11½ and 12½ (1891–93)

207a	**14**	1d. rose (Die 3)		
207b	**15**	2d. lilac (Die 3)		
		ba. Brown-red advert (3rd setting) (9.93) . .		
207c	**18**	4d. green.	—	50·00
207d	**19**	5d. olive-black	—	95·00
207e	**20**	6d. brown (Die 1)	—	£100
		ea. Die 2	—	£150

C. W **12**c. Paper with vert mesh (1890). (a) P 12 × 11½

208	**14**	1d. rose (Die 3)	45·00	4·00
209	**15**	2d. purple (Die 3)	48·00	4·00
210	**16**	2½d. ultramarine (27.12)	45·00	6·50
211	**17**	3d. yellow	50·00	6·50
		a. *Lemon-yellow*	50·00	7·00
212	**20**	6d. brown (Die 1)	85·00	13·00
213	**22**	1s. deep red-brown	£100	24·00

(b) P 12½

214	**14**	1d. rose (Die 3)	£170	£100
215	**15**	2d. purple (Die 3)	£180	90·00
216	**16**	2½d. ultramarine	£200	95·00

(c) Perf compound of 12 and 12½

216a	**20**	6d. brown (Die 1)	£180	£130

D. *Continuation of W* **12**b. *Paper with vert mesh* (1891–1900)

(a) Perf compound of 10 and 12½ (1891–94)

216b	**14**	1d. rose (Die 3)	£175	85·00
		ba. Red-brown advert (1st setting) (2.93) . .	£175	£100
		bb. Brown-red advert (2nd setting) (4.93) . .	£150	70·00
		bc. Mauve advert (2nd setting) (5.93)	£150	70·00
		bd. Green advert (2nd setting) (6.93)	£200	£120
216c	**15**	2d. lilac (Die 3)	£150	55·00
216d	**16**	2½d. blue (1893)	£130	60·00
216e	**17**	3d. yellow	£150	70·00
216f	**18**	4d. green.	£170	£140
216g	**19**	5d. olive-black (1894)	£180	£170
216h	**20**	6d. brown (Die 1)	£190	£190
		i. Die 2 (1892)	£150	£150
		ia. Brown-purple advert (3rd setting)		
		(9.93)	£175	£175
216j	**22**	1s. red-brown	£170 ·	£160

(b) P 10 (1891–95)

217	**13**	½d. black (1895)	2·50	15
218	**14**	1d. rose (Die 3)	3·00	10
		a. *Carmine*	5·50	1·25
		b. Imperf (pair)	£250	£250
		c. Imperf between (pair)	£275	
		d. Imperf horiz (vert pair)	£200	
		e. Mixed perfs 10 and 12½	£250	£120
		f. Red-brown advert (1st setting) (2.93) . . .	12·00	4·00
		g. Red advert (1st setting) (3.93)	12·00	5·00
		h. Brown-red advert (2nd and 3rd settings)		
		(4.93)	6·00	2·50
		i. Blue advert (2nd setting) (4.93)	45·00	20·00
		j. Mauve advert (2nd setting) (5.93)	6·00	2·50
		k. Green advert (2nd setting) (6.93)	45·00	16·00
		l. Brown-purple advert (3rd setting) (9.93) .	6·00	2·50
		Wi. Wmk inverted	15·00	6·00
219	**15**	2d. lilac (Die 3)	6·00	10
		a. *Purple*	7·50	15
		b. Imperf between (pair)	£180	
		c. Mixed perfs 10 and 12½	£200	90·00
		d. Red-brown advert (1st setting) (2.93) . .	20·00	5·00
		e. Red advert (1st setting) (3.93)	20·00	5·00
		f. Brown-red advert (2nd and 3rd settings)		
		(4.93)	10·00	2·50
		g. Sepia advert (2nd setting) (5.93)	14·00	3·00
		h. Green advert (2nd setting) (6.93)	30·00	8·00
		i. Brown-purple advert (3rd setting) (9.93) .	10·00	2·50
220	**16**	2½d. blue (1892)	35·00	3·50
		a. *Ultramarine*	35·00	4·00
		b. Mixed perfs 10 and 12½	£170	80·00
		c. Mauve advert (2nd setting) (5.93)	35·00	6·00
		d. Green advert (2nd setting) (6.93)	55·00	9·00
		e. Brown-purple advert (3rd setting) (9.93) .	35·00	6·00
221	**17**	3d. pale orange-yellow	35·00	5·50
		a. *Orange*	35·00	5·50
		b. *Lemon-yellow*	42·00	6·50
		c. Mixed perfs 10 and 12½	£160	£120
		d. Brown-red advert (2nd and 3rd settings)		
		(4.93)	38·00	9·00
		e. Sepia advert (2nd setting) (5.93)	75·00	22·00
		f. Brown-purple advert (3rd setting) (9.93) .	40·00	9·00
222	**18**	4d. green (1892)	45·00	2·50
		a. *Blue-green*	50·00	3·50
		b. Mixed perfs 10 and 12½	£190	80·00
		c. Brown-red advert (2nd setting) (4.93) . .	60·00	4·00
		d. Brown-purple advert (3rd setting) (9.93) .	55·00	4·00
223	**19**	5d. olive-black (1893)	42·00	10·00
		a. Brown-purple advert (3rd setting) (9.93) .	65·00	14·00
224	**20**	6d. brown (Die 1)	80·00	12·00
		a. Mixed perfs 10 and 12½		
		b. Die 2 (1892)	45·00	3·50
		ba. *Black-brown*	48·00	3·50
		bb. Imperf (pair)	£225	
		bc. Mixed perfs 10 and 12½	90·00	50·00
		bd. Sepia advert (2nd setting) (4.93)	60·00	9·00
		be. Brown-red advert (3rd setting) (9.93) . .	60·00	9·00
		bf. Brown-purple advert (3rd setting) (9.93) .	60·00	9·00
225	**21**	8d. blue (brown-purple advert. 3rd setting)		
		(9.93)	65·00	45·00
226	**22**	1s. red-brown	75·00	5·00
		a. Imperf between (pair)	£350	
		b. Mixed perfs 10 and 12½	£150	£110
		c. Sepia advert (2nd setting) (5.93)	£100	12·00
		d. Black advert (2nd setting) (5.93)	£175	£110
		e. Brown-red advert (3rd setting) (9.93) . .	£100	12·00
		f. Brown-purple advert (3rd setting) (9.93) .	£100	12·00

(c) *Perf compound of* 11 *and* 10 (1895)

226c	13	½d. black	12·00	6·00
226d	14	1d. rose (Die 3)	25·00	3·75
226e	20	6d. brown (Die 2)	£160	70·00

(d) *Perf compound of* 10 *and* 11 (1895–97)

227	13	½d. black (1896)	3·25	20
		a. Mixed perfs 10 and 11	75·00	22·00
228	14	1d. rose (Die 3)	4·00	15
		a. Mixed perfs 10 and 11	80·00	40·00
229	15	2d. purple (Die 3)	7·50	12
		a. Mixed perfs 10 and 11	60·00	40·00
230	16	2½d. blue (1896)	35·00	3·50
		a. *Ultramarine*	35·00	4·00
		b. Mixed perfs 10 and 11	—	60·00
231	17	3d. lemon-yellow (1896)	45·00	5·50
232	18	4d. pale green (1896)	60·00	5·50
		a. Mixed perfs 10 and 11	—	75·00
233	19	5d. olive-black (1897)	45·00	10·00
234	20	6d. deep brown (Die 2) (1896)	50·00	3·75
		a. Mixed perfs 10 and 11	—	55
235	22	1s. red-brown (1896)	70·00	7·00
		a. Mixed perfs 10 and 11	£130	70·00

(e) *P* 11 (1895–1900)

236	13	½d. black (1897)	2·50	15
		Wi. Wmk inverted	40·00	15·00
		a. Thin coarse toned paper (1898)	20·00	50
		b. Ditto. Wmk sideways	—	£130
237	14	1d. rose (Die 3)	3·50	10
		a. *Deep carmine*	5·50	75
		b. Imperf between (pair)	£275	
		Wi. Wmk inverted	15·00	15·00
		c. *Deep carmine/thin coarse toned* (1898)	8·00	75
		d. Ditto. Wmk sideways	—	£190
238	15	2d. Mauve (Die 3)	7·00	12
		a. *Purple*	7·00	12
		Wi. Wmk inverted	15·00	5·00
		b. *Deep purple/thin coarse toned* (1898)	8·00	55
		c. Ditto. Wmk sideways	—	£180
239	16	2½d. blue (1897)	35·00	3·50
		a. Thin coarse toned paper (1898)	45·00	10·00
240	17	3d. pale yellow (1897)	40·00	4·50
		a. *Pale dull yellow/thin coarse toned* (1898)	45·00	6·00
		b. *Orange* (1899)	40·00	5·00
		c. *Dull orange-yellow* (1900)	40·00	5·00
241	18	4d. yellowish green (1897)	40·00	2·25
		a. *Bluish green* (1897)	40·00	2·25
242	19	5d. olive-black/*thin coarse toned* (1899)	40·00	12·00
243	20	6d. brown (Die 2) (1897)	50·00	2·75
		a. *Black-brown*	50·00	2·75
		b. *Brown/thin coarse toned* (1898)	55·00	4·00
244	21	8d. blue (1898)	65·00	45·00
245	22	1s. red-brown (1897)	70·00	5·50

Only the more prominent shades have been included.

Stamps perf compound of 11 and 12½ exist but we do not list them as there is some doubt as to whether they are genuine.

For the ½d. and 2d. with double-lined watermark, see Nos. 271/2.

23 Mount Cook
or Aorangi

24 Lake Taupo and
Mount Ruapehu

25 Pembroke Peak,
Milford Sound

26 Lake Wakatipu and
Mount Earnslaw, inscribed
"WAKITIPU"

27 Lake Wakatipu and Mount
Earnslaw, inscribed
"WAKATIPU"

28 Sacred Huia
Birds

29 White Terrace,
Rotomahana

30 Otira Gorge and
Mount Ruapehu

31 Brown Kiwi

32 Maori War
Canoe

33 Pink Terrace, Rotomahana

34 Kea and Kaka

35 Milford Sound

36 Mount Cook

(Des H. Young (½d.), J. Gaut (1d.), W. Bock (2d., 3d., 9d., 1s.). E. Howard (4d., 6d., 8d.), E. Luke (others). Eng A. Hill (2½d., 1s.), J. A. C. Harrison (5d.), Rapkin (others). Recess Waterlow)

1898 (5 Apr). *No wmk. P* 12 *to* 16.

246	23	½d. purple-brown	3·50	35
		a. Imperf between (pair)	£500	£500
		b. *Purple-slate*	3·75	35
		c. *Purple-black*	6·00	1·50
247	24	1d. blue and yellow-brown	2·00	20
		a. Imperf between (pair)	£550	
		b. Imperf vert (horiz pair)	£425	
		c. Imperf horiz (vert pair)	£425	
		d. *Blue and brown*	2·50	65
		da. Imperf between (pair)	£550	
248	25	2d. lake	20·00	20
		a. Imperf vert (horiz pair)	£375	
		b. *Rosy lake*	20·00	20
		ba. Imperf between (pair)	£500	
		bb. Imperf vert (horiz pair)	£375	
249	26	2½d. sky-blue (inscr "WAKITIPU")	6·00	18·00
		a. *Blue*	6·00	18·00
250	27	2½d. blue (inscr "WAKATIPU")	11·00	1·25
		a. *Deep blue*	11·00	1·50
251	28	3d. yellow-brown	20·00	4·75
252	29	4d. bright rose	12·00	14·00
		a. *Lake-rose*	14·00	14·00
		b. *Dull rose*	12·00	14·00
253	30	5d. sepia	45·00	75·00
		a. *Purple-brown*	27·00	12·00
254	31	6d. green	48·00	22·00
		a. *Grass-green*	55·00	30·00
255	32	8d. indigo	32·00	20·00
		a. *Prussian blue*	32·00	20·00

256	33	9d. purple	32·00	20·00
257	34	1s. vermilion	48·00	14·00
		a. Dull red	48·00	14·00
		ab. Imperf between (pair)	£1000	
258	35	2s. grey-green	90·00	55·00
		a. Imperf between (vert pair)	£1000	£1000
259	36	5s. vermilion	£200	£150
		Set of 13	£450	£250

37 Lake Taupo and
Mount Ruapehu

(Recess Govt Printer, Wellington)

1899 (May)–**03**. *Thick, soft ("Pirie") paper. No wmk. P* 11.

260	27	2½d. blue (6.99)	11·00	1·75
		a. Imperf between (pair)	£400	
		b. Imperf horiz (vert pair)	£275	
		c. Deep blue	11·00	1·75
261	28	3d. yellow-brown (5.00).	17·00	65
		a. Imperf between (pair)	£550	
		b. Imperf vert (horiz pair)	£350	
		c. Deep brown	17·00	65
		ca. Imperf between (pair)	£550	
262	37	4d. indigo and brown (8.99)	7·00	1·25
		a. Bright blue and chestnut	7·00	1·25
		b. Deep blue and bistre-brown	7·00	1·25
263	30	5d. purple-brown (6.99)	17·00	1·25
		a. Deep purple-brown	17·00	2·25
		ab. Imperf between (pair)	£600	
264	31	6d. deep green	48·00	48·00
		a. Yellow-green	60·00	65·00
265		6d. pale rose (5.5.00)	35·00	2·50
		a. Imperf vert (horiz pair)	£350	
		b. Rose-red	35·00	2·50
		ba. Printed double	£300	
		bb. Imperf between (pair)	£500	
		bc. Imperf vert (horiz pair)	£190	
		bd. Showing part of sheet wmk (7.02)*	48·00	18·00
		c. Scarlet	45·00	8·00
		ca. Imperf vert (horiz pair)	£375	
266	32	8d. indigo	26·00	8·00
		a. Prussian blue	26·00	8·00
267	33	9d. deep purple (8.99)	35·00	18·00
		a. Rosy purple	26·00	8·50
268	34	1s. red (5.00)	42·00	6·50
		a. Dull orange-red	42·00	3·00
		b. Dull brown-red	42·00	6·50
		c. Bright red	50·00	18·00
269	35	2s. blue-green (7.99)	75·00	30·00
		a. Laid paper (1.03)	£160	£160
		b. Grey-green	75·00	30·00
270	36	5s. vermilion (7.99)	£200	£130
		a. Carmine-red	£300	£200
		Set of 11	£425	£200

*No. 265bd is on paper without general watermark, but showing the words "LISBON SUPERFINE" wmkd once in the sheet; the paper was obtained from Parsons Bros, an American firm with a branch at Auckland.

1900. *Thick, soft ("Pirie") paper. Wmk double-lined "NZ" and Star, W* **38** *(sideways). P* 11.

271	13	½d. black	3·50	3·00
272	15	2d. bright purple	9·00	3·00
		Wi. Wmk sideways inverted	18·00	8·00

No. 272Wi shows the star to the left of N Z, *as seen from the back of the stamp.*

39 White Terrace,
Rotomahana

41

40 Commemorative of the New Zealand
Contingent in the South African War

(Des J. Nairn (1½d.). Recess Govt Printer, Wellington)

1900 (Mar–Dec). *Thick, soft ("Pirie") paper. W* **38**. *P* 11.

273	23	½d. pale yellow-green (7.3.00)	7·00	2·50
		a. Yellow-green	4·25	10
		b. Green	3·50	10
		ba. Imperf between (pair)	£250	
		c. Deep green	3·50	10
		Wi. Wmk inverted	20·00	8·00
274	39	1d. crimson (7.3.00)	8·00	10
		a. Rose-red	8·00	10
		ab. Imperf between (pair)	£500	£500
		ac. Imperf vert (horiz pair)	£250	
		b. Lake	15·00	2·50
		Wi. Wmk inverted		
275	40	1½d. khaki (7.12.00)	£650	£475
		a. Brown	40·00	40·00
		ab. Imperf vert (horiz pair)	£400	
		ac. Imperf (pair)	£450	
		b. Chestnut	7·50	4·00
		ba. Imperf vert (horiz pair)	£400	
		bb. Imperf horiz (vert pair)	£500	
		c. Pale chestnut	7·50	4·00
		ca. Imperf (pair)	£450	
276	41	2d. dull violet (3.00)	5·50	20
		a. Imperf between (pair)	£600	
		b. Mauve	8·00	1·50
		c. Purple	6·50	20
		ca. Imperf between (pair)	£425	

The above ½d. stamps are slightly smaller than those of the previous printing. A new plate was made to print 240 stamps instead of 120 as previously, and to make these fit the watermarked paper the border design was redrawn and contracted, the centre vignette remaining as before. The 2d. stamp is also from a new plate providing smaller designs.

38

42

(Des G. Bach. Eng. J. A. C. Harrison. Recess Waterlow)

1901 (1 Jan). *Universal Penny Postage. No wmk. P* 12 *to* 16.

277	42	1d. carmine	5·00	2·50

(Recess Govt Printer, Wellington)

1901 (Feb–Dec).　*Thick, soft ("Pirie") paper. W* **38**. (a) *P* 11.
278	42	1d. carmine	5·00	10
		a. Imperf between (pair)	£225	
		b. Deep carmine	5·00	10
		ba. Imperf between (pair)	£225	
		c. Carmine-lake	17·00	7·50

(b) *P* 14
279	23	½d. green (11.01)	9·00	2·75
280	42	1d. carmine	35·00	7·50
		a. Imperf between (pair)	£225	

(c) *Perf compound of* 11 *and* 14
281	23	½d. green	10·00	4·00
		a. Deep green	10·00	4·00
282	42	1d. carmine	£250	£100

(d) *P* 11 *and* 14 *mixed**
283	23	½d. green	55·00	35·00
284	42	1d. carmine	£250	£110

*The term "mixed" is applied to stamps from sheets which were at first perforated 14, or 14 and 11 compound, and either incompletely or defectively perforated. These sheets were patched on the back with strips of paper, and re-perforated 11 in those parts where the original perforation was defective.

(Recess Govt Printer, Wellington)

1901 (Dec.)　*Thin, hard ("Basted Mills") paper. W* **38**. (a) *P* 11.
285	23	½d. green	50·00	50·00
286	42	1d. carmine	60·00	50·00

(b) *P* 14
287	23	½d. green	30·00	10·00
		a. Imperf between (pair)	£325	
288	42	1d. carmine	14·00	2·00
		a. Imperf between (pair)	£325	

(c) *Perf compound of* 11 *and* 14
289	23	½d. green	25·00	25·00
		a. Deep green	25·00	25·00
290	42	1d. carmine	12·00	2·50

(d) *Mixed perfs*
291	23	½d. green	75·00	75·00
292	42	1d. carmine	£100	80·00

(Recess Govt Printer, Wellington)

1902 (Jan).　*Thin, hard ("Cowan") paper. No wmk.* (a) *P* 11.
293	23	½d. green	£100	90·00

(b) *P* 14
294	23	½d. green	9·00	3·25
295	42	1d. carmine	15·00	1·25

(c) *Perf compound of* 11 *and* 14
296	23	½d. green	£100	£100
297	42	1d. carmine	£120	£120

(d) *Mixed perfs*
298	23	½d. green	£100	£100
299	42	1d. carmine	£140	£140

43 "Single" Wmk

SIDEWAYS WATERMARKS. Stamps with W **43** sideways show the star to the left of NZ, *as seen from the back.* Sideways inverted varieties have the star to the right of NZ, *as seen from the back.*

(Recess Govt Printer, Wellington)

1902 (Apr).　*Thin, hard ("Cowan") paper. W* **43**. (a) *P* 11.
300	23	½d. green	55·00	55·00
301	42	1d. carmine	£650	£500

(b) *P* 14
302	23	½d. green	2·25	15
		a. Imperf vert (horiz pair)	£150	
		b. Deep green	2·75	30
		ba. Imperf vert (horiz pair)	£150	
		c. Yellow-green	2·25	25
		d. Pale yellow-green	8·50	2·00
		Wi. Wmk inverted	20·00	10·00
303	42	1d. carmine	3·00	10
		a. Imperf between (pair)	£170	
		b. Booklet pane of 6 (21.8.02)	£190	
		c. Pale carmine	3·00	10
		ca. Imperf between (pair)	£170	
		cb. Booklet pane of 6	£190	
		d. Deep carmine*	28·00	15·00
		Wi. Wmk inverted	40·00	15·00

(c) *Perf compound of* 11 *and* 14
304	23	½d. green	14·00	25·00
		a. Deep green	20·00	27·00
305	42	1d. carmine	£120	80·00
		a. Deep carmine*	£500	£375

(d) *Mixed perfs*
306	23	½d. green	26·00	26·00
		a. Deep green	30·00	30·00
307	42	1d. carmine	35·00	35·00
		a. Pale carmine	35·00	35·00
		b. Deep carmine*	£325	£325

*Nos. 303d, 305a and 307b were printed from a plate made by Waterlow & Sons, known as the "Reserve" plate. The stamps do not show evidence of wearing and the area surrounding the upper part of the figure is more deeply shaded.

A special plate, showing a minute dot between the horizontal rows, was introduced in 1902 to print booklet panes. A special characteristic of the booklet plate was that the pearl in the top left-handed corner was large. Some panes exist with outer edges imperforate.

(Recess Govt Printer, Wellington)

1902 (28 Aug)–**09**.　*Thin, hard ("Cowan") paper. W* **43** (*sideways on 3d., 5d., 6d., 8d., 1s. and 5s.*) (a) *P* 11
308	27	2½d. blue (5.03)	11·00	10·00
		a. Deep blue	12·00	10·00
		Wi. Wmk inverted		
309	28	3d. yellow-brown	16·00	35
		a. Bistre-brown	16·00	35
		b. Pale bistre	25·00	2·75
		Wi. Wmk sideways inverted	16·00	35
310	37	4d. deep blue and deep brown/bluish (27.11.02)	8·50	28·00
		a. Imperf vert (horiz pair)	£425	
311	30	5d. red-brown (4.03)	16·00	5·50
		a. Deep brown	16·00	2·50
		b. Sepia	30·00	12·00
312	31	6d. rose (9.02)	35·00	3·50
		a. Rose-red	35·00	3·50
		ab. Wmk upright	£400	£300
		b. Rose-carmine	35·00	3·50
		ba. Imperf vert (horiz pair)	£300	
		bb. Imperf horiz (vert pair)		
		c. Bright carmine-pink	48·00	5·00
		d. Scarlet	48·00	15·00
		Wi. Wmk sideways inverted	35·00	3·50
313	32	8d. blue (2.03)	24·00	6·00
		a. Steel-blue	24·00	6·00
		ab. Imperf vert (horiz pair)	£450	
		ac. Imperf horiz (vert pair)	£450	
		Wi. Wmk sideways inverted	24·00	6·00
314	33	9d. purple (5.03)	25·00	9·00
		Wi. Wmk inverted	60·00	30·00
315	34	1s. brown-red (11.02)	42·00	3·50
		a. Bright red	45·00	3·75
		b. Orange-red	42·00	3·25
		ba. Error. Wmk W **12**b (inverted)	†	£1200
		c. Orange-brown	55·00	5·50
		Wi. Wmk sideways inverted	42·00	3·25
316	35	2s. green (4.03)	70·00	32·00
		a. Blue-green	70·00	32·00
		Wi. Wmk inverted	£150	50·00
317	36	5s. deep red (6.03)	£190	£120
		Wi. Wmk sideways inverted		
		a. Wmk upright	£200	£130
		b. Vermilion	£190	£120
		ba. Wmk upright	£200	£130

(b) P 14

318	40	1½d. chestnut (2.07)	9·50	26·00
319	41	2d. grey-purple (12.02)	5·50	40
		a. Purple	5·50	40
		ab. Imperf vert (horiz pair)	£325	
		ac. Imperf horiz (vert pair)	£325	
		b. Bright reddish purple	6·50	85
320	27	2½d. blue (1906)	7·00	1·25
		a. Deep blue	7·00	1·50
321	28	3d. bistre-brown (1906)	23·00	90
		a. Imperf vert (horiz pair)	£425	
		b. Bistre	23·00	90
		c. Pale yellow-bistre	38·00	8·00
		Wi. Wmk sideways inverted	23·00	90
322	37	4d. deep blue and deep brown/bluish (1903)	6·00	2·00
		a. Imperf vert (horiz pair)	£350	
		b. Imperf horiz (vert pair)	£350	
		c. Centre inverted	†	£20000
		d. Blue and chestnut/bluish	6·00	60
		e. Blue and ochre-brown/bluish	6·00	60
		Wi. Wmk inverted	20·00	6·00
323	30	5d. black-brown (1906)	38·00	14·00
		a. Red-brown	22·00	5·50
324	31	6d. bright carmine-pink (1906)	48·00	5·50
		a. Imperf vert (horiz pair)	£250	
		b. Rose-carmine	48·00	6·00
		Wi. Wmk sideways inverted	48·00	5·50
325	32	8d. steel-blue (1907)	25·00	4·50
		Wi. Wmk sideways inverted	25·00	4·50
326	33	9d. purple (1906)	25·00	6·00
		Wi. Wmk inverted	60·00	20·00
327	34	1s. orange-brown (1906)	55·00	4·50
		a. Orange-red	50·00	4·50
		b. Pale red	70·00	20·00
		Wi. Wmk sideways, inverted	50·00	4·50
328	35	2s. green (1.06)	60·00	20·00
		a. Blue-green	60·00	20·00
		Wi. Wmk inverted	£150	50·00
329	36	5s. deep red (1906)	£190	£120
		a. Wmk upright	£200	£130
		aWi. Wmk inverted		
		b. Dull red	£190	£120
		ba. Wmk upright	£200	£130

(c) Perf compound of 11 and 14

330	40	1½d. chestnut (1907)	£450	
331	41	2d. purple (1903)	£250	
332	28	3d. bistre-brown (1906)	£450	£450
333	37	4d. blue and yellow-brown (1903)	£300	£300
334	30	5d. red-brown (1906)	£400	£400
335	31	6d. rose-carmine (1907)	£250	£200
		Wi. Wmk sideways inverted	£250	£200
336	32	8d. steel-blue (1907)	£600	£600
		Wi. Wmk sideways inverted	£600	£600
337	33	9d. purple (1906)	£800	£800
338	36	5s. deep red (1906)	£1100	£1000

(d) Mixed perfs

339	40	1½d. chestnut (1907)	£450	
340	41	2d. purple (1903)	£130	
341	28	3d. bistre-brown (1906)	£450	£450
		Wi. Wmk sideways inverted	£450	£450
342	37	4d. blue and chestnut/bluish (1904)	£250	£250
		a. Blue and yellow-brown/bluish	£250	£250
343	30	5d. red-brown (1906)	£375	£375
344	31	6d. rose-carmine (1907)	£250	£200
		a. Bright carmine-pink	£250	£200
		Wi. Wmk sideways inverted	£200	£200
345	32	8d. steel-blue (1907)	£550	£550
346	33	9d. purple (1906)	£700	£700
347	35	2s. blue-green (1906)	£600	£600
348	36	5s. vermilion (1906)	£1100	£1000

Two sizes of paper were used for the above stamps:—
(1) A sheet containing 240 wmks, with a space of 9 mm between each.
(2) A sheet containing 120 wmks, with a space of 24 mm between each vertical row.

Size (1) was used for the ½d., 1d., 2d., and 4d., and size (2) for 2½d., 5d., 9d., and 2s. The paper in each case exactly fitted the design, and had the watermark in register, though in the case of the 4d., the plate of which contained only 80 stamps, the paper was cut up to print it. The 3d., 6d., 8d., and 1s. were printed on variety (1), but with watermark sideways: by reason of this, specimens from the margins of the sheets show parts of the words "NEW ZEALAND POSTAGE" in large letters, and some copies have no watermark at all. For the 1½d. and 5s. stamps variety (1) was also used, but two watermarks appear on each stamp.

(Recess Govt Printer, Wellington)

1904. Printed from new "dot" plates. Thin, hard ("Cowan") paper. W **43**.

(a) P 14.

349	42	1d. rose-carmine	8·00	30
		a. Pale carmine	8·00	30
		Wi. Wmk inverted	75·00	25·00

(b) Perf compound of 11 and 14

350	42	1d. rose-carmine	£130	£130

(c) Mixed perfs

351	42	1d. rose-carmine	26·00	22·00
		a. Pale carmine	26·00	22·00

The above new plates have a minute dot between the stamps in the horizontal rows, but it is frequently cut out by the perforations. However, they can be further distinguished by the notes below.

In 1906 fresh printings were made from four new plates, two of which, marked "W1" and "W2", were supplied by Waterlow Bros and Layton, and the other two, marked "R1" and "R2", by W. R. Royle & Son. The intention was to note which pair of plates wore the best and produced the best results. They can be distinguished as follows:—

(a)	(b)	(c)

(d)	(e)	(f)

(a) Four o'clock flaw in rosette at top right corner. Occurs in all these plates but not in the original Waterlow plates.
(b) Pearl at right strong.
(c) Pearl at right weak.
(d) Dot at left and S-shaped ornament unshaded.
(e) S-shaped ornament with one line of shading within.
(f) As (e) but with line from left pearl to edge of stamp.
"Dot" plates comprise (a) and (d). Waterlow plates comprise (a), (b) and (e). Royle plates comprise (a), (c) and (d) and the line in (f) on many stamps but not all.

(Recess Govt Printer, Wellington)

1906. Thin, hard ("Cowan") paper. W **43**.

(a) Printed from new Waterlow plates. (i) P 14

352	42	1d. deep rose-carmine	18·00	70
		a. Imperf between (pair)	£200	
		b. Aniline carmine	17·00	70
		ba. Imperf between (pair)	£200	
		c. Rose-carmine	17·00	70

(ii) P 11

353	42	1d. aniline carmine	£325	£325

(iii) Perf compound of 11 and 14

354	42	1d. rose-carmine	£300	£300

(iv) Mixed perfs

355	42	1d. deep rose-carmine	£325	£325

(b) Printed from new Royle plates. (i) P 14

356	42	1d. rose-carmine	10·00	90
		a. Imperf between (vert pair)	£200	£200
		b. Bright rose-carmine	12·00	1·00

(ii) P 11

357	42	1d. bright rose-carmine	£150	£150

(iii) Perf compound of 11 and 14

358	42	1d. rose-carmine	85·00	85·00

(iv) Mixed perfs

359	42	1d. rose-carmine	£110	£110

(v) P 14 × 14½ (comb)

360	42	1d. bright rose-carmine	60·00	45·00
		a. Rose-carmine	60·00	45·00

Nos. 360/a are known both with and without the small dot.
See also No. 437.

1905 (15 June)–**06**.   *Stamps supplied to penny-in-the-slot machines.*

(i) *"Dot" plates of 1904.* (ii) Waterlow *"reserve" plate of* 1902

(a) *Imperf top and bottom; zigzag roulette* 9½ *on one or both sides, two large holes at sides*

361	**42**	1d. rose-carmine (i)	£120	
362		1d. deep carmine (ii)	£120	

(b) *As last but rouletted* 14½ (8.7.05)

363	**42**	1d. rose-carmine (i)	£140	
364		1d. deep carmine (ii)		

(c) *Imperf all round, two large holes each side* (6.3.06)

365	**42**	1d. rose-carmine (i)	£180	
366		1d. deep carmine (ii)	£140	

(d) *Imperf all round* (21.6.06)

367	**42**	1d. deep carmine (ii)	£120	

(e) *Imperf all round. Two small indentations on back of stamp* (1.06)

368	**42**	1d. deep carmine (ii)	£130	£130

(f) *Imperf all round; two small pin-holes in stamp* (21.6.06)

369	**42**	1d. deep carmine (ii)	£130	£130

No. 365 *only* exists from strips of Nos. 361 or 363 (resulting from the use of successive coins) which have been separated by scissors. Similarly strips of Nos. 362 and 364 can produce single copies of No. 366 but this also exists in singles from a different machine.

Most used copies of Nos. 361/7 are forgeries and they should only be collected on cover.

44 Maori Canoe, *Te Arawa*

(Des L. J. Steele. Eng W. R. Bock. Typo Govt Printer, Wellington)

1906 (1–17 Nov).   *New Zealand Exhibition, Christchurch. T* **44** *and similar horiz designs. W* **43** *(sideways). P* 14.

370		½d. emerald-green	16·00	23·00
		Wi. Wmk sideways inverted	20·00	25·00
371		1d. vermilion	13·00	15·00
		Wi. Wmk sideways inverted	20·00	20·00
		a. Claret	£7000	£8000
372		3d. brown and blue	45·00	48·00
		Wi. Wmk sideways inverted	£125	£140
373		6d. pink and olive-green (17.11)	£140	£225
		Wi. Wmk sideways inverted	£225	
		Set of 4	£200	£275

Designs:—1d. Maori art; 3d. Landing of Cook; 6d. Annexation of New Zealand.

The 1d. in claret was the original printing, which was considered unsatisfactory.

DOMINION

46   **47** (T **28** reduced)

48 (T **31** reduced)   **49** (T **34** reduced)

(New plates (except 4d.), supplied by Perkins Bacon. Recess (T **46** typo) by Govt Printer, Wellington)

1907–8.   *Thin, hard ("Cowan") paper. W* **43**. (a) *P* 14 *(line).*

374	**23**	½d. green (1907)	27·00	6·00
		a. Imperf (pair)	90·00	
		b. Yellow-green	18·00	2·00
		c. Deep yellow-green	14·00	1·50
375	**47**	3d. brown (6.07)	48·00	17·00
376	**48**	6d. carmine-pink (3.07)	48·00	6·00
		a. Red	75·00	26·00

(b) *P* 14 × 13, 13½ *(comb)*

377	**23**	½d. green (1907)	18·00	3·50
		a. Yellow-green	8·00	85
378	**47**	3d. brown (2.08)	48·00	22·00
		a. Yellow-brown	48·00	25·00
379	**37**	4d. blue and yellow-brown/*bluish* (6.08)	27·00	20·00
380	**48**	6d. pink (2.08)	£250	80·00
381	**49**	1s. orange-red (12.07)	£130	45·00

(c) *P* 14 × 15 *(comb)*

382	**23**	½d. yellow-green (1907)	11·00	60
383	**46**	1d. carmine (1.12.08)	30·00	50
		Wi. Wmk inverted	—	50·00
384	**47**	3d. brown (8.08)	48·00	7·00
		a. Yellow-brown	48·00	7·00
385	**48**	6d. carmine-pink (8.08)	48·00	8·00
386	**49**	1s. orange-red (8.08)	£120	24·00
		a. Deep orange-brown	£300	

The ½d. stamps of this 1907–8 issue have a minute dot in the margin between the stamps, where not removed by the perforation. (See note after No. 351a.) Those perforated 14 can be distinguished from the earlier stamps, Nos. 302/*d*, by the absence of plate wear. This is most noticeable on the 1902 printings as a white patch at far left, level with the bottom of the "P" in "POSTAGE". Such damage is not present on the new plates used for Nos. 374/*c*.

Stamps of T **47, 48** and **49** also have a small dot as described in note after No. 351a.

Stamps in T **46** are typographed but the design also differs from T **42**. The rosettes in the upper corners are altered and the lines on the globe diagonal instead of vertical. The paper is chalk-surfaced.

TYPOGRAPHY PAPERS 1909–30. **De La Rue paper** is chalk-surfaced and has a smooth finish. The watermark is as illustrated. The gum is toned and strongly resistant to soaking.

Jones paper is chalk-surfaced and has a coarser texture, is poorly surfaced and the ink tends to peel. The outline of the watermark commonly shows on the surface of the stamp. The gum is colourless or only slightly toned and washes off readily.

Cowan paper is chalk-surfaced and is white and opaque. The watermark is usually smaller than in the "Jones" paper and is often barely visible.

Wiggins Teape paper is chalk-surfaced and is thin and hard. It has a vertical mesh with a narrow watermark, whereas the other papers have a horizontal mesh and a wider watermark.

50   **51**   **52**

(Eng. P.B. Typo Govt Printer, Wellington)

1909 (8 Nov)–**12**.   *De La Rue chalk-surfaced paper with toned gum. W* **43**. *P* 14 × 15 *(comb).*

387	**50**	½d. yellow-green	2·75	10
		aa. Deep green	2·75	20
		a. Imperf (pair)	£140	
		b. Booklet pane. Five stamps plus label in position 1 (4.10)	£400	
		c. Ditto, but label in position 6 (4.10)	£400	
		d. Booklet pane of 6 (4.10)	£140	
		e. Ditto, but with coloured bars on selvedge (5.12)	£140	

Stamps with blurred and heavy appearance are from booklets.

(Eng W. R. Royle & Son, London. Recess Govt Printer, Wellington)

1909 (8 Nov)–**16**. *T* **51** *and similar portraits.*

(a) W **43**. *P* 14 × 14½ *(comb)*

388	2d. mauve		14·00	4·75
	a. Deep mauve		17·00	4·75
	Wi. Wmk inverted		†	
389	3d. chestnut		17·00	30
390	4d. orange-red		22·00	20·00
	a. Orange-yellow (1912)		9·00	2·25
	Wi. Wmk inverted		—	£100
391	5d. brown (1910)		13·00	60
	a. Red-brown		11·00	60
392	6d. carmine (1910)		24·00	40
	a. Deep carmine (29.10.13)		24·00	50
393	8d. indigo-blue		9·00	65
	a. Deep bright blue		11·00	65
	Wi. Wmk inverted		20·00	15·00
394	1s. vermilion (1910)		42·00	2·00
	Set of 8		£130	27·00

(b) W **43**. *P* 14 *(line)**

395	3d. chestnut (1910)		32·00	3·75
396	4d. orange (1910)		15·00	5·00
397	5d. brown		18·00	3·00
	a. Red-brown (15.9.11)		20·00	3·50
398	6d. carmine		35·00	6·50
399	1s. vermilion		45·00	6·50
	Set of 5		£130	22·00

(c) W **43** *(sideways) (paper with widely spaced watermark as used for Nos. 308 and 320 – see note below No. 348). P* 14 *(line)**

400	8d. indigo-blue (8.16)		13·00	27·00
	a. No wmk		45·00	60·00

(d) W **43**. *P* 14 × 13½ *(comb)*†

401	3d. chestnut (1915)		50·00	50·00
	a. Vert pair. P 14 × 13½ and 14 × 14½		£225	£275
	Wi. Wmk inverted		£120	£120
402	5d. red-brown (1916)		15·00	1·50
	a. Vert pair. P 14 × 13½ and 14 × 14½		50·00	70·00
403	6d. carmine (1915)		55·00	55·00
	a. Vert pair. P 14 × 13½ and 14 × 14½		£225	£275
404	8d. indigo-blue (3.16)		17·00	1·75
	a. Vert pair. P 14 × 13½ and 14 × 14½		50·00	70·00
	b. Deep bright blue		17·00	1·75
	ba. Vert pair. P 14 × 13½ and 14 × 14½		50·00	70·00
	Wi. Wmk inverted		20·00	15·00
	Set of 4		£120	95·00

*In addition to showing the usual characteristics of a line perforation, these stamps may be distinguished by their vertical perforation which measures 13.8. Nos. 388/94 generally measure vertically 14 to 14.3. An exception is 13.8 one vertical side but 14 the other.

†The 3d. and 6d. come in full sheets perf 14 × 13½. The 3d., 5d. and 6d. values also exist in two combinations: (a) five top rows perf 14 × 13½ with five bottom rows perf 14 × 14½ and (b) four top rows perf 14 × 13½ with six bottom rows perf 14 × 14½. The 8d. perf 14 × 13½ only exists from combination (b).

(Eng P.B. Typo Govt Printer, Wellington)

1909 (8 Nov)–**26**. *P* 14 × 15 *(comb).*

(a) W **43**. *De La Rue chalk-surfaced paper with toned gum*

405	**52**	1d. carmine	1·00	10
		a. Imperf (pair)	£170	
		b. Booklet pane of 6 (4.10)	£110	
		c. Ditto, but with coloured bars on selvedge (5.12)	£110	
		Wi. Wmk inverted	20·00	20·00

(b) W **43**. *Jones chalk-surfaced paper with white gum*

406	**52**	1d. deep carmine (1924)	7·50	2·50
		a. On unsurfaced paper. *Pale carmine*	£275	
		b. Booklet pane of 6 with bars on selvedge (1.12.24)	95·00	
		Wi. Wmk inverted	25·00	25·00

(c) W **43**. *De La Rue unsurfaced medium paper with toned gum*

407	**52**	1d. rose-carmine (4.25)	18·00	45·00

(d) W **43** *(sideways). De La Rue chalk-surfaced paper with toned gum*

408	**52**	1d. bright carmine (4.25)	4·25	14·00
		a. No wmk	14·00	26·00
		b. Imperf (pair)	50·00	
		Wi. Wmk sideways inverted	6·00	16·00

(e) No wmk, but bluish "NZ" and Star lithographed on back. Art paper

409	**52**	1d. rose-carmine (1925)	2·25	60
		a. "NZ" and Star in black	8·00	
		b. "NZ" and Star colourless	22·00	

(f) W **43**. *Cowan thick, opaque, chalk-surfaced paper with white gum*

410	**52**	1d. deep carmine (8.25)	4·00	60
		a. Imperf (pair)	60·00	70·00
		b. Booklet pane of 6 with bars and adverts on selvedge	45·00	
		Wi. Wmk inverted	30·00	20·00

(g) W **43**. *Wiggins Teape thin, hard, chalk-surfaced paper with white gum*

411	**52**	1d. rose-carmine (6.26)	16·00	7·00
		Wi. Wmk inverted	35·00	20·00

Examples of No. 405 with a blurred and heavy appearance are from booklets.

No. 406a comes from a sheet on which the paper coating was missing from the right-hand half.

Many stamps from the sheets of No. 408 were without watermark or showed portions of "NEW ZEALAND POSTAGE" in double-lined capitals.

AUCKLAND
EXHIBITION,
1913.

(59)   60

1913 (1 Dec). *Auckland Industrial Exhibition. Nos.* 387aa, 389, 392 *and* 405 *optd with T* **59** *by Govt Printer, Wellington.*

412	**50**	½d. deep green	10·00	20·00
413	**52**	1d. carmine	15·00	24·00
414	**51**	3d. chestnut	£100	£160
415		6d. carmine	£100	£170
		Set of 4	£200	£350

These overprinted stamps were only available for letters in New Zealand and to Australia.

(Des H. L. Richardson. Recess Govt Printer, Wellington, from plates made in London by P.B.)

1915 (30 July)–**30**. *P* 14 × 14½, comb *(See notes below).*

(a) W **43**. *Cowan unsurfaced paper*

416	**60**	1½d. grey-slate	2·50	40
		a. Perf 14 × 13½	1·75	50
		b. Vert pair, 416/a	35·00	50·00
417		2d. bright violet	6·50	17·00
		a. Perf 14 × 13½	6·50	17·00
		b. Vert pair, 417/a	24·00	50·00
418		2d. yellow (15.1.16)	4·00	12·00
		a. Perf 14 × 13½	4·00	12·00
		b. Vert pair, 418/a	18·00	45·00
419		2½d. blue	8·50	4·00
		a. Perf 14 × 13½ (1916)	3·25	1·75
		b. Vert pair, 419/a	35·00	65·00
420		3d. chocolate	6·00	60
		Wi. Wmk inverted	45·00	25·00
		a. Perf 14 × 13½	6·00	50
		aWi. Wmk inverted	55·00	30·00
		b. Vert pair, 420/a	35·00	55·00
		bWi. Wmk inverted	£110	£130
421		4d. yellow	4·25	28·00
		a. Perf 14 × 13½	4·25	28·00
		b. Vert pair, 421/a	26·00	£120
		c. Re-entry (Pl 20 R.1/6)	30·00	
		d. Re-entry (Pl 20 R.4/10)	35·00	
422		4d. bright violet (7.4.16)	7·00	20
		a. Perf 14 × 13½	5·00	15
		b. Imperf (pair)	£950	
		c. Vert pair, 422/a	35·00	65·00
		d. Re-entry (Pl 20 R.1/6)	35·00	
		e. Re-entry (Pl 20 R.4/10)	40·00	
423		4½d. deep green	16·00	13·00
		a. Perf 14 × 13½	10·00	3·00
		b. Vert pair, 423/a	48·00	65·00
424		5d. light blue (4.22)	14·00	12·00
		a. Perf 14 × 13½	6·00	40
		aWi. Wmk inverted	—	90·00
		b. Imperf (pair)	£110	£120
		c. Pale ultramarine (5.30)	11·00	5·50
		ca. Perf 14 × 13½	8·00	3·75
		cb. Vert pair, 424c/ca	55·00	75·00

425	**60**	6d. carmine	5·50	30
		Wi. Wmk inverted	50·00	40·00
		a. Perf 14 × 13½	5·50	20
		aWi. Wmk inverted	£100	48·00
		b. Vert pair, 425/a (1916)	65·00	95·00
		c. Imperf three sides (pair)	£1200	
		d. Carmine-lake. Perf 14 × 13½ (28.1.28). . .	£500	£325
426		7½d. red-brown	27·00	30·00
		a. Perf 14 × 13½ (10.20).	11·00	15·00
		b. Vert pair, 426/a	50·00	75·00
427		8d. indigo-blue (19.4.21)	15·00	28·00
		a. Perf 14 × 13½	13·00	26·00
		b. Vert pair, 427/a	38·00	70·00
428		8d. red-brown (p 14 × 13½) (2.22)	15·00	40
429		9d. sage-green	17·00	3·50
		a. Perf 14 × 13½	13·00	60
		b. Vert pair, 429/a	70·00	£100
		c. Imperf three sides (pair)	£1300	
		d. Imperf (pair)	£1000	
		e. Yellowish olive. Perf 14 × 13½ (12.25). . .	28·00	7·00
430		1s. vermilion	13·00	25
		Wi. Wmk inverted		
		a. Perf 14 × 13½	13·00	95
		aWi. Wmk inverted	—	£125
		b. Imperf (pair)	£2250	
		c. Vert pair, 430/a	75·00	£100
		cWi. Wmk inverted		
		d. Pale orange-red	24·00	3·50
		da. Imperf (pair)	£325	
		db. Orange-brown (1.2.28)	£850	£425
		Set of 15	90·00	90·00

(b) W **43** (sideways on 2d., 3d. and 6d.). Thin paper with widely spaced watermark as used for Nos. 308 and 320–see note below No. 348)

431	**60**	1½d. grey-slate (3.16)	1·25	3·00
		a. No wmk	2·00	6·50
		b. Perf 14 × 13½	1·25	3·00
		ba. No wmk	2·00	6·50
		c. Vert pair, 431/b	20·00	35·00
		ca. Vert pair, 431a/ba	28·00	50·00
432		2d. yellow (p 14, line) (6.16)	4·50	30·00
		a. No wmk	28·00	60·00
433		3d. chocolate (p 14, line) (6.16)	5·50	7·00
		a. No wmk	25·00	45·00
434		6d. carmine (p 14, line) (8.16)	6·00	35·00
		a. No wmk	35·00	70·00
		Set of 4	15·00	65·00

The 1½d., 2½d., 4½d. and 7½d. have value tablets as shown in T **60**. In the other values, the tablets are shortened, and the ornamental border at each side of the crown correspondingly extended.

During the laying-down of plate 20 for the 4d., from the roller-die which also contained dies of other values, an impression of the 4½d. value was placed on R.1/6 and of the 2½d. on R.4/10. These errors were subsequently corrected by re-entries of the 4d. impression, but on R.1/6 traces of the original impression can be found in the right-hand value tablet and above the top frame line, while on R.4/10 the foot of the "2" is visible in the left-hand value tablet with traces of "½" to its right.

Of this issue the 1½d., 2½d., 4d. (both), 4½d., 5d., 6d., 7½d., 9d. and 1s. are known from sheets perforated 14 × 14½ throughout.

All values from 1½d. to 1s. were also produced showing the use of the two different perforations within the same sheet as described beneath No. 404ba. In most instances the top four rows were perforated 14 × 13½ and the bottom six 14 × 14½. For one printing of the 4d. violet and for all printings of the 5d. pale ultramarine with two perforations on the same sheet the arrangement differed in that the top five rows were perforated 14 × 14½ and the bottom five 14 × 13½.

With the exception of Nos. 432/4 any with perforations measuring 14 × 14 or nearly must be classed as 14 × 14½, this being an irregularity of the comb machine, and not a product of the 14-line machine.

(Die eng W. R. Bock. Typo Govt Printer, Wellington, from plates made by P.B. (T **61**) or locally (T **62**))

1915 (30 July)–**34**. P 14 × 15. (a) W **43**. De La Rue chalk-surfaced paper with toned gum.

435	**61**	½d. green	70	10
		a. Booklet pane of 6 with bars on selvedge	95·00	
		b. Yellow-green	3·00	60
		ba. Booklet pane of 6 with bars on selvedge	80·00	
		c. Very thick, hard, highly surfaced paper with white gum (12.15)	11·00	17·00
		Wi. Wmk inverted	30·00	
436	**62**	1½d. grey-black (4.16)	3·00	30
		a. Black	4·50	35
437	**61**	1½d. slate (5.9.16)	5·50	10
		Wi. Wmk inverted	—	£110
438		1½d. orange-brown (9.18)	1·50	10
		Wi. Wmk inverted	75·00	60·00
439		2d. yellow (9.16)	80	10
		a. Pale yellow	3·50	90
		Wi. Wmk inverted	75·00	
440		3d. chocolate (5.19)	6·00	30
		Set of 6	16·00	70

(b) W **43**. Jones chalk-surfaced paper with white gum

441	**61**	½d. green (10.24)	5·50	3·25
		a. Booklet pane of 6 with bars on selvedge (1.12.24)	85·00	
		Wi. Wmk inverted	40·00	
442		2d. dull yellow (7.24)	4·00	12·00
		Wi. Wmk inverted	30·00	
443		3d. deep chocolate (3.25)	15·00	4·00
		Set of 3	22·00	17·00

(c) No wmk, but bluish "NZ" and Star lithographed on back. Art paper

444	**61**	½d. apple-green (4.25)	1·25	50
		a. "NZ" and Star almost colourless . . .	4·25	
445		2d. yellow (7.25)	5·50	26·00

(d) W **43**. Cowan thick, opaque, chalk-surfaced paper with white gum

446	**61**	½d. green (8.25)	40	10
		a. Booklet pane of 6 with bars and adverts on selvedge	85·00	
		ab. Booklet panes of 6 with bars on selvedge (1934)		
		Wi. Wmk inverted	30·00	20·00
		b. Perf 14 (1927)	50	20
		ba. Booklet pane of 6 with bars on selvedge (1928)	45·00	
		bb. Booklet pane of 6 with bars and adverts on selvedge (1928)	45·00	
		bWi. Wmk inverted	40·00	22·00
447		1½d. orange-brown (p 14) (8.29)	8·50	8·50
		a. Perf 14 × 15 (7.33)	45·00	48·00
448		2d. yellow (8.25)	3·25	20
		a. Perf 14 (1929)	2·75	10
		aWi. Wmk inverted	35·00	
449		3d. chocolate (8.25)	6·50	20
		Wi. Wmk inverted	60·00	
		a. Perf 14 (1929)	7·50	1·25
		Set of 4	17·00	8·50

(e) W **43**. Wiggins Teape thin, hard, chalk-surfaced paper

450	**61**	1½d. orange-brown (p 14) (1930).	27·00	55·00
451		2d. yellow (5.26)	6·50	14·00
		Wi. Wmk inverted	24·00	
		a. Perf 14 (10.27)	6·00	14·00
		aWi. Wmk inverted	30·00	30·00

The designs of these stamps also differ as described beneath No. 434. Stamps from booklet panes often have blurred, heavy impressions. Different advertisements can be found on the listed booklet panes.

1915 (24 Sept). No. 435 optd with T **63**.

452	**61**	½d. green	1·40	20

WAR STAMP

61   62   (63)

Type **62** (from local plates) can be identified from Type **61** (prepared by Perkins Bacon) by the shading on the portrait. This is diagonal on Type **62** and horizontal on Type **61**.

64 "Peace" and Lion    65 "Peace" and Lion

(Des and typo D.L.R. from plates by P.B., Waterlow and D.L.R.)

1920 (27 Jan). *Victory. T* **64/5** *and similar designs. W* **43**. (*sideways on* ½*d.,* 1½*d.,* 3*d., and* 1*s.*). *De La Rue chalk-surfaced paper. P* 14.

453		½d. green	1·50	75
		a. Pale yellow-green	20·00	8·50
		Wi. Wmk sideways inverted	48·00	
454		1d. carmine-red	2·75	25
		a. Bright carmine	3·75	35
		Wi. Wmk inverted	15·00	
455		1½d. brown-orange	3·25	20
		Wi. Wmk sideways inverted	25·00	
456		3d. chocolate	10·00	10·00
		Wi. Wmk sideways inverted	—	85·00
457		6d. violet	10·00	11·00
		a. Wmk sideways	—	£250
		Wi. Wmk inverted	—	£125
458		1s. orange-red	20·00	35·00
		Set of 6	42·00	50·00

Designs: *Horiz* (*as T* **65**)—1½d. Maori chief. (*As T* **64**)—3d. Lion; 1s. King George V. *Vert* (*as T* **64**)—6d. "Peace" and "Progress".
The above stamps were placed on sale in London in November, 1919.

2d.   **2d.**

TWOPENCE

(68)   69

1922 (Mar). *Surch with T* **68**.

459	64	2d. on ½d. green (R.)	2·00	60
		Wi. Wmk sideways inverted	35·00	35·00

(Des and eng W. R. Bock. Typo Govt Printer, Wellington)

1923 (1 Oct)–**25**. *Restoration of Penny Postage. W* **43**. *P* 14 × 15.

(a) De La Rue chalk-surfaced paper with toned gum.

460	69	1d. carmine	1·50	25

(b) Jones chalk-surfaced paper with white gum

461	69	1d. carmine (3.24)	3·75	2·25
		Wi. Wmk inverted	25·00	25·00

(c) Cowan unsurfaced paper with very shiny gum

462	69	1d. carmine-pink (4.25)	26·00	22·00

The paper used for No. 462 is similar to that of Nos. 416/30.

70 Exhibition Buildings

(Des H. L. Richardson. Eng and typo Govt Printer, Wellington)

1925 (17 Nov). *Dunedin Exhibition. W* **43**. *Cowan chalk-surfaced paper. P* 14 × 15.

463	70	½d. yellow-green/green	1·75	8·50
		Wi. Wmk inverted	—	85·00
464		1d. carmine/rose	2·00	5·00
		Wi. Wmk inverted	—	85·00
465		4d. mauve/pale mauve	35·00	60·00
		a. "POSTAGF" at right (R.1/2, R.10/1)	£120	£170
		Set of 3	35·00	65·00

(Des H. L. Richardson; plates by B.W. (1d. from sheets), P.B. (1d. from booklets), Royal Mint, London (others). Typo Govt Printer, Wellington).

1926 (12 July)–**34**. *W* **43**. *P* 14. (*a*) *Jones chalk-surfaced paper with white gum.*

466	72	2s. deep blue	42·00	42·00
		Wi. Wmk inverted	50·00	45·00
467		3s. mauve	70·00	85·00
		Wi. Wmk inverted	90·00	£100
		Set of 2	£110	£125

(b) Cowan thick, opaque, chalk-surfaced paper with white gum

468	71	1d. rose-carmine (15.11.26)	40	5
		a. Imperf (pair)	45·00	
		b. Booklet pane of 6 with bars on selvedge (1928)	45·00	
		c. Booklet pane of 6 with bars and adverts on selvedge (1928)	45·00	
		Wi. Wmk inverted	12·00	10·00
		d. Perf 14 × 15 (3.27)	45	5
		da. Booklet pane of 6 with bars and adverts on selvedge (1934)	60·00	
		dWi. Wmk inverted	12·00	10·00
469	72	2s. light blue (5.27)	40·00	14·00
470		3s. pale mauve (9.27)	70·00	80·00
		Set of 3	£100	85·00

(c) Wiggins Teape thin, hard, chalk-surfaced paper with white gum

471	71	1d. rose-carmine (6.30)	13·00	3·50
		Wi. Wmk inverted	25·00	10·00

No. 468 exists in a range of colours including scarlet and deep carmine to magenta but we have insufficient evidence to show that these were issued.

73 Nurse   **74** Smiling Boy

(Typo Govt Printing Office, Wellington)

1929–30. *Anti-Tuberculosis Fund. T* **73** *and similar type. W* **43**. *P* 14.

(a) Inscribed "HELP STAMP OUT TUBERCULOSIS".

544		1d. + 1d. scarlet (11.12.29)	11·00	13·00
		Wi. Wmk inverted	£150	
		First Day Cover		£150

(b) Inscribed "HELP PROMOTE HEALTH"

545		1d. + 1d. scarlet (29.10.30)	16·00	22·00
		First Day Cover		£160

(Des L. C. Mitchell. Dies eng and plates made Royal Mint, London (1d.), Govt Ptg Office, Wellington from W. R. Bock die (2d.). Typo Govt Ptg Office, Wellington).

1931 (31 Oct). *Health Stamps. W* **43** (*sideways*). *P* 14½ × 14.

546	74	1d. + 1d. scarlet	70·00	75·00
547		2d. + 1d. blue	70·00	65·00
		Set of 2	£140	£140
		First Day Cover		£700

71   72

75 New Zealand Lake Scenery

FIVE PENCE

(76)

(Des L. C. Mitchell. Plates, Royal Mint, London. Typo Govt Ptg Office)

1931 (10 Nov)-**35**. *Air. W* **43**. *P* 14 × 14½.
548 **75** 3d. chocolate . . . . 15·00 8·50
    a. Perf 14 × 15 (4.35) £190 £425
549   4d. blackish purple . . . . 17·00 10·00
550   7d. brown-orange . . . . 18·00 7·00
    Set of 3 . . . . 45·00 23·00

1931 (18 Dec). *Air. Surch with T* **76**.
551 **75** 5d. on 3d. green (R.) . . . . 8·50 7·50

77 Hygeia,
Goddess of Health
78 The Path to Health

86 Maori Girl

87 Mitre Peak

 88 Swordfish
89 Harvesting

(Des R. E. Tripe and W. J. Cooch. Eng H. T. Peat. Recess Govt Printing Office, Wellington)

1932 (18 Nov). *Health Stamp. W* **43**. *P* 14.
552 **77** 1d. + 1d. carmine . . . . 14·00 20·00
    Wi. Wmk inverted £150
    First Day Cover £140

(Des J. Berry. Eng H. T. Peat. Recess Govt Printing Office, Wellington)

1933 (8 Nov). *Health Stamp. W* **43**. *P* 14.
553 **78** 1d. + 1d. carmine . . . . 7·00 11·00
    Wi. Wmk inverted £130
    First Day Cover £110

90 Tuatara Lizard
91 Maori Panel
92 Tui

**TRANS-TASMAN
AIR MAIL
"FAITH IN AUSTRALIA."**
(79)

 80 Crusader

93 Capt. Cook at Poverty Bay
94 Mt Egmont

1934 (17 Jan). *Air. T* **75** *in new colour optd with T* **79**. *W* **43**. *P* 14 × 14½.
554 **75** 7d. light blue (B.) . . . . 25·00 35·00
    First Day Cover £150

(Des J. Berry. Recess D.L.R.)

1934 (25 Oct). *Health Stamp. W* **43**. *P* 14 × 13½.
555 **80** 1d. carmine . . . . 4·00 7·00
    Wi. Wmk inverted . . . . 40·00 45·00
    First Day Cover £200

81 Collared Grey
Fantail
82 Brown Kiwi
83 Maori Woman

84 Maori Carved House
85 Mt Cook

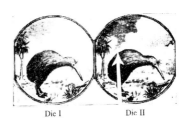

Die I
Die II

"CAPTAIN COQK"
(R. 1/4)

(Des J. Fitzgerald (½d., 4d.), C. H. and R. J. G. Collins (1d.), M. Matthews (1½d.), H. W. Young (2d.), L. C. Mitchell (2½d., 3d., 8d., 1s., 3s.), W. J. Cooch and R. E. Tripe (5d.), T. I. Archer (6d.), I. F. Calder (9d.) and I. H. Jenkins (2s.). Litho Waterlow (9d.). Recess D.L.R. (remainder))

1935 (1 May).   *W* **43**.

556	**81**	½d. bright green, *p* 14 × 13½	1·00	20
		Wi. Wmk inverted	1·50	50
557	**82**	1d. scarlet (Die I), *p* 14 × 13½	1·00	10
		Wi. Wmk inverted	1·75	50
		a. Perf 13½ × 14	40·00	17·00
		b. Die II. Perf 14 × 13½	3·75	75
		ba. Booklet pane of 6 with adverts on selvedge	25·00	
		bWi. Wmk inverted	8·00	1·25
558	**83**	1½d. red-brown, *p* 14 × 13½	3·50	3·75
		a. Perf 13½ × 14	3·50	3·50
		aWi. Wmk inverted	14·00	16·00
559	**84**	2d. orange, *p* 14 × 13½	1·25	30
		Wi. Wmk inverted	50·00	
560	**85**	2½d. chocolate and slate, *p* 13–14 × 13½	3·00	8·00
		Wi. Wmk inverted	20·00	
		a. Perf 13½ × 14	2·75	8·00
561	**86**	3d. brown, *p* 14 × 13½	7·00	60
		Wi. Wmk inverted	—	50·00
562	**87**	4d. black and sepia, *p* 14	2·25	35
		Wi. Wmk inverted	—	50·00
563	**88**	5d. ultramarine, *p* 13–14 × 13½	8·00	11·00
		Wi. Wmk inverted	—	55·00
		a. Perf 13½ × 14	13·00	12·00
564	**89**	6d. scarlet, *p* 13½ × 14	3·50	1·50
		Wi. Wmk inverted	—	30·00
565	**90**	8d. chocolate, *p* 14 × 13½	3·50	1·75
		Wi. Wmk inverted	—	40·00
566	**91**	9d. scarlet and black, *p* 14 × 14½	8·00	2·50
567	**92**	1s. deep green, *p* 14 × 13½	10·00	3·00
		Wi. Wmk inverted	—	50·00
568	**93**	2s. olive-green, *p* 13–14 × 13½	17·00	12·00
		Wi. Wmk inverted	40·00	
		a. "CAPTAIN COQK"	25·00	
		b. Perf 13½ × 14	24·00	15·00
		ba. "CAPTAIN COQK"	35·00	
569	**94**	3s. chocolate & yellow-brown, *p* 13–14 × 13½	15·00	27·00
		a. Perf 13½ × 14	14·00	25·00
		aWi. Wmk inverted	£250	£200
		Set of 14	75·00	65·00

In the 2½d., 5d., 2s. and 3s. perf 13–14 × 13½ the horizontal perforations of each stamp are in two sizes, one half of each horizontal side measuring 13 and the other 14.

See also Nos. 577/90 and 630/1.

95 Bell Block Aerodrome    **96** King George V and Queen Mary

(Des J. Berry. Eng Stamp Printing Office, Melbourne. Recess Govt Printing Office, Wellington)

1935 (4 May).   *Air. W* **43**. *P* 14.

570	**95**	1d. carmine	30	20
		Wi. Wmk inverted	50·00	
571		3d. violet	2·25	1·75
		Wi. Wmk inverted	70·00	
572		6d. blue	4·00	2·25
		Wi. Wmk inverted	90·00	
		Set of 3	6·00	3·75

(Frame by J. Berry. Recess B.W.)

1935 (7 May).   *Silver Jubilee. W* **43**. *P* 11 × 11½.

573	**96**	½d. green	70	45
574		1d. carmine	90	20
575		6d. red-orange	10·00	15·00
		Set of 3	10·50	15·00
		First Day Cover		48·00

97 "The Key to Health"   **98** "Multiple Wmk"

(Des S. Hall. Recess John Ash, Melbourne)

1935 (30 Sept).   *Health Stamp. W* **43**. *P* 11.

576	**97**	1d. + 1d. scarlet	1·50	2·25
		First Day Cover		13·00

WATERMARKS. In W **43** the wmk units are in vertical columns widely spaced and the sheet margins are unwatermarked or wmkd "NEW ZEALAND POSTAGE" in large letters.

In W **98** the wmk units are arranged alternately in horizontal rows closely spaced and are continued into the sheet margins.

Stamps with W **98** sideways show the star to the left of NZ, *as seen from the back*. Sideways inverted varieties have the star to the right, *as seen from the back*.

PRICES

George VI issues (1936–1952)

First column = Unmounted Mint
Second column = Mounted Mint
Third column = Used

COUNTER COIL PAIRS. These were from dispensing machines used by post office counter clerks, the public not having direct access to them. The coils were made up of sections and each section (of 24, 20 or 16 stamps) was divided by a gutter and numbered 1 to 19 (originally in various colours, from 1948 in black), either handstamped or printed, to aid accounting. The figures exist sideways, inverted, upwards or downwards in relation to the stamps. Prices are for unused pairs separated by a numbered gutter (any number), as illustrated.

Counter Coil Pairs

(Litho Govt Ptg Office, Wellington (9d.). Recess Waterlow or D.L.R. (others))

1936–43. W **98.**

577	81	½d. bright green, p 14 × 13½	45	20	5
		Gi. Wmk inverted	1·00	60	25
578	82	1d. scarlet, p 14 × 13½	30	15	5
		Gi. Wmk inverted	4·50	3·00	1·50
579	83	1½d. red-brown, p 14 × 13½	3·00	90	1·25
580	84	2d. orange, p 14 × 13½	15	8	5
		Ea. Coil pair (1945)	£150	£100	
		Wi. Wmk inverted	20·00	15·00	15·00
		b. Perf 12½† (6.41)	1·75	65	10
		bWi. Wmk inverted			
		c. Perf 14 (6.41)	6·00	2·00	70
		d. Perf 14 × 15 (6.41)	12·00	4·50	3·25
581	85	2½d. chocolate & slate, p 13–14 × 13½	75	40	2·25
		Wi. Wmk inverted	4·00	2·00	
		a. Perf 14	95	45	1·25
		aWi. Wmk inverted	5·50	2·75	
		b. Perf 14 × 13½ (1942)	50	25	1·75
582	86	3d. brown, p 14 × 13½	23·00	8·00	15
		Wi. Wmk inverted	38·00	23·00	
583	87	4d. black and sepia, p 14 × 13½	1·75	60	10
		Wi. Wmk inverted	9·50	6·00	
		a. Perf 12½* (1941)	8·00	3·00	70
		aWi. Wmk inverted	†	†	—
		b. Perf 14, line (1941)	40·00	18·00	30·00
		c. Perf 14 × 14½ comb (7.42)	80	30	5
		cWi. Wmk inverted	45·00	28·00	
584	88	5d. ultramarine, p 13–14 × 13½	3·75	1·40	80
		Ea. Coil pair (1945)	£150	£100	
		Wi. Wmk inverted	17·00	10·00	
		b. Perf 12½*† (7.41, 1942)	11·00	4·25	95
		c. Perf 14 × 13½ (1942)	2·00	1·00	65
		cWi. Wmk inverted	35·00	25·00	
585	89	6d. scarlet, p 13½ × 14.	2·50	70	10
		Wi. Wmk inverted	16·00	10·00	
		a. Perf 12½* (1941)	2·25	75	20
		b. Perf 14½ × 14 (1942)	65	25	5
		bEa. Coil pair (1945)	£150	£100	
		bWi. Wmk inverted	—	—	40·00
586	90	8d. chocolate, p 14 × 13½ (wmk sideways)	2·25	1·00	75
		Wi. Wmk sideways inverted	11·00	7·00	
		aa. Wmk upright (1939)	2·25	90	55
		a. Perf 12½* (wmk sideways) (1941)	2·00	80	60
		b. Perf 14 × 14½ (wmk sideways) (1943)	90	55	10
		bEa. Coil pair (1945)	£170	£110	
		bWi. Wmk sideways inverted	—	—	18·00
587	91	9d. red & grey, p 14 × 15 (wmk sideways)	25·00	8·00	1·75
		a. Red & grey-black. Perf 13½ × 14 (1.3.38)	25·00	8·00	1·50
		aWi. Wmk inverted	28·00	10·00	
588	92	1s. deep green, p 14 × 13½	1·50	70	10
		Ea. Coil pair (1945)	£160	£110	
		Wi. Wmk inverted	30·00	15·00	
		b. Perf 12½* (11.41)	32·00	10·00	8·50
589	93	2s. olive-green, p 13–14 × 13½	12·00	5·00	1·25
		a. "CAPTAIN COOK"	28·00	18·00	
		Wi. Wmk inverted	32·00	20·00	
		b. Perf 13½ × 14 (1938)	£130	45·00	2·00
		ba. "CAPTAIN COOK"	£130	45·00	
		c. Perf 12½*† (1941, 1942)	14·00	6·00	1·50
		ca. "CAPTAIN COOK"	25·00	15·00	
		d. Perf 14 × 13½ (1942)	7·50	4·25	85
		da. "CAPTAIN COOK"	35·00	25·00	
		dWi. Wmk inverted	—	—	75·00
590	94	3s. choc & yell-brn, p 13–14 × 13½	15·00	6·50	3·25
		Wi. Wmk inverted	38·00	15·00	
		a. Perf 12½* (1941)	35·00	13·00	22·00
		b. Perf 14 × 13½ (1942)	6·00	4·25	1·50
		Set of 14	65·00	26·00	6·50

*†Stamps indicated with an asterisk were printed and perforated by Waterlow; those having a dagger were printed by D.L.R. and perforated by Waterlow. No. 580d was printed by D.L.R. and perforated by Harrison and No. 583b was printed by Waterlow and perforated by D.L.R. These are all known as "Blitz perfs" because De La Rue were unable to maintain supplies after their works were damaged by enemy action. All the rest, except the 9d., were printed and perforated by D.L.R.

On stamps printed and perforated by De La Rue the perf 14 × 13½ varies in the sheet and is sometimes nearer 13½. 2d. perf 14 × 15 is sometimes nearer 14 × 14½.

2½d., 5d., 2s. and 3s. In perf 13–14 × 13½ one half the length of each horizontal perforation measures 13 and the other 14. In perf 14 × 13½ the horizontal perforation is regular.

4d. No. 583b is line-perf measuring 14 exactly and has a blackish sepia frame. No. 583c is a comb-perf measuring 14 × 14.3 or 14 × 14.2 and the frame is a warmer shade.

2s. No. 589b is comb-perf and measures 13.5 × 13.75.

For 9d. typograpned, see Nos. 630/1.

99 N.Z. Soldier at   100 Wool
Anzac Cove

(Des L. C. Mitchell. Recess John Ash, Melbourne)

1936 (27 Apr). *Charity. 21st Anniv of "Anzac" Landing at Gallipoli.* W **43**. P 11.

591	99	½d. + ½d. green	25	90
592		1d. + 1d. scarlet	25	90
		Set of 2	50	1·75
		First Day Cover		2·50

(Des L. C. Mitchell. Recess John Ash, Melbourne)

1936 (1 Oct). *Congress of British Empire Chambers of Commerce, Wellington. Industries Issue. T* **100** *and similar horiz designs.* W **43**. P 11½.

593		½d. emerald-green	15	25
594		1d. scarlet	15	20
595		2½d. blue	90	4·00
596		4d. violet	80	3·50
597		6d. red-brown	90	3·25
		Set of 5	2·50	10·00
		First Day Cover		13·00

Designs:—1d. Butter; 2½d. Sheep; 4d. Apples; 6d. Exports.

105 Health Camp   106 King George VI and
Queen Elizabeth

(Des J. Berry. Recess John Ash, Melbourne)

1936 (2 Nov). *Health Stamp.* W **43**. P 11.

598	105	1d. + 1d. scarlet	65	2·75
		First Day Cover		4·00

(Recess B.W.)

1937 (13 May). *Coronation.* W **98**. P 14 × 13½.

599	106	1d. carmine	25	12	10
600		2½d. Prussian blue	90	40	1·10
601		6d. red-orange	1·25	55	1·00
		Set of 3	2·25	95	2·00
		First Day Cover			2·50

107 Rock climbing   108   King George VI   108a

(Des G. Bull and J. Berry. Recess John Ash, Melbourne)

1937 (1 Oct).   *Health Stamp.* W **43**. P 11.
602   **107**   1d. + 1d. scarlet. . . . .   1·50 — 70   2·50
      First Day Cover . . . .   4·00

(Des W. J. Cooch. Recess B.W.)

1938–44. W **98**. P 14 × 13½.
603   **108**   ½d. green (1.3.38) . . . .   3·50   1·00   5
      Wi. Wmk inverted . . . .   8·00   4·00   1·00
604   ½d. brown-orange (10.7.41) . . . .   10 —   5   5
      Wi. Wmk inverted . . . .
605   1d. scarlet (1.7.38) . . . .   3·50 — 1·00   5
      Wi. Wmk inverted . . . .   8·00   4·00   1·00
606   1d. green (21.7.41) . . . .   10 —   5   5
      Ea. Horiz coil pair (16.2.45) . . . .   5·00   3·00
      Wi. Wmk inverted . . . .   25·00 15·00 25·00
607   **108a** 1½d. purple-brown (26.7.38) . . . .   16·00   5·50   70
      Wi. Wmk inverted . . . .   20·00 10·00   2·00
608   1½d. scarlet (1.2.44) . . . . 10 —   5   5
      Wi. Wmk inverted . . . .   —   —   40·00
609   3d. blue (26.9.44) . . . .   10 —   5   5
      Ea. Horiz coil pair (16.2.45) . . . .   5·00   3·00
      Wi. Wmk inverted . . . .   —   —   30·00
      Set of 7 . . . .   21·00   7·00   70
For other values see Nos. 680/89.

109 Children playing   110 Beach Ball

(Des J. Berry. Recess B.W.)

1938 (1 Oct).   *Health Stamp.* W **98**. P 14 × 13½.
610   **109**   1d. scarlet . . . .   1·40 ✔ 60   1·40
      First Day Cover . . . .   3·50

(Des S. Hall. Recess Note Printing Branch, Commonwealth Bank of Australia, Melbourne)

1939 (16 Oct).   *Health Stamps. Surcharged with new value.* W **43**. P 11.
611   **110**   1d. on ½d. + ½d. green . . . .   1·50   75   3·25
612   2d. on 1d. + 1d. scarlet . . . .   1·75   90   3·25
      Set of 2 . . . .   3·25 ✔ 1·50   6·50
      First Day Cover . . . .   8·50

111 Arrival of the Maoris, 1350   115 Signing Treaty of
                                       Waitangi, 1840

(Des L. C. Mitchell (½d., 3d., 4d.); J. Berry (others). Recess B.W.)

1940 (2 Jan–8 Mar).   *Centenary of Proclamation of British Sovereignty.* T **111**, **115** *and similar designs.* W **98**. P 14 × 13½ (2½d.), 13½ × 14 (5d.) or 13½ (others).
613   ½d. blue-green   25   10   5
614   1d. chocolate and scarlet . . . .   1·25   40   5
615   1½d. light blue and mauve   30   12   20
616   2d. blue-green and chocolate . . . . . .   1·25   40   5
617   2½d. blue-green and blue   45   20   25
618   3d. purple and carmine . . . .   2·00 1·00 35
619   4d. chocolate and lake . . . .   6·50 3·00 70
620   5d. pale blue and brown . . . .   3·25 1·75 2·50
621   6d. emerald-green and violet . . . .   6·00 2·25 35
622   7d. black and red . . . .   1·25   85   4·00
623   8d. black and red (8.3) . . . .   5·50 2·00 1·50
624   9d. olive-green and orange . . . .   6·00 3·50 1·25
625   1s. sage-green and deep green . . . . .   9·00 4·75 2·25
      Set of 13 . . . .   38·00 18·00 12·00
      First Day Covers (2) . . . .   32·00
Designs: *Horiz (as T* 111*)*—1d. H.M.S. *Endeavour*, chart of N.Z., and Capt. Cook; 1½d. British Monarchs; 2d. Tasman with *Heemskerk* and chart; 3d. Landing of immigrants, 1840; 4d. Road, Rail, Sea and Air Transport; 6d. *Dunedin* and "Frozen Mutton Route" to London; 7d., 8d. Maori Council; 9d. Gold mining in 1861 and 1940. (As T **115**)—5d. H.M.S. *Britomart* at Akaroa, 1840. *Vert (as T* 111*)*—1s. Giant Kauri tree.

1940 (1 Oct).   *Health Stamps. As T* **110**, *but without extra surcharge.* W **43**. P 11.
626   **110**   1d. + ½d. blue-green . . . .   2·50 1·25 7·00
627   2d. + 1d. brown-orange . . . .   2·50 1·25 7·00
      Set of 2 . . . .   5·00 2·50 14·00
      First Day Cover . . . .   20·00

1ᴰ   1ᴰ

■   ■   2ᴰ   **1941**

(123)   Inserted "2"   (124)

1941.   *Surch as T* **123**.
628   **108**   1d. on ½d. green (1.5.41)   25   10   5
629   **108a** 2d. on 1½d. purple-grown (4.41) .   25   10   5
      a. Inserted "2" £450 £275 £300
      Set of 2   50   20   10
The surcharge on No. 629 has only one figure, at top left, and there is only one square to obliterate the original value at bottom right.
The variety "Inserted 2" occurs on the 10th stamp, 10th row. It is identified by the presence of remnants of the damaged "2", and by the spacing of "2" and "D" which is variable and different from the normal.

(Typo Govt Printing Office, Wellington)

1941. *As T* **91**, *but smaller* (17½ × 20½ *mm*). P 14 × 15. (*a*) W **43**.
630   **91**   9d. scarlet and black (5.41) . . . . .   50·00 24·00 7·00
      Wi. Wmk inverted . . . .

                        (*b*) W **98**
631   **91**   9d. scarlet and black (29.4.41) . . . .   1·75   90   75
      Wi. Wmk inverted . . . .   40·00 28·00 25·00

1941 (4 Oct).   *Health Stamps. Nos.* 626/7 *optd with T* **124**.
632   **110**   1d. + ½d. blue-green   25   15   1·25
633   2d. + 1d. brown-orange   25   15   1·25
      Set of 2 . . . .   50 ✔ 30   2·50
      First Day Cover . . . .   8·00

PUZZLED ?
Then you need
PHILATELIC TERMS ILLUSTRATED
to tell you all you need to know about printing methods, papers, errors, varieties, watermarks, perforations, etc. 192 pages, some in full colour, soft cover. Third Edition.

125 Boy and Girl   126 Princess Margaret
   on Swing

(Des S. Hall. Recess Note Printing Branch, Commonwealth Bank of
Australia, Melbourne)

1942 (1 Oct). *Health Stamps. W* **43**. *P* 11.
634 **125** 1d. + ½d. blue-green   15   10   35
635   2d. + 1d. orange-red   15   10   30
          Set of 2   30   20   65
          First Day Cover . . . .   3·00

(Des J. Berry. Recess B.W.)

1943 (1 Oct). *Health Stamps. T* **126** *and similar triangular design. W* **98**.
P 12.
636 1d. + ½d. green   10   5   20
     a. Imperf between (vert pair) £3500
637 2d. + 1d. red-brown   10   5   10
     a. Imperf between (vert pair) . . . . £3500   — £3500
          Set of 2   20   10   30
          First Day Cover . . . .   3·00
Design:—2d. Queen Elizabeth II as Princess.

✚ TENPENCE ✚
(128)

1944 (1 May). *No.* 615 *surch with T* **128**.
662 10d. on 1½d. light blue and mauve   10   5   10

129 Queen Elizabeth II as   130 Statue of Peter Pan,
Princess and Princess Margaret   Kensington Gardens

(Recess B.W.)

1944 (9 Oct). *Health Stamps. W* **98**. *P* 13½.
663 **129** 1d. + ½d. green   10   5   10
664   2d. + 1d. blue   10   5   10
          Set of 2   20   10   20
          First Day Cover . . . .   2·00

(Des J. Berry. Recess B.W.)

1945 (1 Oct). *Health Stamps. W* **98**. *P* 13½.
665 **130** 1d. + ½d. green and buff   5   5   5
          Wi. Wmk inverted . . . . 40·00 28·00
666   2d. + 1d. carmine and buff   5   5   10
          Wi. Wmk inverted . . . . 50·00 35·00
          Set of 2   10   10   15
          First Day Cover   90

131 Lake Matheson   132 King George VI and
                         Parliament House, Wellington

133 St. Paul's Cathedral   139 "St. George"
                           (Wellington College
                            War Memorial
                             Window)

Printer's guide mark
(R. 12/3)

Completed rudder
(R. 2/4 of Pl. 42883
and R. 3/2 of Pl. 42796)

(Des J. Berry. Photo Harrison (1½d. and 1s.). Recess B.W. (1d. and 2d.) and
Waterlow (others))

1946 (1 Apr). *Peace issue. T* **131**/3, **139** *and similar designs. W* **98**
(sideways on 1½d.). *P* 13 (1d., 2d.), 14 × 14½ (1½d., 1s.), 13½ *(others)*.
667 ½d. green and brown   10   5   15
     a. Printer's guide mark . . . . 1·50 1·00
     Wi. Wmk inverted . . . . 40·00 25·00
668 1d. green   10   5   5
     Wi. Wmk inverted . . . . 30·00 20·00
669 1½d. scarlet   10   5   10
     Wi. Wmk sideways inverted   10   5   10
670 2d. purple   15   5   5
671 3d. ultramarine and grey   20   10   10
     a. Completed rudder . . . . 3·00 2·00

672	4d. bronze-green and orange	20	10	15
	Wi. Wmk inverted	80·00	50·00	
673	5d. green and ultramarine	20	10	10
674	6d. chocolate and vermilion	15	10	10
675	8d. black and carmine	15	10	10
676	9d. blue and black	15	10	10
677	1s. grey-black	15	10	15
	Set of 11	1·50	85	1·00
	First Day Cover			2·00

Designs: *Horiz* (as *T* **132**)—2d. The Royal Family. (As *T* **131**)—3d. R.N.Z.A.F. badge and aeroplanes; 4d. Army badge, tank and plough; 5d. Navy badge, H.M.S. *Achilles* (cruiser) and *Dominion Monarch* (liner); 6d. N.Z. coat of arms, foundry and farm; 9d. Southern Alps and Franz Josef Glacier. *Vert* (as *T* **139**)—1s. National Memorial Campanile.

142 Soldier helping Child over Stile

(Des J. Berry. Recess Waterlow)

1949 (24 Oct). *Health Stamps.* W **98**. P 13½.

678	**142**	1d. + ½d. green and orange-brown	5	5	5
		a. Yellow-green & orange-brown	2·75	1·25	2·75
		Wi. Wmk inverted	11·00	6·50	
679		2d. + 1d. chocolate & orange-brn	5	5	5
		Set of 2	10	5	10
		First Day Cover..........			50

144 King George VI

145 Statue of Eros

Plate 1   Plate 2

(Des W. J. Cooch. Recess T **108a**, B.W.; T **144**, D.L.R.)

1947–52. W **98** (*sideways on "shilling" values*). (a) P 14 × 13½.

680	**108a**	2d. orange	15	10	5
		Ea. Horiz coil pair (17.11.47) ...	5·00	3·00	
		Wi. Wmk inverted	40·00	28·00	
681		4d. bright purple	35	15	10
		Ea. Horiz coil pair (17.11.47) ...	7·00	4·00	
682		5d. slate	50	20	35
		Ea. Horiz coil pair (16.4.48)	5·00	3·00	
683		6d. carmine	40	15	5
		Ea. Horiz coil pair (1949)	5·00	3·00	
		Wi. Wmk inverted	30·00	20·00	
684		8d. violet	65	25	15
		Ea. Horiz coil pair (1949)	7·00	4·00	
685		9d. purple-brown	70	30	10
		Ea. Horiz coil pair (1951)	9·00	5·50	
		Wi. Wmk inverted	20·00	12·00	

(b) P 14

686	**144**	1s. red-brown & carmine (Plate 1)	1·40	60	20
		Ea. Vert coil pair (1949)	6·00	3·50	
		Wi. Wmk sideways inverted ...	7·00	4·50	
		b. Wmk upright (Plate 1)	50	20	20
		bEa. Vert coil pair	90·00	55·00	
		c. Wmk upright (Plate 2)	85	35	15
		cEa. Vert coil pair	6·00	3·50	
		cWi. Wmk inverted	30·00	20·00	
687		1s. 3d. red-brown & blue (Plate 2)	70	30	30
		Ea. Vert coil pair (1949)	6·50	3·75	
		Wi. Wmk sideways inverted ...	4·00	2·50	2·50
		a. Wmk upright (14.1.52)	1·75	80	3·00
		aWi. Wmk inverted			
688		2s. brown-orange & grn (Plate 1)	1·25	60	50
		Wi. Wmk sideways inverted ...	11·00	5·50	
		a. Wmk upright (Plate 1)	1·00	50	1·25
689		3s. red-brown and grey (Plate 2) .	1·75	80	1·00
		Wi. Wmk sideways inverted ...	14·00	9·00	
		Set of 10	6·00	2·75	2·25

In head-plate 2 the diagonal lines of the background have been strengthened and result in the upper corners and sides appearing more deeply shaded.

(Des J. Berry. Recess Waterlow)

1947 (1 Oct). *Health Stamps.* W **98** (*sideways*). P 13½.

690	**145**	1d. + ½d. green	5	5	5
		Wi. Wmk sideways inverted	20·00	12·00	
691		2d. + 1d. carmine	5	5	5
		Wi. Wmk sideways inverted ...	32·00	18·00	
		Set of 2	10	5	10
		First Day Cover			45

146 Port Chalmers, 1848

148 First Church, Dunedin

(Des J. Berry. Recess B.W.)

1948 (23 Feb). *Centennial of Otago.* T **146**, **148** *and similar designs.* W **98** (*sideways on* 3d.). P 13½.

692	1d. blue and green	8	5	10
	Wi. Wmk inverted	17·00	11·00	
693	2d. green and brown	8	5	10
694	3d. purple	8	5	10
695	6d. black and rose	8	5	10
	Wi. Wmk inverted			
	Set of 4	30	15	35
	First Day Cover			60

Designs. *Horiz*—2d. Cromwell, Otago; 6d. University of Otago.

150 Boy Sunbathing and Children Playing

151 Nurse and Child

(Des E. Linzell. Recess B.W.)

1948 (1 Oct). *Health Stamps. W* **98**. *P* 13½.
696   **150**   1d. + ½d. blue and green   5   5   5
                 Wi. Wmk inverted . . . .   16·00   10·00
697   2d. + 1d. purple and scarlet   5   5   5
                 Set of 2 . . . .   10⬤   5   10
                 First Day Cover   45

1949 ROYAL VISIT ISSUE. Four stamps were prepared to commemorate
this event: 2d. Treaty House, Waitangi; 3d. H.M.S. *Vanguard*; 5d. Royal
portraits; 6d. Crown and sceptre. The visit did not take place and the
stamps were destroyed, although a few examples of the 3d. later
appeared on the market. A similar set was prepared in 1952, but was,
likewise, not issued.

(Des J. Berry. Photo Harrison)

1949 (3 Oct). *Health Stamps. W* **98**. *P* 14 × 14½.
698   **151**   1d. + ½d. green   5   5   5
699   2d. + 1d. ultramarine   5   5   5
                 a. No stop below "D" of "1 D." .   6·00   3·50   10·00
                 Set of 2 . . . .   10⬤   5   10
                 First Day Cover   45

1½d.

POSTAGE
(152)

153 Queen Elizabeth II
and Prince Charles

1950 (28 July). *As Type F* **6**, *but without value, surch with T* **152**. *W* **98**
(*inverted*). *Chalk-surfaced paper. P* 14.
700   F **6**   1½d. carmine . . . .   5⬤   5   5
                 Wi. Wmk upright . . . .   1·25   65   1·25
Originally issued with the watermark inverted, this later appeared with it
upright.

(Des J. Berry and R. S. Phillips. Photo Harrison)

1950 (2 Oct). *Health Stamps. W* **98**. *P* 14 × 14½.
701   **153**   1d. + ½d. green   5   5   5
                 Wi. Wmk inverted . . . .   4·00   2·50
702   2d. + 1d. plum   5   5   5
                 Wi. Wmk inverted . . . .   13·00   8·00
                 Set of 2 . . . .   10⬤   10   10
                 First Day Cover   50

154 Christchurch
Cathedral

155 Cairn on Lyttleton Hills

(Des L. C. Mitchell (2d.), J. A. Johnstone (3d.) and J. Berry (others). Recess
B.W.)

1950 (20 Nov). *Centennial of Canterbury, N.Z. W* **154/5** *and similar
designs. W* **98** (*sideways on* 1d. *and* 3d.). *P* 13½.
703   1d. green and blue   8   5   12
704   2d. carmine and orange   10   5   10

705   3d. dark blue and blue   10   5   10
706   6d. brown and blue   15   10   25
707   1s. reddish purple and blue   15   10   30
       Set of 5 . . . .   50⬤   25   80
       First Day Cover . . . .   1·25
Designs: *Vert* (as *T* **154**)—3d. John Robert Godley. *Horiz* (as *T* **155**)—6d.
Canterbury University College; 1s. Aerial view of Timaru.

159 "Takapuna" class Yachts

(Des J. Berry and R. S. Phillips. Recess B.W.)

1951 (1 Nov). *Health Stamps. W* **98**. *P* 13½.
708   **159**   1½d. + ½d. scarlet and yellow   10   5   10
709   2d. + 1d. deep green and yellow .   10   5   10
                 Wi. Wmk inverted . . . .   40·00   25·00
                 Set of 2 . . . .   20⬤   10   20
                 First Day Cover   45

PRICES

Elizabeth II issues (from 1952)

First column = Unmounted Mint
Second column = Used

3D

160 Princess Anne   **161** Prince Charles   (162)

(From photographs by Marcus Adams. Photo Harrison)

1952 (1 Oct). *Health Stamps. W* **98**. *P* 14 × 14½.
710   **160**   1½d. + ½d. carmine-red   10   5
711   **161**   2d. + 1d. brown   10   5
                 Set of 2 . . . .   20⬤   10
                 First Day Cover   40

1952–53. *Nos.* 604 *and* 606 *surch as T* **162**.
712   **108**   1d. on ½d. brown-orange (11.9.53)   8   10
                 a. "D" omitted . . . .   †   —
713   3d. on 1d. green (12.12.52*)   10   5
                 Set of 2 . . . .   15⬤   15
*Earliest known date used.

163 Buckingham Palace   **164** Queen Elizabeth II

165 Coronation State Coach   **166** Westminster Abbey

167 St. Edward's Crown and Royal Sceptre

(Des L. C. Mitchell (1s. 6d.), J. Berry (others). Recess D.L.R. (2d., 4d.)
Waterlow (1s. 6d.) Photo Harrison (3d., 8d.))

1953 (25 May). *Coronation.* W **98**. *P* 13 (2*d.*, 4*d.*), 13½ (1*s.* 6*d.*) *or* 14 × 14½
(3*d.*, 8*d.*).

714	**163**	2d. deep bright blue	15	15
715	**164**	3d. brown	15	5
716	**165**	4d. carmine	70	1·50
717	**166**	8d. slate-grey	60	70
718	**167**	1s. 6d. purple and ultramarine	1·25	80
		Set of 5	2·50	2·75
		First Day Cover		3·50

168 Girl Guides   **169** Boy Scouts

(Des J. Berry. Photo Harrison)

1953 (7 Oct). *Health Stamps.* W **98**. *P* 14 × 14½.

719	**168**	1½d. + ½d. blue	10	5
720	**169**	2d. + 1d. deep yellow-green	10	15
		Set of 2	20	20
		First Day Cover		40

170 Queen Elizabeth II   **171** Queen Elizabeth II and
Duke of Edinburgh

(Des L. C. Mitchell. Recess Waterlow)

1953 (9 Dec). *Royal Visit.* W **98**. *P* 13 × 14 (3*d.*) *or* 13½ (4*d.*).

721	**170**	3d. dull purple	10	5
		Wi. Wmk inverted	—	60
722	**171**	4d. deep ultramarine	10	20
		Set of 2	20	25
		First Day Cover		80

172   **173** Queen Elizabeth II **174**

Die I   Die II

(Des L. C. Mitchell (T **172**/3), J. Berry (T **174**). Recess D.L.R. (T **173**),
B.W. (others))

1953 (15 Dec)–**58**. W **98**. *P* 14 × 13½ (T **172**), 14 (T **173**) *or* 13½ (T **174**).

723	**172**	½d. slate-black	15	15
724		1d. orange	15	5
		Wi. Wmk inverted	30	20
725		1½d. brown-lake	20	5
		Wi. Wmk inverted	—	£200
726		2d. bluish green	20	5
		Ea. Horiz coil pair (4.54)	1·50	
		Wi. Wmk inverted	—	£200
727		3d. vermilion	20	5
		Ea. Horiz coil pair (4.54)	90	
		Wi. Wmk inverted	40	20
728		4d. blue	40	15
		Ea. Horiz coil pair (4.54)	1·40	
729		6d. purple	70	40
		Ea. Horiz coil pair (4.54)	2·25	
		Wi. Wmk inverted	£200	
730		8d. carmine	60	25
		Ea. Horiz coil pair (4.54)	2·00	
		Wi. Wmk inverted	—	£200
731	**173**	9d. brown and bright green	60	10
		Ea. Horiz coil pair (5.54)	7·50	
		Eb. Vert coil pair (4.55)	1·75	
		Wi. Wmk inverted	£100	£100
732		1s. black and carmine-red (Die I)	65	5
		a. Die II (1958)	50·00	9·00
		Eb. Horiz coil pair (I) (5.54)	10·00	
		Ec. Vert coil pair (I) (4.55)	1·75	
		Wi. Wmk inverted (I)	—	£125
733		1s. 6d. black and bright blue	1·75	15
		Eb. Horiz coil pair (8.54)	10·00	
		Ec. Vert coil pair (4.55)	3·50	
		Wi. Wmk inverted	£100	
733*a*		1s. 9d. black and red-orange	5·50	50
		aEb. Vert coil pair (12.57)	12·00	
		Eo. White opaque paper (2.2.59)	4·25	50
		Eob. Vert coil pair (7.59)	10·00	
		aWi. Wmk inverted	£100	
733*b*	**174**	2s. 6d. brown	20·00	4·00
734		3s. bluish green	9·00	25
		Wi. Wmk inverted	—	£200
735		5s. carmine	16·00	2·25
736		10s. deep ultramarine	35·00	14·00
		Set of 16	80·00	20·00

1s. Dies I and II. The two dies of the Queen's portrait differ in the shading
on the sleeve at right. The long lines running upwards from left to right are
strong in Die I and weaker in Die II. In the upper part of the shading the fine
cross-hatching is visible in Die I only between the middle two of the four
long lines, but in Die II it extends clearly across all four lines.

In the lower part of the shading the strength of the long lines in Die I
makes the cross-hatching appear subdued, whereas in Die II the weaker
long lines make the cross-hatching more prominent.

Centre plates 1A, 1B and 2B are Die I; 3A and 3B are Die II.

For stamps as T **172** but with larger figures of value see Nos. 745/51.

1958 NEW PAPER. A new white opaque paper first came into use in August 1958 and was used for later printings of Nos. 733a, 745, 747/9, O159, O161, O163/4, O166 and L54. It is slightly thicker than the paper previously used, but obviously different in colour (white, against cream) and opacity (the previous paper being *relatively* transparent).

175 Young Climber and Mts Aspiring and Everest

(Des J. Berry. Recess; vignette litho B.W.)

1954 (4 Oct). *Health Stamps. W* **98**. *P* 13½.
737	**175**	1½d. + ½d. sepia and deep violet	10	10
738		2d. + 1d. sepia and blue-black	10	10
		Set of 2	20	20
		First Day Cover		40

176 Maori Mail-carrier

177 Queen Elizabeth II

178 Douglas "DC 3" Airliner

(Des R. M. Conly (2d.), J. Berry (3d.), A. G. Mitchell (4d.). Recess D.L.R.)

1955 (18 July). *Centenary of First New Zealand Postage Stamps. W* **98**. *P* 14 (2d.), 14 × 14½ (3d.) or 13 (4d.).
739	**176**	2d. sepia and deep green	5	10
		Wi. Wmk inverted	—	50·00
740	**177**	3d. brown-red	5	5
741	**178**	4d. black and bright blue	15	25
		Set of 3	20	35
		First Day Cover		65

179 Children's Health Camps Federation Emblem

180

(Des E. M. Taylor. Recess B.W.)

1955 (3 Oct). *Health Stamps. W* **98** (*sideways*). *P* 13½ × 13.
742	**179**	1½d. + ½d. sepia and orange-brown	10	25
743		2d. + 1d. red-brown and green	10	15
744		3d. + 1d. sepia and deep rose-red	10	10
		a. Centre omitted		
		Set of 3	25	45
		First Day Cover		70

1955–60. *As Nos. 724/30Ea but larger figures of value and stars omitted from lower right corner. W* **2**. *P* 14 × 13½.
745	**180**	1d. orange (12.7.56)	45	5
		Wi. Wmk inverted	60	45
		Eo. White opaque paper (2.6.59)	30	5
		EoWi. Wmk inverted	60	45
746		1½d. brown-lake (1.12.55)	60	60
747		2d. bluish green (19.3.56)	40	5
		Ea. Horiz coil pair (8.56)	2·25	
		Eo. White opaque paper (10.11.59)	45	5
		Eoa. Horiz coil pair (1.60)	4·00	
748		3d. vermilion (1.5.56)	65	50
		Wi. Wmk inverted	1·00	60
		Eo. White opaque paper (20.6.59)	85	5
		Eoa. Horiz coil pair (1.60)	2·50	
		EoWi. Wmk inverted	95	30
749		4d. blue (3.2.58)	1·75	25
		Ea. Horiz coil pair (4.59)	4·50	
		Eo. White opaque paper (9.9.59)	2·50	70
		Eoa. Horiz coil pair (2.60)	17·00	
750		6d. purple (20.10.55)	4·50	10
		Ea. Horiz coil pair (5.56)	9·50	
751		8d. chestnut (*white opaque paper*) (1.12.59)	3·75	5·00
		Ea. Horiz coil pair (4.60)	16·00	
		Set of 7	11·00	5·50

Nos. 748/Ei were only issued in booklets (q.v.). No. 748Eo first came in booklets (see B4) and later in sheets (1.10.59). The price for No. 748EoWi is for the inverted watermark from booklets but it has also been reported with selvedge from a sheet.

White opaque paper. See note above No. 737.

181 "The Whalers of Foveaux Strait"

182 "Farming"   183 Takahe

(Des E. R. Leeming (2d.), L. C. Mitchell (3d.), M. R. Smith (8d.). Recess D. L. R.)

1956 (16 Jan). *Southland Centennial. W* **98**. *P* 13½ × 13 (8d.) or 13 × 12½ (*others*).
752	**181**	2d. deep blue-green	10	10
753	**182**	3d. sepia	5	5
		Wi. Wmk inverted	—	70·00
754	**183**	8d. slate-violet and rose-red	40	80
		Set of 3	50	85
		First Day Cover		1·75

184 Children picking Apples

(Des L. C. Mitchell, after photo by J. F. Louden. Recess B.W.)

1956 (24 Sept). *Health Stamps.* W **98**. P 13 × 13½.

755	**184**	1½d. + ½d. purple-brown		10	20
		a. *Blackish brown*		60	4·00
756		2d. + 1d. blue-green		10	15
757		3d. + 1d. claret		10	10
		Set of 3		25	40
		First Day Cover			75

185 New Zealand Lamb and Map

186 Lamb, *Dunedin* and *Port Brisbane* (refrigerated freighter)

(Des M. Goaman. Photo Harrison)

1957 (15 Feb). *75th Anniv of First Export of N.Z. Lamb.* W **98** (*sideways inverted on* 4d.). P 14 × 14½ (4d.) or 14½ × 14 (8d.).

758	**185**	4d. blue		50	60
		Wi. Wmk sideways		7·00	5·50
759	**186**	8d. deep orange-red		75	90
		Set of 2		1·25	1·50
		First Day Cover			2·75

187 Sir Truby King

(Des M. R. Smith. Recess B.W.)

1957 (14 May). *50th Anniv of Plunket Society.* W **98**. P 13.

760	**187**	3d. bright carmine-red		10	5
		Wi. Wmk inverted		25·00	
		First Day Cover			40

188 Life-savers in Action

189 Children on Seashore

(Des L. Cutten (2d.), L. C. Mitchell (3d.). Recess Waterlow)

1957 (25 Sept). *Health Stamps.* W **98** (*sideways*). P 13½.

761	**188**	2d. + 1d. black and emerald		10	10
762	**189**	3d. + 1d. ultramarine and rose-red		10	10
		Set of 2		20	20
		First Day Cover			50
MS762b		Two sheets each 112 × 96 mm with Nos. 761 and 762 in blocks of 6 (2 × 3) *Per pair*		12·00	18·00
		First Day Covers (2)			24·00
MS762c		As last but with wmk upright *Per pair*		16·00	32·00
		First Day Covers (2)			48·00

2d

(190)

191 Girls' Life Brigade Cadet

192 Boys' Brigade Bugler

1958 (6 Jan–Mar). *No.* 746 *surch as T* **190**.

763	**180**	2d. on 1½d. brown-lake		15	5
		a. Smaller dot in surch		10	5
		b. Error. Surch on No. 725 (3.58)		£110	£150

Diameter of dot on No. 763 is 4½mm; on No. 763a 3¾ mm. Forgeries of No. 763b are known.

No. 765Ea. An incomplete Jubilee line reveals a "Tent" (R.4/1 (margin)).

(Des J. Berry. Photo Harrison)

1958 (20 Aug). *Health Stamps.* W **98**. P 14 × 14½.

764	**191**	2d. + 1d. green		12	10
765	**192**	3d. + 1d. blue		12	10
		Ea. Phantom "Tent"		3·50	
		Set of 2		20	20
		First Day Cover			50
MS765a		Two sheets each 104 × 124 mm with Nos. 764/5 in blocks of 6 (3 × 2) *Per pair*		12·00	14·00
		First Day Covers (2)			22·00

192a Sir Charles Kingsford Smith and *Southern Cross*

193 Seal of Nelson

(Des J. E. Lyle. Eng F. D. Manley. Recess Commonwealth Bank of Australia Note Ptg Branch)

1958 (27 Aug). *30th Anniv of First Air Crossing of the Tasman Sea.* W **98** (*sideways*). P 14 × 14½.

766	**192a**	6d. deep ultramarine		20	30
		First Day Cover			1·00

(Des M. J. Macdonald. Recess B.W.)

1958 (29 Sept). *Centenary of City of Nelson. W* **98**. *P* 13½ × 13.
767　**193**　3d. carmine . . . . 5 　 5
　　　　　First Day Cover 35

194 "Pania" Statue　　　**196** Maori Sheep-
　　Napier　　　　　　　　　　shearer

195 Australian Gannets on Cape
Kidnappers

(Des M. R. Smith (2d.), J. Berry (3d.), L. C. Mitchell (8d.). Photo
Harrison)

1958 (3 Nov). *Centenary of Hawke's Bay Province. W* **98** (*sideways on*
3d.). *P* 14½ × 14 (3d.) *or* 13½ × 14½ (*others*).
768　**194**　2d. yellow-green . . . . 5 　 5
769　**195**　3d. blue . . . . 15 　 5
770　**196**　8d. red-brown . . . . 45 　 90
　　　　　Set of 3 . . . . 60 　 90
　　　　　First Day Cover . . . . 2·00

197 "Kiwi" Jamboree　　**198** Careening H.M.S.
　　Badge　　　　　　　　*Endeavour* at Ship Cove

(Des Mrs. S. M. Collins. Recess B.W.)

1959 (5 Jan). *Pan-Pacific Scout Jamboree, Auckland. W* **98**.
P 13½ × 13.
771　**197**　3d. sepia and carmine . . . . 10 　 5
　　　　　First Day Cover 40

(Des G. R. Bull and G. R. Smith. Photo Harrison)

1959 (2 Mar). *Centenary of Marlborough Province. T* **198** *and similar
horiz designs. W* **98** (*sideways*) *P* 14½ × 14.
772　**198**　2d. green . . . . 15 　 10
773　**198**　3d. deep blue . . . . 15 　 5
774　**198**　8d. light brown . . . . 75 　 80
　　　　　Set of 3 . . . . 80 　 85
　　　　　First Day Cover . . . . 2·00
Designs:—3d. Shipping wool, Wairau Bar, 1857; 8d. Salt industry,
Grassmere.

201 Red Cross Flag

(Photo Harrison)

1959 (3 June). *Red Cross Commemoration. W* **98** (*sideways*).
P 14½ × 14.
775　**201**　3d. + 1d. red and ultramarine . . . . 10 　 10
　　　　　a. Red Cross omitted £950
　　　　　First Day Cover 40

202 Grey Teal　　　　**203** New Zealand
　　　　　　　　　　　　　　　Stilt

(Des Display Section, G.P.O. Photo Harrison)

1959 (16 Sept). *Health Stamps. W* **98** (*sideways*). *P* 14 × 14½.
776　**202**　2d. + 1d. greenish yellow, ol & rose-red . . . 15 　 15
777　**203**　3d. + 1d. black, pink and light blue . . . . . . 15 　 15
　　　　　a. Pink ptg omitted . . . . 95·00
　　　　　Eb. Pink ptg shifted to left (at least 2½ mm) 18·00
　　　　　Wi. Wmk sideways inverted . . . . 3·00 　 3·00
　　　　　Set of 2 . . . . 30 　 30
　　　　　First Day Cover 60
MS777c Two sheets each 95 × 109 mm with Nos. 776/7
in blocks of 6 (3 × 2) . . . . *Per pair* 6·00 　 14·00
　　　　　First Day Covers (2) . . . . 24·00

204 "The Explorer"　　**205** "The Gold Digger"

(Des G. R. Bull and G. R. Smith. Photo Harrison)

1960 (16 May). *Centenary of Westland Province. T* **204**/5 *and similar
vert design. W* **98**. *P* 14 × 14½.
778　**204**　2d. deep dull green . . . . 15 　 10
779　**204**　3d. orange-red . . . . 15 　 5
780　**205**　8d. grey-black . . . . 40 　 1·50
　　　　　Set of 3 . . . . 60 　 1·50
　　　　　First Day Cover . . . . 2·75
Design:—8d. "The Pioneer Woman".

207 Manuka　　　　**208** Karaka　　　　**209** Kowhai
(Tea Tree)　　　　　　　　　　　　　　Ngutu-kaka
　　　　　　　　　　　　　　　　　　　(Kaka Beak)

No. 783Ed. "F" for "E" in "ZEALAND". Occurs on R.3/1 black Pl. 2.

209a Titoki   210 Kowhai   211 Puarangi
                                          (Hibiscus)

211a Matua Tikumu   212 Pikiarero   212a Koromiko
(Mountain Daisy)   (Clematis)

213 Rata   214 National Flag   215 Timber Industry

216 Trout   217 Tiki   218 Aerial Top
                                           Dressing

219 Taniwha   220 Butter Making
(Maori Rock Drawing)

221 Tongariro National Park   221a Tongariro National Park
    and Château   and Château

222 Sutherland Falls   224 Pohutu Geyser

223 Tasman Glacier

(Des Harrison (½d.), G. F. Fuller (1d., 3d., 6d.), A. G. Mitchell (2d., 4d., 5d.,
8d., 3s., 10s., £1), P.O. Public Relations Division (7d.), P.O. Publicity
Section (9d.), J. Berry (1s., 1s. 6d.), R. E. Barwick (1s. 3d.), J. C. Boyd
(1s. 9d.), D. F. Kee (2s.), L. C. Mitchell (2s. 6d., 5s.).
Photo D.L.R. (½d., 1d., 2d., 3d., 4d., 6d., 8d.) or Harrison (others))

1960 (11 July)–**66**. *Ordinary or chalk-surfaced paper (2½d., 5d., 7d.,*
*1s. 9d. (No. 795), 3s. (No. 799)). W **98** (sideways on 5d., 1s. 3d.,*
1s. 6d., 2s. 6d., 3s. and 10s. or sideways inverted on 2½d.) P 14 × 14½
(1s. 3d., 1s. 6d., 2s., 5s., £1) or 14½ × 14 (others).

781	**207**	½d. grey, green and cerise (1.9.60)	5	5
		a. Grey omitted	30·00	
		b. Green omitted	45·00	
		Ep. "Chambon" perf	1·25	
782	**208**	1d. orange, green, lake & brown (1.9.60)	5	5
		a. Orange omitted	£110	
		b. Coil. Perf 14½ × 13. Wmk sideways		
		(11.63)	60	1·25
		c. Chalky paper ('65?)	10	10
		cEp. "Chambon" perf	2·00	
783	**209**	2d. carmine, black, yellow and green ...	12	5
		a. Black omitted	£130	
		b. Yellow omitted	£140	
		Ec. Vert coil pair	2·50	
		Ed. "ZFALAND"	35·00	
		Ep. "Chambon" perf	1·40	
784	**209a**	2½d. red, yellow, black & green (1.11.61)	35	5
		a. Red omitted	£110	
		b. Yellow omitted	40·00	
		c. Green omitted	55·00	
		d. Red and green omitted	£225	
		Wi. Wmk sideways	—	20·00
		Ef. Vert coil pair (8.62)	2·00	
785	**210**	3d. yellow, green, yellow-brown and deep		
		greenish blue (1.9.60)	20	5
		a. Yellow omitted	30·00	
		b. Green omitted	30·00	
		c. Yellow-brown omitted	30·00	
		Ed. Vert coil pair (9.60)	1·60	
		e. Coil. Perf 14½ × 13 (C). Wmk sideways		
		(3.10.63)	60	90
		Ep. "Chambon" perf	1·25	
		f. Chalky paper (1965?)	25	15
		fEd. Vert coil pair	8·00	
		fEp. "Chambon" perf	2·75	
786	**211**	4d. purple, buff, yellow-green & lt blue ..	30	5
		a. Purple omitted	60·00	
		b. Buff omitted	£130	
		Ec. Vert coil pair	1·75	
		Ep. "Chambon" perf	1·60	
		d. Chalky paper (1965?)	£150	7·00
787	**211a**	5d. yellow, deep green, black & violet		
		(14.5.62)	40	5
		a. Yellow omitted	85·00	
788	**212**	6d. lilac, green & dp bluish grn (1.9.60) .	40	5
		a. No wmk	17·00	12·00
		ab. Lilac omitted	55·00	
		ac. Green omitted	42·00	
		Eb. Vert coil pair	3·50	
		Ep. "Chambon" perf	1·50	
		c. Chalky paper (1966?)	40	50
		cEb. Vert coil pair	3·75	
		cEp. "Chambon" perf	2·75	
788d	**212a**	7d. red, green, yellow & pale red (16.3.66)	35	70
		Wi. Wmk inverted	3·50	4·25
789	**213**	8d. rose-red, yellow, green & grey (1.9.60)	40	10
		Eb. Vert coil pair (9.60)	4·00	
		Ep. "Chambon" perf	2·75	
790	**214**	9d. red and ultramarine (1.9.60)	30	5
		a. Red omitted	£120	
791	**215**	1s. brown and deep green	25	5
		Ea. Horiz coil pair	5·00	
792	**216**	1s. 3d. carmine, sepia & bright blue	70	10
		a. Carmine omitted	£120	
		Eb. Carmine, sepia and greyish blue ...	70	10
		Ec. Vert coil pair (8.62)	5·50	
		Wi. Wmk sideways inverted	—	45·00

793	**217**	1s. 6d. olive-green and orange-brown ..	50		10
		Eb. Vert coil pair (7.60)	6·50		
794	**218**	1s. 9d. bistre-brown	10·00	15	
		Ea. Horiz coil pair (7.60)	22·00		
795		1s. 9d. orange-red, blue, green and yellow			
		(4.11.63)	6·00	50	
		Ea. Horiz coil pair (11.63)	11·00		
		Eb. Red ptg (aircraft) shifted 20 mm to			
		right	55·00		
796	**219**	2s. black and orange-buff	2·25		5
		a. Chalky paper (1966)	1·75	1·25	
797	**220**	2s. 6d. yellow and light brown	1·75	60	
		a. Yellow omitted	£225		
798	**221**	3s. blackish brown	35·00	90	
799	**221**a	3s. bistre, blue and green (1.4.64)	7·50	1·50	
		Wi. Wmk sideways inverted	26·00		
800	**222**	5s. blackish green	5·50	70	
		a. Chalky paper (1966)	2·25	4·25	
801	**223**	10s. steel-blue	8·00	1·75	
		a. Chalky paper (1966)	3·50	8·50	
802	**224**	£1 deep magenta	7·00	7·50	
		Set of 23	60·00	13·50	

Counter Coil Pairs

In this issue the coils are made up of 24 sections of 20 stamps (2d. to 6d. and 8d.) and the gutters numbered 1 to 23. The others (1s. to 1s. 9d.) are made up of 20 sections of 16 stamps and the gutters numbered 1 to 19 as in the earlier issue. The figures are printed in red or black. See also the general notes after No. 576.

"Chambon" Perforations

When the first supplies of this issue were printed a conventional single-row comb, perforating twelve stamps at a time, was used by De La Rue. Soon afterwards it was thought that the work could be speeded up and a double-row comb of unusual layout was supplied experimentally by Messrs. Chambon. This is unique in the history of perforating in that at one strike a horizontal row of stamps was completely perforated; at the same time half the vertical sides of all the adjacent stamps in the rows above and below were also perforated. The next strike completed the half perforated row, perforated completely another row and half the vertical sides of the next. This process was repeated throughout the sheet.

The junction of successive strokes occurs half way up the stamps and is therefore much more noticeable when defective than when a conventional comb is used in which the junctions are in the corners. A typical example of the 2d. is shown alongside. It will be seen that in the upper stamp two perforation holes have come close together causing a very thin tooth, while on the lower stamp two holes are wide apart leaving an abnormally wide tooth. Combinations of wide, narrow and normal teeth in a strip of three are many. The ¾d., 1d., 2d., 3d., 4d., 6d. and 8d. from sheets and the 2d., 3d., 4d., 6d. and 8d. from Counter Coils are known. This comb was found unsatisfactory and after about six to eight weeks was discarded. Since then these stamps have been perforated by a conventional two-row comb. *Our prices are for strips of three* showing typical "Chambon" perforations although extreme variations are worth more. Although strips of three are sufficient to identify the perforations, blocks of six show them more clearly, the prices of these being double.

Nos. 782b and 785e were replaced by coils with upright watermark perf 14½ × 14, in 1966.

CHALKY PAPER. The chalk-surfaced paper is not only whiter but also thicker, making the watermark difficult to see. Examples of the 4d. value can be found on a thick surfaced paper. These should not be confused with the rare chalk-surfaced printing, No. 786d., which can be identified by its positive reaction to the silver test.

225 Sacred   **226** New Zealand
Kingfisher   Pigeon

(Des Display Section, G.P.O. Recess B.W.)

1960 (10 Aug). *Health Stamps. W* **98**. *P* 13½.

803	**225**	2d. + 1d. sepia and turquoise-blue	30	30
804	**226**	3d. + 1d. deep purple-brown and orange ..	30	35
		Set of 2	60	65
		First Day Cover		90
MS804b		Two sheets each 95 × 107 mm with Nos. 803		
		and 804 in blocks of 6. P 11½ × 11	*Per pair* 26·00	32·00
		First Day Covers (2)		38·00

227 "The Adoration of the Shepherds"
(Rembrandt)

(Photo Harrison)

1960 (1 Nov). *Christmas. W* **98**. *P* 12.

805	**227**	2d. red and deep brown/*cream*	15	5
		a. Red omitted	£300	
		First Day Cover		1·50

228 Great Egret   **229** New Zealand
Falcon

(Des Display Section, G.P.O. Recess B.W.)

1961 (2 Aug). *Health Stamps. W* **98**. *P* 13½.

806	**228**	2d. + 1d. black and purple	20	20
807	**229**	3d. + 1d. deep sepia and yellow-green . . .	20	20
		Set of 2	40	40
		First Day Cover		65
MS807a		Two sheets each 97 × 121 mm with Nos.		
		806/7 in blocks of 6 (3 × 2).	*Per pair* 22·00	22·00
		First Day Covers (2)		27·00

2½d   2½d

(230)   (231)

232 "Adoration of the
Magi" (Dürer)

1961 (1 Sept). *No. 748 surch with T **230** (wide setting).*
808 180 2½d. on 3d. vermilion . . . .   10 ━ 5
          a. Narrow setting (T **231**)   10   5
          b. Pair, wide and narrow . . . . 15·00 20·00
   The difference in the settings is in the overall width of the new value,
caused by two different spacings between the "2", "½" and "d".

(Photo Harrison)

1961 (16 Oct). *Christmas. W **98** (sideways). P 14½ × 14.*
809 **232** 2½d. multicoloured . . . .   5 ✔ 5
          Wi. Wmk sideways inverted . . . . 30·00 12·00
          First Day Cover . . . .   1·10

233 Morse Key and Port Hills, Lyttelton

(Des A. G. Mitchell (3d.) and L. C. Mitchell (8d.). Photo Harrison)

1962 (1 June). *Telegraph Centenary. T **233** and similar horiz design.
W **98** (sideways). P 14½ × 14.*
810   3d. sepia and bluish green   10   5
          a. Green omitted £300
811   8d. black and brown-red   35   70
          a. Imperf (pair) £800
          b. Black omitted £300
          Set of 2 . . . .   45 ━ 75
          First Day Cover . . . .   1·50
Design:—8d. Modern teleprinter.
   No. 811a comes from a sheet with the two top rows imperforate and the
third row imperforate on three sides.

235 Red-fronted   236 Saddleback
    Parakeet

(Des Display Section, G.P.O. Photo D.L.R.)

1962 (3 Oct). *Health Stamps. W **98**. P 15 × 14.*
812 **235** 2½d. + 1d. multicoloured   20   25
          a. Orange omitted . . . .
          Eb. Printed on the gummed side £180
          Wi. Wmk inverted . . . . 30·00
813 **236** 3d. + 1d. multicoloured   20   25
          a. Orange omitted £750
          Set of 2 . . . .   40 ━ 50
          First Day Cover   80
MS813b Two sheets each 96 × 101 mm with Nos. 812/3
in blocks of 6 (3 × 2) . . . . *Per pair* 30·00 30·00
          First Day Covers (2) . . . .   38·00
No. 812Eb comes from a miniature sheet.

237 "Madonna in Prayer"
(Sassoferrato)

(Photo Harrison)

1962 (15 Oct). *Christmas. W **98**. P 14½ × 14.*
814 **237** 2½d. multicoloured . . . .   10 ✔ 5
          First Day Cover   80

238   Prince Andrew   239

(Design after photographs by Studio Lisa, London. Recess D.L.R.)

1963 (7 Aug). *Health Stamps. W **98**. P 14.*
815 **238** 2½d. + 1d. dull ultramarine (*shades*)   10   10
          Ea. Ultramarine   15   12
          Eb. Deep blue   25   35
816 **239** 3d. + 1d. carmine   10   10
          Set of 2 . . . .   20 ✔ 20
          First Day Cover   65
MS816a Two sheets each 93 × 100 mm with Nos. 815/
16 in blocks of 6 (3 × 2) . . . . *Per pair* 18·00 22·00
          First Day Covers (2) . . . .   27·00
No. 815Eb comes from the Miniature sheet.

240 "The Holy Family" (Titian)

(Photo Harrison)

1963 (14 Oct). *Christmas. W **98** (sideways). P 12½.*
817 **240** 2½d. multicoloured . . . .   5 ✔ 5
          a. Imperf (pair) £150
          b. Yellow omitted £250
          Wi. Wmk sideways inverted   30   12
          First Day Cover   65

241 Steam Locomotive *Pilgrim*   242 Diesel Express and
and "DG" Diesel Electric Loco   Mt Ruapehu

(Des Commercial Art Section, N.Z. Railways. Photo D.L.R.)

1963 (25 Nov).   *Railway Centenary. W* **98** (*sideways*). *P* 14.
818   **241**   3d. multicoloured   30   10
              a. Blue (sky) omitted £250
819   **242**   1s. 9d. multicoloured . . . .   2·00   1·25
              a. Red (value) omitted £650
              Set of 2 . . . .   2·25 ◣1·25
              First Day Cover . . . .   3·25

242*a* "Commonwealth
Cable"

(Des P. Morriss. Photo Note Ptg Branch, Reserve Bank of Australia)

1963 (3 Dec).   *Opening of COMPAC (Trans-Pacific Telephone Cable). No
wmk. P* 13½.
820   **242***a*   8d. red, blue, black and yellow . . . .   50 ◣1·25
                First Day Cover . . . .   2·50

243 Road Map and   244 Silver Gulls
Car Steering-wheel

(Des L. C. Mitchell. Photo Harrison)

1964 (1 May).   *Road Safety Campaign. W* **98**. *P* 15 × 14.
821   **243**   3d. black, ochre-yellow and blue . . . . . .   5 ◣   5
                First Day Cover   50

(Des Display Section G.P.O., after Miss T. Kelly. Photo Harrison)

1964 (5 Aug).   *Health Stamps. T* **244** *and similar horiz design. Multicoloured. W* **98**. *P* 14½.
822   2½d. + 1d. Type **244**   10   15
        a   Red (beak and legs) omitted . . . .   80·00
823   3d. + 1d. Little Penguin   10   15
        Wi. Wmk inverted . . . .   40·00
              Set of 2 . . . .   20 ◣   30
              First Day Cover   60
MS823*a* Two sheets each 171 × 84 mm with Nos. 822/3
in blocks of 8 (4 × 2) . . . . *Per pair* 38·00   45·00
              First Day Covers (2) . . . .   50·00

246 Rev. S. Marsden taking first
Christian service at Rangihoua
Bay, 1814

7^D

POSTAGE

(247)

(Des L. C. Mitchell. Photo Harrison)

1964 (12 Oct).   *Christmas. W* **98** (*sideways*). *P* 14 × 13½.
824   **246**   2½d. multicoloured . . . .   5 ◣   5
                First Day Cover   50

1964 (14 Dec).   *As Type* F **6**, *but without value, surch with T* **247**. *W* **98**.
Unsurfaced paper. P 14 × 13½.
825   F **6**   7d. carmine-red . . . .   25 ◣   80

248 Anzac Cove

(Des R. M. Conly. Photo Harrison)

1965 (14 Apr).   *50th Anniv of Gallipoli Landing. T* **248** *and similar horiz
design. W* **98**. *P* 12½.
826   4d. yellow-brown   5   5
827   5d. green and red   5   25
              Set of 2 . . . .   10 ◣   30
              First Day Cover   50
Design:—5d. Anzac Cove and poppy.

250 I.T.U. Emblem and Symbols   250*a* Sir Winston
                                              Churchill

(Photo Harrison)

1965 (17 May).   *I.T.U. Centenary. W* **98**. *P* 14½ × 14.
828   **250**   9d. blue and pale chocolate . . . .   30 ◣   50
                First Day Cover   85

(From photograph by Karsh. Photo Note Ptg Branch, Reserve Bank of
Australia)

1965 (24 May).   *Churchill Commemoration. No wmk. P* 13½.
829   **250***a*   7d. black, pale grey and light blue . . . . .   15 ◣   50
                First Day Cover   75

251 Wellington Provincial Council Building

(Des from painting by L. B. Temple (1867). Photo Harrison)

1965 (26 July).   *Centenary of Government in Wellington. W* **98** (*sideways*). *P* 14½ × 14.
830   **251**   4d. multicoloured . . . .   5 ◣   5
                First Day Cover   40

252 Kaka   253 Collared Grey Fantail
                                        (after Miss T. Kelly)

(Des Display Section, G.P.O. Photo Harrison)

1965 (4 Aug). *Health Stamps. W* **98**. *P* 14 × 14½.
831	252	3d. + 1d. multicoloured		20	15
832	253	4d. + 1d. multicoloured		20	15
		a. Green ("POSTAGE HEALTH" and on			
		leaves) omitted		£110	
		Set of 2		40 ✎ 30	
		First Day Cover			65

MS832*b* Two sheets each 100 × 109 mm with Nos.
831/2 in blocks of 6 (3 × 2) . . . . *Per pair*   24·00   35·00
     First Day Covers (2) . . . .   40·00

254 I.C.Y. Emblem   **255** "The Two Trinities"
                                      (Murillo)

(Litho D.L.R.)

1965 (28 Sept). *International Co-operation Year. W* **98** (*sideways inverted*). *P* 14.
833	254	4d. carmine-red and light yellow-olive	. . . .	15 ✎	5
		Wi. Wmk sideways	. . . .	3·25	
		First Day Cover	. . . .		40

(Photo Harrison)

1965 (11 Oct). *Christmas. W* **98**. *P* 13½ × 14.
834	255	3d. multicoloured	. . . .	5 ✎	5
		a. Gold (frame) omitted	. . . .	£600	
		First Day Cover	. . . .		40

No. 834a comes from a sheet in which the fourth and part of the third
stamp in each of the lower five rows has the gold frame omitted. The gold
plate number is also omitted.

256 Arms of New Zealand   **259** "Progress"
                                        Arrowhead

(Des Display Section, G.P.O. Photo D.L.R.)

1965 (30 Nov). *11th Commonwealth Parliamentary Conference. T* **256**
and similar horiz designs. Multicoloured. P 14.
835	4d. Type **256**	25	20
	a. Blue (incl value) omitted	. . . .	£300	
	Eb. Printed on the gummed side	. . . .		
836	9d. Parliament House, Wellington and Badge	. . .	45	1·00
837	2s. Wellington from Mt Victoria	. . . .	80	3·25
	a. Carmine omitted	. . . .	£250	
	Set of 3	. . . .	1·40 ✎ 4·00	
	First Day Cover	. . . .		6·00

(Des Display Section, G.P.O. Photo Harrison)

1966 (5 Jan). *Fourth National Scout Jamboree, Trentham. W* **98**.
P 14 × 15.
838	259	4d. gold and myrtle-green	10 ✎	5
		a. Gold (arrowhead) omitted	. . . .	£450	
		First Day Cover	. . . .		40

260 New Zealand   **262** "The Virgin with Child"
     Bell Bird   (Maratta)

(Des Display Section, G.P.O. Photo Harrison)

1966 (3 Aug). *Health Stamps. T* **260** *and similar vert design. Multicoloured. W* **98** (*sideways*). *P* 14 × 14½.
839	3d. + 1d. Type **260**	. . . .	15	20
840	4d. + 1d. Weka Rail	. . . .	15	20
	a. Deep brown (values and date) omitted	. . . .	£650	
	Set of 2	. . . .	30 ✎ 40	
	First Day Cover	. . . .		65

MS841 Two sheets each 107 × 91 mm. Nos. 839/40 in
blocks of 6 (3 × 2) . . . . *Per pair*   16·00   27·00
     First Day Covers (2) . . . .   30·00
In No. 840a besides the value, "1966" and "Weka" are also omitted and
the bird, etc. appears as light brown.

(Photo Harrison)

1966 (3 Oct). *Christmas. W* **98** (*sideways*). *P* 14½.
842	262	3d. multicoloured	. . . .	5 ✎ 5
		a. Red omitted	. . . .	£100	
		First Day Cover	. . . .		40

263 Queen Victoria and   **264** Half-sovereign of
   Queen Elizabeth II   1867 and Commemorative
                                   Dollar Coin

(Des Display Section, G.P.O. Photo Harrison)

1967 (3 Feb). *Centenary of New Zealand Post Office Savings Bank. W* **98**
(*sideways on* 4d.). *P* 14 × 14½.
843	263	4d. black, gold and maroon	. . . .	8	5
		Wi. Wmk sideways inverted	. . . .	40·00	
844	264	9d. gold, silver, black, lt blue & dp grn	. . .	10	15
		Set of 2	. . . .	15 ✎ 20	
		First Day Cover	. . . .		65

(New Currency. 100 cents = 1 dollar)

265 Manuka (Tea Tree)   **266** Pohutu Geyser

1967 (10 July)-**70**.　*Decimal Currency. Designs as earlier issues, but with values inscr in decimal currency as T* **265/6**. *Chalky paper.* W **98** (*sideways on* 8 *c.,* 10 *c.,* 20 *c.,* 50 *c. and* $2). *P* 13½ × 14 (½ *c. to* 3 *c.,* 5 *c. and* 7 *c.*), 14½ × 14 (4 *c.,* 6 *c.,* 8 *c.,* 10 *c.,* 25 *c.,* 30 *c. and* $1) *or* 14 × 14½ (15 *c.,* 20 *c.,* 50 *c. and* $2).

845	265	½ c.　pale blue, yellow-green and cerise　..	10 •	5
846	208	1 c.　yellow, carmine, green & lt brown　...	10 •	5
		a.　Booklet pane. Five stamps plus one printed label	1·50	
847	209	2 c.　carmine, black, yellow and green　...	10 •	5
848	210	2½ c.　yellow, green, yellow-brown and deep bluish green	10 •	5
		a.　Deep bluish green omitted*	£400	
		b.　Imperf (pair)†	45·00	
		Ec.　Vert coil pair (1969)	1·50	
849	211	3 c.　purple, buff, yellow-green and light greenish blue	12 •	5
		Ea.　Vert coil pair (1969)	1·50	
850	211*a*	4 c.　yellow, deep green, black and violet　..	30 •	5
		Ea.　Horiz coil pair (1969)	80	
851	212	5 c.　lilac, yellow-olive and bluish green　..	55 *	5
852	212*a*	6 c.　red, green, yellow and light pink　....	70 •	10
		Ea.　Horiz coil pair (1969)	1·75	
853	213	7 c.　rose-red, yellow, green and grey　...	85 •	10
854	214	8 c.　red and ultramarine	85 •	5
		a.　Red omitted	£170	
		Eb.　Horiz coil pair (1969)	2·75	
855	215	10 c.　brown and deep green	60 •	15
856	217	15 c.　olive-green and orange-brown　....	60 •	60
		Wi.　Wmk inverted	8·00	
857	219	20 c.　black and buff	2·00 •	10
		Ea.　Vert coil pair (1969)	6·00	
858	220	25 c.　yellow and light brown	4·00 •	90
859	221*a*	30 c.　olive-yellow, green & greenish blue　..	3·50 •	25
		Wi.　Wmk inverted	24·00	
		a.　No wmk (1970)	3·50	3·75
860	222	50 c.　blackish green	3·50 •	75
861	223	$1　Prussian blue	14·00 •	1·75
		Wi.　Wmk inverted	65·00	
862	266	$2　deep magenta	8·50 •	10·00
		Set of 18	30·00	13·00

* This occurred on one horizontal row of ten, affecting the background colour so that the value is also missing. In the row above and the row below, the colour was partially omitted. The price is for a vertical strip.

The 2½ c. value has been seen with the yellow omitted, but only on a used example.

† This comes from a sheet of which the six right-hand vertical rows were completely imperforate and the top, bottom and left-hand margins had been removed.

The 4 c., 30 c. and 50 c. exist with PVA gum as well as gum arabic. No. 859a exists with PVA gum only.

For $4 to $10 in the "Arms" type, see under Postal Fiscal stamps.

For the 15 c. and $2 in changed colours see Nos. 874 and 879.

Counter Coil Pairs:

The 2½ c., 3 c., 4 c. and 6 c. are made up in 20 sections of 20 stamps; the 10 c. (873) and 20 c. are in 20 sections of 10 stamps, all with gutters numbered 1 to 19; the 8 c. and 15 c. (874) are in 30 sections of 10 stamps numbered 1 to 29. They are generally in bad condition as about 50% have the whole sides guillotined off the stamps and are joined crookedly.

See also general notes after No. 576.

268 Running with Ball

(Des L. C. Mitchell. Photo Harrison)

1967 (2 Aug).　*Health Stamps. Rugby Football. T* **268** *and similar multicoloured design.* W **98** (*sideways on* 2½ *c.*). *P* 14½ × 14 (2½ *c.*) *or* 14 × 14½ (3 *c.*).

867	2½ c. + 1 c.　Type **268**	10	10
868	3 c. + 1 c.　Positioning for a place-kick (*horiz*)　..	10	10
	Set of 2	20	20
	First Day Cover		50
MS869	Two sheets: (*a*)　76 × 130 mm (867); (*b*)　130 × 76 mm (868). Containing blocks of six		
	Per pair	18·00	22·00
	First Day Covers (2)		27·00

270 *Kaita* (trawler) and Catch　　　**271** Brown Trout

272 Apples and Orchard

273 Forest and Timber

274 Sheep and the "Woolmark"

275 Consignments of Beef and Herd of Cattle

276 Dairy Farm, Mt Egmont and Butter Consignment　　　**277** Fox Glacier, Westland National Park

(Des Display Section, G.P.O. (7, 8, 10, 18, 20, 25 c. and 28 c. from photo),
R. M. Conly (7½ c.). Litho B.W. (7, 8, 18, 20 c.) or photo D.L.R. (7½ c.)
and Harrison (10, 25, 28 c.). Others (15 c., $2) as before)

1967-69. *Chalky paper (except 7, 8, 18, 20 c.). No wmk (7, 8, 20 c.) or
W 98 (sideways on 7½, 10, 15, 25 c., upright on 18, 28 c., $2). P 13½ (7,
7½ c.), 13 × 13½ (8, 18, 20 c.), 14½ × 14 (10, 25 c.) or 14 × 14½ (15, 28 c., $2).*
870	270	7 c. multicoloured (3.12.69)	75 •	75
871	271	7½ c. multicoloured* (29.8.67)	30 •	70
		a. Wmk upright (10.68)	50	60
872	272	8 c. multicoloured (8.7.69)	75 •	70
873	273	10 c. multicoloured (2.4.68)	50 •	5
		a. Green (background) omitted	£170	
		Eb. Horiz coil pair	2·75	
874	217	15 c. apple-green, myrtle-green and car-		
		mine† (19.3.68)	90 •	40
		Ea. Vert coil pair	3·50	
875	274	18 c. multicoloured (8.7.69)	1·40 •	55
876	275	20 c. multicoloured (8.7.69)	1·40 •	20
		Ea. Horiz coil pair	7·00	
877	276	25 c. multicoloured (10.12.68)	5·50 •	2·00
878	277	28 c. multicoloured (30.7.68)	60 •	5
		Wi. Wmk inverted		
879	266	$2 black, ochre & pale blue (10.12.68) .	35·00	18·00
		Set of 10	42·00 •	21·00

* No. 871 was originally issued to commemorate the introduction of the
brown trout into New Zealand.
† No. 874 is slightly larger than No. 856, measuring 21 × 25 mm and the
inscriptions and numerals differ in size.

278 "The Adoration   279 Mount Aspiring,   280 Sir James
of the Shepherds"   Aurora Australis and   Hector (founder)
(Poussin)   Southern Cross

(Photo Harrison)

1967 (3 Oct). *Christmas. W 98 (sideways). P 13½ × 14.*
880	278	2½ c. multicoloured	5 ✔	5
		First Day Cover		35

(Des J. Berry. Litho D.L.R.)

1967 (10 Oct). *Centenary of the Royal Society of New Zealand. W 98
(sideways on 4 c.). P 14 (4 c.) or 13 × 14 (8 c.).*
881	279	4 c. multicoloured	15	20
		Wi. Wmk sideways inverted	2·50	
882	280	8 c. multicoloured	15 ✔	25
		Set of 2	30	45
		First Day Cover		65

281 Open Bible   282 Soldiers and Tank

(Des Display Section, G.P.O. Litho D.L.R.)

1968 (23 Apr). *Centenary of Maori Bible. W 98. P 13½.*
883	281	3 c. multicoloured	5 ✔	5
		a. Gold (inscr etc.) omitted	£100	
		Wi. Wmk inverted	25·00	
		First Day Cover		45

(Des L. C. Mitchell. Litho D.L.R.)

1968 (7 May). *New Zealand Armed Forces. T 282 and similar horiz
designs. Multicoloured. W 98 (sideways). P 14 × 13½.*
884		4 c. Type 282	30	15
		Wi. Wmk inverted	9·00	
885		10 c. Airmen, "Canberra" and "Kittyhawk" aircraft	50	35
886		28 c. Sailors, H.M.N.Z.S. *Achilles*, 1939, and		
		H.M.N.Z.S. *Waikato*, 1968	70	2·00
		Wi. Wmk inverted	7·00	
		Set of 3	1·40 ✔	2·25
		First Day Cover		3·25

285 Boy breasting Tape, and   287 Placing Votes in
Olympic Rings   Ballot Box

(Des L.C. Mitchell. Photo Harrison)

1968 (7 Aug). *Health Stamps. T 285 and similar horiz design. Multicoloured. P 14½ × 14.*
887		2½ c.+1 c. Type 285	10	10
888		3 c.+1 c. Girl swimming and Olympic rings	10	10
		a. Red ring omitted	£750	
		Set of 2	20 ✔	20
		First Day Cover		50
MS889		Two sheets each 145×95 mm. Nos 887/8 in		
		blocks of six . . . . Per pair	13·00	18·00
		First Day Covers (2)		24·00

No. 888a occurred in a miniature sheet and only six copies are known
(one being used).

(Des J. Berry. Photo Japanese Govt Ptg Bureau, Tokyo)

1968 (19 Sept). *75th Anniv of Universal Suffrage in New Zealand. P 13.*
890	287	3 c. ochre, olive-green and light blue	5 ✔	5
		First Day Cover		30

288 Human Rights   289 "The Nativity"
Emblem   (G. van Honthorst)

(Photo Japanese Govt Ptg Bureau, Tokyo)

1968 (19 Sept). *Human Rights Year. P 13.*
891	288	10 c. scarlet, yellow and deep green	10 ✔	25
		First Day Cover		40

(Photo Harrison)

1968 (1 Oct). *Christmas. W 98 (sideways). P 14 × 14½.*
892	289	2½ c. multicoloured	5 ✔	5
		First Day Cover		35

290 I.L.O. Emblem

(Photo Harrison)

1969 (11 Feb). *50th Anniv of International Labour Organization.* W **98** *(sideways).* P 14½ × 14.

| 893 | **290** | 7 c. black and carmine-red | . . . . | 15 ✔ | 30 |
| | | *First Day Cover* | . . . . | | 70 |

291 Supreme Court Building, Auckland

292 Law Society's Coat of Arms

293 "Justice" (from Memorial Window in University of Canterbury, Christchurch)

(Des R. M. Conly. Litho B.W.)

1969 (8 Apr). *Centenary of New Zealand Law Society.* P 13½ × 13 (3 c.) or 13 × 13½ (others).

894	**291**	3 c. multicoloured *(shades)*	. . . .	10	5
		Ea. Blue printed double	. . . .	£110	
895	**292**	10 c. multicoloured	. . . .	30	60
896	**293**	18 c. multicoloured *(shades)*	. . . .	40	90
		Set of 3	. . . .	70 ✔	1·40
		First Day Cover	. . . .		2·00

295 Student being conferred with Degree

(Des R. M. Conly. Litho B.W.)

1969 (3 June). *Centenary of Otago University* T **295** *and similar multicoloured design.* P 13 × 13½ (3 c.) or 13½ × 13 (10 c.).

897		3 c. Otago University *(vert)*	. . . .	10	10
898		10 c. Type **295**	. . . .	20 ✔	25
		Set of 2	. . . .	30 ✔	35
		First Day Cover	. . . .		85

296 Boys playing Cricket

298 Dr. Elizabeth Gunn (founder of First Children's Health Camp)

(Des R. M. Conly (4 c.); L. C. Mitchell (others). Litho B.W.)

1969 (6 Aug). *Health Stamps.* T **296** *and similar horiz design and T* **298**. P 12½ × 13 (No. 901) or 13 × 12½ (others).

899		2½ c. + 1 c. multicoloured	. . . .	30	40
900		3 c. + 1 c. multicoloured	. . . .	30	40
901		4 c. + 1 c. brown and ultramarine	. . . .	30	1·00
		Set of 3	. . . .	80 ✔	1·60
		First Day Cover	. . . .		2·25
MS902		Two sheets each 144 × 84 mm. Nos. 899/900 in blocks of six	. . . . *Per pair*	20·00	32·00
		First Day Covers (2)	. . . .		38·00

Design:—3 c. Girls playing cricket.

299 Oldest existing House in New Zealand, and Old Stone Mission Store, Kerikeri

300 View of Bay of Islands

(Litho D.L.R.)

1969 (18 Aug). *Early European Settlement in New Zealand, and 150th Anniv of Kerikeri.* W **98** *(sideways).* P 13 × 13½.

903	**299**	4 c. multicoloured	. . . .	20	25
904	**300**	6 c. multicoloured	. . . .	30	1·00
		Set of 2	. . . .	50 ✔	1·25
		First Day Cover	. . . .		1·75

301 "The Nativity" (Federico Fiori (Barocci))

(Photo Harrison)

1969 (1 Oct). *Christmas.* P 13 × 14. A. W **98**. B. *No wmk.*

				A		B	
905	**301**	2½ c. multicoloured	. . . . .	5 ✔	5	5	5
		First Day Cover	. . . . . .		30		

302 Captain Cook. Transit of Venus and "Octant"

303 Sir Joseph Banks (naturalist) and Outline :
of H.M.S. *Endeavour*

304 Dr. Daniel Solander (botanist) and his
Plant

305 Queen Elizabeth II and Cook's Chart, 1769

(Des Eileen Mayo. Photo; portraits embossed Harrison)

1969 (9 Oct).   *Bicentenary of Captain Cook's Landing in New Zealand.*
P 14½ × 14.
906	**302**	4 c.	black, cerise and blue	75	35
907	**303**	6 c.	slate-green, purple-brown & black . .	1·00	2·50
908	**304**	18 c.	purple-brown, slate-green & black . .	2·50	2·50
909	**305**	28 c.	cerise, black and blue	4·00	4·50
			Set of 4	7·50	9·00
			First Day Cover		14·00
MS910		109 × 90 mm. Nos. 906/9	18·00	28·00
			First Day Cover		30·00

The miniature sheet exists additionally inscribed on the selvedge at
bottom. "A SOUVENIR FROM NEW ZEALAND STAMP EXHIBITION,
NEW PLYMOUTH 6TH–11TH OCTOBER, 1969". These were not sold
from Post Offices.

306 Girl, Wheat
Field and
C.O.R.S.O. Emblem

307 Mother feeding her Child,
Dairy Herd and C.O.R.S.O.
Emblem

(Des L. C. Mitchell. Photo Japanese Govt Printing Bureau, Tokyo)

1969 (18 Nov).   *25th Anniv of C.O.R.S.O. (Council of Organizations for*
Relief Services Overseas). P 13.
911	**306**	7 c. multicoloured	30	1·00
912	**307**	8 c. multicoloured	30	1·00
		Set of 2	60	2·00
		First Day Cover		3·00

GIBBONS STAMP MONTHLY
—finest and most informative magazine for all
collectors. Obtainable from your newsagent or
by postal subscription—details on request.

308 "Cardigan Bay" (champion trotter)

(Des L. C. Mitchell. Photo Courvoisier)

1970 (28 Jan).   *Return of "Cardigan Bay" to New Zealand. P* 11½.
913	**308**	10 c. multicoloured	20	25
		First Day Cover		50

309 Red Admiral
Butterfly

310 Queen Elizabeth II and New
Zealand Coat of Arms

(Des Enid Hunter (½ c., 1 c., 2 c., 18 c., 20 c.), Eileen Mayo (2½ c. to 7 c.),
D. B. Stevenson (7½ c., 8 c.), M. Cleverley (10 c., 15 c., 25 c., 30 c., $1,
$2), M. V. Askew (23 c., 50 c.). Photo Harrison (½ c. to 20 c.), Enschedé
(23 c., 50 c.), Courvoisier ($1, $2) or Litho B.W. (25 c., 30 c.))

1970 (12 Mar)**-76**. *Various designs at T* **309/10**. *W* **98** *(sideways on* 10,
15 *and* 20 *c.) or No wmk* (23 *c. to* $2).

(a) *Size as T* **309**. *P* 13½ × 13
914		½ c. multicoloured (2.9.70)	15 .	20
915		1 c. multicoloured (2.9.70)	12 •	5
	Wi.	Wmk inverted	30·00	
	a.	Wmk sideways inverted (booklets) (6.7.71)	60	80
	b.	Booklet pane. No. 915a × 3 with three *se-*		
		tenant printed labels (6.7.71)	2·00	
916		2 c. multicoloured (2.9.70)	12 •	5
	a.	Black (inscr, etc.) omitted	90·00	
	Wi.	Wmk inverted	2·25	
917		2½ c. multicoloured (2.9.70)	40 •	10
918		3 c. black, brown and orange (2.9.70)	15 .	5
	Wi.	Wmk inverted	40	60
	a.	Wmk sideways inverted (booklets) (6.7.71)	40	60
	aWi.	Wmk sideways	17·00	
	Eb.	Horiz coil pair	2·25	
919		4 c. multicoloured (2.9.70)	20 •	5
	Wi.	Wmk inverted	3·00	
	a.	Wmk sideways inverted (booklets) (6.7.71)	40	60
	Eb.	Horiz coil pair	2·5C	
920		5 c. multicoloured (4.11.70)	45 •	10
	Ea.	Horiz coil pair	5·00	
921		6 c. blackish grn, yell-grn & carm (4.11.70) . .	45 •	20
	Ea.	Horiz coil pair	5·00	
922		7 c. multicoloured (4.11.70)	55 •	30
923		7½ c. multicoloured (4.11.70)	1·00 •	1·50
924		8 c. multicoloured (4.11.70)	65 •	30
	Ea.	Horiz coil pair	5·00	

(b) *Size as T* **310**. *Various Perfs*
925		10 c. multicoloured (*p* 14½ × 14)	40 •	15
	Ea.	Horiz coil pair	7·00	
	Wi.	Wmk sideways inverted	6·00	
926		15 c. black, flesh and pale brown (*p* 13½ × 13)		
		(20.1.71)	1·50 •	40
927		18 c. chestnut, black & apple-grn (*p* 13 × 13½)		
		(20.1.71)	1·50 •	40
	Wi.	Wmk inverted	25·00	
928		20 c. black & yell-brn (*p* 13½ × 13) (20.1.71) . .	1·50 •	40
	Ea.	Horiz coil pair	7·50	
929		23 c. multicoloured (*p* 13½ × 12½) (1.12.71) . . .	80 •	15
930		25 c. multicoloured (*p* 13 × 13½) (1.9.71)	1·75 •	15
	Ea.	Black (inscr) printed double		
	b.	Perf 14 (11.76?)	70	40
931		30 c. multicoloured (*p* 13 × 13½) (1.9.71)	2·25 •	20
	a.	Perf 14 (9.76?)	2·50	2·25
932		50 c. multicoloured (*p* 13½ × 12½) (1.9.71) . . .	80 •	20
	a.	Apple green (hill) omitted	25·00	
	b.	Buff (shore) omitted	50·00	
933		$1 multicoloured (*p* 11½) (14.4.71)	2·00 •	80

934	$2 multicoloured (*p* 11½) (14.4.71)		4·75 •	1·75
	Set of 21		18·00	6·50
	Presentation Pack (contains ½ c. to 8 *c.)*			
	(sold at 85 *c.)*		6·00	
	Presentation Pack (contains ½ c. to 50 *c.)*			
	(sold at $2.66)		20·00	
	Presentation Pack (contains ½ c. to 20 *c.)*			
	(sold at $1.50) (5.3.73)		14·00	
	Presentation Pack (contains ½ c. to $2) *(sold*			
	at $5.75) (5.3.73)		25·00	
	First Day Covers (7)			16·00

Designs: *Vert*—½ c. Glade Copper Butterfly; 1 c. Type **309**; 2 c. Tussock Butterfly; 2½ c. Magpie Moth; 3 c. Lichen Moth; 4 c. Puriri Moth; 5 c. Scarlet Parrot Fish; 6 c. Sea Horses; 7 c. Leather Jacket (fish); 7½ c. Garfish; 8 c. John Dory (fish); 18 c. Maori Club; 25 c. Hauraki Gulf Maritime Park; 30 c. Mt Cook National Park. *Horiz*—10 c. Type **310**; 15 c. Maori fish hook; 20 c. Maori tattoo pattern; 23 c. Egmont National Park; 50 c. Abel Tasman National Park; $1 Geothermal Power; $2 Agricultural Technology.

Although issued as a definitive, No. 925 was put on sale on the occasion of the Royal Visit to New Zealand.

See also Nos. 1008, etc.

New Zealand · expo'70   **7**c

311 Geyser Restaurant

312 U.N. H.Q. Building

(Des M. Cleverley. Photo Japanese Govt Printing Bureau, Tokyo)

1970 (8 Apr). *World Fair, Osaka. T* **311** *and similar horiz designs. Multicoloured. P* 13.

935	7 c. Type **311**		40	80
936	8 c. New Zealand Pavilion		40	80
937	18 c. Bush Walk		60	80
	Set of 3		1·25	2·25
	First Day Cover			3·00

(Des R. M. Conly (3 c.), L. C. Mitchell (10 c.). Litho D.L.R.)

1970 (24 June). *25th Anniv of United Nations. T* **312** *and similar vert design. P* 13½.

938	3 c. multicoloured		5	5
939	10 c. scarlet and yellow		10	15
	Set of 2		15	20
	First Day Cover			55

Design:—10 c. Tractor on horizon.

313 Soccer

(Des L. C. Mitchell. Litho D.L.R.)

1970 (5 Aug). *Health Stamps. T* **313** *and similar multicoloured design. P* 13½.

940	2½ c. + 1 c. Netball (*vert*)		10	15
941	3 c. + 1 c. Type **313**		10	15
	Set of 2		20	30
	First Day Cover			60
MS942	Two sheets: (*a*) 102 × 125 mm (940); (*b*)			
	125 × 102 mm (941), containing blocks of six			
	Per pair		15·00	20·00
	First Day Covers (2)			24·00

314 "The Virgin adoring the Child" (Correggio)

315 "The Holy Family" (stained glass window, Invercargill Presbyterian Church)

(Litho D.L.R.)

1970 (1 Oct). *Christmas. T* **314/15** *and similar design. P* 12½.

943	2½ c. multicoloured		5	5
944	3 c. multicoloured		5	5
	a. Green (inscr and value) omitted		£150	
945	10 c. black, orange and silver		30	70
	Set of 3		35	70
	First Day Cover			95

Design: *Horiz*—10 c. Tower of Roman Catholic Church, Sockburn.

Souvenir Pack 1970

1970 (1 Dec). *Comprises Nos. 906/9, 911/13, 935/41 and 943/5. Sold at* $1.95.

SP945a   Souvenir Pack . . . .   28·00

316 Chatham Islands Lily

(Des Eileen Mayo. Photo Japanese Govt Printing Bureau, Tokyo)

1970 (2 Dec). *Chatham Islands. T* **316** *and similar horiz design. Multicoloured. P* 13.

946	1 c. Type **316**		10	15
947	2 c. Shy Albatross		15	25
	Set of 2		25	40
	First Day Cover			60

4c **NEW ZEALAND**

317 Country Women's Institute Emblem

(Des L. C. Mitchell. Photo Japanese Govt Ptg Bureau, Tokyo)

1971 (10 Feb). *50th Anniversaries of Country Women's Institutes and Rotary International in New Zealand. T* **317** *and similar horiz design. Multicoloured. P* 13.

948	4 c. Type **317**		5	5
949	10 c. Rotary emblem and map of New Zealand . .		10	20
	Set of 2		15	25
	First Day Cover			55

5c   One Ton Cup,1971

318 *Rainbow II* (yacht)

(Des J. Berry (5 c.), G. F. Fuller (8 c.). Litho B.W.)

1971 (3 Mar). *One Ton Cup Racing Trophy. T* **318** *and similar horiz design. Multicoloured. P* 13½ × 13.

950	5 c.	Type **318**	15	20
951	8 c.	One Ton Cup	25	55
		Set of 2	40	75
		First Day Cover		1·00

319 Civic Arms of Palmerston North

(Des R. M. Conly. Photo Japanese Govt Ptg Bureau, Tokyo)

1971 (12 May). *City Centenaries. T* **319** *and similar horiz designs. Multicoloured. P* 13.

952	3 c.	Type **319**	10	8
953	4 c.	Arms of Auckland	10	10
954	5 c.	Arms of Invercargill	15	40
		Set of 3	30	50
		First Day Cover		70

320 Antarctica on Globe   **321** Child on Swing

(Des Eileen Mayo. Photo Japanese Govt Ptg Bureau, Tokyo)

1971 (9 June). *Tenth Anniv of Antarctic Treaty. P* 13.

955	**320**	6 c. multicoloured	1·50	1·50

(Des Eileen Mayo. Photo Japanese Govt Ptg Bureau, Tokyo)

1971 (9 June). *25th Anniv of U.N.I.C.E.F. P* 13.

956	**321**	7 c. multicoloured	50	70
		First Day Cover (Nos. 955/6)		2·75

4c   **4**c   **4**c

(322)   (322a)   (322b)

T **322**. Photo, showing screening dots; thin bars, wide apart.
T **322a**. Typo, without screening dots; thick bars, closer together.
T **322b**. Typo; bars similar to T **322**.

1971–73. *No.* 917 *surcharged.*

(a) In photogravure, by Harrison (23.6.71*)

957	**322**	4 c. on 2½ c. multicoloured	15	10

(b) Typographically, by Harrison (13.7.72*)

957a	**322a**	4 c. on 2½ c. multicoloured	40	12
		ab. Albino surch	£110	
		ac. Surch double, one albino	15·00	

(c) Typographically, locally (18.6.73*)

957b	**322b**	4 c. on 2½ c. multicoloured	15	10

* Earliest known postmarks.

323 Satellite-tracking Aerial

(Des M. Cleverley. Photo Courvoisier)

1971 (14 July). *Opening of Satellite Earth Station. T* **323** *and similar horiz design. P* 11½.

958	8 c.	black, drab-grey and vermilion	60	1·00
959	10 c.	black, turquoise-green & pale bluish violet	65	1·00
		Set of 2	1·25	2·00
		First Day Cover		2·50

Design:—10 c. Satellite.

324 Girls playing Hockey

(Des L. C. Mitchell. Litho Harrison)

1971 (4 Aug). *Health Stamps. T* **324** *and similar horiz designs. Multicoloured. W* **98** *(sideways on* 5 *c.). P* 13½ × 13.

960	3 c. + 1 c.	Type **324**	20	20
961	4 c. + 1 c.	Boys playing hockey	20	25
962	5 c. + 1 c.	Dental Health	70	1·25
		Set of 3	1·00	1·50
		First Day Cover		1·75
MS963		Two sheets each 122 × 96 mm. Nos. 960/1 in blocks of six ...... Per pair	17·00	25·00
		First Day Covers (2)		28·00

325 "Madonna bending over   **326** "Tiffany" Rose
the Crib" (Maratta)

(Des Enid Hunter (10 c.), D. A. Hatcher (others). Photo Harrison)

1971 (6 Oct). *Christmas. T* **325** *and similar vert designs. Multicoloured. P* 13 × 13½.

964	3 c.	Type **325**	10	10
965	4 c.	"The Annunciation" (stained-glass window) (21½ × 38 mm)	10	5
966	10 c.	"The Three Kings" (21½ × 38 mm)	70	1·25
		Set of 3	80	1·25
		First Day Cover		1·60

Souvenir Pack 1971

1971 (6 Oct). *Comprises Nos.* 946/56, 958/62 *and* 964/6. *Sold at* $1.50.

SP966a	Souvenir Pack	18·00	

(Des A. G. Mitchell. Photo Courvoisier)

1971 (3 Nov). *First World Rose Convention, Hamilton. T* **326** *and similar vert designs showing roses. Multicoloured. P* 11½.

967	2 c.	Type **326**	15	20
968	5 c.	"Peace"	35	30
969	8 c.	"Chrysler Imperial"	60	1·00
		Set of 3	1·00	1·40
		First Day Cover		1·50

327 Lord Rutherford and   328 Benz (1895)
     Alpha Particles

(Des M. Cleverley. Litho B.W.)

1971 (1 Dec). *Birth Centenary of Lord Rutherford (scientist). T* **327** *and similar horiz design. Multicoloured. P* 13½ × 13.
970	1 c. Type **327**	25	35
971	7 c. Lord Rutherford and formula	85	1·25
	Set of 2	1·10	1·60
	First Day Cover		1·75

(Des A. G. Mitchell. Litho B.W.)

1972 (2 Feb). *International Vintage Car Rally. T* **328** *and similar horiz designs. Multicoloured. P* 14.
972	3 c. Type **328**	20	5
973	4 c. Oldsmobile (1904)	25	5
974	5 c. Ford "Model T" (1914)	35	15
975	6 c. Cadillac Service car (1915)	55	65
976	8 c. Chrysler (1924)	1·25	1·50
977	10 c. Austin "7" (1923)	1·25	1·50
	Set of 6	3·50	3·50
	First Day Cover		3·75

329 Coat of Arms of   330 Black Scree
     Wanganui   Cotula

(Des M. Cleverley. Litho Harrison)

1972 (5 Apr). *Anniversaries. T* **329** *and similar designs. P* 13 × 13½ (3, 5 *and* 8 *c.) or* 13½ × 13 (*others*).
978	3 c. multicoloured	12	10
979	4 c. red-orange, brown-bistre and black	15	10
980	5 c. multicoloured	25	20
981	8 c. multicoloured	1·50	2·00
982	10 c. multicoloured	1·50	2·00
	Set of 5	3·25	4·00
	First Day Cover		5·00

Designs and Events: *Vert*—3 c. Type **329** (Centenary of Wanganui Council govt); 5 c. De Havilland DH89 "Rapide" *Dominie* and Boeing "737" (25th Anniv National Airways Corp); 8 c. French frigate and Maori palisade (Bicent of landing by Marion du Fresne). *Horiz*—4 c. Postal Union symbol (Tenth Anniv of Asian-Oceanic Postal Union); 10 c. Stone cairn (150th Anniv of New Zealand Methodist Church).

(Des Eileen Mayo. Litho Harrison)

1972 (7 June). *Alpine Plants. T* **330** *and similar vert designs. Multicoloured. P* 13½.
983	4 c. Type **330**	30	12
	Ea. Inscr and face value printed double*	20·00	9·00
984	6 c. North Island Eidelweiss	75	80
985	8 c. Haast's Buttercup	1·25	1·50
986	10 c. Brown Mountain Daisy	1·75	2·00
	Set of 4	3·50	4·00
	First Day Cover		5·00

* This shows a double impression of "NEW ZEALAND" and the "4 c" and bar at the top, resulting from incorrect tension of the blanket.

331 Boy playing   332 "Madonna with
     Tennis   Child" (Murillo)

(Des L. C. Mitchell. Litho Harrison)

1972 (2 Aug). *Health Stamps. T* **331** *and similar vert design. P* 13 × 13½.
987	3 c. + 1 c. light grey and chestnut	20	25
988	4 c. + 1 c. light red-brown, grey and lemon	20	25
	Set of 2	40	50
	First Day Cover		70
MS989	Two sheets each 107 × 123 mm. Nos. 987/8 in blocks of six	*Per pair* 18·00	25·00
	First Day Covers (2)		28·00

Design:—No. 988, Girl playing tennis.

(Des D. A. Hatcher. Photo Courvoisier)

1972 (4 Oct). *Christmas. T* **332** *and similar vert designs. Multicoloured. P* 11½.
990	3 c. Type **332**	10	5
991	5 c. "The Last Supper" (stained-glass window, St. John's Church, Levin)	15	5
992	10 c. Pohutukawa flower	55	1·00
	Set of 3	70	1·00
	First Day Cover		1·50

Souvenir Pack 1972

1972 (4 Oct). *Comprises Nos. 967/88 and 990/2. Sold at* $1.95.
| SP992a | Souvenir Pack | 22·00 |

333 Lake   334 Old Pollen Street
     Waikaremoana

(Des D. A. Hatcher. Photo Courvoisier)

1972 (6 Dec). *Lake Scenes. T* **333** *and similar vert designs. Multicoloured. P* 11½.
993	6 c. Type **333**	1·00	1·50
994	8 c. Lake Hayes	1·10	1·50
995	18 c. Lake Wakatipu	2·00	3·00
996	23 c. Lake Rotomahana	2·25	3·25
	Set of 4	5·75	8·50
	First Day Cover		11·00
	Souvenir Postcards (4)	4·00	

(Des Miss V. Jepsen (3 c.), B. Langford (others). Litho Harrison)

1973 (7 Feb). *Commemorations. T* **334** *and similar horiz designs. Multicoloured (except* 8 *c.). P* 13½ × 13.
997	3 c. Type **334**	15	10
998	4 c. Coal-mining and pasture	15	8
999	5 c. Cloister	15	15
1000	6 c. Forest, birds and lake	50	70
1001	8 c. Rowers (light grey, indigo and gold)	45	1·00
	Ea. Gold printed double	80·00	
1002	10 c. Graph and people	50	1·40
	Set of 6	1·75	3·00
	First Day Cover		3·50

Events:—3 c. Centennial of Thames Borough; 4 c. Centennial of Westport Borough; 5 c. Centennial of Canterbury University; 6 c. 50th Anniv of Royal Forest and Bird Protection Society; 8 c. Success of N.Z. Rowers in 1972 Olympics; 10 c. 25th Anniv of E.C.A.F.E.

335 Class "W" Locomotive   336 "Maori Woman
                                      and Child"

337 Prince Edward   338 "Tempi Madonna"
                               (Raphael)

(Des R. M. Conly. Litho Harrison)

1973 (4 Apr). *New Zealand Steam Locomotives. T* **335** *and similar horiz designs. Multicoloured. P* 14 × 14½.
1003	3 c. Type **335**	45	10
1004	4 c. Class "X"	55	10
1005	5 c. Class "Ab"	60	15
1006	10 c. Class "Ja"	2·50	2·00
	Set of 4	3·50	2·10
	First Day Cover		3·00

1973–76. *As Nos. 914 etc., but no wmk.*
1008	1 c. multicoloured (7.9.73)	60	20
	a. Booklet pane. No. 1008 × 3 with three se-tenant printed labels (8.74)	2·00	
	b. Red (wing markings) omitted	£100	
	c. Blue (spots on wings) omitted	45·00	
1009	2 c. multicoloured (6.73?)	25	10
1010	3 c. black, light brown and orange (1974)	1·50	40
	Ea. Horiz coil pair	4·00	
1011	4 c. multicoloured (7.9.73)	50	5
	a. Bright green (wing veins) inverted	£275	
	b. Purple-brown omitted	£170	
	c. Orange-yellow omitted	£170	
	d. Greenish blue (background) omitted	£140	
	e. Bright green (wing veins) omitted	6·00	
	f. Apple green (wings) omitted	90·00	
	Eg. Horiz coil pair	2·25	
1012	5 c. multicoloured (1973)	1·75	65
	Ea. Horiz coil pair	3·50	
1013	6 c. blackish green, yellow-green and rose-carmine (7.9.73)	40	25
	Ea. Horiz coil pair (1973)	3·25	
1014	7 c. multicoloured (1974)	3·00	2·00
1015	8 c. multicoloured (1974)	3·75	1·50
	a. Blue-green (background) omitted	80·00	
	Eb. Horiz coil pair	6·00	
1017	10 c. multicoloured, *p* 13½ × 13 (6.73?)	60	5
	a. Silver (Arms) omitted	£130	
	b. Imperf (vert pair)	£180	
	c. Deep blue (Queen's head, face value, etc.) omitted	£150	
	d. Red omitted	:20·00	
	Ee. Horiz coil pair	4·00	
1018	15 c. blk, flesh & pale brn, *p* 13½ × 13 (2.8.76)	1·25	15
1019	18 c. chestnut, black and apple-green (1974)	1·00	60
	a. Black (inscr, etc.) omitted	£160	
1020	20 c. black and yellow-brown (1974)	80	15
	Ea. Horiz coil pair	6·00	
	Set of 12	14·00	5·50

(Des and photo Courvoisier)

1973 (6 June). *Paintings by Frances Hodgkins. T* **336** *and similar vert designs. Multicoloured. P* 11½.
1027	5 c. Type **336**	40	15
1028	8 c. "Hilltop"	75	85
1029	10 c. "Barn in Picardy"	1·00	1·00
1030	18 c. "Self Portrait Still Life"	1·50	1·00
	Set of 4	3·25	3·00
	First Day Cover		4·50

GIBBONS STAMP MONTHLY
—finest and most informative magazine for all collectors. Obtainable from your newsagent or by postal subscription—details on request.

(Des and litho Harrison)

1973 (1 Aug). *Health Stamps. P* 13 × 13½.
1031	**337** 3 c. + 1 c. dull yellowish green and reddish brown	25	25
1032	4 c. + 1 c. rose-red and blackish brown	25	25
	Set of 2	50	50
	First Day Cover		70
MS1033	Two sheets each 96 × 121 mm with Nos. 1031/2 in blocks of 6 (3 × 2) *Per pair*	15·00	23·00
	First Day Covers (2)		28·00

(Des A. G. Mitchell. Photo Enschedé)

1973 (3 Oct). *Christmas. T* **338** *and similar vert designs. Multicoloured. P* 12½ × 13½.
1034	3 c. Type **338**	10	5
1035	5 c. "Three Kings" (stained-glass window, St. Theresa's Church, Auckland)	10	5
1036	10 c. Family entering church	25	50
	Set of 3	40	50
	First Day Cover		1·25

Souvenir Pack 1973

1973 (3 Oct). *Comprises Nos. 997/1006 and 1027/36. Sold at* $2.25.
SP1036a	Souvenir Pack	22·00	

339 Mitre Peak   340 Hurdling

(Des D. A. Hatcher. Photo Enschedé)

1973 (5 Dec). *Mountain Scenery. T* **339** *and similar multicoloured designs. P* 13 × 13½ (6, 8 c.) *or* 13½ × 13 (*others*).
1037	6 c. Type **339**	80	90
1038	8 c. Mt Ngauruhoe	1·00	1·50
1039	18 c. Mt Seiton (*horiz*)	1·75	3·00
1040	23 c. Burnett Range (*horiz*)	2·00	3·00
	Set of 4	5·00	7·50
	First Day Cover		8·00
	Souvenir Postcards (4)	8·50	

(Des M. Cleverley. Litho Harrison)

1974 (9 Jan). *Tenth British Commonwealth Games, Christchurch. T* **340** *and similar vert designs. 5 c. black and violet-blue, others multicoloured. P* 13 × 14.
1041	4 c. Type **340**	10	5
1042	5 c. Ball-player	15	5
1043	10 c. Cycling	20	15
1044	18 c. Rifle-shooting	35	65
1045	23 c. Bowls	50	85
	Set of 5	1·10	1·60
	First Day Cover		2·25

No. 1042 does not show the Games emblem, and commemorates the Fourth Paraplegic Games, held at Dunedin.

341 Queen Elizabeth II　　**342** "Spirit of Napier" Fountain

(Des D. A. Hatcher and A. G. Mitchell. Litho Harrison)

1974 (5 Feb). *New Zealand Day. Sheet* 131 × 74 *mm, containing T* **341** *and similar horiz designs, size* 37 × 20 *mm. Multicoloured. P* 13.
MS1046　4 c. × 5 Treaty House, Waitangi; Signing Waitangi Treaty; Type **341**; Parliament Buildings Extensions; Children in Class . . . . 80　1·75
　　　　First Day Cover . . . . 2·25

(Des Miss V. Jepsen. Photo Courvoisier)

1974 (3 Apr). *Centenaries of Napier and U.P.U. T* **342** *and similar vert designs. Multicoloured. P* 11½.
1047　4 c. Type **342** . . . . 10　8
1048　5 c. Clock Tower, Berne . . . . 10　15
1049　8 c. U.P.U. Monument, Berne . . . . . . 35　90
　　　　Set of 3 . . . . 50　1·00
　　　　First Day Cover . . . . 1·10

343 Boeing Seaplane, 1919　　**344** Children, Cat and Dog

(Des R. M. Conly. Litho Harrison)

1974 (5 June). *History of New Zealand Airmail Transport. T* **343** *and similar horiz designs. Multicoloured. P* 14 × 13.
1050　3 c. Type **343** . . . . 25　10
1051　4 c. Lockheed "Electra", 1937 . . . . 30　15
1052　5 c. Bristol Freighter, 1958 . . . . 35　15
1053　23 c. Empire "S 30" flying-boat, 1940 . . . . . . 1·50　1·75
　　　　Set of 4 . . . . 2·25　2·00
　　　　First Day Cover . . . . 2·50

(Des B. Langford. Litho Harrison)

1974 (7 Aug). *Health Stamps. P* 13 × 13½.
1054　**344**　3 c. + 1 c. multicoloured . . . . 15　25
1055　–　4 c. + 1 c. multicoloured . . . . 20　25
1056　–　5 c. + 1 c. multicoloured . . . . 90　1·10
　　　　Set of 3 . . . . 1·10　1·40
　　　　First Day Cover . . . . 1·60
MS1057　145 × 123 mm. No. 1055 in block of ten . . . 18·00　27·00
　　　　First Day Cover . . . . 30·00
Nos. 1055/6 are as T **344**, showing children and pets.

THE WORLD CENTRE FOR FINE STAMPS IS 399 STRAND

345 "The Adoration of the Magi" (Konrad Witz)　　**346** Great Barrier Island

(Des Eileen Mayo. Photo Courvoisier)

1974 (2 Oct). *Christmas. T* **345** *and similar horiz designs. Multicoloured. P* 11½.
1058　3 c. Type **345** . . . . 5　5
1059　5 c. "The Angel Window" (stained-glass window, Old St. Pauls Church, Wellington) . . 10　5
1060　10 c. Madonna Lily . . . . 30　50
　　　　Set of 3 . . . . 40　55
　　　　First Day Cover . . . . 1·25

Souvenir Pack 1974

1974 (2 Oct). *Comprises Nos.* 1037/56 *and* 1058/60. *Sold at* $2.70.
SP1060a　Souvenir Pack . . . . 22·00

(Des D. A. Hatcher. Photo Enschedé)

1974 (4 Dec). *Off-shore Islands. T* **346** *and similar horiz designs. Multicoloured. P* 13½ × 13.
1061　6 c. Type **346** . . . . 30　40
1062　8 c. Stewart Island . . . . 40　80
1063　18 c. White Island . . . . 70　1·50
1064　23 c. The Brothers . . . . 1·00　2·00
　　　　Set of 4 . . . . 2·25　4·25
　　　　First Day Cover . . . . 5·00

347 Crippled Child

(Des Miss V. Jepsen (3 c., 5 c.), A. G. Mitchell (10 c., 18 c.). Litho Harrison)

1975 (5 Feb). *Anniversaries and Events. T* **347** *and similar horiz designs. Multicoloured. P* 13½.
1065　3 c. Type **347** . . . . 10　5
1066　5 c. Farming family . . . . 15　10
1067　10 c. I.W.Y. symbols . . . . 20　55
1068　18 c. Medical School Building, Otago University 35　80
　　　　Set of 4 . . . . 70　1·40
　　　　First Day Cover . . . . 1·75
Commemorations:—3 c. 40th Anniv of N.Z. Crippled Children Society; 5 c. 50th Anniv of Women's Division, Federated Farmers of N.Z.; 10 c. International Women's Year; 18 c. Centenary of Otago Medical School.

348 Scow *Lake Erie*

(Des R. M. Conly. Litho Harrison)

1975 (2 Apr). *Historic Sailing Ships. T* **348** *and similar horiz designs. P* 13½ × 13.
1069　4 c. black and red . . . . 20　5
1070　5 c. black and turquoise-blue . . . . 30　5
1071　8 c. black and yellow . . . . 40　45

1072	10 c. black and olive-yellow	40	5
1073	18 c. black and light brown	85	1·25
1074	23 c. black and slate-lilac	1·00	1·75
	Set of 6	2·75	3·50
	First Day Cover		4·00

Ships:—5 c. Schooner *Herald*; 8 c. Brigantine *New Zealander*; 10 c. Topsail schooner *Jessie Kelly*; 18 c. Barque *Tory*; 23 c. Full-rigged clipper *Rangitiki*.

349 Lake Sumner Forest Park

(Des and photo Enschedé)

1975 (4 June). *Forest Park Scenes. T* **349** *and similar horiz designs. Multicoloured. P* 13.

1075	6 c. Type **349**	50	70
1076	8 c. North-west Nelson	60	1·00
1077	18 c. Kaweka	1·25	2·00
1078	23 c. Coromandel	1·50	2·25
	Set of 4	3·50	5·50
	First Day Cover		6·00

350 Girl feeding Lamb   **351** "Virgin and Child" (Zanobi Machiavelli)

(Des Margaret Chapman. Litho Harrison)

1975 (6 Aug). *Health Stamps. T* **350** *and similar horiz designs. Multicoloured. P* 13½ × 13.

1079	3 c. + 1 c. Type **350**	15	15
1080	4 c. + 1 c. Boy with hen and chicks	15	15
1081	5 c. + 1 c. Boy with duck and duckling	50	50
	Set of 3	70	1·10
	First Day Cover		1·25
MS1082	123 × 146 mm. No. 1080 × 10	14·00	20·00
	First Day Cover		25·00

(Des Enid Hunter. Photo Harrison)

1975 (1 Oct). *Christmas. T* **351** *and similar horiz designs. Multicoloured. P* 13 × 13½ (3 c.) *or* 13½ × 13 *(others)*.

1083	3 c. Type **351**	10	5
	a. Red omitted*		
1084	5 c. "Cross in Landscape" (stained-glass window, Greendale Church)	15	5
	a. Brown (face value) omitted	£160	
1085	10 c. "I saw three ships . . ." (carol)	35	65
	Set of 3	60	65
	First Day Cover		1·00

*This occurred in the last two vertical rows of the sheet with the red partially omitted on the previous row.

Used copies of No. 1083 have been seen with the orange ("Christmas 1975") omitted.

Souvenir Pack 1975

1975 (1 Oct). *Comprises Nos.* 1061/81 *and* 1083/5. *Sold at* $2.95.

SP 1085a	Souvenir Pack	18·00

352 "Sterling   **353** Queen Elizabeth II   **353a** Maripi
Silver"   (photograph by   (knife)
                W. Harrison)

353b Paua   **353c** "Beehive" (section of Parliamentary Buildings, Wellington)

(Des A. G. Mitchell (1 to 14 c.), I. Hulse (20 c. to $2), R. Conly ($5). Photo Harrison (1 to 10 c.), Courvoisier (11 to 14 c.), Heraclio Fournier (20 c. to $5))

1975 (26 Nov)–**81**. (*a*) *Vert designs as T* **352** *showing garden roses. Multicoloured. P* 14½ (6 *to* 8 c.) *or* 14½ × 14 (*others*).

1086	1 c. Type **352**	5	5
1087	2 c. "Lilli Marlene"	5	5
1088	3 c. "Queen Elizabeth"	50	10
	a. Perf 14½ (6.79)	40	5
1089	4 c. "Super Star"	10	5
1090	5 c. "Diamond Jubilee"	10	5
1091	6 c. "Cresset"	90	60
	a. Perf 14½ × 14 (8.76?)	10	5
1092	7 c. "Michele Meilland"	1·50	50
	a. Perf 14½ × 14 (6.76?)	20	5
1093	8 c. "Josephine Bruce"	1·50	60
	a. Perf 14½ × 14 (8.76?)	25	5
1094	9 c. "Iceberg"	15	5
	Presentation Pack (sold at 65 c.) (28.2.76)	4·25	

(*b*) *Type* **353**. *P* 14½ × 14 (7.12.77)

1094a	10 c. multicoloured	85	30
	ab. Perf 14½ (2.79)	20	5

(*c*) *Vert designs as T* **353a** *showing Maori artefacts. P* 11½ (24.11.76)

1095	11 c. reddish brown, lemon & blackish brn	35	15
1096	12 c. reddish brown, lemon & blackish brn	30	10
1097	13 c. reddish brown, greenish blue and blackish brown	45	25
1098	14 c. reddish brown, lemon & blackish brn	30	15

Designs:—12 c. Putorino (flute); 13 c. Wahaika (club); 14 c. Kotiate (club).

(*d*) *Horiz designs as T* **353b** *showing Seashells. Multicoloured. P* 13

1099	20 c. Type **353b** (29.11.78)	15	20
1100	30 c. Toheroa (29.11.78)	25	30
1101	40 c. Coarse Dosinia (29.11.78)	30	35
1102	50 c. Spiny Murex (29.11.78)	40	45
1103	$1 Scallop (26.11.79)	70	85
	a. Imperf between (vert pair)	£400	
1104	$2 Circular Saw (26.11.79)	1·00	1·75

(*e*) *Type* **353c**. *P* 13 (2.12.81)

1105	$5 multicoloured	3·00	2·00
	Set of 21	7·50	6·00
	Presentation Pack (Nos. 1086/94a, 1099/ 1104, 1232/6) *(Sold at* $8.30) (4.2.81)	9·00	
	First Day Covers (6)		14·00

Faked "missing colour errors" exist of No. 1094a, involving parts of the portrait.

A used example of No. 1099 exists with the black colour omitted so that the body of the shell appears in blue instead of green.

No. 1103a occurs on the top two rows of the sheet; the lower stamp being imperforate on three edges except for two perforation holes at the foot of each vertical side.

354 Family and League of Mothers Badge

(Des A. P. Derrick. Litho J.W.)

1976 (4 Feb). *Anniversaries and Metrication. T* **354** *and similar horiz designs. Multicoloured. P* 13½ × 14.

1110	6 c. Type **354**	8	5
1111	7 c. Weight, temperature, linear measure and capacity	10	5
1112	8 c. *William Bryan* (immigrant ship), mountain and New Plymouth	20	10
1113	10 c. Two women shaking hands and Y.W.C.A. badge	15	40
1114	25 c. Map of the world showing cable links	30	1·25
	Set of 5	70	1·60
	First Day Cover		1·75

Anniversaries:—6 c. League of Mothers, 50th Anniv; 7 c. Metrication; 8 c. Centenary of New Plymouth; 10 c. 50th Anniv of New Zealand Y.W.C.A.; 25 c. Centenary of link with International Telecommunications Network.

355 Gig

356 Purakaunui Falls

(Des G. F. Fuller. Litho Harrison)

1976 (7 Apr). *Vintage Farm Transport. T* **355** *and similar horiz designs. Multicoloured. P* 13½ × 13.

1115	6 c. Type **355**	15	20
1116	7 c. Thorneycroft lorry	20	5
1117	8 c. Scandi wagon	50	20
1118	9 c. Traction engine	30	40
1119	10 c. Wool wagon	30	75
1120	25 c. Cart	80	1·75
	Set of 6	2·00	2·75
	First Day Cover		3·00

(Des and photo Courvoisier)

1976 (2 June). *Waterfalls. T* **356** *and similar vert designs. Multicoloured. P* 11½.

1121	10 c. Type **356**	40	15
1122	14 c. Marakopa Falls	75	70
1123	15 c. Bridal Veil Falls	80	80
1124	16 c. Papakorito Falls	90	90
	Set of 4	2·50	2·25
	First Day Cover		2·75

357 Boy and Pony

358 "Nativity"
(Spanish carving)

(Des Margaret Chapman. Litho Harrison)

1976 (4 Aug). *Health Stamps. T* **357** *and similar vert designs. Multicoloured. P* 13 × 13½.

1125	7 c. + 1 c. Type **357**	15	25
1126	8 c. + 1 c. Girl and calf	15	25
1127	10 c. + 1 c. Girls and bird	40	60
	Set of 3	65	1·00
	First Day Cover		1·25
MS1128	96 × 121 mm. Nos. 1125/7 × 2	6·00	9·00
	First Day Cover		11·00

(Des Margaret Chapman (18 c.), D. A. Hatcher (others). Photo Harrison)

1976 (6 Oct). *Christmas. T* **358** *and similar horiz designs. Multicoloured. P* 14 × 14½ (7 c.) *or* 14½ × 14 (*others*).

1129	7 c. Type **358**	15	5
1130	11 c. "Resurrection" (stained-glass window, St. Joseph's Catholic Church, Grey Lynn)	25	30
1131	18 c. Angels	40	60
	Set of 3	70	85
	First Day Cover		1·25

Souvenir Pack 1976

1976 (6 Oct). *Comprises Nos.* 1110/31. *Sold at* $2.95.

SP1131a	Souvenir Pack		18·00

359 Arms of Hamilton

360 Queen Elizabeth II

(Des P. L. Blackie. Litho Harrison)

1977 (19 Jan). *Anniversaries. T* **359** *and similar vert designs. Multicoloured. P* 13 × 13½.

1132	8 c. Type **359**	15	10
	a. Horiz strip of 3, Nos. 1132/4	45	
1133	8 c. Arms of Gisborne	15	10
1134	8 c. Arms of Masterton	15	10
1135	10 c. A.A. emblem	15	20
	a. Horiz pair. Nos. 1135/6	30	90
1136	10 c. Arms of the College of Surgeons	15	20
	Set of 5	75	60
	First Day Cover		1·50

Events:—Nos. 1132/4, City Centenaries; No. 1135, 75th Anniv of the Automobile Association in New Zealand; No. 1136, 50th Anniv of Royal Australasian College of Surgeons.

Designs of each value were printed in the same sheet horizontally se-tenant.

(Des and photo Harrison from photographs by Warren Harrison)

1977 (23 Feb). *Silver Jubilee. Sheet* 178 × 82 *mm containing T* **360** *and similar vert designs showing different portraits. P* 14 × 14½.

MS1137	8 c. × 5 multicoloured	70	1·50
	a. Imperf	£1400	
	ab. Ditto, and silver omitted	£2000	
	b. Silver omitted	£550	
	c. Indian red omitted	£250	
	First Day Cover		1·75

MINIMUM PRICE

The minimum price quoted is 5p which represents a handling charge rather than a basis for valuing common stamps. For further notes about prices see introductory pages.

361 Physical Education   (362)
and Maori Culture

(Des A. G. Mitchell. Litho Harrison)

1977 (6 Apr). *Education. T **361** and similar vert designs. Multicoloured.
  P 13 × 13½.
1138   8 c. Type **361**   40   50
       a. Horiz strip of 5. Nos. 1138/42 .... 1·75
1139   8 c. Geography, science and woodwork   40   50
1140   8 c. Teaching the deaf, kindergarten and wood-
            work   40   50
1141   8 c. Tertiary and language classes   40   50
1142   8 c. Home science, correspondence school and
            teacher training   40   50
            Set of 5 .... 1·75   2·00
            First Day Cover ....   2·50
Nos. 1138/42 were printed horizontally *se-tenant* throughout the sheet.

1977 (Apr). *Coil Stamps. Nos. 1010/11 surch as T **362** by Govt Printer,
  Wellington.*
1143   7 c. on 3 c. Lichen Moth (19.4)   20   40
1144   8 c. on 4 c. Puriri Moth (21.4)   20   40
       a. Bright green (wing veins) omitted ..... 85·00
            Set of 2   40   80
Forged "7 c." surcharges, similar to No. 1143, but in smaller type, are
known applied to Nos. 918 and 1010.

363 Karitane Beach   364 Girl with Pigeon

(Des D. A. Hatcher. Photo Heraclio Fournier)

1977 (1 June). *Seascapes. T **363** and similar horiz designs. Multicoloured.
  P 14½.*
1145   10 c. Type **363**   20   15
1146   16 c. Ocean Beach, Mount Maunganui   35   45
1147   18 c. Piha Beach   40   50
1148   30 c. Kaikoura Coast   50   70
             Set of 4 .... 1·25   1·60
             First Day Cover ....   1·75

(Des A. P. Derrick. Litho Harrison)

1977 (3 Aug). *Health Stamps. T **364** and similar vert designs. Multicoloured. P 13 × 13½.*
1149   7 c. + 2 c. Type **364**   15   20
1150   8 c. + 2 c. Boy with frog   20   25
1151   10 c. + 2 c. Girl with butterfly   35   50
             Set of 3   65   85
             First Day Cover ....   1·25
MS1152 97 × 120 mm. Nos. 1149/51 × 2 .... 5·50 10·00
             First Day Cover ....   13·00
Stamps from the miniature sheet are without white border and together
form a composite design.

365 "The Holy Family" (Correggio)

(Des Margaret Chapman (23 c.), graphics for all values produced by printer.
Photo Courvoisier)

1977 (5 Oct). *Christmas. T **365** and similar vert designs. Multicoloured.
  P 11½.*
1153   7 c. Type **365**   15   5
1154   16 c. "Madonna and Child" (stained-glass win-
             dow, St. Michael's and All Angels, Dune-
             din)   25   30
1155   23 c. "Partridge in a Pear Tree"   40   60
             Set of 3   70   85
             First Day Cover ....   1·00

366 Merryweather Manual   367 Town Clock and
     Pump, 1860   Coat of Arms,
                                       Ashburton

(Des R. M. Conly. Litho Harrison)

1977 (7 Dec). *Fire Fighting Appliances. T **366** and similar horiz designs.
  Multicoloured. P 14 × 13.*
1156   10 c. Type **366**   15   10
1157   11 c. 2-wheel hose, reel and ladder, 1880   15   15
1158   12 c. Shand Mason steam fire engine, 1873 ...   20   25
1159   23 c. Chemical fire engine, 1888   30   40
             Set of 4   70   80
             First Day Cover ....   1·40

Souvenir Pack 1977

1977 (7 Dec). *Comprises Nos. 1132/42, 1145/51 and 1153/9. Sold at
  $3.75.*
SP1159a Souvenir Pack ....   12·00

(Des P. L. Blackie (No. 1162), Harrison (No. 1163), P. J. Durrant (others).
Litho Harrison)

1978 (8 Mar). *Centenaries. T **367** and similar multicoloured designs.
  P 14.*
1160   10 c. Type **367**   15   5
       a. Horiz pair. Nos. 1160/1   30   50
1161   10 c. Stratford and Mt Egmont   15   5
1162   12 c. Early telephone   15   15
1163   20 c. Bay of Islands (horiz)   20   30
             Set of 4   60   85
             First Day Cover ....   1·25
Centenaries commemorated are those of the towns of Ashburton and
Stratford, of the telephone in New Zealand, and of the Bay of Islands
County.
The 10 c. values were printed together, *se-tenant*, in horizontal pairs
throughout the sheet.

368 Students and   **369**   **370** Maui Gas
Ivey Hall, Lincoln   Drilling Platform
College

(Des A. P. Derrick. Litho Harrison)

1978 (26 Apr). *Land Resources and Centenary of Lincoln College of Agriculture. T* **368** *and similar vert designs. Multicoloured. P* 14½.
1164	10 c. Type **368**	15	10
1165	12 c. Sheep grazing	20	25
1166	15 c. Fertiliser ground spreading	20	30
1167	16 c. Agricultural Field Days	20	30
1168	20 c. Harvesting grain	25	40
1169	30 c. Dairy farming	40	70
	Set of 6	1·25	1·90
	First Day Cover		2·25

(Photo Harrison)

1978 (3 May–9 June). *Coil Stamps. P* 14½ × 14 (10 c.) *or* 14 × 13 (*others*).
1170	**369**	1 c. bright purple (9.6)	5	20
1171		2 c. bright orange (9.6)	5	20
1172		5 c. red-brown (9.6)	5	20
1173		10 c. bright blue	8	20
		Set of 4	20	70

(Des R. M. Conly. Litho Harrison)

1978 (7 June). *Resources of the Sea. T* **370** *and similar vert designs. Multicoloured. P* 13 × 14.
1174	12 c. Type **370**	20	15
1175	15 c. Trawler	30	25
1176	20 c. Map of 200 mile fishing limit	40	35
1177	23 c. Humpback Whale and Bottle-nosed Dolphins	50	40
1178	35 c. Kingfish, snapper, grouper and squid	75	75
	Set of 5	1·90	1·75
	First Day Cover		2·00

371 First Health   **372** "The Holy   **373** Sir Julius
Charity Stamp   Family" (El Greco)   Vogel

(Des A. G. Mitchell. Litho Harrison)

1978 (2 Aug). *Health Stamps. Health Services Commemorations. T* **371** *and similar vert design. P* 13 × 14.
1179	10 c. + 2 c. black, red and gold	25	25
1180	12 c. + 2 c. multicoloured	25	30
	Set of 2	50	55
	First Day Cover		75
MS1181	97 × 124 mm. Nos. 1179/80 × 3	3·50	4·75
	First Day Cover		6·50

Designs and commemorations:—10 c. Type **371** (50th anniversary of health charity stamps); 12 c. Heart operation (National Heart Foundation).

(Des R. M. Conly. Photo Courvoisier)

1978 (4 Oct). *Christmas. T* **372** *and similar multicoloured designs. P* 11½.
1182	7 c. Type **372**	12	5
1183	16 c. All Saints' Church, Howick	25	30
1184	23 c. Beach scene	30	45
	Set of 3	60	70
	First Day Cover		95

Souvenir Pack 1978

1978 (4 Oct). *Comprises Nos.* 1160/9, 1174/84. *Sold at* $2.50.
SP1184*a*	Souvenir Pack	9·50

(Des A. G. Mitchell. Litho J.W.)

1979 (7 Feb). *Statesmen. T* **373** *and similar vert designs in sepia and drab. P* 13 × 13½.
1185	10 c. Type **373**	30	40
	a. Horiz strip of 3. Nos. 1185/7	90	
1186	10 c. Sir George Grey	30	40
1187	10 c. Richard John Seddon	30	40
	Set of 3	90	1·10
	First Day Cover		1·40

Nos. 1185/7 were printed together, *se-tenant*, in horizontal strips of 3 throughout the sheet.
Nos. 1185/7 have matt, almost invisible gum.

374 Riverlands Cottage,   **375** Whangaroa Harbour
Blenheim

(Des P. Leitch. Litho Enschedé)

1979 (4 Apr). *Architecture* (1st series). *T* **374** *and similar horiz designs. P* 13½ × 13.
1188	10 c. black, new blue and deep blue	12	12
1189	12 c. black, pale green and bottle green	15	20
1190	15 c. black and grey	20	25
1191	20 c. black, yellow-brown and sepia	25	30
	Set of 4	65	80
	First Day Cover		1·00

Designs:—12 c. The Mission House, Waimate North; 15 c. "The Elms", Tauranga; 20 c. Provincial Council Buildings, Christchurch.
See also Nos. 1217/20 and 1262/5.

(Photo Heraclio Fournier)

1979 (6 June). *Small Harbours. T* **375** *and similar multicoloured designs. P* 13.
1192	15 c. Type **375**	20	10
1193	20 c. Kawau Island	25	30
1194	23 c. Akaroa Harbour (*vert*)	30	35
1195	35 c. Picton Harbour (*vert*)	45	50
	Set of 4	1·10	1·10
	First Day Cover		1·50

376 Children with Building Bricks

(Des W. Kelsall. Litho J.W.)

1979 (6 June). *International Year of the Child. P* 14.
1196	**376**	10 c. multicoloured	15	10
		First Day Cover		30

377 Demoiselle   (378)

(Des P. Blackie (12 c.), G. Fuller (others). Litho Harrison)

1979 (25 July).   *Health Stamps. Marine Life. T* **377** *and similar multicoloured designs. P* 13 × 13½ (12 c.) *or* 13½ × 13 (*others*).

1197	10 c.+2 c. Type **377**		25	30
	a. Horiz pair. Nos. 1197/8		50	60
1198	10 c.+2 c. Sea Urchin		25	30
	Eb. Emerald printed double		£100	
1199	12 c.+2 c. Fish and underwater cameraman (*vert*)		25	30
	Set of 3		70	80
	First Day Cover			1·00
MS1200	144 × 72 mm. Nos. 1197/9, each × 2. P 14 × 14½ (12 c.) or 14½ × 14 (others)		4·00	5·50
	First Day Cover			7·00

Nos. 1197/8 were printed together, *se-tenant*, in horizontal pairs throughout the sheet.

1979 (31 Aug)–**80**.   *Nos. 1091a, 1092a, 1093a and 1094ab surch as T* **378** *by Govt Printer, Wellington.*

1201	4 c. on 8 c. "Josephine Bruce" (24.9.79)		5	5
1202	14 c. on 10 c. Type **353**		35	20
	a. Surch double, one albino			
1203	17 c. on 6 c. "Cresset" (9.10.79)		35	50
1203a	20 c. on 7 c. "Michele Meilland" (29.9.80)		20	5
	Set of 4		85	70

379 "Madonna and   380 Chamber, House of
Child" (sculpture by   Representatives
Ghiberti)

(Des D. Hatcher. Photo Courvoisier)

1979 (3 Oct).   *Christmas. T* **379** *and similar vert designs. Multicoloured. P* 11½.

1204	10 c. Type **379**		15	5
1205	25 c. Christ Church, Russell		30	40
1206	35 c. Pohutukawa (tree)		40	55
	Set of 3		75	90
	First Day Cover			1·10

Souvenir Pack 1979

1979 (3 Oct).   *Comprises Nos. 1185/99 and 1204/6. Sold at* $4.25.

SP1206a	Souvenir Pack		6·00

(Des D. Hatcher. Litho J.W.)

1979 (26 Nov).   *25th Commonwealth Parliamentary Conference, Wellington. T* **380** *and similar vert designs. Multicoloured. P* 13½.

1207	14 c. Type **380**		15	5
1208	20 c. Mace and Black Rod		20	20
1209	30 c. Wall hanging from the "Beehive"		30	45
	Set of 3		60	60
	First Day Cover			90

381 1855 1d. Stamp

(Des D. Hatcher (14 c. (all designs)), R. Conly (others). Litho Harrison)

1980 (17 Feb).   *Anniversaries and Events. T* **381** *and similar designs. P* 13½ × 13 (14 c. (*all designs*)) *or* 14 (*others*).

1210	14 c. black, brown-red and yellow		20	20
	a. Horiz strip of 3. Nos. 1210/12		60	
	ab. Black (inscription) omitted (*strip of* 3)		90·00	
1211	14 c. black, deep turquoise-blue and yellow		20	20
1212	14 c. black, dull yellowish green and yellow		20	20
	Ea. Dull yellowish green (1s. stamp) printed triple		†	
1213	17 c. multicoloured		20	25
1214	25 c. multicoloured		25	30
1215	30 c. multicoloured		25	35
	Set of 6		1·10	1·40
	First Day Cover			1·60
MS1216	146 × 96 mm. Nos. 1210/12. P 14½ × 14 (*sold at* 52 c.)		2·75	4·50
	First Day Cover			6·00

Designs and commemorations: (38 × 22 *mm*)—No. 1210, Type **381**; No. 1211, 1855 2d. stamp; No. 1212, 1855 1s. stamp (125th anniversary of New Zealand stamps). (40 × 23 *mm*)—No. 1213, Geyser, wood-carving and building (centenary of Rotorua (town)); No. 1214, *Earina autumnalis* and *thelymitra venosa* (International Orchid Conference, Auckland); No. 1215, Ploughing and Golden Plough Trophy (World Ploughing Championships, Christchurch).

The premium on No. **MS**1216 was used to help finance the "Zeapex 80" International Stamp Exhibition, Auckland.

Nos. 1210/12 were printed together, *se-tenant*, in horizontal strips of 3 throughout the sheet.

382 Ewelme Cottage, Parnell   383 Auckland Harbour

(Des P. Leitch. Litho Enschedé)

1980 (2 Apr).   *Architecture (2nd series). T* **382** *and similar horiz designs. Multicoloured. P* 13½ × 12½.

1217	14 c. Type **382**		15	10
1218	17 c. Broadgreen, Nelson		25	30
1219	25 c. Courthouse, Oamaru		30	40
1220	30 c. Government Buildings, Wellington		35	45
	Set of 4		95	1·10
	First Day Cover			1·25

(Des D. Hatcher. Photo Heraclio Fournier)

1980 (4 June).   *Large Harbours. T* **383** *and similar horiz designs. Multicoloured. P* 13.

1221	30 c. Type **383**		30	25
1222	30 c. Wellington Harbour		35	30
1223	35 c. Lyttelton Harbour		40	40
1224	50 c. Port Chalmers		65	65
	Set of 4		1·50	1·40
	First Day Cover			1·75

384 Surf-fishing   **385** "Madonna and
Child with Cherubim"
(sculpture by Andrea
della Robbia)

(Des Margaret Chapman. Litho Enschedé)

1980 (6 Aug). *Health Stamps. Fishing. T* **384** *and similar horiz designs. Multicoloured. P* 13 × 12½.

1225	14 c. + 2 c. Type **384**		25	30
	a. Horiz pair. Nos. 1225/6		50	60
1226	14 c. + 2 c. Wharf-fishing		25	30
1227	17 c. + 2 c. Spear-fishing		25	30
	Set of 3		70	80
	First Day Cover			1·10
MS1228	148 × 75 mm. Nos. 1225/7 each × 2.			
	P 13½ × 13		2·25	3·00
	First Day Cover			3·50

Nos. 1225/6 were printed together, *se-tenant*, in horizontal pairs throughout the sheet.

(Des P. Durrant. Photo Courvoisier)

1980 (1 Oct). *Christmas. T* **385** *and similar vert designs. Multicoloured. P* 11½.

1229	10 c. Type **385**		15	5
1230	25 c. St. Mary's Church, New Plymouth		25	25
1231	35 c. Picnic scene		40	45
	Set of 3		70	70
	First Day Cover			90

Souvenir Pack 1980

1980 (1 Oct). *Comprises Nos.* 1207/15, 1217/27 *and* 1229/31. *Sold at* $6.25.

SP1231a	Souvenir Pack	6·00

386 Te Heu Heu   **387** Lt.-Col. the Hon W. H. A.
(chief)   Feilding and Borough of
Feilding Crest

(Des R. Conly. Litho Heraclio Fournier)

1980 (26 Nov). *Maori Personalities. Vert designs as T* **386**. *Multicoloured. P* 12½ × 13.

1232	15 c. Type **386**		10	5
1233	25 c. Te Hau (chief)		15	5
1234	35 c. Te Puea (princess)		20	10
1235	45 c. Ngata (politician)		30	15
1236	60 c. Te Ata-O-Tu (warrior)		35	20
	Set of 5		1·00	50
	First Day Cover			1·40

(Des R. Conly. Litho Harrison)

1981 (4 Feb). *Commemorations. T* **387** *and similar horiz design. P* 14½.

1237	20 c. multicoloured	20	20
1238	25 c. black and brown-ochre	25	25
	Set of 2	45	45
	First Day Cover		60

Designs and Commemorations:—20 c. type **387** (Centenary of Feilding (town)); 25 c. I.Y.D. emblem and cupped hands (International Year of the Disabled).

388 The Family at Play   **389** Kaiauai River

(Des A. Derrick. Litho J.W.)

1981 (1 Apr). *"Family Life." T* **388** *and similar vert designs. Multicoloured. P* 13½ × 13.

1239	20 c. Type **388**		20	10
1240	25 c. The family, young and old		25	25
1241	30 c. The family at home		30	30
1242	35 c. The family at church		35	40
	Set of 4		1·00	95
	First Day Cover			1·25

(Des D. Hatcher. Photo Heraclio Fournier)

1981 (3 June). *River Scenes. T* **389** *and similar multicoloured designs. P* 13½ × 13 (30, 35 c.) *or* 13 × 13½ (*others*).

1243	30 c. Type **389**		30	30
1244	35 c. Mangahao		40	40
1245	40 c. Shotover (*horiz*)		45	45
1246	60 c. Cleddau (*horiz*)		75	75
	Set of 4		1·75	1·75
	First Day Cover			2·25

390 St. Paul's Cathedral   **391** Girl with Starfish

(Des and litho Harrison)

1981 (29 July). *Royal Wedding. T* **390** *and similar horiz design. Multicoloured. P* 14½.

1247	20 c. Type **390**		20	30
	a. Pair. Nos. 1247/8		40	60
	ab. Deep grey (inscriptions and date) omitted		£800	
	Eac. Deep grey printed double		£425	
1248	20 c. Prince Charles and Lady Diana Spencer		20	30
	Set of 2		40	60
	First Day Cover			80

* No. 1247Eac shows a double impression of the deep grey resulting from problems with the litho blanket.

Nos. 1247/8 were printed together, *se-tenant*, in horizontal and vertical pairs throughout the sheet.

(Des P.O. Litho Harrison)

1981 (5 Aug). *Health Stamps. Children playing by the Sea. T* **391** *and similar vert designs. Multicoloured. P* 14½.

1249	20 c. + 2 c. Type **391**		25	35
	a. Horiz pair. Nos. 1249/50		50	70
1250	20 c. + 2 c. Boy fishing		25	35
1251	25 c. + 2 c. Children exploring rock pool		25	30
	Set of 3		70	90
	First Day Cover			1·25
MS1252	100 × 125 mm. Nos. 1249/51, each × 2		2·00	2·50
	First Day Cover			3·25

The 20 c. values were printed together, *se-tenant*, in horizontal pairs throughout the sheet, forming a composite design.

The stamps from No. **MS**1252 were printed together, *se-tenant*, in two horizontal strips of 3, each forming a composite design.

392 "Madonna Suckling the Child" (painting, d'Oggiono)

393 Tauranga Mission House

396 Kaiteriteri Beach, Nelson (Summer)

397 Labrador

(Des Margaret Chapman. Photo Courvoisier)

1981 (7 Oct). *Christmas. T* **392** *and similar vert designs. Multicoloured. P* 11½.

1253	14 c.	Type **392**	15	5
1254	30 c.	St. John's Church, Wakefield	35	35
1255	40 c.	Golden Tainui (flower)	45	45
		Set of 3	85	75
		First Day Cover		1·10

Souvenir Pack 1981

1981 (7 Oct). *Comprises Nos.* 1237/55. *Sold at* $8.25.
SP1255a Souvenir Pack .... 5·00

(Des A. Derrick. Litho Walsall)

1982 (3 Feb). *Commemorations. T* **393** *and similar vert designs. Multicoloured. P* 14½.

1256	20 c.	Type **393**	25	5
	a.	Horiz pair. Nos. 1256/7	50	60
1257	20 c.	Water tower, Hawera	25	5
1258	25 c.	Cat	25	35
1259	30 c.	Dunedin (refrigerated sailing ship)	35	40
1260	35 c.	Scientific research equipment	40	45
		Set of 5	1·40	1·60
		First Day Cover		2·00

Commemorations:—No. 1256, Centenary of Tauranga (town); No. 1257, Centenary of Hawera (town); No. 1258, Centenary of S.P.C.A. (Society for the Prevention of Cruelty to Animals in New Zealand); No. 1259, Centenary of Frozen Meat Exports; No. 1260, International Year of Science. The 20 c. values were printed together, *se-tenant*, in horizontal pairs throughout the sheet.

394 Map of New Zealand

395 Alberton, Auckland

(Des A. G. Mitchell. Litho Leigh-Mardon Ltd, Melbourne)

1982 (1 Apr–13 Dec). *P* 12½.

1261	**394**	24 c. pale yellowish green and ultramarine	20	10
	a.	Perf 14½ × 14 (13.12.82)	20	5
		First Day Cover		60

(Des P. Leitch. Litho Walsall)

1982 (7 Apr). *Architecture* (3rd series). *T* **395** *and similar horiz designs. Multicoloured. P* 14 × 14½.

1262	20 c.	Type **395**	20	15
1263	25 c.	Caccia Birch, Palmerston North	25	25
1264	30 c.	Railway station, Dunedin	30	30
1265	35 c.	Post Office, Ophir	35	40
		Set of 4	1·00	1·00
		First Day Cover		1·40

(Des D. Hatcher. Photo Heraclio Fournier)

1982 (2 June). *"The Four Seasons". New Zealand Scenes. T* **396** *and similar horiz designs. Multicoloured. P* 13 × 13½.

1266	35 c.	Type **396**	40	40
1267	40 c.	St. Omer Park, Queenstown (Autumn)	45	45
1268	45 c.	Mt. Ngauruhoe, Tongariro National Park (Winter)	50	50
1269	70 c.	Wairarapa farm (Spring)	75	75
		Set of 4	1·90	1·90
		Presentation Pack (1 Sept)	2·50	
		First Day Cover		2·40
		Souvenir Postcards (4)	1·50	

(Des R. Conly. Litho Enschedé)

1982 (4 Aug). *Health Stamps. Dogs. T* **397** *and similar vert designs. Multicoloured. P* 13 × 13½.

1270	24 c. + 2 c. Type **397**		35	40
	a. Horiz pair. Nos. 1270/1		70	80
1271	24 c. + 2 c. Border Collie		35	40
1272	30 c. + 2 c. Cocker Spaniel		45	45
	Set of 3		1·10	1·25
	First Day Cover			1·60
MS1273	98 × 125 mm. Nos. 1270/2, each × 2. P 14 × 13½		2·25	2·50
	First Day Cover			3·25

The 24 c. values were printed together, *se-tenant*, in horizontal pairs throughout the sheet.

398 "Madonna with Child and Two Angels" (painting by Piero di Cosimo)

(Des Margaret Chapman. Photo Heraclio Fournier)

1982 (6 Oct). *Christmas. T* **398** *and similar vert designs. Multicoloured. P* 14 × 13½.

1274	18 c.	Type **398**	20	5
1275	35 c.	Rangiatea Maori Church, Otaki	35	30
1276	45 c.	Surf life-saving	50	40
		Set of 3	95	65
		First Day Cover		1·25

Souvenir Pack 1982

1982 (6 Oct). *Comprises Nos.* 1256/60, 1262/76. *Sold at* $8.95.
SP1276a Souvenir Pack .... 8·50

THE WORLD CENTRE FOR FINE STAMPS IS 399 STRAND

CHANGES IN STAMP PAPER. Following the closure of the paper mill producing the Australian security paper used for Nos. 1277/95, some new printings from August 1986 onwards were on Clark paper manufactured in

Great Britain. This is a creamy paper often with matt cream gum and, usually, shows a white reaction under U.V. light. Clark paper has, so far, been used on the following printings of stamps initially produced on the Australian paper:

1c. printing of August 1987 with five kiwis in sheet margin
2c. printing of August 1987 (four kiwis)
3c. printing of August 1987 (four kiwis)
5c. printing of 1 May 1987 (three kiwis) (non-fluorescent)
     printing of 4.3.88 (four kiwis)
     printing of 12.5.88 (five kiwis)
     printing of 21.2.89 (six kiwis)
10c. printing of 4 March 1987 (two kiwis)
20c. printing of November 1987 (one kiwi)
30c. (No. 1288) part printing of January 1987 (two kiwis)
40c. (No. 1286) part printing of 15 August 1986 (two kiwis)
40c. (No. 1289) part original printing and part printing of 26 May 1987 (one kiwi)
     printing of August 1987 (two kiwis)
     printing of April 1988 (three kiwis)
     printing of 23 September 1988 (four kiwis)
50c. printing of January 1988 (two kiwis)
$1 printing of 25 June 1987 (one kiwi) (non-fluorescent or fluorescent)
     printing of 8 June 1989 (two kiwis)
$3 printing of 1 May 1987 (one kiwi)
$4 printing of August 1987 (one kiwi)

399 Nephrite   **399a** Grapes   **399b** Kokako

(Des P. Durrant (Nos. 1277/82), D. Little (Nos. 1283/7), Janet Marshall (Nos. 1288/97). Litho Leigh-Mardon Ltd, Melbourne)

1982 (1 Dec)–**89**. *Multicoloured*. P 14½ × 14 (*Nos. 1277/87*) or 14½ (*Nos. 1288/97*). (*a*) *Minerals*. T **399** and similar vert designs.

1277	1 c. Type **399**		5	5
	a. Perf 12½		25	10
1278	2 c. Agate		5	5
	a. Perf 12½		75	75
1279	3 c. Iron Pyrites		5	5
1280	4 c. Amethyst		5	5
1281	5 c. Carnelian		5	5
1282	9 c. Native Sulphur		5	5

        (*b*) *Fruits*. T **399a** and similar vert designs

1283	10 c. Type **399a** (7.12.83)	5	5
1284	20 c. Citrus Fruit (7.12.83)	12	5
1285	30 c. Nectarines (7.12.83)	20	5
1286	40 c. Apples (7.12.83)	25	10
1287	50 c. Kiwifruit (7.12.83)	30	10

        (*c*) *Native Birds*. T **399b** and similar vert designs

1288	10 c. Kakapo (1.5.86)	20	15
	Ea. Brown (background) double		
1289	40 c. Mountain ("Blue") Duck (2.2.87)	25	15
1290	45 c. New Zealand Falcon (1.5.86)	30	20
1291	60 c. New Zealand Teal (2.2.87)	35	25
1292	$1 Type **399b** (24.4.85)	65	20
1293	$2 Chatham Island Robin (24.4.85)	1·40	50
1294	$3 Stitchbird (23.4.86)	2·00	1·40
1295	$4 Saddleback (23.4.86)	2·75	2·00
1296	$5 Takahe (20.4.88)	3·25	2·50
1297	$10 Little Spotted Kiwi (19.4.89)	6·00	5·00
	Set of 21	16·00	11·50
	Presentation Pack (contains Nos. 1261 and 1277/87) (7.12.83)	2·25	
	Presentation Pack (contains Nos. 1292/3) (7.8.85)	3·25	
	Presentation Pack (contains Nos. 1294/5) (25.6.86)	6·00	
	Presentation Pack (contains Nos. 1292/7 optd "SPECIMEN" in red) (sold in support of the 1990 Auckland International Stamp Exhibition at $12.50) (19.4.89)	7·50	
	First Day Covers (8)		25·00

400 Old Arts Building,   **401** Queen Elizabeth II
Auckland University

(Des G. Emery (35 c.), P. Durrant (others). Litho Cambec Press, Melbourne (35 c.), J.W. (others))

1983 (2 Feb). *Commemorations.* T **400** and similar vert designs. Multicoloured. P 13 × 13½ (35 c.) or 14 × 13½ (others).

1303	24 c. Salvation Army Centenary logo	25	10
1304	30 c. Type **400**	30	35
1305	35 c. Stylised Kangaroo and Kiwi	35	35
1306	40 c. Rainbow Trout	40	45
1307	45 c. Satellite over Earth	45	50
	Set of 5	1·50	1·50
	First Day Cover		2·00

Commemorations:—24 c. Centenary of Salvation Army; 30 c. Centenary of Auckland University; 35 c. Closer Economic Relationship agreement with Australia; 40 c. Centenary of introduction of Rainbow Trout into New Zealand; 45 c. World Communications Year.

(Des P. Durrant. Litho Harrison)

1983 (14 Mar). *Commonwealth Day.* T **401** and similar horiz designs. Multicoloured. P 13½.

1308	24 c. Type **401**	20	10
1309	35 c. Maori rock drawing	30	40
1310	40 c. Woolmark and wool-scouring symbols	35	45
1311	45 c. Coat of arms	40	55
	Set of 4	1·10	1·40
	Presentation Pack	1·90	
	First Day Cover		1·60

402 "Boats, Island Bay"   **403** Mt Egmont
(Rita Angus)

(Des D. Hatcher. Litho Leigh-Mardon Ltd, Melbourne)

1983 (6 Apr). *Paintings by Rita Angus.* T **402** and similar vert designs. Multicoloured. P 14½.

1312	24 c. Type **402**	25	10
1313	30 c. "Central Otago Landscape"	30	45
1314	35 c. "Wanaka Landscape"	35	50
1315	45 c. "Tree"	45	70
	Set of 4	1·25	1·60
	Presentation Pack	2·00	
	First Day Cover		2·00

(Des P. Durrant. Photo Heraclio Fournier)

1983 (1 June). *Beautiful New Zealand* and similar multicoloured designs. P 13.

1316	35 c. Type **403**	30	35
1317	40 c. Cooks Bay	35	40
1318	45 c. Lake Matheson (*horiz*)	40	45
1319	70 c. Lake Alexandrina (*horiz*)	65	70
	Set of 4	1·50	1·75
	Presentation Pack (27 June)	2·25	
	First Day Cover		2·25
	Souvenir Postcards (4)	1·50	

HEALTH   POSTAGE
2ᶜ   24ᶜ

Tabby

New Zealand 1983

404 Tabby

18c NEW ZEALAND
Christmas 1983

405 "The Family of the
Holy Oak Tree" (Raphael)

(Des R. Conly. Litho Harrison)

1983 (3 Aug). *Health Stamps. Cats. T* **404** *and similar vert designs.
Multicoloured. P* 14.

1320	24 c. + 2 c. Type **404**		25	25
	a. Horiz pair. Nos. 1320/1		50	50
1321	24 c. + 2 c. Siamese		25	25
1322	30 c. + 2 c. Persian		40	30
	Set of 3		90	80
	First Day Cover			1·40
MS1323	100 × 126 mm. Nos. 1320/2, each × 2		1·50	1·75
	First Day Cover			2·25

The 24 c. values were printed together, *se-tenant*, in horizontal pairs
throughout the sheet.

(Des R. Conly (45 c.), M. Wyatt (others). Photo Courvoisier)

1983 (5 Oct). *Christmas. T* **405** *and similar vert designs. Multicoloured.
P* 12 × 11½.

1324	18 c. Type **405**		12	5
1325	35 c. St. Patrick's Church, Greymouth		30	35
1326	45 c. "The Glory of Christmas" (star and flowers)		40	45
	Set of 3		75	75
	First Day Cover			1·40

Souvenir Pack 1983

1983 (5 Oct). *Comprises Nos. 1303/26. Sold at* $10.95.

SP1326a	Souvenir Pack		9·50

Antarctic
Research

NEW ZEALAND   24c

406 Geology

(Des R. Conly. Litho Cambec Press, Melbourne)

1984 (1 Feb). *Antarctic Research. T* **406** *and similar horiz designs.
Multicoloured. P* 13½ × 13.

1327	24 c. Type **406**		25	10
1328	40 c. Biology		35	40
1329	58 c. Glaciology		50	55
1330	70 c. Meteorology		60	70
	Set of 4		1·60	1·60
	Presentation Pack (15 Feb)		2·50	
	First Day Cover			2·25
MS1331	126 × 110 mm. Nos. 1327/30		1·75	2·25
	First Day Cover			2·75

NEW ZEALAND 24c

407 *Mountaineer*, Lake Wakatipu

408 Mount Hutt

(Des M. Wyatt. Litho Cambec Press, Melbourne)

1984 (4 Apr). *New Zealand Ferry Boats. T* **407** *and similar horiz designs.
Multicoloured. P* 13½ × 13.

1332	24 c. Type **407**		30	10
1333	40 c. *Waikana*, Otago		40	40
1334	58 c. *Britannia*, Waitemata		55	55
1335	70 c. *Wakatere*, Firth of Thames		65	65
	Set of 4		1·75	1·60
	Presentation Pack (18 Apr)		2·25	
	First Day Cover			2·25
	Souvenir Postcards (4)		1·50	

(Des D. Little. Litho Cambec Press, Melbourne)

1984 (6 June). *Ski-slope Scenery. T* **408** *and similar horiz designs.
Multicoloured. P* 13½ × 13.

1336	35 c. Type **408**		40	40
1337	40 c. Coronet Park		45	45
1338	45 c. Turoa		50	50
1339	70 c. Whakapapa		75	75
	Set of 4		1·90	1·90
	Presentation Pack (20 June)		2·00	
	First Day Cover			2·50

Hamilton's Frog

New Zealand 24c

409 Hamilton's Frog

(Des. A. G. Mitchell. Litho Cambec Press, Melbourne)

1984 (11 July). *Amphibians and Reptiles. T* **409** *and similar horiz designs.
Multicoloured. P* 13½.

1340	24 c. Type **409**		30	30
	a. Horiz pair. Nos. 1340/1		60	60
1341	24 c. Great Barrier Skink		30	30
1342	30 c. Harlequin Gecko		35	35
1343	58 c. Otago Skink		70	70
1344	70 c. Gold-striped Gecko		75	75
	Set of 5		2·25	2·25
	First Day Cover			3·00

Nos. 1340/1 were printed together, *se-tenant*, in horizontal pairs
throughout the sheet.

24

New Zealand

410 Clydesdales ploughing Field

(Des Margaret Chapman. Litho Harrison)

1984 (1 Aug). *Health Stamps. Horses. T* **410** *and similar horiz designs.
Multicoloured. P* 14½.

1345	24 c. + 2 c. Type **410**		30	30
	a. Horiz pair. Nos. 1345/6		60	60
1346	24 c. + 2 c. Shetland ponies		30	30
1347	30 c. + 2 c. Thoroughbreds		45	35
	Set of 3		1·00	85
	First Day Cover			1·50
MS1348	148 × 75 mm. Nos. 1345/7, each × 2		1·40	1·75
	First Day Cover			2·25

Nos. 1345/6 were printed together, *se-tenant*, in horizontal pairs
throughout the sheet.

MACHINE LABELS. An automatic machine dispensing labels, ranging in
value from 1 c. to $99.99, was installed at the Queen Street Post Office,
Auckland, on 3 September 1984 for a trial period. The oblong designs,
framed by simulated perforations at top and bottom and vertical rules at
the sides, showed the "Southern Cross", face value and vertical column of
six horizontal lines between the "NEW ZEALAND" and "POSTAGE"
inscriptions. The trial period ended abruptly on 16 October 1984.

Similar labels, with the face value and inscriptions within a plain
oblong, were introduced on 12 February 1986 and from 22 August 1988
they were printed on paper showing New Zealand flags.

411 "Adoration of the Shepherds"
(Lorenzo di Credi)

(Des R. Conly (45 c.), P. Durrant (others). Photo Heraclio Fournier)

1984 (26 Sept). *Christmas. T* **411** *and similar multicoloured designs.
P* 13½ × 14 (18 c.) or 14 × 13½ (others).

1349	18 c. Type **411**	20	10
1350	35 c. Old St. Paul's, Wellington (*vert*)	40	35
1351	45 c. "The Joy of Christmas" (*vert*)	50	45
	Set of 3	1·00	80
	First Day Cover		1·40

Souvenir Pack 1984

1984 (26 Sept). *Comprises Nos. 1327/30, 1332/47 and 1349/51. Sold at* $10.95.

SP1351a	Souvenir Pack	8·75

412 Mounted Riflemen, South
Africa, 1901

(Des R. Conly. Litho Harrison)

1984 (7 Nov). *New Zealand Military History. T* **412** *and similar horiz designs. Multicoloured. P* 15 × 14.

1352	24 c. Type **412**	30	10
1353	40 c. Engineers. France, 1917	45	45
1354	58 c. Tanks of 2nd N.Z. Divisional Cavalry, North Africa, 1942	60	60
1355	70 c. Infantryman in jungle kit, and 25-pounder gun, Korea and South-East Asia, 1950–72	70	75
	Set of 4	1·90	1·75
	Presentation Pack (12 Dec)	2·40	
	First Day Cover		2·50
MS1356	122 × 106 mm. Nos. 1352/5	1·60	1·90
	First Day Cover		3·00

Post Office Yearbook 1984

1984 (7 Nov). *Comprises Nos. 1327/56 in hardbound book with slip case.*

YB1356a	Yearbook	50·00

413 St. John Ambulance Badge

(Des Lindy Fisher. Litho J.W.)

1985 (16 Jan). *Centenary of St. John Ambulance in New Zealand. P* 14.

1357	**413**	24 c. black, gold and bright rosine	25	10
1358		30 c. black, silver and bright ultramarine	35	30
1359		40 c. black and grey	40	45
		Set of 3	90	75
		First Day Cover		1·50

The colours of the badge depicted are those for Bailiffs and Dames Grand Cross (24 c.), Knights and Dames of Grace (30 c.) and Serving Brothers and Sisters (40 c.).

414 Nelson Horse-drawn Tram.　　　**415** Shotover Bridge
1862

(Des R. Conly. Litho Cambec Press, Melbourne)

1985 (6 Mar). *Vintage Trams. T* **414** *and similar horiz designs. Multicoloured. P* 13½.

1360	24 c. Type **414**	25	10
1361	30 c. Graham's Town steam tram, 1871	35	35
1362	35 c. Dunedin cable car, 1881	35	45
1363	40 c. Auckland electric tram, 1902	35	45
1364	45 c. Wellington electric tram, 1904	40	55
1365	58 c. Christchurch electric tram, 1905	50	75
	Set of 6	2·00	2·40
	Presentation Pack (20 Mar)	2·75	
	First Day Cover		3·00

TARAPEX '86. To support this National Philatelic Exhibition the New Zealand Post Office co-operated with the organisers in the production of a set of "postage imprint labels". Five of the designs showed drawings of Maoris, taken from originals by Arthur Herbert Messenger, and the sixth the Exhibition logo.

The sheetlets of 6 gummed and perforated labels were released by the Exhibition organisers on 3 April 1985. Although such labels were valid for postage, and could be so used by the general public, the sheetlets were not available from any New Zealand post office counter or from the Philatelic Bureau.

(Des R. Freeman. Photo Courvoisier)

1985 (12 June). *Bridges of New Zealand. T* **415** *and similar multicoloured designs. Granite paper. P* 11½.

1366	35 c. Type **415**	40	35
1367	40 c. Alexandra Bridge	45	40
1368	45 c. South Rangitikei Railway Bridge (*vert*)	50	50
1369	70 c. Twin Bridges (*vert*)	70	70
	Set of 4	1·90	1·75
	Presentation Pack (20 Nov)	2·75	
	First Day Cover		2·50

416 Queen　　　　**417** Princess of Wales
Elizabeth II (from　　and Prince William
photo by Camera
Press)

(Des B. Clinton. Litho Leigh-Mardon Ltd, Melbourne)

1985 (1 July). *Multicoloured, background colours given. P* 14½ × 14.

1370	**416**	25 c. rosine	40	5
1371		35 c. new blue	90	10
		Set of 2	1·10	15
		First Day Cover		1·50

Examples of the 25 c. value exist with the orders on the sash omitted. These are believed to originate from unissued sheets sent for destruction in March 1986.

(Des D. Little. Litho Cambec Press, Melbourne)

1985 (31 July).   *Health Stamps. T 417 and similar vert designs showing photographs by Lord Snowdon. Multicoloured. P 13½.*

1372	25 c. +2 c. Type **417**	35	35
	a. Horiz pair. Nos. 1372/3	70	70
1373	25 c. +2 c. Princess of Wales and Prince Henry ..	35	35
1374	35 c. +2 c. Prince and Princess of Wales with Princes William and Henry	35	35
	Set of 3	95	95
	First Day Cover		1·40
MS1375	118 × 84 mm. Nos. 1372/4, each × 2.	1·40	1·75
	First Day Cover		2·00

Nos. 1372/3 were printed together, *se-tenant,* in horizontal pairs throughout the sheet.

418 The Holy Family in the Stable

419 H.M.N.Z.S. *Philomel* (1914–47)

(Des Eileen Mayo. Photo Enschedé)

1985 (18 Sept).   *Christmas. T 418 and similar vert designs. Multicoloured. P 13½ × 12½.*

1376	18 c. Type **418**	20	5
1377	40 c. The shepherds	40	45
1378	50 c. The angels	45	50
	Set of 3	95	90
	First Day Cover		1·50

Examples of the 18 c. and 50 c. stamps exist showing the spelling error "CRISTMAS". These are believed to originate from unissued sheets sent for destruction in March 1986. The New Zealand Post Office has stated that no such stamps were issued and that existing examples were removed unlawfully during the destruction process.

Souvenir Pack 1985

1985 (18 Sept).   *Comprises Nos. 1352/5, 1357/69, 1372/4 and 1376/8. Sold at $11.*

SP1378a	Souvenir Pack	8·00

(Des P. Durrant. Litho Cambec Press, Melbourne)

1985 (6 Nov).   *New Zealand Naval History. T 419 and similar horiz designs. Multicoloured. P 13½.*

1379	25 c. Type **419**	35	10
1380	45 c. H.M.N.Z.S. Achilles (1936–46)	55	60
1381	60 c. H.M.N.Z.S. Rotoiti (1949–65)	75	80
1382	75 c. H.M.N.Z.S. Canterbury (from 1971)	85	90
	Set of 4	2·25	2·25
	First Day Cover		2·75
MS1383	124 × 108 mm. Nos. 1379/82	2·25	2·50
	First Day Cover		3·25

Post Office Yearbook 1985

1985 (6 Nov).   *Comprises Nos. 1292/3 and 1357/83 in hardbound book with slip case.*

YB1383a	Yearbook	32·00

GIBBONS STAMP MONTHLY

—finest and most informative magazine for all collectors. Obtainable from your newsagent or by postal subscription—details on request.

420 Police Computer Operator

421 Indian "Power Plus" 1000cc Motor Cycle (1920)

(Des A. G. Mitchell. Litho Leigh-Mardon Ltd, Melbourne)

1986 (15 Jan).   *Centenary of New Zealand Police. T 420 and similar vert designs, each showing historical aspects over modern police activities. Multicoloured. P 14½ × 14.*

1384	25 c. Type **420**	25	30
	a. Horiz strip of 5. Nos. 1384/8	1·10	
1385	25 c. Detective and mobile control room	25	30
1386	25 c. Policewoman and badge	25	30
1387	25 c. Forensic scientist, patrol car and policeman with child	25	30
1388	25 c. Police College, Porirua, patrol boat and dog handler	25	30
	Set of 5	1·10	1·40
	First Day Cover		1·75

Nos. 1384/8 were printed together, *se-tenant,* in horizontal strips of 5 throughout the sheet.

(Des M. Wyatt. Litho J.W.)

1986 (5 Mar).   *Vintage Motor Cycles. T 421 and similar horiz designs. Multicoloured. P 13 × 12½.*

1389	35 c. Type **421**	40	30
1390	45 c. Norton "CS1" 500cc (1927)	50	35
1391	60 c. B.S.A. "Sloper" 500cc (1930).	65	50
1392	75 c. Triumph "Model H" 550cc (1915)	75	70
	Set of 4	2·10	1·75
	First Day Cover		2·25

422 Tree of Life

423 Knights Point

(Des Margaret Clarkson. Litho J.W.)

1986 (5 Mar).   *International Peace Year. T 422 and similar horiz design. Multicoloured. P 13 × 12½.*

1393	25 c. Type **422**	30	30
	a. Horiz pair. Nos. 1393/4	60	60
1394	25 c. Peace dove	30	30
	Set of 2	60	60
	First Day Cover		85

Nos. 1393/4 were printed together, *se-tenant,* in horizontal pairs throughout the sheet.

(Des P. Durrant. Photo Heraclio Fournier)

1986 (11 June).   *Coastal Scenery. T 423 and similar horiz designs. Multicoloured. P 14.*

1395	55 c. Type **423**	85	45
1396	60 c. Becks Bay	85	45
1397	65 c. Doubtless Bay	90	50
1398	80 c. Wainui Bay	75	65
	Set of 4	2·25	1·90
	Presentation Pack (22 Oct)	3·50	
	First Day Cover		2·40
MS1399	124 × 99 mm. No. 1398 (sold at $1.20)	85	90

The 40 c. premium on No. **MS1399** was to support the Auckland International Stamp Exhibition to be held in 1990.

No. **MS1399** exists overprinted for "Stockholmia". Such miniature sheets were only available at this International Exhibition in Stockholm and were not placed on sale in New Zealand.

424 "Football"
(Kylie Epapara)

425 "A Partridge in
a Pear Tree"

(Litho Leigh-Mardon Ltd, Melbourne)

1986 (30 July). *Health Stamps. Children's Paintings* (1st series). *T* **424**
and similar multicoloured designs. P 14½ × 14 (30 c.) *or* 14 × 14½ (45 c.).

1400	30 c. + 3 c. Type **424**		30	30
	a. Horiz pair. Nos. 1400/1		60	60
1401	30 c. + 3 c. "Children at Play" (Phillip Kata)		30	30
1402	45 c. + 3 c. "Children Skipping" (Mia Flannery)			
	(horiz)		40	40
	Set of 3		90	90
	First Day Cover			1·40
MS1403	144 × 81 mm. Nos. 1400/2, each × 2		2·00	2·25
	First Day Cover			2·75

Nos. 1400/1 were printed together, *se-tenant*, in horizontal pairs
throughout the sheet.

No. **MS**1403 exists overprinted for "Stockholmia". Such miniature
sheets were only available at this International Stamp Exhibition in
Stockholm and were not placed on sale in New Zealand.

See also Nos. 1433/6.

(Des Margaret Halcrow-Cross. Photo Heraclio Fournier)

1986 (17 Sept). *Christmas. "The Twelve Days of Christmas"* (carol).
T **425** *and similar vert designs. Multicoloured. P* 14½.

1404	25 c. Type **425**		20	10
1405	55 c. "Two turtle doves"		45	45
1406	65 c. "Three French hens"		50	50
	Set of 3		1·00	95
	First Day Cover			1·60

Souvenir Pack 1986

1986 (17 Sept). *Comprises Nos. 1379/82, 1384/98, 1400/2 and 1404/6.
Sold at* $13.90.
SP1406a Souvenir Pack . . . . 9·75

426 Conductor and Orchestra

427 Jetboating

(Des R. Freeman. Litho Leigh-Mardon Ltd, Melbourne)

1986 (5 Nov). *Music in New Zealand. T* **426** *and similar vert designs.
P* 14½ × 14.

1407	30 c. multicoloured		25	10
1408	60 c. black, new blue and yellow-orange		45	50
1409	80 c. multicoloured		70	75
1410	$1 multicoloured		80	85
	Set of 4		2·00	2·00
	First Day Cover			2·75

Designs:—60 c. Cornet and brass band; 80 c. Piper and Highland pipe
band; $1 Guitar and country music group.

Post Office Yearbook 1986

1986 (5 Nov). *Comprises Nos. 1294/5 and 1384/410 in hardbound book
with slip case.*
YB1410a Yearbook . . . . 28·00

(Des M. Wyatt. Litho Leigh-Mardon Ltd, Melbourne)

1987 (14 Jan). *Tourism. T* **427** *and similar vert designs. Multicoloured.
P* 14½ × 14.

1411	60 c. Type **427**		50	45
1412	70 c. Sightseeing flights		60	55
1413	80 c. Camping		70	65
1414	85 c. Windsurfing		70	65
1415	$1.05, Mountaineering		90	80
1416	$1.30, River rafting		1·10	95
	Set of 6		4·00	3·75
	First Day Cover			4·25

428 Southern Cross Cup

429 Hand writing Letter
and Postal Transport

(Des R. Proud. Litho Leigh-Mardon Ltd, Melbourne)

1987 (2 Feb). *Yachting Events. T* **428** *and similar horiz designs showing
yachts. Multicoloured. P* 14 × 14½.

1417	40 c. Type **428**		35	15
1418	80 c. Admiral's Cup		70	70
1419	$1.05, Kenwood Cup		85	1·00
1420	$1.30, America's Cup		1·10	1·10
	Set of 4		2·75	2·75
	First Day Cover			3·50

(Des Communication Arts Ltd. Litho C.P.E. Australia Ltd, Melbourne)

1987 (1 Apr). *New Zealand Post Ltd Vesting Day. T* **429** *and similar horiz
design. Multicoloured. P* 13½.

1421	40 c. Type **429**		40	40
	a. Horiz pair. Nos. 1421/2		80	80
1422	40 c. Posting letter, train and mailbox		40	40
	Set of 2		80	80
	First Day Cover			1·10

Nos. 1421/2 were printed together, *se-tenant*, in horizontal pairs
throughout the sheet.

430 Avro "626" and Wigram
Airfield, 1937

431 Urewera National
Park and Fern Leaf

(Des P. Leitch. Litho Leigh-Mardon Ltd, Melbourne)

1987 (15 Apr). *50th Anniv of Royal New Zealand Air Force. T* **430** *and
similar horiz designs. Multicoloured. P* 14 × 14½.

1423	40 c. Type **430**		35	15
1424	70 c. "P-40 Kittyhawk" over World War II Pacific
airstrip		55	60
1425	80 c. Short "Sunderland" flying boat and Pacific
lagoon		60	70
1426	85 c. A-4 "Skyhawk" and Mt. Ruapehu		65	75
	Set of 4		2·00	2·00
	First Day Cover			2·50
MS1427	115 × 105 mm. Nos. 1423/6		2·25	2·50
	First Day Cover			3·00

No. **MS**1427 overprinted on the selvedge with the "CAPEX" logo was
available from the New Zealand stand at this International Philatelic
Exhibition in Toronto.

(Des Tracey Purkis. Litho Leigh-Mardon Ltd, Melbourne)

1987 (17 June). *Centenary of National Parks Movement. T* **431** *and similar vert designs. Multicoloured.* P 14½.

1428	70 c. Type **431**		80	55
1429	80 c. Mt. Cook and buttercup		85	60
1430	85 c. Fiordland and pineapple shrub		70	65
1431	$1.30, Tongariro and tussock		1·00	95
	Set of 4		2·75	2·50
	First Day Cover			3·00
MS1432	123 × 99 mm. No. 1431 (*sold at* $1.70)		1·75	1·75
	First Day Cover			1·90

The 40 c. premium on No. **MS**1432 was to support the 1990 Auckland International Stamp Exhibition.

No. **MS**1432 overprinted on the selvedge with the "CAPEX" logo was available from the New Zealand stand at this International Philatelic Exhibition in Toronto.

432 "Kite Flying"
(Lauren Baldwin)

433 "Hark the Herald
Angels Sing"

(Adapted D. Little. Litho Leigh-Mardon Ltd, Melbourne)

1987 (29 July). *Health Stamps. Children's Paintings (2nd series). T* **432** *and similar multicoloured designs.* P 14½.

1433	40 c. + 3 c. Type **432**		35	35
	a. Horiz pair. Nos. 1433/4		70	70
1434	40 c. + 3 c. "Swimming" (Ineke Schoneveld)		35	35
1435	60 c. + 3 c. "Horse Riding" (Aaron Tylee) (*vert*)		50	50
	Set of 3		1·10	1·10
	First Day Cover			1·40
MS1436	100 × 117 mm. Nos. 1433/5, each × 2		2·25	2·25
	First Day Cover			2·75

Nos. 1433/4 were printed together, *se-tenant*, in horizontal pairs throughout the sheet.

(Des Ellen Giggenbach. Litho Leigh-Mardon Ltd, Melbourne)

1987 (16 Sept). *Christmas. T* **433** *and similar vert designs. Multicoloured.* P 14½.

1437	35 c. Type **433**		30	10
1438	70 c. "Away in a Manger"		55	55
1439	85 c. "We Three Kings of Orient Are"		65	65
	Set of 3		1·40	1·25
	First Day Cover			1·50

Souvenir Pack 1987

1987 (16 Sept). *Comprises Nos.* 1407/26, 1428/31, 1433/5 *and* 1437/9. *Sold at* $22.14.

SP1439a	Souvenir Pack		18·00

434 Knot ("Pona")

435 "Geothermal"

(Des Nga Puna Waihanga. Litho Security Printers (M), Malaysia)

1987 (4 Nov). *Maori Fibre-work. T* **434** *and similar vert designs. Multicoloured.* Wmkd Multiple "SPM" *in curve.* P 12.

1440	40 c. Type **434**		35	10
1441	60 c. Binding ("Herehere")		45	45
1442	80 c. Plait ("Whiri")		60	65

1443	85 c. Cloak weaving ("Korowai") with flax fibre ("Whitau")		65	70
	Set of 5		1·90	1·75
	First Day Cover			2·00

Post Office Yearbook 1987

1987 (4 Nov). *Comprises Nos.* 1289, 1291 *and* 1411/43 *in hardbound book with slip case.*

YB1443a	Yearbook		45·00

(Des Fay McAlpine. Litho Leigh-Mardon Ltd, Melbourne)

1988 (13 Jan). *Centenary of Electricity. T* **435** *and similar horiz designs, each showing radiating concentric circles representing energy generation.* P 14 × 14½.

1444	40 c. multicoloured		30	35
1445	60 c. black, rosine and brownish black		40	45
1446	70 c. multicoloured		50	55
1447	80 c. multicoloured		55	60
	Set of 4		1·60	1·75
	First Day Cover			2·25

Designs:—60 c. "Thermal"; 70 c. "Gas"; 80 c. "Hydro".

436 Queen Elizabeth II
and 1882 Queen Victoria
1d. Stamp

437 "Mangopare"

(Des A. G. Mitchell (40 c.), M. Conly and M. Stanley ($1). Litho Leigh-Mardon Ltd, Melbourne)

1988 (13 Jan). *Centenary of Royal Philatelic Society of New Zealand. T* **436** *and similar multicoloured designs.* P 14 × 14½.

1448	40 c. Type **436**		30	35
	a. Horiz pair. Nos. 1448/9		60	70
1449	40 c. As Type **436**, but 1882 Queen Victoria 2d.		30	35
	Set of 2		60	70
	First Day Cover			95
MS1450	107 × 160 mm. $1 "Queen Victoria" (Chalon) (*vert*). P 14½ × 14		70	75
	First Day Cover			1·10

Nos. 1448/9 were printed together, *se-tenant*, in horizontal pairs throughout the sheet.

No. **MS**1450 overprinted on the selvedge with the "SYDPEX" logo was available from the New Zealand stand at this International Philatelic Exhibition in Sydney and from the Philatelic Bureau at Wanganui.

(Des S. Adsett. Litho Leigh-Mardon Ltd, Melbourne)

1988 (2 Mar). *Maori Rafter Paintings. T* **437** *and similar vert designs. Multicoloured.* P 14½.

1451	40 c. Type **437**		40	35
1452	40 c. "Koru"		40	35
1453	40 c. "Raupunga"		40	35
1454	60 c. "Koiri"		55	45
	Set of 4		1·60	1·40
	First Day Cover			1·75

438 "Good Luck"

439 Paradise
Shelduck

(Des Communication Arts Ltd. Litho CPE Australia Ltd, Melbourne)

1988 (18 May). *Greetings Booklet Stamps. T* **438** *and similar multi-coloured designs. P* 13½.

1455	40 c. Type **438**		25	30
	a. Booklet pane. Nos. 1455/9		1·10	
1456	40 c. "Keeping in touch"		25	30
1457	40 c. "Happy birthday"		25	30
1458	40 c. "Congratulations" (41 × 27 mm)		25	30
1459	40 c. "Get well soon" (41 × 27 mm)		25	30
	Set of 5		1·10	1·40
	First Day Cover			2·00

Nos. 1455/9 only exist from $2 stamp booklets.

(Des Pauline Morse. Litho Leigh-Mardon Ltd, Melbourne)

1988 (7 June–2 Nov). *Native Birds. Multicoloured. P* 14½ × 14.

1460	10 c. Banded Dotterel (2.11)		5	8
1461	20 c. Yellowhead (2.11)		12	15
1462	30 c. Silvereye (2.11)		20	25
1463	40 c. Brown Kiwi (2.11)		25	30
1464	50 c. Kingfisher (2.11)		30	35
1465	60 c. Spotted Shag (2.11)		40	40
1466	70 c. Type **439**		45	50
1467	80 c. Fiordland Crested Penguin (2.11)		55	55
1468	90 c. South Island Robin (2.11)		60	60
	Set of 9		2·50	2·75
	Presentation Pack (16 Nov)		3·00	
	First Day Covers (2)			3·50

440 Milford Track

441 Kiwi and Koala at Campfire

(Des H. Thompson. Litho Leigh-Mardon Ltd, Melbourne)

1988 (8 June). *Scenic Walking Trails. T* **440** *and similar vert designs. Multicoloured. P* 14½.

1469	70 c. Type **440**		50	55
1470	80 c. Heaphy Track		55	60
1471	85 c. Copland Track		60	65
1472	$1.30, Routeburn Track		90	95
	Set of 4		2·25	2·50
	Presentation Pack (29 June)		3·00	
	First Day Cover			3·25
MS1473	124 × 99 mm. No. 1472 (sold at $1.70)		1·25	1·40
	First Day Cover			1·90

The 40 c. premium on No. **MS**1473 was to support the 1990 Auckland International Stamp Exhibition.

(Des R. Harvey. Litho Leigh-Mardon Ltd, Melbourne)

1988 (21 June). *Bicentenary of Australian Settlement. P* 14½.

1474	**441**	40 c. multicoloured		30	30
		First Day Cover			55
		Souvenir Postcard (30 July)		60	

A stamp in a similar design was also issued by Australia.

442 Swimming

443 "O Come All Ye Faithful"

(Des R. Proud. Litho Leigh-Mardon Ltd, Melbourne)

1988 (27 July). *Health Stamps. Olympic Games. Seoul. T* **442** *and similar horiz designs. Multicoloured. P* 14½.

1475	40 c. + 3 c. Type **442**		30	35
1476	60 c. + 3 c. Athletics		45	50
1477	70 c. + 3 c. Canoeing		50	55
1478	80 c. + 3 c. Show-jumping		60	65
	Set of 4		1·60	1·90
	First Day Cover			2·40
MS1479	120 × 90 mm. Nos. 1475/8		1·90	2·00
	First Day Cover			2·50

(Des Fay McAlpine. Litho Leigh-Mardon Ltd, Melbourne)

1988 (14 Sept). *Christmas. Carols. T* **443** *and similar vert designs, each showing illuminated verses. Multicoloured. P* 14½.

1480	35 c. Type **443**		25	30
1481	70 c. "Hark the Herald Angels Sing"		50	55
1482	80 c. "Ding Dong Merrily on High"		55	60
1483	85 c. "The First Nowell"		60	65
	Set of 4		1·75	1·90
	First Day Cover			2·40

Souvenir Pack 1988

1988 (14 Sept). *Comprises Nos. 1440/9, 1451/4, 1469/72, 1474/8 and 1480/3. Sold at* $17.75.

SP1483a	Souvenir Pack		13·00

444 "Lake Pukaki" (John Gully)

445 Brown Kiwi

(Litho Leigh-Mardon Ltd, Melbourne)

1988 (5 Oct). *New Zealand Heritage* (1st issue). *The Land. T* **444** *and similar horiz designs showing 19th-century paintings. Multicoloured. P* 14 × 14½.

1484	40 c. Type **444**		30	35
1485	60 c. "On the Grass Plain below Lake Arthur" (William Fox)		40	45
1486	70 c. "View of Auckland" (John Hoyte)		50	55
1487	80 c. "Mt. Egmont from the Southward" (Charles Heaphy)		55	60
1488	$1.05, "Anakiwa, Queen Charlotte Sound" (John Kinder)		75	80
1489	$1.30, "White Terraces, Lake Rotomahana" (Charles Barraud)		90	95
	Set of 6		3·00	3·25
	First Day Cover			3·75

See also Nos. 1505/10 and 1524/9.

(Des A. G. Mitchell. Eng. G. Prosser of B.A.B.N. Recess Leigh-Mardon Ltd, Melbourne)

1988 (19 Oct). *Booklet Stamp. P* 14½ (*and around design*).

1490	**445**	$1 bronze-green		60	65
		a. Booklet pane. No. 1490 × 6		3·50	
		First Day Cover			95

No. 1490 were only issued in $6 stamp booklets with the horizontal edges of the booklet pane imperforate. Each circular stamp is also separated by vertical perforations.

446 Humpback Whale and Calf

447 Clover

(Des Lindy Fisher. Litho Govt Ptg Office, Wellington)

1988 (2 Nov). *Whales. T* **446** *and similar horiz designs. Multicoloured.*
P 13½.

1491	60 c. Type **446**	45	45
1492	70 c. Killer Whales	55	55
1493	80 c. Southern Right Whale	60	60
1494	85 c. Blue Whale	85	65
1495	$1.05, Southern Bottlenose Whale and calf	80	80
1496	$1.30, Sperm Whale	95	95
	Set of 6	3·50	3·50
	Presentation Pack (16 Nov)		4·00
	First Day Cover		4·00

Although inscribed "ROSS DEPENDENCY" Nos. 1491/6 were available
from post offices throughout New Zealand.

Post Office Yearbook 1988

1988 (2 Nov). *Comprises No.* 1296 *and Nos.* 1448/96 *in hardbound book*
with slip case.

YB1496a	Yearbook	38·00

(Des Heather Arnold. Litho Leigh-Mardon Ltd, Melbourne)

1989 (18 Jan). *Wild Flowers. T* **447** *and similar horiz designs. Multi-*
coloured. P 14½.

1497	40 c. Type **447**	35	35
1498	60 c. Lotus	45	45
1499	70 c. Montbretia	55	55
1500	80 c. Wild Ginger	60	60
	Set of 4	1·75	1·75
	Presentation Pack		2·00
	First Day Cover		2·25

448 Katherine Mansfield

449 Moriori Man and Map
of Chatham Islands

(Des A. G. Mitchell. Litho Harrison)

1989 (1 Mar). *New Zealand Authors. T* **448** *and similar vert designs.*
Multicoloured. P 12½.

1501	40 c. Type **448**	30	35
1502	60 c. James K. Baxter	40	45
1503	70 c. Bruce Mason	50	55
1504	80 c. Ngaio Marsh	55	60
	Set of 4	1·60	1·75
	First Day Cover		2·25

(Des D. Gunson. Litho Leigh-Mardon Ltd, Melbourne)

1989 (17 May). *New Zealand Heritage* (2nd issue). *The People. T* **449** *and*
similar horiz designs. P 14 × 14½.

1505	40 c. multicoloured	30	35
1506	60 c. orange-brn, brownish grey & reddish brn	45	50
1507	70 c. yellow-green, brownish grey and deep olive	50	55
1508	80 c. brt greenish bl, brownish grey & dp dull bl	60	65
1509	$1.05, grey, brownish grey and grey-black	80	85
1510	$1.30, brt rose-red, brownish grey & lake-brn	1·00	1·10
	Set of 6	3·25	3·50
	First Day Cover		4·00

Designs:—60 c. Gold prospector; 70 c. Settler ploughing; 80 c. Whaling;
$1.05, Missionary preaching to Maoris; $1.30, Maori village.

STANLEY GIBBONS
STAMP COLLECTING SERIES

Introductory booklets on *How to Start, How to*
Identify Stamps and *Collecting by Theme.* A
series of well illustrated guides at a low price.
Write for details.

450 White Pine (Kahikatea) **451** Duke and Duchess of York
with Princess Beatrice

(Des D. Gunson. Litho Questa)

1989 (7 June). *Native Trees. T* **450** *and similar vert designs. Multi-*
coloured. P 14 × 14½.

1511	80 c. Type **450**	60	65
1512	85 c. Red Pine (Rimu)	65	70
1513	$1.05, Totara	80	85
1514	$1.30, Kauri	1·00	1·10
	Set of 4	2·75	3·00
	First Day Cover		3·50
MS1515	102 × 125 mm. No. 1514 (sold at $1.80)	1·40	1·50
	First Day Cover		1·75

The 50 c. premium on No. **MS**1515 was to support the 1990 Auckland
International Stamp Exhibition.

(Des and litho Leigh-Mardon Ltd, Melbourne)

1988 (26 July). *Health Stamps. T* **451** *and similar vert designs. Multi-*
coloured. P 14½.

1516	40 c. + 3 c. Type **451**	30	35
	a. Horiz pair. Nos. 1516/17	60	70
1517	40 c. + 3 c. Duchess of York with Princess Beatrice	30	35
1518	80 c. + 3 c. Princess Beatrice	60	65
	Set of 3	1·10	1·25
	First Day Cover		1·50
MS1519	120 × 89 mm. Nos. 1516/18, each × 2	2·50	2·75
	First Day Cover		3·25

Nos. 1516/17 were printed together, *se-tenant*, in horizontal pairs
throughout the sheet.

452 One Tree Hill, Auckland, **453** Windsurfing
through Bedroom Window

(Des H. Chapman. Litho Leigh-Mardon Ltd, Melbourne)

1989 (13 Sept). *Christmas T* **452** *and similar vert designs showing Star of*
Bethlehem. Multicoloured. P 14½.

1520	35 c. Type **452**	25	30
1521	65 c. Shepherd and dog in mountain valley	50	55
1522	80 c. Star over harbour	60	65
1523	$1 Star over globe	75	80
	Set of 4	1·90	2·10
	First Day Cover		2·25

Souvenir Pack 1989

1989 (13 Sept). *Comprises Nos.* 1484/9, 1491/514, 1516/18 *and* 1520/3.
Sold at $28.50.

SP1523a	Souvenir Pack	21·00

(Des M. Bailey. Litho Leigh-Mardon Ltd, Melbourne)

1989 (11 Oct). *New Zealand Heritage* (3rd issue). *The Sea. T* **453** *and*
similar horiz designs. Multicoloured. P 14 × 14½.

1524	40 c. Type **453**	30	35
1525	60 c. Fishes of many species	45	50
1526	65 c. Marlin and game fishing launch	50	55
1527	80 c. Rowing boat and yachts in harbour	60	65
1528	$1 Coastal scene	75	80
1529	$1.50, Container ship and tug	1·10	1·25
	Set of 6	3·50	3·75
	First Day Cover		4·00

454 Games Logo

(Des Heather Arnold. Litho Leigh-Mardon Ltd, Melbourne)

1989 (8 Nov). *14th Commonwealth Games, Auckland.* T **454** *and similar*
horiz designs. Multicoloured. P 14½.
1530 40 c. Type **454** . . . . ~~30~~ 35 –
1531 40 c. Goldie (games kiwi mascot) . . . . ~~30~~ 35 –

1532	40 c. Gymnastics		~~30~~	35 –
1533	50 c. Weightlifting		~~35~~	40 –
1534	65 c. Swimming		~~50~~	55
1535	80 c. Cycling		~~60~~	65 –
1536	$1 Lawn bowling		~~75~~	80 –
1537	$1.80, Hurdling		~~1·40~~	1·50 –
	Set of 8		4·00 ✓	4·50
	Presentation Pack		5·75	
	First Day Cover			4·75

Post Office Yearbook 1989

1989 (8 Nov). *Comprises No.* 1297 *and Nos.* 1497/537 *in hardbound book*
with slip case.
YB1537a Yearbook . . . . 39·00

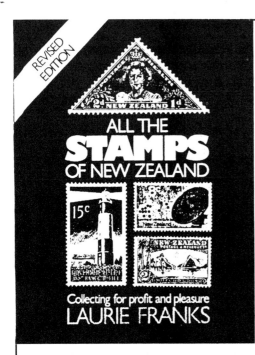

Index to New Zealand Stamp Designs from 1946

The following index is intended to facilitate the identification of all New Zealand stamps from 1946 onwards. Portrait stamps are usually listed under surnames only, views under the name of the town or city and other issues under the main subject or a prominent word and date chosen from the inscription. Simple abbreviations have occasionally been resorted to and when the same design or subject appears on more than one stamp, only the first of each series is indicated.

STAMP BOOKLETS

PRICES quoted are for complete booklets.

COMPOSITION. In Booklet Nos. B1 to B29 all booklet panes are of six stamps (or five stamps and one label). Initially these were in vertical format (2 × 3), but from No. B16 onwards they were horizontal (3 × 2). Booklet Nos. B1 to B25 are stapled.

1901. *White card covers with postal information. Interleaved with wax paper.*
B1   1s. ½d. booklet. Twelve 1d. (No. 278) in panes of 6   ......   £1000
B2   2s. 6½d. booklet. Thirty 1d. (No. 278) in panes of 6   .... £1100

1902 (21 Aug)–**05.** *White card covers with postal information. Interleaved with wax paper.*
B3   1s. ½d. booklet. Twelve 1d. in panes of 6 (Nos. 303b or 303cb)   £800
B4   2s. ½d. booklet. Twenty-four 1d. in panes of 6 (Nos. 303b or 303cb) (21.5.05) £1200
B5   2s. 6½d. booklet. Thirty 1d. in panes of 6 (Nos. 303b or 303cb) £1200
  Cover price of Nos. B1/5 included an extra ½d. to cover cost of manufacture.

1910 (Apr)–**12.** *White card covers with postal information. Interleaved with wax paper (No. B6) or with advertisements (No. B7).*
B6   2s. booklet. Eleven ½d. in pane of 5 plus label (Nos. 387b or 387c) and pane of 6 (No. 387d), and eighteen 1d. in panes of 6 (No. 405b) £1000
B7   2s. booklet. Twelve ½d. and eighteen 1d. each in panes of 6 with bars on the selvedge (Nos. 387e and 405c) (5.12) . £600
  Booklet No. B6 contained stamps to a face value of 1s. 11½d. with the additional ½d. being used to cover cost of manufacture.

INTERLEAVES. Booklet Nos. B8 to B29 are interleaved with advertisements.

1915–25. *White card covers with postal information.*
B 8 2s. booklet. Twelve ½d. and eighteen 1d. each in panes of 6 with bars on the selvedge (Nos. 435a or 435ba and 405c) £550
B 9 2s. booklet. Twelve ½d. and eighteen 1d. each in panes of 6 with bars on the selvedge (Nos. 441a and 406b) (1.12.24) £550
B10 2s. booklet. Twelve ½d. and eighteen 1d. each in panes of 6 with bars and advertisements on the selvedge (Nos. 446a and 410b) (1925) £550

1928–34. *White card covers with postal information.*
B11 2s. booklet. Twelve ½d. and eighteen 1d. each in panes of 6 with bars on the selvedge (Nos. 446ba and 468b) ... £500
  a. As No. B11, but panes with bars and advertisements on the selvedge (Nos. 446bb and 468c) £500
B12 2s. booklet. Twenty-four 1d. in panes of 6 with bars and advertisements on the selvedge (No. 468c) (1930) ... £800
B13 2s. booklet. Twelve ½d. and eighteen 1d. each in panes of 6 with bars on the selvedge (Nos. 446ab and 468b) (1934) £500
B14 2s. booklet. Twenty-four 1d. in panes of 6 with bars and advertisements on the selvedge (No. 468da) (1934) .. £400

WATERMARKS. Booklet Nos. B15 and B17/28 can be found containing panes with inverted watermarks.

1935. *White card cover with postal information.*
B15 2s. booklet. Twenty-four 1d. in panes of 6 with advertisements on the selvedge (No. 557ba) £125

1936. *White card cover with postal information.*
B16 2s. booklet. Twenty-four 1d. (No. 578) in horizontal panes of 6 . . . . 85·00

PUZZLED ?

Then you need
PHILATELIC TERMS ILLUSTRATED
to tell you all you need to know about printing methods, papers, errors, varieties, watermarks, perforations, etc. 192 pages, some in full colour, soft cover. Third Edition.

(Type A (*Illustration reduced. Actual size* 70 × 48 *mm*))

1938 (1 July). *Cream cover as Type A.*
B17 2s. booklet. Twenty-four 1d. (No. 605) in panes of 6 .... £150

1938 (Nov). *Cream (2s.) or blue (2s. 3d.) covers as Type A.*
B18 2s. booklet. Twelve ½d. (No. 603) and eighteen 1d. (No. 605) each in panes of 6 . . . . £150
B19 2s. 3d. booklet. Eighteen 1½d. (No. 607) in panes of 6 .... £150

Type AB (*Illustration reduced. Actual size* 71½ × 48 *mm.*)

1954 (Apr). *Black and green on cream cover, Type AB.*
B20 4s. booklet. Twelve 1d (No. 724) and twelve 3d. (No. 727) each in panes of 6 . . . . 8·00

1956 (1 May). *Black and green on cream cover. Type AB.*
B21 4s. booklet. Twelve 1d. (No. 724) and twelve 3d. (No. 748) each in panes of 6 plus one pane of air mail labels ... 17·00

1957 (5 Sept). *Black and green on cream cover, Type AB.*
B22 4s. booklet. Twelve 1d. (No. 745) and twelve 3d. (No. 748) each in panes of 6 plus one pane of air mail labels ... 16·00

1959 (20 June). *Black and green on cream cover, Type AB.*
B23 4s. booklet. Twelve 1d. (No. 745Eo) and twelve 3d. (No. 748Eo) each in panes of 6 plus one pane of air mail labels . . . . 20·00

Type B (*Illustration reduced. Actual size* 71½ × 48 *mm.*)

1960 (1 Sept).   *Black and red on cream cover, as Type* B.
B24   4s. booklet. Twelve 1d. (No. 782) and twelve 3d. (No. 785)
        in panes of 6 plus one pane of air mail labels . . . . . .   7·00

1962 (21 May).   *Black and red on cream cover, Type* B.
B25   4s. 6d. booklet. Twelve ½d. (No. 781), twelve 1d. (No. 782)
        and twelve 3d. (No. 785) each in panes of 6 plus one
        pane of air mail labels . . . .   18·00

1964.   *Black and carmine on cream cover, as Type* B. *Stitched.*
B26   4s. 3d. booklet. Six ½d. (No. 781), twelve 1d. (No. 782) and
        twelve 3d. (No. 785) each in panes of 6 plus one pane
        of air mail labels . . . .   10·00

Type C Maori Art (*Illustration reduced. Actual size* 71½ × 48 *mm.*)

1967 (10 July).   *Black and carmine on pale lemon cover, Type* C. *Stitched.*
B27   50 c. booklet. Six ½ c. (No. 845), eleven 1 c. (No. 846) and
        twelve 3 c. (No. 849) all in panes of 6 except one pane
        of the 1 c. which has five stamps with *se-tenant* label
        (No. 846a) plus one pane of air mail labels . . . .   9·00

Type D Native Trees (*Illustration reduced. Actual size* 71½ × 48 *mm.*)

1971 (6 July).   *Multicoloured on cream cover, Type* D. *Stitched.*
B28   75 c. booklet. Nine 1 c. (No. 915a), six 3 c. (No. 918a) and
        twelve 4 c. (No. 919a), all in panes of 6 except one
        pane of 1 c. which has three stamps and three printed
        labels (No. 915b) plus one pane of air mail labels . .   14·00

1974 (Aug).   *Multicoloured on cream cover. Type* D. *Stitched.*
B29   75 c. booklet. As No. B28, but containing stamps without
        watermark: Nos. 1008, 1010 and 1011 . . . .   10·00

STANLEY GIBBONS
STAMP COLLECTING SERIES

Introductory booklets on *How to Start, How to
Identify Stamps* and *Collecting by Theme.* A
series of well illustrated guides at a low price.
Write for details.

Type E Garden Rose "Josephine Bruce" (*Illustration reduced. Actual
size* 80 × 58 *mm.*)

1977 (Apr).   *Multicoloured Folded Card Cover, Type* E.
B30   80 c. booklet. Ten 8 c. (No. 1093a) attached by the selvedge   2·50

Type F (*Illustration reduced. Actual size* 89 × 49 *mm.*)

1977 (Apr).   *Blue and black Folded Card Cover, Type* F.
B31 $1 booklet. Ten 10 c. (No. 1017) attached by the selvedge .   6·00

Two Settings of Booklet Cover for No. B32:
      Setting I.   Inscription at foot. "c" aligned at top of "10" (similar to Type
                         G).
      Setting II. Inscription at top. "c" aligned on bottom of "10".

1978 (Aug)–79.   *Black and ultramarine cover as Type* G. *Folded.*
B32 $1 booklet. Ten 10 c. (No. 1094a) attached by selvedge
        (Cover Setting I) . . . .   8·50
      a. Cover Setting II . . . .   8·50
      b. Containing ten 10 c. (No. 1094ab) (Cover Setting I)
        (1979) . . . .   2·00

Type G (*Illustration reduced. Actual size* 80 × 58 *mm.*)

1978 (Aug).   *Black and orange cover. Type* G. *Folded.* (*Setting* I).
B33 $1.20 booklet. Ten 12 c. (No. 1096) attached by the
selvedge . . . .   3·00

1980 (Mar).   *Black and red cover as Type* G. *Folded* (*Setting* I).
B34 $1.40 booklet. Ten 14 c. (No. 1098) attached by the
selvedge . . . .   3·00

Type H (*Illustration reduced. Actual size* 80 × 58 *mm.*)

1980 (12 May).   *Black and green cover. Type* H. *Folded.*
B35 $1.40* booklet. Ten 14 c. (No. 1098) attached by the
selvedge . . . .   3·00
The cover of No. B35 is inscribed "1.54" which included a premium
payable when purchased from commercial outlets authorised to sell
booklets. It was available at $1.40 (value of contents) from the Post Office
Philatelic Bureau.

Type J (*Illustration reduced. Actual size* 95 × 50 *mm*)

1981.   *Black and blue cover. Type* J. *Folded.*
B36 $2 booklet. Ten 20 c. (No. 1099) attached by the selvedge .   2·00

Type K (*Illustration reduced. Actual size* 95 × 50 *mm*)

1981.   *Black and green cover. Type* K. *Folded.*
B37 $2* booklet. Ten 20 c. (No. 1099) attached by the selvedge   2·00
*The cover of No. B37 is inscribed "$2.20". See note below No. B35.

1982 (1 Apr)–**83.**   *Black and green cover as Type* G. *Folded.* A. *No.* 1261.
B. *No* 1261a (1983).
                                                              A   B
B38 $2.40 booklet. Ten 24 c. attached by the selvedge   3·00   2·00

1982 (1 Apr)–**84.**   *Black and blue cover as Type* H. *Folded.* A. *No.* 1261. B.
No. 1261a (1984).
                                                              A   B
B39 $2.40* booklet. Ten 24 c. attached by the sel-
vedge . . . .   3·00   2·00
*The cover of No. B39 is inscribed "$2.64". See note below No. B35.

Type L Lake Tekapo, South Island
(*Illustration reduced. Actual size* 83 × 60 *mm*)

1985 (2 July).   *Multicoloured cover as Type* L *with design continuing on
back cover. Folded. Pane attached by selvedge.*
B40 $2.50 booklet. (Type L). Ten 25 c. (No. 1370) . . . .   2·00
B41 $2.50* booklet (Tongariro National Park, North Island). Ten
25 c. (No. 1370) . . . .   2·00
*The cover of Booklet No. B41 is inscribed $2.75. See note below No.
B35.

1986 (1 May).   *Multicoloured covers as Type* L, *but* 115 × 60 *mm, with the
design continuing on back cover. Folded. Pane attached by selvedge.*
B42 $3 booklet (Matukituki Valley, Otago). Ten 30 c. (No. 1288)   2·00
B43 $3* booklet (Stream and native bush, Canterbury). Ten
30 c. (No. 1288) . . . .   2·00
*The cover of Booklet No. B43 is inscribed $3.30. See note below No.
B35.

1987 (2 Feb–June).   *Multicoloured covers as Type* L, *but* 115 × 60 *mm,
with the design continuing on back cover. Folded. Pane attached by
selvedge.*
B44 $4 booklet (Ahuriri Valley, Otago). Ten 40 c. (No. 1289) . .   3·25
a. Revised "NZ POST" logo without crown (June) . . . . .
B45 $4* booklet (Totaranui Beach, Abel Tasman National Park,
Nelson). Ten 40 c. (No. 1289) . . . .   3·25
a. Revised "NZ POST" logo without crown (June) . . . . .
*The cover of booklet No. B45 is inscribed $4.40. See note below No.
B35.
Nos. B44a and B45a overprinted on the front cover with the "CAPEX"
logo were available from the New Zealand stand at this International
Philatelic Exhibition in Toronto.

1988 (Jan).   *Multicoloured covers as Type* L, *but* 115 × 60 *mm, with the
design continuing on back cover. New "NZ POST" logo as shown on
Type* N. *Folded. Pane attached by selvedge.*
B46 $4 booklet (Wellington by night). Ten 40 c. (No. 1289) . . .   3·25
B47 $4* booklet (Katiki Point). Ten 40 c. (No. 1289) . . . .   3·25
*The cover of Booklet No. B47 is inscribed $4.40. See note below No.
B35.

Type M (*Illustration reduced. Actual size* 100 × 60 *mm*)

1988 (18 May).   *"Personal Message Stamps". Multicoloured cover. Type*
M. *Folded. Pane attached by selvedge.*
B48 $2 booklet. Five different 40 c. in *se-tenant* pane (No.
1455a) . . . .   1·10

Type N (*Illustration reduced. Actual size* 88×60 *mm*)

1988 (7 June). *"Fast Post" Service. Black, bright scarlet and new blue cover. Type N. Folded. Pane attached by selvedge.*
B49 $7 booklet. Ten 70 c. (No. 1466) . . . . 4·50

Type O (*Illustration reduced. Actual size* 116×59 *mm*)

1988 (14 Sept). *Christmas. Multicoloured cover. Type O. Folded. Pane attached by selvedge.*
B50 $3.50 booklet. Ten 35 c. (No. 1480) . . . . 3·00

Type P (*Illustration reduced. Actual size* 85×55 *mm*)

1988 (19 Oct). *Multicoloured cover. Type P. Folded. Pane attached by selvedge.*
B51 $6 booklet. Six $1 (booklet pane No. 1490a) . . . . 4·00

Type Q Mt Cook from the Hooker Valley, South Canterbury
(*Illustration reduced. Actual size* 88×60 *mm*)

1988 (2 Nov). *Multicoloured cover, Type Q, with design continuing on back cover. Folded. Pane attached by selvedge.*
B52 $4 booklet. Ten 40 c. (No. 1463) . . . . 2·75

1989 (13 Sept). *Christmas. Multicoloured cover as Type O. Folded. Pane attached by selvedge.*
B53 $3.50 booklet. Ten 35 c. (No. 1520) . . . . 2·50

EXPRESS DELIVERY STAMPS

POSTAGE DUE STAMPS

E 1

(Typo Govt Printing Office, Wellington)

D 1

(I)

(II)

1903 (9 Feb).   *Value in first colour. W **43** (sideways). P* 11.
E1   E **1**   6d. red and violet . . . .   30·00   20·00
            Wi. Wmk sideways inverted . . . .   30·00   20·00

1926–36.   *Thick, white, opaque chalk-surfaced "Cowan" paper. W **43.**

(a) P 14×14½
E2   E **1**   6d. vermilion and bright violet . . . .   25·00   16·00
            Wi. Wmk inverted . . . .   85·00

(b) P 14×15 (1936)
E3   E **1**   6d. carmine and bright violet . . . .   26·00   35·00

3D.
(a)
Large "D"

5D.
(b)
Small "D"

(Typo Govt Printing Office, Wellington)

1899 (1 Dec).   *W **12**b. Coarse paper. P* 11.

I. Type I. *Circle of 14 ornaments, 17 dots over "N.Z.", "N.Z." large.*

(a) *Large "D"*
D1   D **1**   ½d. carmine and green . . . .   11·00   20·00
            a. No stop after "D" (Right pane R. 2/3) . .   80·00   £100
D2   8d. carmine and green . . . .   60·00   75·00
D3   1s. carmine and green . . . .   65·00   60·00
D4   2s. carmine and green £120   £130
            Set of 4 . . . .   £225   £250
To avoid further subdivision the 1s. and 2s. are placed with the *pence*
values, although the two types of "D" do not apply to the higher values.

(b) *Small "D"*
D6   D **1**   5d. carmine and green . . . .   18·00   18·00
D7   6d. carmine and green . . . .   20·00   18·00
D8   10d. carmine and green . . . .   70·00   80·00
            Set of 3 . . . .   £100   £100

1937–39.   *Thin, hard, chalk-surfaced "Wiggins Teape" paper. W **43.**
(a) P 14×14½
E4   E **1**   6d. carmine and bright violet . . . .   40·00   20·00   22·00
(b) P 14×15 (1939)
E5   E **1**   6d. vermilion and bright violet . . .   65·00   30·00   55·00

II. Type II. *Circle of 13 ornaments, 15 dots over "N.Z.", "N.Z." small.*
(a) *Large "D"*
D 9   D **1**   ½d. vermilion and green . . . .   2·25   11·00
            a. No stop after "D" (Right pane R.2/3) . .   50·00   70·00
D10   1d. vermilion and green . . . .   7·00   1·00
D11   2d. vermilion and green . . . .   45·00   9·00
D12   3d. vermilion and green . . . .   12·00   3·50
            Set of 4 . . . .   60·00   22·00

E 2 Express Mail Delivery Van

(Des J. Berry. Eng Stamp Ptg Office, Melbourne. Recess Govt Ptg Office,
Wellington)

1939 (16 Aug).   *W **43**. P* 14.
E6   E **2**   6d. violet . . . .   1·50   75   1·75
            Wi. Wmk inverted . . . .   29·00   18·00

(b) *Small "D"*
D14   D **1**   1d. vermilion and green . . . .   10·00   1·25
D15   2d. vermilion and green . . . .   20·00   3·00
D16   4d. vermilion and green . . . .   22·00   9·00
            Set of 3 . . . .   48·00   12·00
Nos. D9/16 were printed from a common frame plate of 240 (4 panes of
60) used in conjunction with centre plates of 120 (2 panes of 60) for the ½d.
and 4d. or 240 for the other values. Sheets of the 1d. and 2d. each
contained two panes with large "D" and two panes with small "D".

D 2   D 3

(Des W. R. Bock. Typo Govt Printing Office)

1902 (28 Feb).   *No wmk. P* 11.
D17   D **2**   ½d. red and deep green   85   4·25

1904–08.   *"Cowan" unsurfaced paper. W **43** (sideways inverted). (a) P* 11
D18   D **2**   ½d. red and green (4.04) . . . .   1·50   1·50
            a. Imperf between (horiz pair) £450
D19   1d. red and green (5.12.05) . . . .   7·00   3·25
D20   2d. red and green (5.4.06) . . . .   90·00   90·00
            Set of 3 . . . .   90·00   90·00

PUZZLED ?

Then you need
PHILATELIC TERMS ILLUSTRATED
to tell you all you need to know about printing
methods, papers, errors, varieties, watermarks,
perforations, etc. 192 pages, some in full
colour, soft cover. Third Edition.

<table>
<tbody>
<tr><td colspan="5">(b) P 14</td></tr>
</tbody>
</table>

D21	D 2	1d. carmine and green (12.06)	7·50	70
		a. Rose-pink and green (9.07)	6·00	40
		Wi. Wmk sideways	6·00	4·00
D22		2d. carmine and green (10.06)	7·50	2·75
		a. Rose-pink and green (6.08)	4·25	65
		Wi. Wmk sideways	4·25	65

1919 (Jan)–**20.** "De La Rue" chalky paper. Toned gum. W **43**. P 14 × 15.

D23	D 2	½d. carmine and green (6.19)	3·25	1·50
D24		1d. carmine and green	4·00	20
		Wi. Wmk inverted		
D25		2d. carmine and green (8.20)	6·00	2·00
		Set of 3	12·00	3·25

1925 (May). "Jones" chalky paper. White gum. W **43**. P 14 × 15.

D26	D 2	½d. carmine and green	27·00	27·00

1925 (July). No wmk, but bluish "N Z" and Star lithographed on back. P 14 × 15.

D27	D 2	½d. carmine and green	1·75	14·00
D28		2d. carmine and green	2·50	12·00
		Set of 2	4·25	26·00

1925 (Nov)–**35.** "Cowan" thick, opaque chalky paper. W **43**.

<table><tbody><tr><td>(a) P 14 × 15</td></tr></tbody></table>

D29	D 2	½d. carmine and green (12.26)	1·75	4·50
D30		1d. carmine and green	3·25	80
D31		2d. carmine and green (6.26)	11·00	3·75
D32		3d. carmine and green (6.35)	32·00	32·00
		Set of 4	42·00	35·00

<table><tbody><tr><td>(b) P 14</td></tr></tbody></table>

D33	D 2	½d. carmine and green (10.28)	15·00	22·00
D34		1d. rose and pale yellow-green (6.28)	3·25	50
D35		2d. carmine and green (10.29)	6·50	1·75
D36		3d. carmine and green (5.28)	15·00	25·00
		Set of 4	35·00	45·00

PRICES

George VI issues (1937–1952)

First column = Unmounted Mint
Second column = Mounted Mint
Third column = Used

1937–38. "Wiggins Teape" thin, hard chalky paper. W **43**. P 14 × 15.

D37	D 2	½d. carmine & yellow-green (2.38) . . .	9·00	4·50	16·00
D38		1d. carmine & yellow-green (1.37) . . .	8·00	4·00	3·50
D39		2d. carmine & yellow-green (6.37) . . .	10·00	4·50	6·00
D40		3d. carmine & yellow-grn (11.37) . . .	38·00	13·00	30·00
		Set of 4	60·00	23·00	50·00

(Des J. Berry. Typo Govt Printing Office, Wellington)

1939–49. P 15 × 14. (a) W **43** (sideways inverted) (16.8.39).

D41	D 3	½d. turquoise-green	3·00	1·50	3·50
D42		1d. carmine	1·25	55	30
		Wi. Wmk sideways	—	—	1·50
D43		2d. bright blue	4·00	2·00	2·75
D44		3d. orange-brown	12·00	4·75	14·00
		Wi. Wmk sideways			
		Set of 4	18·00	8·00	17·00

<table><tbody><tr><td>(b) W 98 sideways</td></tr></tbody></table>

D45	D 3	1d. carmine (4.49)	2·50	70	1·50*
D46		2d. bright blue (12.46)	1·00	45	2·50
		Wi. Wmk sideways inverted	4·00	2·00	70
D47		3d. orange-brown (6.45)	3·00	1·50	5·00
		a. Wmk upright (1943)	25·00	12·00	23·00
		Wi. Wmk sideways inverted	4·00	2·00	4·50
		Set of 3	6·00	2·40	6·00*

*The use of Postage Due stamps ceased in 1951, our used price for No. D45 being for stamps postmarked after this date (price for examples clearly cancelled 1949–51, £25).

THE WORLD CENTRE FOR
FINE STAMPS IS 399 STRAND

OFFICIAL STAMPS

1892–1906. Contemporary issues handstamped "O.P.S.O." diagonally.

(a) Stamps of 1873 type. W **12**b. P 12½.

O 1	**3**	½d. rose (V.)	—	£400

(b) Stamps of 1892–97 optd in rose or magenta. W **12**b.

O 2	**13**	½d. black (p 10)	—	£150
		a. Violet opt	—	£160
O 3		½d. black (p 10 × 11)	—	£150
O 4	**14**	1d. rose (p 12 × 11½)	—	£160
O 5		1d. rose (p 11)	—	£160
O 6	**15**	2d. purple (p 11)	—	£300
O 7		2d. mauve-lilac (p 10)	—	£300
		a. Violet opt		
O 8	**16**	2½d. blue (p 11)	—	£200
O 9		2½d. ultramarine (p 10)	—	£200
O10		2½d. ultramarine (p 10 × 11)	—	£200
O11	**19**	5d. olive-black (p 12 × 11½)	—	£325
O12	**20**	6d. brown (p 12 × 11½)	—	£400

(c) Stamps of 1898–1903 optd in violet. P 11. (i) No wmk

O13	**23**	½d. green (p 14) (No. 294)	—	£140
O14	**26**	2½d. blue (p 12–16) (No. 249a)	—	£350
O15	**27**	2½d. blue (No. 260)	—	£275
O16	**37**	4d. indigo and brown (No. 262)	—	£325
O17	**30**	5d. purple-brown (No. 263)	—	£375
		a. Green opt	—	£350
O18	**32**	8d. indigo (No. 266)	—	£400

(ii) W **38**

O19	**42**	1d. carmine (No. 278)	—	£150

(iii) W **43** (sideways on 3d., 1s.)

O20	**42**	1d. carmine (p 14) (No. 303)	—	£150
		a. Green opt	—	£150
O21	**27**	2½d. blue (No. 308)	—	£250
O22	**28**	3d. yellow-brown (No. 309)	—	£300
O23	**34**	1s. orange-red (No. 315b)	—	£600
O24	**35**	2s. green (No. 316)	—	£600

The letters signify "On Public Service Only," and stamps so overprinted were used by the Post Office Department on official correspondence between the department and places abroad.

OFFICIAL.

(O 3)

1907–08. Stamps of 1902–6 optd with Type O **3** (vertically upwards). W **43** (sideways on 3d., 6d., 1s. and 5s.). P 14.

O59	**23**	½d. green (p 14)	5·50	50
		a. Perf compound of 11 and 14	60·00	
		b. Mixed perfs	60·00	
O60	**42**	1d. carmine (No. 303)	5·50	6·00
		a. Booklet pane of 6*	30·00	
O60b		1d. rose-carmine (Waterlow) (No. 352)	5·50	30
		ba. Perf compound of 11 and 14	£250	£190
		bb. Mixed perfs	£250	£190
O60c		1d. carmine (Royle)	5·50	25
		ca. Perf compound of 11 and 14	£170	£160
		cb. Mixed perfs	£170	£160
O61	**41**	2d. purple	6·50	1·25
		a. Bright reddish purple	6·50	1·00
		ab. Mixed perfs	£140	£140
O63	**28**	3d. bistre-brown	35·00	1·75
		Wi. Wmk sideways inverted	35·00	1·75
O64	**31**	6d. bright carmine-pink	£110	15·00
		a. Imperf vert (horiz pair)	£700	
		b. Mixed perfs	£325	£325
		Wi. Wmk sideways inverted	£110	15·00
O65	**34**	1s. orange-red	85·00	15·00
		Wi. Wmk sideways inverted	85·00	15·00
O66	**35**	2s. blue-green	70·00	45·00
		a. Imperf between (pair)	£900	
		b. Imperf vert (horiz pair)	£600	
		Wi. Wmk inverted		
O67	**36**	5s. deep red	£150	£150
		Wi. Wmk sideways inverted	£150	£150
		a. Wmk upright	£700	£500
		Set of 8	£425	£200

*Though issued in 1908, a large quantity of booklets was mislaid and not utilized until they were found in 1930.

1908–09. *Optd as Type* O **3**. *W* **43**.

O69	**23**	½d. green (*p* 14×15)	6·00	1·25
O70	**46**	1d. carmine (*p* 14×15)	48·00	1·00
O71	**48**	6d. pink (*p* 14×13, 13½)	£140	30·00
O72		6d. pink (*p* 14×15) (1909)	£110	26·00
O72*a*	F **4**	£1 rose-pink (*p* 14) (No. F89)	£600	£450

1910. *No.* 387 *optd with Type* O **3**.

O73	**50**	½d. yellow-green	3·00	30
		a. Opt inverted (reading downwards)	†	£1200

1910–16. *Nos.* 389 *and* 392/4 *optd with Type* O **3**. *P* 14×14½.

O74	**51**	3d. chestnut	14·00	80
		a. Perf 14×13½ (1915)	60·00	70·00
		ab. Vert pair, O74/a	£300	£350
O75	–	6d. carmine	18·00	3·75
		a. Deep carmine (1913)	24·00	4·25
		Wi. Wmk inverted		
O76	–	8d. indigo-blue (R.) (5.16)	13·00	18·00
		Wi. Wmk inverted	30·00	30·00
		a. Perf 14×13½	13·00	18·00
		ab. Vert pair, O76/a	45·00	60·00
		aWi. Wmk inverted	30·00	30·00
O77	–	1s. vermilion	45·00	12·00
		Set of 4	80·00	30·00

1910–25. *Optd with Type* O **3**. (*a*) *W* **43**. *De La Rue chalk-surfaced paper with toned gum.*

O78	**52**	1d. carmine (No. 405)	2·00	10
		Wi. Wmk inverted and reversed	—	£100

(*b*) *W* **43**. *Jones chalk-surfaced paper with white gum*

O79	**52**	1d. deep carmine (No. 406) (1925)	7·00	3·00

(*c*) *No wmk, but bluish "NZ" and Star lithographed on back. Art paper*

O80	**52**	1d. rose-carmine (No. 409) (1925)	4·25	6·50

(*d*) *W* **43**. *Cowan thick, opaque, chalk-surfaced paper with white gum*

O81	**52**	1d. deep carmine (No. 410) (1925)	5·50	1·25

1913–25. *Postal Fiscal stamps optd with Type* O **3**.

(i) *Chalk-surfaced De La Rue paper.* (*a*) *P* 14 (1913–14)

O82	F **4**	2s. blue (30.9.14)	30·00	18·00
O83		5s. yellow-green (13.6.13)	65·00	65·00
O84		£1 rose-carmine (1913)	£550	£450
		Set of 3	£575	£475

(*b*) *P* 14½×14, *comb* (1915)

O85	F **4**	2s. deep blue (Aug)	30·00	18·00
		a. No stop after "OFFICIAL"	£120	80·00
O86		5s. yellow-green (Jan)	65·00	65·00
		a. No stop after "OFFICIAL"	£200	£200
		Set of 2	95·00	75·00

(ii) *Thick, white, opaque chalk-surfaced Cowan paper.* *P* 14½×14 (1925)

O87	F **4**	2s. blue	55·00	55·00
		a. No stop after "OFFICIAL"	£160	£160

The overprint on these last and on Nos. O69 and O72*a* is from a new set of type, giving a rather sharper impression than Type O **3**, but otherwise resembling it closely.

1915 (12 Oct)–**34**. *Optd with Type* O **3**. *P* 14×15. (*a*) *On Nos.* 435/40 (*De La Rue chalk-surfaced paper with toned gum*).

O88	**61**	½d. green	80	10
O89	**62**	1½d. grey-black (6.16)	4·75	2·50
O90	**61**	1½d. slate (12.16)	2·50	40
O91		1½d. orange-brown (4.19)	2·75	30
O92		2d. yellow (4.17)	2·75	12
O93		3d. chocolate (11.19)	6·00	35
		Set of 6	18·00	3·50

(*b*) *On Nos.* 441 *and* 443 (*Jones chalk-surfaced paper with white gum*)

O94	**61**	½d. green (1924)	3·50	1·75
O95		3d. deep chocolate (1924)	24·00	4·00
		Set of 2	27·00	5·75

(*c*) *On Nos.* 446/7 *and* 448a/9 (*Cowan thick, opaque, chalk-surfaced paper with white gum*)

O96	**61**	½d. green (1925)	50	10
		Wi. Wmk inverted	25·00	
		a. Perf 14 (1929)	1·25	35
		ab. No stop after "OFFICIAL"	18·00	18·00
O97		1½d. orange-brown (*p* 14) (1929)	8·50	11·00
		a. No stop after "OFFICIAL"	35·00	42·00
		b. Perf 14×15 (1934)	17·00	20·00
O98		2d. yellow (*p* 14) (1931)	1·50	20
		a. No stop after "OFFICIAL"	27·00	17·00
O99	**61**	3d. chocolate (1925)	3·50	40
		a. No stop after "OFFICIAL"	35·00	22·00
		b. Perf 14 (1930)	15·00	1·75
		ba. No stop after "OFFICIAL"	60·00	23·00
		Set of 4	12·50	11·00

1915 (Dec)–**27**. *Optd with Type* O **3**. *P* 14×14½. (*a*) *Nos.* 420, 422, 425, 428 *and* 429a/30 (*Cowan unsurfaced paper*).

O100	**60**	3d. chocolate	3·00	70
		Wi. Wmk inverted	10·00	4·00
		a. Perf 14×13½	3·00	70
		ab. Vert pair, O100/a	35·00	50·00
		aWi. Wmk inverted	10·00	4·00
O101		4d. bright violet (*p* 14×13½) (4.25)	12·00	2·00
		a. Re-entry (Pl 20 R.1/6)	40·00	
		b. Re-entry (Pl 20 R.4/10)	45·00	
		c. Perf 14×14½ (4.27)	14·00	1·00
O102		6d. carmine (6.16)	3·75	75
		Wi. Wmk inverted	85·00	
		a. Perf 14×13½	3·75	60
		ab. Vert pair, O102/a	50·00	50·00
O103		8d. red-brown (*p* 14×13½) (8.22)	70·00	80·00
O104		9d. sage-green (*p* 14×13½) (4.25)	35·00	30·00
O105		1s. vermilion (9.16)	5·00	2·00
		Wi. Wmk inverted	£125	85·00
		a. Perf 14×13½	15·00	7·00
		ab. Vert pair, O105/a	65·00	90·00
		aWi. Wmk inverted	£125	85·00
		c. Pale orange-red	24·00	6·50
		Set of 6	£120	£100

(*b*) *No.* 433 (*Thin paper with widely spaced sideways wmk*)

O106	**60**	3d. chocolate (*p* 14) (7.16)	3·00	4·00
		a. No wmk	30·00	50·00

1927–33. *Optd with Type* O **3**. *W* **43**. *P* 14.

O111	**71**	1d. rose-carmine (No. 468)	1·00	10
		a. No stop after "OFFICIAL"	17·00	9·00
		Wi. Wmk inverted	—	25·00
		b. Perf 14×15	1·25	10
O112	**72**	2s. light blue (No. 469) (2.28)	70·00	65·00
O113	F **6**	5s. green (1933)	£250	£250
		Set of 3	£300	£275

PRICES
George VI issues (1936–1952)
First column = Unmounted Mint
Second column = Mounted Mint
Third column = Used

Official (O **4**) *Official* (O **5**)

1936–61. *Pictorial issue optd horiz or vert* (2*s.*) *with Type* O **4**.

(*a*) *W* **43** (*Single "N Z" and Star*)

O115	**82**	1d. scarlet (Die 1) (*p* 14×13½)	1·00	60	15
		a. Perf 13½×14	70·00	45·00	32·00
O116	**83**	1½d. red-brown (*p* 13½×14)	16·00	9·50	15·00
		a. Perf 14×13½	£3500		
O118	**92**	1s. deep green (*p* 14×13½)	18·00	11·00	18·00
		Wi. Wmk inverted	—	—	40·00
O119	F **6**	5s. green (*p* 14) (12.38)	50·00	20·00	17·00
		Set of 4	75·00	35·00	45·00

The watermark of No. O119 is almost invisible.

Only four examples of No. O116a exist. The error occurred when a sheet of No. 558a was found to have a block of four missing. This was replaced by a block of No. 558 and the sheet was then sent for overprinting.

(*b*) *W* **98** (*Mult "N Z" and Star*)

O120	**81**	½d. bright green, *p* 14×13½ (7.37)	3·00	1·40	3·00
O121	**82**	1d. scarlet, *p* 14×13½ (11.36)	1·50	60	10
		Wi. Wmk inverted	2·00	85	1·00
O122	**83**	1½d. red-brown, *p* 14×13½ (7.36)	6·00	2·50	4·00
O123	**84**	2d. orange, *p* 14×13½ (1.38)	75	25	5
		Wi. Wmk inverted	—	—	50·00
		a. Perf 12½ (1942)	£110	45·00	30·00
		c. Perf 14 (1942)	16·00	5·50	6·50
O124	85	2½d. chocolate and slate, *p* 13–14×13½ (26.7.38)	16·00	7·00	20·00
		a. Perf 14 (1938)	5·50	2·75	9·00
O125	**86**	3d. brown, *p* 14×13½ (1.3.38)	27·00	12·00	2·00
		Wi. Wmk inverted	—	—	20·00

O126	87	4d. black & sepia, p 14 × 13½ (8.36)	3·50	1·50	60
		a. Perf 14 (8.41)	3·00	1·25	60
		b. Perf 12½ (1941)	2·00	95	90
		c. Perf 14 × 14½ (10.42)	3·00	1·25	40
		cWi. Wmk inverted	—	—	20·00
O127	89	6d. scarlet, p 13½ × 14 (12.37) . . .	4·00	1·50	40
		Wi. Wmk inverted			
		a. Perf 12½ (1941)	4·50	2·25	1·75
		b. Perf 14½ × 14 (7.42)	2·00	95	25
O128	90	8d. chocolate, p 12½ (wmk sideways) (1942)	7·00	3·00	6·00
		a. Perf 14 × 14½ (wmk sideways) (1942)	5·50	3·00	6·00
		b. Perf 14 × 13½	†	†	£1400
O129	91	9d. red and grey-black (G.) (No. 587a), p 13½ × 14 (1.3.38) . . .	48·00	24·00	35·00
O130		9d. scarlet and black (Blk.) (No. 631), p 14 × 15 (1943).	13·00	6·50	18·00
O131	92	1s. deep green, p 14 × 13½ (2.37)	8·00	2·75	70
		a. Perf 12½ (1942)	6·50	2·25	70
O132	93	2s. olive-grn, p 13–14 × 13½ (5.37)	30·00	15·00	12·00
		a. "CAPTAIN COOK"	35·00	22·00	
		b. Perf 13½ × 14 (1939)	70·00	30·00	5·50
		ba. "CAPTAIN COOK"	75·00	42·00	
		c. Perf 12½ (1942)	55·00	22·00	20·00
		ca. "CAPTAIN COOK"	65·00	35·00	
		d. Perf 14 × 13½ (1944)	22·00	12·00	7·00
		da. "CAPTAIN COOK"	75·00	42·00	
O133	F 6	5s. green, C, p 14 (3.43)	22·00	8·00	4·25
		Wi. Wmk inverted (2.8.50)	22·00	8·00	4·25
		a. Perf 14 × 13½, Yellow-green, O (10.61)	15·00	7·50	11·00
		Set of 14	£140	70·00	80·00

The opt on No. O127a was sometimes applied at the top of the stamp, instead of always at the bottom, as on No. O127.
See notes on perforations after No. 590b.

1938–51. Nos. 603 etc., optd with Type O 4.

O134	108	½d. green (1.3.38)	7·00	2·50	60
O135		½d. brown-orange (1946)	1·25	65	80
O136		1d. scarlet (1.7.38)	7·00	2·50	15
O137		1d. green (10.7.41)	55	20	5
O138	108a	1½d. purple-brown (26.7.38)	55·00	22·00	18·00
O139		1½d. scarlet (2.4.51)	6·00	2·00	90
O140		3d. blue (16.10.41)	1·25	45	5
		Set of 7	70·00	27·00	18·00

1940 (2 Jan–8 Mar). Centennial. Nos. 613, etc., optd with Type O 5.

O141		½d. blue-green (R.)	40	20	35
		a. "ff" joined, as Type O 4	26·00	16·00	25·00
O142		1d. chocolate and scarlet	2·00	65	5
		a. "ff" joined, as Type O 4	28·00	16·00	25·00
O143		1½d. light blue and mauve	1·00	50	2·00
O144		2d. blue-green and chocolate	2·00	80	10
		a. "ff" joined, as Type O 4	28·00	16·00	25·00
O145		2½d. blue-green and ultramarine	1·75	1·00	2·25
		a. "ff" joined, as Type O 4	28·00	16·00	27·00
O146		3d. purple and carmine (R.)	4·50	2·25	80
		a. "ff" joined, as Type O 4	26·00	16·00	25·00
O147		4d. chocolate and lake	27·00	10·00	2·00
		a. "ff" joined, as Type O4	50·00	28·00	30·00
O148		6d. emerald-green and violet	16·00	7·00	2·00
		a. "ff" joined, as Type O 4	40·00	24·00	30·00
O149		8d. black and red (8.3)	12·00	5·00	12·00
		a. "ff" joined, as Type O 4	40·00	24·00	40·00
O150		9d. olive-green and vermilion	6·00	3·50	7·00
O151		1s. sage-green and deep green	27·00	12·00	4·00
		Set of 11	90·00	38·00	30·00

1947–49. Nos. 680, etc., optd with Type O 4.

O152	108a	2d. orange	50	25	5
O153		4d. bright purple	2·00	1·00	50
O154		6d. carmine	5·50	2·25	55
O155		8d. violet	8·00	4·00	5·50
O156		9d. purple-brown	9·00	4·50	6·50
O157	144	1s. red-brown and carmine (wmk upright) (Plate 1) . . .	8·00	4·00	85
		a. Wmk sideways (Plate 1) (1949)	8·00	4·00	2·50
		aWi. Wmk sideways inverted	25·00	15·00	
		b. Wmk upright (Plate 2)	15·00	8·00	9·00
		bWi. Wmk inverted	42·00	28·00	20·00
O158		2s. brown-orange and green (wmk sideways) (Plate I) . .	15·00	7·50	9·00
		a. Wmk upright (Plate 1)	20·00	10·50	14·00
		Set of 7	42·00	21·00	21·00

    6d

O 6   (O 7)
Queen Elizabeth II

(Des J. Berry. Recess B.W.)

1954 (1 Mar)–**63.** W 98. P 14 × 13½.

O159	O 6	1d. orange		30	15
		Eo. White opaque paper (8.7.59)		30	20
O160		1½d. brown-lake		45	2·50
O161		2d. bluish green		30	15
		Eo. White opaque paper (11.12.58) . . .		50	20
O162		2½d. olive (White opaque paper) (1.3.63)		3·00	1·50
O163		3d. vermilion		30	10
		Eo. White opaque paper (1960)		40	10
		Eoi. Wmk inverted		7·50	3·00
O164		4d. blue		50	15
		Ea. Printed on gummed side		£110	
		Eo. White opaque paper (1.9.61)		80	50
O165		9d. carmine		70	60
O166		1s. purple		50	10
		Eo. White opaque paper (2.10.61) . . .		2·00	75
O167		3s. slate (White opaque paper) (1.3.63)		30·00	45·00
		Set of 9		32·00	45·00

See note re white opaque paper after No. 736.

1959 (1 Oct). No. O160 surch with Type O 7.

O168	O 6	6d. on 1½d. brown-lake		20	85

1961 (1 Sept). No. O161 surch as Type O 7.

O169	O 6	2½d. on 2d. bluish green		35	1·00

Owing to the greater use of franking machines by Government Departments, the use of official stamps was discontinued on 31 March 1965, but they remained on sale at the G.P.O. until 31 December 1965.

OFFICIAL STAMP BOOKLET

1908 (1 July). White card cover. Interleaved with wax paper.

OB1	10s. booklet. One hundred and twenty 1d. in panes of 6 (No. O 60a)	£600

PROVISIONALS ISSUED AT REEFTON AND USED BY THE POLICE DEPARTMENT

1907 (Jan). Current stamps of 1906, overwritten "Official," in red ink, and marked "Greymouth—PAID—3" inside a circular postmark stamp. P 14.

P1	23	½d. green	£425	£600
P2	40	1d. carmine	£425	£650
P3	38a	2d. purple	£650	£800
P4	28	3d. bistre	£550	£700
P5	31	6d. pink	£750	£850
P6	34	1s. orange-red	£1000	£1200
P7	35	2s. green	—	£5000

THE WORLD CENTRE FOR
FINE STAMPS IS 399 STRAND

LIFE INSURANCE DEPARTMENT

PRICES
Edward VII and George V issues (1902–1937)

First column = Mounted Mint
Second column = Used

L 1   Lighthouse   L 2

(Des W. B. Hudson and J. F. Rogers; eng A. E. Cousins. Typo Govt Printing Office, Wellington)

1891 (2 Jan)–**98.   A. W 12**c. P 12 × 11½.

L 1	L 1	½d. bright purple	55·00	7·00
L 2		1d. blue	55·00	9·00
		Wi. Wmk inverted and reversed	—	30·00
		a. Wmk **12**b	90·00	18·00
L 3		2d. brown-red	85·00	4·00
		a. Wmk **12**b	95·00	9·00
L 4		3d. deep brown	£190	20·00
L 5		6d. green	£275	60·00
L 6		1s. rose	£650	£125
		Set of 6	£1100	£200

B.   W 12b (1893–98). (a) P 10 (1893)

L 7	L 1	½d. bright purple	55·00	5·00
L 8		1d. blue	55·00	1·25
L 9		2d. brown-red	70·00	3·75
		Set of 3	£160	9·00

(b) Perf compound of 11 and 10 (1896)

L 9a	L 1	½d. bright purple	90·00	24·00
L 9b		1d. blue	55·00	10·00
		Set of 2	£140	32·00

(c) Perf compound of 10 and 11 (1897)

L10	L 1	½d. bright purple	—	60·00
L11		1d. blue		

(d) Mixed perfs 10 and 11 (1897)

L12	L 1	2d. brown-red	£550	£550

(e) P 11 (1897–98)

L13	L 1	½d. bright purple	55·00	2·50
		a. Thin coarse toned paper (1898)	55·00	4·50
L14		1d. blue	55·00	75
		a. Thin coarse toned paper (1898)	60·00	90
		Wi. Wmk inverted and reversed	£100	18·00
L15		2d. brown-red	65·00	2·75
		a. Chocolate	95·00	20·00
		b. Thin coarse toned paper (1898)	65·00	3·00
		Set of 3	£160	5·50

1902–04.   W 43 (sideways). (a) P 11.

L16	L 1	½d. bright purple (1903)	55·00	2·75
		Wi. Wmk sideways inverted	55·00	2·75
L17		1d. blue (1902)	55·00	90
		Wi. Wmk sideways inverted	55·00	90
L18		2d. brown-red (1904)	75·00	3·75
		Wi. Wmk sideways inverted	75·00	3·75
		Set of 3	£170	6·50

(b) Perf compound of 11 and 14

L19	L 1	½d. bright purple (1903)	£1000	
L20		1d. blue (1904)	90·00	10·00
		Wi. Wmk sideways inverted	90·00	10·00

Nos. L16/17 and L20 are known without watermark from the margins of the sheet.

1905–6.   Redrawn, with "V.R." omitted. W **43** (sideways). (a) P 11.

L21	L 2	2d. brown-red (12.05)	£1200	80·00
		Wi. Wmk sideways inverted	£1200	80·00

(b) P 14

L22	L 2	1d. blue (1906)	£140	27·00
		Wi. Wmk sideways inverted	£140	27·00

(c) Perf compound of 11 and 14

L23	L 2	1d. blue (wmk sideways inverted) (1906)	£325	£150
		a. Mixed perfs	—	£350

1913 (2 Jan)–**37.**   New values and colours. W **43**.

(a) "De La Rue paper". P 14 × 15

L24	L 2	½d. green	6·00	70
		a. Yellow-green	6·00	70
L25		1d. carmine	6·00	60
		a. Carmine-pink	11·00	90
L26		1½d. black (1917)	28·00	5·50
L27		1½d. chestnut-brown (1919)	1·25	2·25
L28		2d. bright purple	32·00	15·00
		Wi. Wmk inverted	—	40·00
L29		2d. yellow (1920)	3·50	2·00
L30		3d. yellow-brown	32·00	22·00
L31		6d. carmine-pink	22·00	17·00
		Set of 8	£120	55·00

(b) "Cowan" paper. (i) P 14 × 15

L31a	L 2	½d. yellow-green (1925)	12·00	3·00
L31b		1d. carmine-pink (1925)	17·00	3·00
		Wi. Wmk inverted	24·00	5·00
		Set of 2	29·00	6·00

(ii) P 14

L32	L 2	½d. yellow-green (1926)	5·50	1·50
		Wi. Wmk inverted	—	8·00
L33		1d. scarlet (1931)	1·50	1·50
		Wi. Wmk inverted	10·00	2·50
L34		2d. yellow	3·25	3·00
		Wi. Wmk inverted	20·00	17·00
L35		3d. brown-lake (1931)	16·00	20·00
L36		6d. pink (1925)	17·00	18·00
		Set of 5	45·00	40·00

(c) "Wiggins Teape" paper. P 14 × 15

L36a	L 2	½d. yellow-green (3.37)	2·25	4·00
L36b		1d. scarlet (3.37)	6·50	1·50
L36c		6d. pink (7.37)	22·00	26·00
		Set of 3	28·00	28·00

For descriptions of the various types of paper, see after No. 518.
In the 1½d. the word "POSTAGE" is in both the side-labels instead of at left only.

PRICES
George VI issues (1937–1952)

First column = Unmounted Mint
Second column = Mounted Mint
Third column = Used

1944–47.   W **98**. P 14 × 15.

L37	L 2	½d. yellow-green (7.47)	1·50	60	2·75
L38		1d. scarlet (6.44)	1·50	75	1·25
L39		2d. yellow (1946)	3·50	1·50	2·75
L40		3d. brown-lake (10.46)	9·00	4·75	8·00
L41		6d. pink (7.47)	7·00	3·50	13·00
		Set of 5	20·00	10·00	25·00

L 3 Castlepoint Lighthouse   L 4 Taiaroa Lighthouse

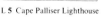   

L 5 Cape Palliser Lighthouse   L 6 Cape Campbell Lighthouse

L 7 Eddystone
Lighthouse

L 8 Stephens Island
Lighthouse

L 13 Moeraki Point
Lighthouse

L 15 Baring Head
Lighthouse

L 9 The Brothers Lighthouse

L 10 Cape Brett
Lighthouse

L 14 Puysegur Point Lighthouse

(L 16)

(Des J. Berry. Recess B.W.)

1947 (1 Aug)–**65.** *W* **98** *(sideways on* 1*d.,* 2*d.,* 2½*d.).* P 13½.

L42	L **3**	½d. grey-green and orange-red ..	80	40	70
L43	L **4**	1d. olive-green and pale blue ...	50	30	30
L44	L **5**	2d. deep blue and grey-black ...	70	40	25
L45	L **6**	2½d. black and bright blue *(white opaque paper)* (4.11.63)	6·50	3·25	8·50
L46	L **7**	3d. mauve and pale blue	1·75	80	45
L47	L **8**	4d. brown and yellow-orange ...	1·75	80	50
		a. Wmk sideways *(white opaque paper)* (13.10.65)	5·00	2·50	12·00
L48	L **9**	6d. chocolate and blue	1·75	80	1·50
L49	L **10**	1s. red-brown and blue	1·75	80	1·25
		Set of 8	14·00	6·75	12·00

(Des J. Berry. Litho B.W.)

1969 (27 Mar)–**77.** *Types* L **13**·**14** *and similar designs. No wmk. Chalk-surfaced paper* (8, 10 *c.), ordinary paper (others).* P 14 (8, 10 *c.), or* 13½ *(others).*

L56		½ c. greenish yellow, red and deep blue	1·75	2·00
L57		2½ c. ultramarine, green and pale buff	1·00	1·25
L58		3 c. reddish brown and yellow	75	75
		a. Chalk-surfaced paper (16.6.77)	65	1·25
L59		4 c. lt new blue, yellowish grn & apple-grn ..	1·00	1·00
		a. Chalk-surfaced paper (16.6.77)	65	1·25
L60		8 c. multicoloured (17.11.76)	45	1·25
L61		10 c. multicoloured (17.11.76)	45	1·25
L62		15 c. black, light yellow and ultramarine	60	1·50
		a. Perf 14. Chalk-surfaced paper (24.12.76) .	1·25	1·50
		Set of 7	4·75	8·00

Designs: *Horiz*—4 c. Cape Egmont Lighthouse. *Vert*—3 c. Baring Head Lighthouse; 8 c. East Cape; 10 c. Farewell Spit; 15 c. Dog Island Lighthouse.

1978 (8 Mar). *No.* L57 *surch with Type* L **16**. *Chalky paper.*

L63	L **14**	25 c. on 2½ c. ultramarine, grn & buff	75	1·00

2ᶜ

(L 11)

10ᶜ

(L 12)

1967 (10 July)–**68.** *Decimal currency. Stamps of* 1947–65, *surch as Type* L **12** *or* L **11** (2 c.).

L50	L **4**	1 c. on 1d. (No. L43)	1·75	4·00
		a. Wmk upright *(white opaque paper)* (10.5.68)	1·60	3·25
L51	L **6**	2 c. on 2½d. (No. L45)	3·50	7·00
L52	L **7**	2½ c. on 3d. (No. L46)	1·75	4·00
		a. Wmk sideways *(white opaque paper)* (4.68?)	2·50	4·25
L53	L **8**	3 c. on 4d. (No. L47a)	3·50	4·75
L54	L **9**	5 c. on 1s. (No. L48)	2·00	5·00
		Eo. White opaque paper	5·00	7·50
L55	L **10**	10 c. on 1s. (No. L49)	3·00	9·50
		a. Wmk sideways *(white opaque paper)*	1·25	4·00
		Set of 6	12·00	25·00

See note *re* white opaque paper below No. L736.

L 17

(Des A. G. Mitchell. Litho Harrison)

1981 (3 June). P 14½.

L64	L **17**	5 c. multicoloured	5	5
L65		10 c. multicoloured	5	8
L66		20 c. multicoloured	12	15
L67		30 c. multicoloured	20	25
L68		40 c. multicoloured	25	30
L69		50 c. multicoloured	30	35
		Set of 6	85	1·00
		First Day Cover		1·90

POSTAL FISCAL STAMPS

As from 1 April 1882 fiscal stamps were authorised for postal use and conversely postage stamps became valid for fiscal use. Stamps in the designs of 1867 with "STAMP DUTY" above the Queen's head were withdrawn and although some passed through the mail quite legitimately they were mainly "philatelic" and we no longer list them. The issue which was specifically authorised in 1882 was the one which had originally been put on sale for fiscal use in 1880.

Although all fiscal stamps were legally valid for postage only values between 2s. and £1 were stocked at ordinary post offices. Other values could only be obtained by request from the G.P.O., Wellington or from offices of the Stamp Duties Department. Later the Arms types above £1 could also be obtained from the head office in Auckland, Christchurch, Dunedin and also a branch post office at Christchurch North where there was a local demand for them.

It seems sensible to list under Postal Fiscals the Queen Victoria stamps up to the £1 value and the Arms types up to the £5 because by 1931 the higher values were genuinely needed for postal purposes. Even the £10 was occasionally used on insured airmail parcels.

Although 2s. and 5s. values were included in the 1898 pictorial issue, it was the general practice for the Postal Department to limit the postage issues to 1s. until 1926 when the 2s. and 3s. appeared. These were then dropped from the fiscal issues and when in turn the 5s. and 10s. were introduced in 1953 and the £1 in 1960 no further printings of these values occurred in the fiscal series.

FORGED POSTMARKS. Our prices are for stamps with genuine postal cancellations. Beware of forged postmarks on stamps from which fiscal cancellations have been cleaned off.

Many small post offices acted as agents for government departments and it was the practice to use ordinary postal date-stamps on stamps used fiscally, so that when they are removed from documents they are indistinguishable from postally used specimens unless impressed with the embossed seal of the Stamp Duties Department.

Date-stamps very similar to postal date-stamps were sometimes supplied to offices of the Stamp Duties Department and it is not clear when this practice ceased. Prior to the Arms types the only sure proof of the postal use of off-cover fiscal stamps is when they bear a distinctive duplex, registered or parcel post cancellation, but beware of forgeries of the first two.

PRICES

Victoria to George V issues (1882–1936)

First column = Mounted Mint

Second column = Used

F 1   F 2   F 3

(Die eng W. R. Bock. Typo Govt Ptg Office)

1882 (Feb). *W* **12***a. P* 12 × 11½.

F1	**F 1**	1d. lilac	....	£160	£300
F2		1d. blue	....	75·00	25·00

The 1d. fiscal was specifically authorised for postal use in February 1882 owing to a shortage of the 1d. Type **5** and pending the introduction of the 1d. Type **14** on 1 April.

The 1d. lilac had been replaced by the 1d. blue in 1878 but postally used copies with 1882 duplex postmarks are known although most postally used examples are dated from 1890 and these must have been philatelic.

(Des and dies eng W. R. Bock. Typo Govt Ptg Office)

1882 (early). *W* **12***a. P* 12 × 11½.

F3	**F 2**	1s. grey green	....
F4	**F 3**	1s. grey-green and red	....

Copies of these are known postally used in 1882 and although not specifically authorised for postal use it is believed that their use was permitted where there was a shortage of the 1s. postage stamp.

The 2s. value Type **F 3** formerly listed is not known with 1882–83 postal date-stamps.

WMK TYPE F 5. The balance of the paper employed for the 1867 issue was used for early printings of Type **F 4** introduced in 1880 before changing over to the "N Z" and Star watermark. The values we list with this watermark are known with 1882–83 postal date-stamps. Others have later

dates and are considered to be philatelic but should they be found with 1882–83 postal dates we would be prepared to add them to the list.

In the following list the 4d., 6d., 8d. and 1s. are known with early 1882 postal date-stamps and, like Nos. F3/4, it is assumed that they were used to meet a temporary shortage of postage stamps.

F 4   F 5

The 12s. 6d. value has the head in an oval (as Type **10**), and the 15s. and £1 values have it in a broken circle (as Type **7**).

(Dies eng W. R. Bock. Typo Govt Ptg Office)

1882 (1 Apr). *Type F* **4** *and similar types. "De La Rue" paper.*

A. W 12*a* (6 *mm*). (*a*) *P* 12 (1882)

F 5		4d. orange-red (*wmk F* **5**)	....	—	£120
F 6		6d. lake-brown	....	—	£120
F 7		8d. green (*wmk F* **5**)	....		
F 8		1s. pink	....		
F 9		2s. blue	....	45·00	4·50
F10		2s. 6d. grey-brown	....	80·00	4·50
		a. Wmk F **5**			
F11		3s. mauve	....	£100	5·50
F12		4s. brown-rose	....	£100	11·00
F13		5s. green	....	£130	11·00
		a. *Yellow-green*	....	£130	11·00
F14		6s. rose	....	£140	27·00
F15		7s. ultramarine	....	£150	40·00
F16		7s. 6d. bronze-grey	....	£150	45·00
F17		8s. deep blue	....	£150	40·00
F18		9s. orange	....	£140	45·00
F19		10s. brown-red	....	£130	14·00
		a. Wmk F **5**			
F20		15s. green	....	£170	45·00
F21		£1 rose-pink	....	£170	45·00

(*b***) *P* 12½ (1886)**

F22		2s. blue	....	45·00	4·50
F23		2s. 6d. grey-brown	....	80·00	4·50
F24		3s. mauve	....	£100	5·50
F25		4s. purple-claret	....	£100	11·00
		a. *Brown-rose*	....	£100	11·00
F26		5s. green	....	£130	11·00
		a. *Yellow-green*	....	£130	11·00
F27		6s. rose	....	£140	27·00
F28		7s. ultramarine	....	£150	40·00
F29		8s. deep blue	....	£150	40·00
F30		9s. orange	....	£140	45·00
F31		10s. brown-red	....	£130	14·00
F32		15s. green	....	£170	45·00
F33		£1 rose-pink	....	£170	45·00

B. W 12*b* (7 *mm*). *P* 12½ (1888)

F34		2s. blue	....	45·00	4·50
F35		2s. 6d. grey-brown	....	80·00	4·50
F36		3s. mauve	....	£100	5·50
F37		4s. brown-rose	....	£100	11·00
		a. *Brown-red*	....	£100	11·00
F38		5s. green	....	£130	11·00
		a. *Yellow-green*	....	£130	11·00
F39		6s. rose	....	£140	27·00
F40		7s. ultramarine	....	£150	40·00
F41		7s. 6d. bronze-grey	....	£150	45·00
F42		8s. deep blue	....	£150	40·00
F43		9s. orange	....	£140	45·00
F44		10s. brown-red	....	£130	12·00
		a. *Maroon*	....	£130	12·00
F45		£1 pink	....	£170	45·00

C. W 12*c* (4 *mm*). *P* 12½ (1890)

F46		2s. blue	....	70·00	11·00
F47		3s. mauve	....	£140	27·00
F48		4s. brown-red	....	£110	15·00
F49		5s. green	....	£130	12·00

F50	6s. rose	£150	27·00
F51	7s. ultramarine	£160	40·00
F52	8s. deep blue	£160	40·00
F53	9s. orange	£140	45·00
F54	10s. brown-red	£130	13·00
F55	15s. green	£225	60·00

D. *Continuation of W* **12***b. P* 11 (1895–1901)

F56	2s. blue		27·00	5·50
F57	2s. 6d. grey-brown		80·00	4·50
	a. Inscr "COUNTERPART" (1901)*	£150	£110	
F58	3s. mauve		£100	5·50
F59	4s. brown-red		£100	10·00
F60	5s. yellow-green		£130	12·00
F61	6s. rose		£140	27·00
F62	7s. pale blue		£150	40·00
F63	7s. 6d. bronze-grey		£150	45·00
F64	8s. deep blue		£150	40·00
F65	9s. orange		£140	45·00
	a. Imperf between (horiz pair)			
F66	10s. brown-red		£130	12·00
	a. Maroon		£130	45·00
F67	15s. green		£170	45·00
F68	£1 rose-pink		£170	45·00

*The plate normally printed in yellow and inscribed "COUNTERPART" just above the bottom value panel, was for use on the counterparts of documents but was issued in error in the colour of the normal fiscal stamp and accepted for use.

E. W **43** (*sideways*)
(i) *Unsurfaced "Cowan" paper.* (*a*) *P* 11 (1903)

F69	2s. 6d. grey-brown	80·00	4·50
F70	3s. mauve	£100	5·50
F71	4s. orange-red	£100	10·00
F72	6s. rose	£140	27·00
F73	7s. pale blue	£150	40·00
F74	8s. deep blue	£140	40·00
F75	10s. brown-red	£130	14·00
	a. Maroon	£130	14·00
F76	15s. green	£170	45·00
F77	£1 rose-pink	£170	45·00

(*b*) *P* 14 (1906)

F78	2s. 6d. grey-brown	80·00	4·50
F79	3s. mauve	£100	5·50
F80	4s. orange-red	£100	7·50
F81	5s. yellow-green	70·00	7·50
F82	6s. rose	£140	27·00
F83	7s. pale blue	£150	40·00
F84	7s. 6d. bronze-grey	£150	45·00
F85	8s. deep blue	£150	40·00
F86	9s orange	£140	45·00
F87	10s. maroon	£130	12·00
F88	15s. green	£170	45·00
F89	£1 rose-pink	£170	45·00

(*c*) *P* 14½ × 14, *comb* (*clean-cut*) (1907)

F90	2s. blue	25·00	4·00
F91	2s. 6d. grey-brown	80·00	4·50
F92	3s. mauve	£100	5·50
F93	4s. orange-red	90·00	7·50
F94	6s. rose	£140	27·00
F95	10s. maroon	£130	12·00
F96	15s. green	£170	45·00
F97	£1 rose-pink	£170	45·00

(ii) *Chalk-surfaced "De La Rue" paper.* (*a*) *P* 14 (1913)

F 98	2s. blue	25·00	4·00
F 99	2s. 6d grey-brown	27·00	4·50
F100	3s. purple	70·00	5·50
F101	4s. orange-red	70·00	7·00
F102	5s. yellow-green	70·00	7·50
F103	6s. rose	£100	14·00
F104	7s. pale blue	£100	15·00
F105	7s. 6d. bronze-grey	£150	45·00
F106	8s. deep blue	£130	24·00
F107	9s. orange	£140	45·00
F108	10s. maroon	£130	12·00
F109	15s. green	£170	40·00
F110	£1 rose-carmine	£170	45·00

(*b*) *P* 14½ × 14, *comb* (1913–21)

F111	2s. deep blue	25·00	4·00
F112	2s. 6d. grey-brown	27·00	4·50
F113	3s. purple	70·00	5·50
F114	4s. orange-red	70·00	7·00
F115	5s. yellow-green	70·00	7·50
F116	6s. rose	£100	14·00
F117	7s. pale blue	£100	15·00
F118	8s. deep blue	£130	24·00

F119	9s. orange	£130	45·00
F120	10s. maroon	£130	12·00
F121	12s. 6d. deep plum (1921)	£1700	£450
F122	15s. green	£170	40·00
F123	£1 rose-carmine	£170	45·00

The "De La Rue" paper has a smooth finish and has toned gum which is strongly resistant to soaking.

(ii) *Chalk-surfaced "Jones" paper. P* 14½ × 14, *comb* (1924)

F124	2s. deep blue	25·00	4·00
F125	2s. 6d. deep grey-brown	27·00	4·50
F126	3s. purple	70·00	5·50
F127	5s. yellow-green	70·00	7·50
F128	10s. brown-red	£130	12·00
F129	12s. deep purple	£1700	£450
F130	15s. green	£170	40·00

The "Jones" paper has a coarser texture, is poorly surfaced and the ink tends to peel. The outline of the watermark commonly shows on the surface of the stamp. The gum is colourless or only slightly toned and washes off readily.

(iv) *Thick, opaque, chalk-surfaced "Cowan" paper. P* 14½ × 14, *comb* (1925–30)

F131	2s. blue	25·00	4·00
F132	2s. 6d. deep grey-brown	27·00	4·50
F133	3s. mauve	£100	10·00
F134	4s. orange-red	70·00	7·00
F135	5s. yellow-green	70·00	7·50
F136	6s. rose	£100	14·00
F137	7s. pale blue	£100	15·00
F138	8s. deep blue	£130	24·00
	a. Error. Blue (as 2s.) (1930)		
F139	10s. brown-red	£130	12·00
F140	12s. 6d. blackish purple	£1700	£450
F141	15s. green	£170	40·00
F142	£1 rose-pink	£170	45·00

The "Cowan" paper is white and opaque and the watermark, which is usually smaller than in the "Jones" paper, is often barely visible.

(v) *Thin, hard, chalk-surfaced "Wiggins Teape" paper. P* 14½ × 14, *comb* (1926)

F143	4s. orange-red	75·00	7·00
F144	£1 rose-pink	£180	80·00

The "Wiggins Teape" paper has a vertical mesh with narrow watermark, whereas other chalk-surfaced papers with this perforation have a horizontal mesh and wider watermark.

F 6   (F 7)

(Des H. L. Richardson. Typo Govt Ptg Office)

1931–40. *As Type* F **6** (*various frames*). W **43.** *P* 14.

(i) *Thick, opaque, chalk-surfaced "Cowan" paper, with horizontal mesh* (1931–35)

F145	1s. 3d. lemon (4.31)	10·00	28·00
F146	1s. 3d. orange-yellow	4·00	2·50
F147	2s. 6d. deep brown	12·00	1·75
F148	4s. red	14·00	2·25
F149	5s. green	15·00	3·50
F150	6s. carmine-rose	22·00	7·00
F151	7s. blue	25·00	8·50
F152	7s. 6d. olive-grey	55·00	48·00
F153	8s. slate-violet	28·00	18·00
F154	9s. brown-orange	30·00	20·00
F155	10s. carmine-lake	24·00	5·00
F156	12s. 6d. deep plum (9.35)	£140	£140
F157	15s. sage-green	60·00	17·00
F158	£1 pink	60·00	15·00
F159	25s. greenish blue	£200	£275
F160	30s. brown (1935)	£250	£120
F161	35s. orange-yellow	£1900	£1900
F162	£2 bright purple	£300	50·00
F163	£2 10s. red	£175	£200
F164	£3 green	£300	£150
F165	£3 10s. rose (1935)	£1200	£950
F166	£4 light blue (1935)	£300	£120
F167	£4 10s. deep olive-grey (1935)	£1300	£1000
F168	£5 indigo-blue	£325	90·00

(ii) Thin, hard "Wiggins Teape" paper with vertical mesh (1936–40)

(a) Chalk-surfaced (1936–39)

F169	1s. 3d. pale orange-yellow	3·50	60
F170	2s. 6d. dull brown	16·00	1·25
F171	4s. pale red-brown	20·00	2·00
F172	5s. green	22·00	4·25
F173	6s. carmine-rose	25·00	8·00
F174	7s. pale blue	27·00	14·00
F175	8s. slate-violet	38·00	28·00
F176	9s. brown-orange	45·00	28·00
F177	10s. pale carmine-lake	38·00	5·50
F178	15s. sage-green	70·00	20·00
F179	£1 pink	55·00	17·00
F180	30s. brown (1.39)	£150	95·00
F181	35s. orange-yellow	£2250	£2000
F182	£2 bright purple (1937)	£300	60·00
F183	£3 green (1937)	£300	£150
F184	£5 indigo-blue (1937)	£375	£110

(b) Unsurfaced (1940)

F185	7s. 6d. olive-grey	75·00	90·00

PRICES
George VI issues (1939–1952)

First column = Unmounted Mint
Second column = Mounted Mint
Third column = Used

1939. *No.* F161 *surch with Type* F **7**.

F186	35/- on 35s. orange-yellow	£300	£200	£200

Because the 35s. orange-yellow could so easily be confused with the 1s. 3d. in the same colour it was surcharged.

1940 (June). *New values surch as Type* F **7**. *W* **43**. *"Wiggins Teape" chalk-surfaced paper. P* 14.

F187	3/6 on 3s. 6d. grey-green	22·00	9·50	8·50
F188	5/6 on 5s. 6d. lilac	38·00	15·00	23·00
F189	11/- on 11s. yellow	£100	50·00	65·00
F190	22/- on 22s. scarlet	£225	£120	£160
	Set of 4	£325	£170	£225

These values were primarily needed for fiscal use.

1940–58. *As Type* F **6** *(various frames). W* **98**.

(i) *P* 14. *"Wiggins Teape" chalk-surfaced paper with vertical mesh*
(1940–56)

F191	1s. 3d. orange-yellow	3·50	1·60	30
F192	1s. 3d. yellow and black (*wmk inverted*) (14.6.55)	1·00	50	15
	Wi. Wmk upright (9.9.55)	25·00	10·00	25·00
	b. Error. Yellow and blue (wmk inverted) (7.56)	3·00	1·50	5·50
F193	2s. 6d. deep brown	5·00	2·25	15
	Wi. Wmk inverted (3.49)	5·00	2·25	15
F194	4s. red-brown	7·50	3·50	25
	Wi. Wmk inverted (3.49)	12·00	5·50	30
F195	5s. green	12·00	5·50	50
	Wi. Wmk inverted (1.5.50)	17·00	7·50	60
F196	6s. carmine-rose	22·00	11·00	2·50
	Wi. Wmk inverted (1948)	22·00	11·00	2·50
F197	7s. pale blue	25·00	12·00	4·25
F198	7s. 6d. olive-grey (*wmk inverted*) (21.12.50)	48·00	25·00	45·00
F199	8s. slate-violet	32·00	15·00	13·00
	Wi. Wmk inverted (6.12.50)	38·00	17·00	12·00
F200	9s. brown-orange (1.46)	24·00	10·00	18·00
	Wi. Wmk inverted (9.1.51)	30·00	12·00	24·00
F201	10s. carmine-lake	20·00	8·50	2·25
	Wi. Wmk inverted (4.50)	23·00	10·00	2·50
F202	15s. sage-green	38·00	19·00	17·00
	Wi. Wmk inverted (8.12.50)	45·00	22·00	25·00
F203	£1 pink	24·00	11·00	3·50
	Wi. Wmk inverted (1.2.50)	35·00	17·00	12·00
F204	25s. greenish blue (1946)	£275	£160	£300
	Wi. Wmk inverted (7.53)	£275	£160	£350
F205	30s. brown (1946)	£200	£110	£110
	Wi. Wmk inverted (9.49)	£180	95·00	95·00
F206	£2 bright purple (1946)	65·00	32·00	18·00
	Wi. Wmk inverted (17.6.52)	60·00	30·00	18·00
F207	£2 10s. red (*wmk inverted*) (9.8.51)	£225	£130	£190
F208	£3 green (1946)	80·00	40·00	45·00
	Wi. Wmk inverted (17.6.52)	75·00	38·00	35·00

F209	£3 10s. rose (11.48)	£1200	£750	£1000
	Wi. Wmk inverted (5.52)	£1200	£750	£1000
F210	£4 lt. blue (*wmk inverted*) (12.5.52)	£100	55·00	48·00
F211	£5 indigo-blue	£150	80·00	45·00
	Wi. Wmk inverted (11.9.50)	£130	65·00	45·00
	Set of 21	£2250	£1200	£1600

I.

II.

3s. 6d.

Type I. Broad serifed capitals.

Type II. Taller capitals, without serifs.

Surcharged as Type F **7**

F212	3/6 on 3s. 6d. grey-green (I) (1942)	18·00	7·50	5·00
	Wi. Wmk inverted (12.10.50)	18·00	7·50	5·00
F213	3/6 on 3s. 6d. grey-green (II) (6.53)	15·00	12·00	27·00
	Wi. Wmk inverted (6.53)	28·00	14·00	35·00
F214	5/6 on 5s. 6d. lilac (1944)	22·00	11·00	9·00
	Wi. Wmk inverted (13.9.50)	22·00	11·00	9·00
F215	11/- on 11s. yellow (1942)	55·00	28·00	40·00
F216	22/- on 22s. scarlet (1954)	£170	95·00	£120
	Wi. Wmk inverted (1.3.50)	£170	95·00	£120
	Set of 5	£250	£140	£180

(ii) *P* 14 × 13½. *"Wiggins Teape" unsurfaced paper with horizontal mesh*
(1956–58)

F217	1s. 3d. yellow and black (11.56)	1·50	70	55
	Wi. Wmk inverted	3·75	1·90	2·50
F218	£1 pink (20.10.58)	32·00	16·00	20·00
	Set of 2	32·00	16·00	20·00

We do not list values above £5 as they were mainly employed for revenue purposes.

No. F192b is an error, as no colour change was intended.

The inverted watermarks on this issue came about through the supply of inferior paper during 1949–53 as for technical reasons it was necessary to feed the paper into the machine in a certain way which resulted in whole printings with the watermark inverted for most values.

PRICES
Elizabeth II issues (from 1953)

First column = Unmounted Mint
Second column = Used

F **8**

1967 (10 July)–**84**. *Decimal currency. W* **98** *(sideways inverted). Unsurfaced paper. P* 14 *(line).*

F219	F **8**	$4 deep reddish violet	10·00	7·00
		Ea. Comb perf, wmk sideways (17.9.68)	2·00	75
		Wai. Wmk sideways inverted (8.7.84)	13·00	
F220		$6 emerald	12·00	9·00
		Ea. Comb perf, wmk sideways (17.9.68)	3·00	1·50
		Wai. Wmk sideways inverted. *Yellowish green* (8.7.84)	16·00	
F221		$8 light greenish blue	17·00	14·00
		Ea. Comb perf, wmk sideways (20.6.68)	4·00	3·50
F222		$10 deep ultramarine	25·00	20·00
		Ea. Comb perf, wmk sideways (20.6.68)	5·00	4·00
		Wai. Wmk sideways inverted. *Royal Blue* (12.7.84)	25·00	
		Set of 4	12·50	9·00

1986 (Apr). *As Nos.* F220/2 *but without wmk. Chalk-surfaced paper.*

F223	F **8**	$6 bright green	4·00	4·50
F224		$8 light greenish blue	6·50	7·50
F225		$10 deep ultramarine	8·00	9·00
		Set of 3	17·00	19·00

No further printings were made of the $4 after the introduction of a $5 postage stamp in 1981.

ANTARCTIC EXPEDITIONS

VICTORIA LAND

These issues were made under authority of the New Zealand Postal Department and, while not strictly necessary, they actually franked correspondence to New Zealand. They were sold to the public at a premium.

1908 (15 Jan). *Shackleton Expedition. T* **42** *of New Zealand (p* 14), *optd* "King Edward VII Land", *in two lines, reading up, by Coulls, Culling and Co., Wellington.*
A1   1d. rose-carmine (No. 356 Royle) (G.) . . . .   £400   35·00
     a. Opt double . . . .   —   £1500
A1b 1d. rose-carmine (No. 352c Waterlow) (G.) £1300   £800
Nos. A1/1b were used on board the expedition ship, *Nimrod*, and at the Cape Royds base in McMurdo Sound. Due to adverse conditions Shackleton landed in Victoria Land, rather than King Edward VII Land the intended destination.

1911 (9 Feb)–**13**. *Scott Expedition. Stamps of New Zealand optd* "VICTORIA LAND.", *in two lines by Govt Printer, Wellington.*
A2 **50** ½d. deep green (No. 387aa) (18.1.13) £500   £500
A3 **52** 1d. carmine (No. 405) . . . .   45·00   70·00
          a. No stop after "LAND" £375   £550
Nos. A2/3 were used at the Cape Evans base on McMurdo Sound or on the *Terra Nova*.

Cook Islands

1892   12 Pence   = 1 Shilling
20 Shillings = 1 Pound
1967   100 Cents   = 1 New Zealand Dollar

A group of islands in the S. Pacific under New Zealand control until it became a territory in free association with New Zealand in 1965.

PRICES FOR STAMPS ON COVER TO 1945

Nos. 1/4   *from* × 5
Nos. 5/74   *from* × 4
Nos. 75/145 *from* × 3

PRICES

Victoria to George V issues (1892–1936)

First column = Mounted Mint
Second column = Used

BRITISH PROTECTORATE

1

2 Queen Makea Takau

3 White Tern or Torea

(Des F. Moss. Typo Govt Printing Office, Wellington)

1892 (19 Apr). *No wmk. P* 12½.

A. *Toned paper.* B. *White paper.*

			A.		B.	
1	**1**	1d. black	26·00	30·00	26·00	30·00
		a. Imperf between (vert pair)	£8500	—		†
2		1½d. mauve	38·00	38·00	38·00	38·00
		a. Imperf (pair)	—	£9000		—
3		2½d. blue	38·00	38·00	38·00	38·00
4		10d. carmine	£140	£130	£160	£130
		Set of 4	£200	£200	£225	£200

(Eng A. E. Cousins. Typo Govt Printing Office, Wellington)

1893 (28 July)**–1900**. *W* **12**b *of New Zealand (N Z and Star wide apart)* (*sideways on T* **3**). (*a*) *P* 12 × 11½.

5	**2**	1d. brown	24·00	30·00
6		1d. blue (3.4.94)	6·00	2·50
		a. Perf 12 × 11½ and 12½ mixed	—	£300
7		1½d. mauve	6·00	6·00
8		2½d. rose	23·00	23·00
		a. Rose-carmine	55·00	55·00
		ab. Perf 12 × 11½ and 12½ mixed	—	—
9		5d. olive-black	12·00	13·00
10		10d. green	48·00	48·00
		Set of 6	£110	£110

(*b*) *P* 11 (July 1896–1900)

11	**3**	½d. blue (11.99)	3·50	4·75
12	**2**	1d. blue	3·00	4·50
13		1d. brown/cream (4.99)	5·50	12·00
		a. Wmk sideways		
14		1½d. deep lilac	4·25	6·00
		a. Deep mauve (1900)	4·25	6·00
15	**3**	2d. brown/thin toned (7.98)	5·00	6·50
		a. Deep brown (1900)	3·75	6·50
16	**2**	2½d. pale rose	30·00	38·00
		a. Deep rose (1900)	8·00	9·00
17		5d. olive-black	16·00	17·00
18	**3**	6d. purple/thin toned (7.98)	20·00	28·00
		a. Bright purple (1900)	13·00	19·00
19	**2**	10d. green	13·00	20·00
20	**3**	1s. red/thin toned (7.98)	50·00	70·00
		a. Deep carmine (1900)	38·00	48·00
		Set of 10	90·00	£130

ONE HALF PENNY

(4)

(5)

1899 (24 Apr). *No. 12 surch with T* **4** *by Govt Printer, Rarotonga.*

21	**2**	½d. on 1d. blue	32·00	42·00
		a. Surch inverted	£800	£850
		b. Surch double	£900	£750

NEW ZEALAND TERRITORY

1901 (8 Oct). *No. 13 optd with T* **5** *by Govt Printer, Rarotonga.*

22	**2**	1d. brown	£130	£125
		a. Crown inverted	£1300	£1300
		c. Optd with crown twice	£1400	£1500

1902. *No wmk. P* 11.

(*a*) *Medium white Cowan paper* (Feb)

23	**3**	½d. blue-green	5·50	6·50
24	**2**	1d. dull rose	8·00	10·00
		Set of 2	13·00	16·00

(*b*) *Thick white Pirie paper* (May)

25	**3**	½d. yellow-green	3·25	3·50
		a. Imperf between (horiz pair)	£1100	
26	**2**	1d. rose-red	8·00	10·00
		a. Rose-lake	7·50	6·50
27		2½d. dull blue	7·00	18·00
		Set of 3	17·00	28·00

1902 (Sept). *W* **14** *of New Zealand (single-lined NZ and Star, close together; sideways on T* **2**). *P* 11.

28	**3**	½d. yellow-green	1·40	3·25
		a. Grey-green	14·00	22·00
29	**2**	1d. rose-pink	1·75	3·50
30		1½d. deep mauve	2·50	7·00
31	**3**	2d. deep brown	3·75	9·50
		a. No figures of value	£1500	£1600
		b. Perf 11 × 14		
32	**2**	2½d. deep blue	3·75	6·50
33		5d. olive-black	27·00	35·00
34	**3**	6d. purple	22·00	27·00
35	**2**	10d. green	48·00	70·00
36	**3**	1s. carmine	48·00	60·00
		a. Perf 11 × 14	£500	
		Set of 9	£140	£200

1909–11. *W* **43** *of New Zealand.*

37	**3**	½d. green (*p* 14½ × 14) (1911)	4·50	6·00
38	**2**	1d. deep red (*p* 14)	14·00	20·00
		a. Wmk sideways (24.12.09)	7·50	9·00
		Set of 2	12·00	15·00

1913–19. *W* **43** *of New Zealand (sideways on T* **3**). *Chalk-surfaced paper.*

39	**3**	½d. deep green (*p* 14) (1915)	1·00	6·00
		a. Wmk upright	1·25	6·00
40	**2**	1d. red (*p* 14) (7.13)	2·00	3·75
41		1d. red (*p* 14 × 14½) (1914)	4·00	4·75
42		1½d. deep mauve (*p* 14) (1915)	55·00	40·00
43		1½d. deep mauve (*p* 14 × 15) (1916)	4·00	3·25
44	**3**	2d. deep brown (*p* 15 × 14) (1919)	5·00	24·00
45	**2**	10d. green (*p* 14 × 15) (1918)	13·00	42·00
46	**3**	1s. carmine (*p* 15 × 14) (1919)	20·00	45·00
		Set of 6	40·00	£110

**THE WORLD CENTRE FOR
FINE STAMPS IS 399 STRAND**

RAROTONGA

APA PENE

(8)

1919 (Apr–July). *Contemporary stamps of New Zealand surch as T* **8**.

(a) *Typographed. P* 14 × 15

50	**61**	½d. green (R.) (June)		20	45
51	**52**	1d. carmine (B.) (June)		20	40
52	**61**	1½d. orange-brown (R.) (June)		25	75
53		2d. yellow (R.)		30	70
54		3d. chocolate (B.) (July)		1·25	2·50

(b) *Recess.* (a) *P* 14 × 14½. (b) *P* 14 × 13½

55	**60**	2½d. blue (R.) (a) (June)		95	2·00
		a. Vert pair. Nos. 55/6		20·00	29·00
56		2½d. blue (R.) (b)		1·60	5·00
57		3d. chocolate (B.) (a)		70	1·50
		a. Vert pair. Nos. 57/8		20·00	35·00
58		3d. chocolate (B.) (b)		1·00	4·25
59		4d. violet (B.) (a)		1·00	3·75
		a. Vert pair. Nos. 59/60		22·00	40·00
60		4d. violet (B.) (b)		1·50	5·50
61		4½d. deep green (B.) (a)		1·10	5·00
		a. Vert pair. Nos. 61/2		25·00	40·00
62		4½d. deep green (B.) (b)		2·00	5·50
63		6d. carmine (B.) (a) (June)		1·50	5·00
		a. Vert pair. Nos. 63/4		40·00	60·00
64		6d. carmine (B.) (b)		2·50	6·50
65		7½d. red-brown (B.)		1·25	5·50
66		9d. sage-green (R.) (a)		2·00	6·50
		a. Vert pair. Nos. 66/7		50·00	75·00
67		9d. sage-green (R.) (b)		3·25	6·50
68		1s. vermilion (B.) (a) (June)		3·25	11·00
		a. Vert pair. Nos. 68/9		65·00	90·00
69		1s. vermilion (B.) (b)		7·00	16·00
		Set of 12		11·50	38·00

9 Capt. Cook landing

10 Warf at Avarua

11 "Capt. Cook" (Dance)

12 Palm Tree

13 Huts at Arorangi

14 Avarua Harbour

(Des, eng and recess Perkins, Bacon & Co)

1920 (23 Aug). *No wmk. P* 14.

70	**9**	½d. black and green		2·25	6·00
71	**10**	1d. black and carmine-red		1·60	4·00
72	**11**	1½d. black and dull blue		6·50	8·50
73	**12**	3d. black and chocolate		2·00	5·50
74	**13**	6d. brown and yellow-orange		1·75	8·00
75	**14**	1s. black and violet		5·00	17·00
		Set of 6		17·00	45·00

RAROTONGA

(15)

1921 (Oct). *Postal Fiscal stamps at Type* F **4** *of New Zealand optd with* T **15**. W **43** *(sideways). Chalk-surfaced "De La Rue" paper. P* 14½ × 14.

76	2s. deep blue (R.)		26·00	38·00
	a. Carmine opt		£140	£150
77	2s. 6d. grey-brown (B.)		18·00	35·00
78	5s. yellow-green (R.)		26·00	42·00
79	10s. maroon (B.)		45·00	50·00
80	£1 rose-carmine (B.)		75·00	90·00
	Set of 5		£170	£225

See also Nos. 85/9.

16 Te Po,
Rarotongan Chief

17 Harbour, Rarotonga
and Mt Ikurangi

(2½d. from a print; 4d. des A. H. Messenger. Plates by P.B. Recess Govt Ptg Office, Wellington)

1924–27. W **43** *of New Zealand. P* 14.

81	**9**	½d. black and green (13.5.26)		3·00	3·50
82	**10**	1d. black and deep carmine (10.11.24)		3·00	1·50
83	**16**	2½d. red-brown and steel blue (15.10.27)		2·50	11·00
84	**17**	4d. green and violet (15.10.27)		2·75	11·00
		Set of 4		10·00	24·00

1926 (Feb–May). *As Nos.* 76/80, *but thick, opaque white chalk-surfaced "Cowan" paper.*

85	2s. blue (C.)		£100	£120
86	2s. 6d. deep grey-brown (B.)		50·00	60·00
87	5s. yellow-green (R.) (May)		35·00	50·00
88	10s. brown-red (B.) (May)		48·00	65·00
89	£1 rose-pink (B.) (May)		75·00	85·00
	Set of 5		£275	£350

1926–28. T **72** *("Admiral" Type) of New Zealand, overprinted with* T **15**.

(a) *"Jones" chalk-surfaced paper*

90	2s. deep blue (R.) (10.26)		10·00	38·00
	Wi. Wmk inverted			

(b) *"Cowan" thick chalk-surfaced paper*

91	2s. light blue (R.) (18.6.27)		15·00	38·00
92	3s. bright mauve (R.) (30.1.28)		16·00	40·00
	Set of 3		38·00	£100

TWO PENCE   COOK ISLANDS.

(18)   (19)

1931. *Surch with* T **18**. *P* 14. (a) *No wmk.*

93	**11**	2d. on 1½d. black and blue (R.)		3·50	2·25

(b) *W* **43** *of New Zealand*

94	**11**	2d. on 1½d. black and blue (R.)		1·25	3·00

1931 (12 Nov)–**32**. *Postal Fiscal stamps as Type* F **6** *of New Zealand. W* **43**. *Thick, opaque, white chalk-faced "Cowan" paper. P* 14.

(a) *Optd with* T **15**

95	2s. 6d. deep brown (B.)		7·50	17·00
96	5s. green (R.)		16·00	38·00
97	10s. carmine-lake (B.)		30·00	55·00
98	£1 pink (B.)		55·00	80·00

(b) *Optd with* T **19** (3.32)

98a	£3 green (R.)		80·00	£140
98b	£5 blue (R.)		£170	£225

The £3 and £5 values were mainly used for fiscal purposes.

20 Capt. Cook landing   21 Capt. Cook

22 Double Maori Canoe   23 Natives working Cargo

24 Port of Avarua   25 R.M.S. *Monowai*

26 King George V

(Des L. C. Mitchell. Recess P.B.)

1932 (16 Mar). *No wmk. P 13.*

99	**20**	½d. black and deep green	2·25	6·50
		a. Perf 14	28·00	50·00
100	**21**	1d. black and lake	2·25	2·75
		a. Centre inverted	£1600	£1600
		b. Perf 13 and 14 mixed	£150	
		c. Perf 14	15·00	16·00
101	**22**	2d. black and brown	2·00	3·75
		a. Perf 14	8·00	11·00
102	**23**	2½d. black and deep blue	5·00	22·00
		a. Perf 14	11·00	22·00
103	**24**	4d. black and bright blue	15·00	25·00
		a. Perf 14	7·00	25·00
		b. Perf 14×13	48·00	75·00
		c. Perf comp of 14 and 13	60·00	
104	**25**	6d. black and orange	24·00	38·00
		a. Perf 14	2·75	9·00
105	**26**	1s. black and violet (*p* 14)	4·25	25·00
		Set of 7	23·00	75·00

No. 100b comes from the first vertical column of one sheet which was reperforated 14 at left.

(Recess from P.B. plates at Govt Printing Office, Wellington)

1933–36. *W 43 of New Zealand (Single N Z and Star). P 14.*

106	**20**	½d. black and deep green	40	70
		Wi. Wmk inverted		
107	**21**	1d. black and scarlet (1935)	45	70
		Wi. Wmk inverted and reversed		
108	**22**	2d. black and brown (1936)	35	20
109	**23**	2½d. black and deep blue	25	80
110	**24**	4d. black and bright blue	25	35
111	**25**	6d. black and orange-yellow (1936)	55	2·25
112	**26**	1s. black and violet (1936)	13·50	17·00
		Set of 7	14·00	20·00

SILVER JUBILEE OF KING GEORGE V. 1910 - 1935.

(27)

Normal letters

B K E N

B K E N

Narrow letters

1935 (7 May). *Silver Jubilee. Optd with T 27 (wider vertical spacing on 6d.). Colours changed. W 43 of New Zealand. P 14.*

113	**21**	1d. red-brown and lake	50	70
		a. Narrow "K" in "KING"	2·75	
		b. Narrow "B" in "JUBILEE"	3·75	
114	**23**	2½d. dull and deep blue (R.)	75	1·00
		a. Narrow first "E" in "GEORGE"	3·50	5·00
115	**25**	6d. green and orange	2·75	4·50
		a. Narrow "N" in "KING"	16·00	
		Set of 3	3·50	5·50
		First Day Cover		15·00

1936 (15 July)–**44.** *Stamps of New Zealand optd with T 19. W 43.*

(a) Thick, white, opaque chalk-surfaced "Cowan" paper. P 14

(i) As T 72 ("Admiral" type)

116	2s. blue	12·00	32·00
117	3s. mauve	13·00	38·00
	Set of 2	25·00	70·00

(ii) As Type F 6 ("Arms" type)

118	2s. 6d. deep brown	15·00	28·00
119	5s. green (R.)	16·00	35·00
120	10s. carmine-lake	32·00	55·00
121	£1 pink	50·00	75·00
	Set of 4	£100	£170

(b) Thin, hard, chalk-surfaced "Wiggins, Teape" paper

122	2s. 6d. dull brown (12.40)	70·00	65·00
123	5s. green (R.) (10.40)	£200	£200
123a	10s. pale carmine-lake (11.44)	£120	£120
123b	£3 green (R.) (date?)	£300	£400
	Set of 4	£600	£700

PRICES

George VI issues (1937–1952)

First column = Unmounted Mint
Second column = Mounted Mint
Third column = Used

COOK IS'DS.

(28)

IS'DS.

Small second "S"
(R. 1/2)

1937 (1 June). *Coronation. Nos. 599/601 of New Zealand optd with T 28.*

124	1d. carmine	30	15	10
	a. Small second "S"	3·25		
125	2½d. Prussian blue	50	15	20
	a. Small second "S"	3·75		
126	6d. red-orange	50	20	20
	a. Small second "S"	3·75		
	Set of 3	1·10	40	45
	First Day Cover			1·00

29 King George VI   30 Native Village

31 Native Canoe   32 Tropical Landscape

(Des J. Berry (2s., 3s., and frame of 1s.). Eng B.W. Recess Govt Ptg. Office, Wellington)

1938 (2 May). *W* **43** *of New Zealand. P* 14.

127	29	1s. black and violet	2·75	1·25	2·25
128	30	2s. black and red-brown	5·00	2·25	4·00
129	31	3s. light blue and emerald-green	11·00	4·50	7·00
		Set of 3	17·00	7·25	12·00

(Recess B.W.)

1940 (2 Sept). *Surch as in T* **32**. *W* **98** *of New Zealand. P* 13½ × 14.

130	32	3d. on 1½d. black and purple	10	5	15

Type **32** was not issued without surcharge.

1943-50. *Postal Fiscal stamps as Type* F **6** *of New Zealand optd with T* **19**. *W* **98**. *"Wiggins, Teape" chalk-surfaced paper. P* 14.

131		2s. 6d. dull brown (3.46)	20·00	8·00	26·00
	Wi.	Wmk inverted (2.4.51)	5·50	2·25	9·00
132		5s. green (R.) (11.43)	5·50	2·75	12·00
	Wi.	Wmk inverted (5.54)	12·00	5·00	18·00
133		10s. carmine-lake (10.48)	40·00	20·00	48·00
	Wi	Wmk inverted (10.51)	26·00	13·00	35·00
134		£1 pink (11.47)	27·00	14·00	35·00
	Wi.	Wmk inverted (19.5.54)	27·00	14·00	35·00
135		£3 green (R.) (1946?)	£325	£140	£450
	Wi.	Wmk inverted (28.5.53)	60·00	28·00	£130
136		£5 blue (R.) (25.10.50)	£200	95·00	£250
	Wi.	Wmk inverted (19.5.54)	£200	95·00	£250
		Set of 6	£300	£140	£450

The £3 and £5 were mainly used for fiscal purposes.

(Recess Govt Ptg Office, Wellington)

1944-46. *W* **98** *of New Zealand (sideways on* ½d., 1d., 1s., *and* 2s.). *P* 14.

137	20	½d. black and deep green (11.44)	85	45	1·25
	Wi.	Wmk sideways inverted	3·50	2·00	
138	21	1d. black and scarlet (3.45)	2·00	1·00	35
	Wi.	Wmk sideways inverted	6·00	4·00	
139	22	2d. black and brown (2.46)	1·25	60	1·00
140	23	2½d. black and deep blue (5.45)	65	30	70
141	24	4d. black and blue (4.44)	1·00	40	1·40
142	25	6d. black and orange (6.44)	90	45	60
143	29	1s. black and violet (9.44)	90	40	90
144	30	2s. black and red-brown (8.45)	7·00	2·50	8·50
145	31	3s. light blue and emer-grn (6.45)	12·00	6·50	15·00
		Set of 9	24·00	11·00	27·00

COOK ISLANDS
(33)

1946 (1 June). *Peace. Nos.* 668, 670, 674·5 *of New Zealand optd with T* **33** *(reading up and down at sides on* 2d.).

146		1d. green	10	5	5
147		2d. purple (B.)	10	5	15
148		6d. chocolate and vermilion	15	10	15
149		8d. black and carmine (B.)	15	10	15
		Set of 4	45	20	45
		First Day Cover			1·00

34 Ngatangiia Channel, Rarotonga

35 Capt. Cook and Map of Hervey Islands

36 Rarotonga and Rev. John Williams

37 Aitutaki and Palm Trees

38 Rarotonga Airfield

39 Penrhyn Village

40 Native Hut

41 Map and Statue of Capt. Cook   **42** Native Hut and Palms   **43** M.V. *Matua*

(Des J. Berry. Recess Waterlow)

1949 (1 Aug)–**61.** *W* **98** *of New Zealand (sideways on shilling values). P* 13½ × 13 *(horiz)* or 13 × 13½ *(vert).*

150	34	½d. violet and brown	10	5	45
151	35	1d. chestnut and green	1·25	55	85
152	36	2d. reddish brown and scarlet	60	30	80
153	37	3d. green and ultramarine	35	15	80
		Wi. Wmk inverted			
		a. Wmk sideways (white opaque paper) (22.5.61)	2·00	1·00	2·50

154	38	5d. emerald-green and violet	70	30	90
155	39	6d. black and carmine	1·00	50	1·00
156	40	8d. olive-green and orange	40	25	2·00
		Wi. Wmk inverted	40·00	20·00	22·00
157	41	1s. light blue and chocolate	3·75	1·60	2·75
158	42	2s. yellow-brown and carmine	3·00	1·25	6·00
		Wi. Wmk sideways inverted*			
159	43	3s. light blue and bluish green	4·75	2·25	8·00
		Set of 10	14·00	6·50	21·00

* See note above New Zealand T **29**.
See note on white opaque paper below No. 736 of New Zealand.

1953 (25 May). *Coronation. As Nos. 715 and 717 of New Zealand, but inscr* "COOK ISLANDS".

160	3d. brown	80	45
161	6d. slate-grey	1·10	80
	Set of 2	1·90	1·25
	First Day Cover		2·50

1/6

(44)

1960 (1 Apr). *No.* 154 *surch with T* **44**.

| 162 | 38 | 1s. 6d. on 5d. emerald-green and violet . . | 15 | 35 |

45 Tiare Maori

46 Fishing God

47 Frangipani

48 White Tern

49 Hibiscus

50 Skipjack Tuna

51 Oranges

52 Queen Elizabeth II

53 Island Scene

54 Administration Centre, Mangaia

55 Rarotonga

(Des J. Berry. Recess (1s. 6d.), litho (others) B.W.)

1963 (4 June). *Wmk T* **98** *of New Zealand* (*sideways*). *P* 13½ × 13 (1*d.*, 2*d.*, 8*d.*), 13 × 13½ (3*d.*, 5*d.*, 6*d.*, 1*s.*) *or* 13½ (*others*).

163	45	1d. emerald-green and yellow	20	10
164	46	2d. brown-red and yellow	8	10
165	47	3d. yellow, yellow-green & reddish vio . . .	25	10
166	48	5d. blue and black	2·25	30
167	49	6d. red, yellow and green	75	25
168	50	8d. black and blue	85	45
169	51	1s. orange-yellow and yellow-green	40	25
170	52	1s. 6d. bluish violet	2·75	2·25
171	53	2s. bistre-brown and grey-blue	75	90
172	54	3s. black and yellow-green	1·25	1·40
173	55	5s. bistre-brown and blue	8·50	4·00
		Set of 11	16·00	9·00

56 Eclipse and Palm

(Des L. C. Mitchell. Litho B.W.)

1965 (31 May). *Solar Eclipse Observation, Manuae Island. W* **98** *of New Zealand. P* 13½.

| 174 | 56 | 6d. black, yellow and light blue . . . . | 10 | 5 |
| | | First Day Cover . . . . | | 25 |

SELF-GOVERNMENT

57 N.Z. Ensign and Map

58 London Missionary Society Church

59 Proclamation of Cession, 1900

60 Nikao School

(Des R. M. Conly (4d.), L. C. Mitchell (10d., 1s.), J. Berry (1s. 9d.). Litho
B.W.)

1965 (16 Sept). *Internal Self-Government. W 98 of New Zealand
(sideways). P 13½.*

175	**57**	4d. red and blue	....	10	5
176	**58**	10d. multicoloured	....	10	10
177	**59**	1s. multicoloured	....	10	10
178	**60**	1s. 9d. multicoloured	....	15	40
		Set of 4	....	40	60
		First Day Cover	....		1·00

In Memoriam
Sɪʀ Wɪɴꜱᴛᴏɴ Cʜᴜʀᴄʜɪʟʟ
1874 - 1965   **Airmail**

(**61**)   (**62**)

1966 (24 Jan). *Churchill Commemoration. Nos. 171/3 and 175/7 optd
with T 61, in red.*

179	**57**	4d. red and blue	....	75	30
		Ea. "I" for "1" in "1874" (R.6/5)	......	2·50	
180	**58**	10d. multicoloured	....	1·50	45
		a. Opt inverted	....	£200	
		Eb. "I" for "1" in "1874" (R.6/5)	......	3·75	
181	**59**	1s. multicoloured	....	1·50	65
		a. Opt inverted	....	£150	
		Eb. "I" for "1" in "1874" (R.6/5)	......	3·75	
182	**53**	2s. bistre-brown and grey-blue	......	2·00	1·25
		Ea. "I" for "1" in "1874" (R.6/5, R.12/5)	.	4·75	
183	**54**	3s. black and yellow-green	....	2·00	1·25
		Ea. "I" for "1" in "1874" (R.6/5, R.12/5)	.	5·50	
184	**55**	5s. bistre-brown and blue	....	2·50	1·75
		Ea. "I" for "1" in "1874" (R.6/5, R.12/5)	.	12·00	
		Set of 6	....	9·00	5·00
		First Day Cover	....		9·50

1966 (22 Apr). *Air. Various stamps optd with T 62 or surch also.*

185	**49**	6d. red, yellow and green	....	1·25	20
186	**50**	7d. on 8d. black and blue	....	1·25	25
187	**47**	10d. on 3d. yellow, yellow-green and reddish violet	....	1·00	15
188	**51**	1s. orange-yellow and yellow-green	....	1·00	15
189	**52**	1s. 6d. bluish violet	....	1·50	1·25
190	**54**	2s. 3d. on 3s. black and yellow-green	...	1·25	65
191	**55**	5s. bistre-brown and blue	....	1·75	1·50
192	**53**	10s. on 2s. bistre-brown and grey-blue	...	2·25	6·00
193	–	£1 pink (No. 134)	....	9·00	15·00
		Eu. Wmk upright	....	12·00	17·00
		a. Aeroplane omitted	....	20·00	32·00
		Eau. Aeroplane omitted and wmk upright	..	24·00	35·00
		Set of 9	....	18·00	23·00

Nos. 193a and 193au occurred in all stamps of the last vertical row as
insufficient aeroplane symbols were available.

There are also numerous other varieties on all values, notably aeroplanes
of different sizes and broken first "i" with dot missing owing to damaged
type.

PRINTERS. The following stamps were printed in photogravure by
Heraclio Fournier, Spain *except where otherwise stated.*

63 "Adoration of the Magi" (Fra Angelico)

64 "Adoration of the Shepherds" (J. de Ribera)

1966 (28 Nov). *Christmas. T 63/4 and similar multicoloured designs.*
A. *P 13 × 12 (horiz) or 12 × 13 (vert).*
B. *P 13 × 14½ (horiz) or 14½ × 13 (vert).*

			A		B	
194		1d. Type **63**	....	25	15	5 5
195		2d. "The Nativity" (Mem-ling) (vert)	....	11·00	5·50	5 5
196		4d. "Adoration of the Magi" (Velazquez) (horiz)	....	60	40	5 5
197		10d. "Adoration of the Magi" (Bosch) (horiz)	......	2·00	1·25	12 10
198		1s. 6d. Type **64**	....	4·00	2·50	20 20
		Set of 5	....	16·00	9·00	40 40
		First Day Cover	....			65

68 Tennis, and Queen Elizabeth II

(Des V. Whiteley)

1967 (12 Jan). *2nd South Pacific Games, Nouméa. T* **68** *and similar horiz designs in orange-brown, black and new blue (1d.) or multicoloured (others). P* 13½. (*a*) *Postage.*

199	½d.	Type **68**	5	5
200	1d.	Netball and Games emblem	5	5
201	4d.	Boxing and Cook Islands' team badge	5	5
202	7d.	Football and Queen Elizabeth II	5	5

(*b*) *Air*

203	10d.	Running and Games emblem	10	5
204	2s. 3d.	Running and Cook Islands' team badge	15	15
		Set of 6	35	25
		First Day Cover		60

77 Avarua, Rarotonga, and Cook Islands 10d. Stamp of 1892

(New Currency. 100 cents = 1 dollar)

1c	2½c	2½c
(74)	(I)	(II)

These occur on alternative vertical rows within the sheet.

78 S.S. *Moana Roa*, "DC-3" Aircraft, Map and Captain Cook

1967 (3 Apr–6 June). *Decimal Currency. Nos.* 134/6, 163/70 *and* 172/5 *surch as T* **74** *by the Government Printer. Sterling values unobliterated except No.* 218.

205	45	1 c. on 1d. emerald-green & yellow (4.5) .		45	1·10
206	46	2 c. on 2d. brown-red & yellow		5	5
207	47	2½ c. on 3d. yellow, yellow-green and reddish violet (I)		20	10
208		2½ c. on 3d. yellow, yellow-green and reddish violet (II)		20	10
209	57	3 c. on 4d. red and blue		15	5
210	48	4 c. on 5d. blue and black (4.5)		80	25
211	49	5 c. on 6d. red, yellow and green		15	5
212	56	5 c. on 6d. black, yellow and light blue ...		2·00	40
213	50	7 c. on 8d. black and blue		15	5
214	51	10 c. on 1s. orange-yellow & yellow-green .		15	5
215	52	15 c. on 1s. 6d. bluish violet (R.) (4.5.67) ..		2·00	1·50
216	54	30 c. on 3s. black and yellow-green (R.) (4.5.67)		12·00	5·50
217	55	50 c. on 5s. bistre-brown and blue (R.) (4.5.67)		3·50	1·50
218	58	$1 and 10s. on 10d. multicoloured (R.) (4.5.67)		12·00	6·50
219	–	$2 on £1 pink (R.) (6.6.67)		£140	£140
220	–	$6 on £3 green (R.) (6.6.67)		£200	£200
221	–	$10 on £5 blue (R.) (6.6.67)		£300	£300
		Ei. Wmk inverted		£300	£300
		Set of 14 (Nos. 205/18)		28·00	15·00

The surcharge on No. 218 is $1 and its equivalent of 10s. in the old currency. The "10d." is obliterated by three bars.

A large number of minor varieties exist in these surcharges, such as wrong fount letter "C" and figures.

1967 (3 July). *75th Anniv of First Cook Islands Stamps. P* 13½.

222	75	1 c. (1d.) multicoloured	5	5
223	76	3 c. (4d.) multicoloured	15	5
224	77	8 c. (10d.) multicoloured	30	5
225	78	18 c. (1s. 9d.) multicoloured	85	20
		Set of 4	1·25	30
		First Day Cover		65
MS226		134 × 109 mm. Nos. 222/5	2·00	2·50
		First Day Cover		3·00

The face values are expressed in decimal currency and in the sterling equivalent.

Each value was issued in sheets of 8 stamps and 1 label.

79 Hibiscus   80 Queen Elizabeth II

75 Village Scene. Cook Islands 1d. Stamp of 1892 and Queen Victoria (from "Penny Black")

76 Post Office, Avarua, Rarotonga and Queen Elizabeth II

81 Queen Elizabeth and Flowers

Two types of $4
I. Value 32½ mm long. Coarse screen.
II. Value 33½ mm long. Finer screen.

(Floral designs from paintings by Mrs. Kay W. Billings)

1967–71. *Multicoloured designs as T* **79/81.** *P* 14 × 13½. A. *Without fluorescent security markings.* B. *With fluorescent security markings.*

			A		B	
227	½ c. Type **79**	5	5	5	5
228	1 c. *Hibiscus syriacus* (27 × 37 mm)	5	5	5	5
229	2 c. Frangipani (27 × 37 mm)	10	5	10	5
230	2½ c. *Clitoria ternatea* (27 × 37 mm)	15	5	15	5
231	3 c. "Suva Queen" (27 × 37 mm)	15	5	15	5
232	4 c. Water Lily ("WALTER LILY") (27 × 37 mm)	45	60		†
233	4 c. Water Lily (27 × 37 mm)	30	20	30	5
234	5 c. *Bauhinia bipinnata rosea* (27 × 37 mm)	15	5	15	5
235	6 c. Hibiscus (27 × 37 mm)	20	5	20	5
236	8 c. *Allamanda cathartica* (27 × 37 mm)	20	5	20	5
237	9 c. Stephanotis (27 × 37 mm)	20	5	20	5
238	10 c. *Poinciana regia flamboyant* (27 × 37 mm)	25	5	25	5
239	15 c. Frangipani (27 × 37 mm)	40	5	40	5
240	20 c. Thunbergia (27 × 37 mm)	75	35	75	25
241	25 c. Canna Lily (27 × 37 mm)	65	25	70	25
242	30 c. *Euphorbia pulcherrima poinsettia* (27 × 37 mm)	65	50	80	50
243	50 c. *Gardinia taitensis* (27 × 37 mm)	90	55	90	55
244	$1 Type **80**	1·75	80	1·75	80
245	$2 Type **80**	3·50	1·50	3·50	1·50
246	$4 Type **81** (I)	3·25	3·75	45·00	48·00
246c	$4 Type **81** (II)		†	11·00	8·50
247	$6 Type **81**	4·00	5·00	12·00	6·00
247c	$8 Type **81**	9·00	12·00	17·00	10·00
248	$10 Type **81**	9·00	12·00	19·00	12·00
	Set of 17 (*Nos. 227/43*)	5·00	2·50		
	Set of 16 (*Nos. 227/43*)			4·75	2·00

Dates of issue:—Nos. 227/238A, 31.7.67; Nos. 239/243A, 11.8.67; Nos. 244/245A, 31.8.67; Nos. 246/247A, 30.4.68; No. 248A, 12.7.68; No. 247cA, 21.4.69; Nos. 227/243B, 9.2.70; Nos. 244/245B, 12.10.70; No. 246cB, 14.7.71; No. 246B, 11.11.70; No. 247B, 12.2.71; No. 247cB, 3.5.71; No. 248B, 14.6.71.

The "WALTER" spelling error occurred on all stamps in one of the four post office sheets which went to make up the printing sheet and this was corrected in later supplies.

FLUORESCENT PAPER. This is on paper treated with fluorescent security markings, in the form of faint multiple coats of arms. Stamps exist with these markings inverted. In addition an invisible synthetic gum has been used which prevents curling and is suitable for use in the tropics without interleaving the stamps.

Some of the above are known with these markings omitted and can be distinguished when in unused condition from the original printings without markings by their synthetic invisible gum.

COOK ISLANDS ¹c

97 "Ia Orana Maria"

1967 (24 Oct). *Gauguin's Polynesian Paintings. T* **97** *and similar designs. Multicoloured. P* 13.

249	1 c. Type **97**	5	5
250	3 c. "Riders on the Beach"	5	5
251	5 c. "Still Life with Flowers"	5	5
252	8 c. "Whispered Words"	10	5
253	15 c. "Maternity"	20	10

254	22 c. "Why are you angry?"	25	15
	Set of 6	60	35
	First Day Cover		65
MS255	156 × 132 mm. Nos. 249/54	85	1·25
	First Day Cover		1·50

The 5 c. includes an inset portrait of Queen Elizabeth.

98 "The Holy Family"   (99)
(Rubens)

HURRICANE
RELIEF
PLUS 5c

1967 (4 Dec). *Christmas. Renaissance Paintings. T* **98** *and similar designs. Multicoloured. P* 12 × 13.

256	1 c. Type **98**	5	5
257	3 c. "Adoration of the Magi" (Dürer)	8	5
258	4 c. "The Lucca Madonna" (J. van Eyck)	10	5
259	8 c. "The Adoration of the Shepherds" (J. da Bassano)	15	5
260	15 c. "Adoration of the Shepherds" (El Greco)	20	5
261	25 c. "Madonna and Child" (Correggio)	20	10
	Set of 6	70	25
	First Day Cover		60

1968 (12 Feb). *Hurricane Relief. Nos.* 231A, 233A, 251, 238A, 241A *and* 243/4A *surch as T* **99** *by Govt Printer, Rarotonga.*

262	3 c. + 1 c. "Suva Queen"	15	10
263	4 c. + 1 c. Water Lily	15	10
264	5 c. + 2 c. "Still Life with Flowers"	15	10
	a. Black surch albino		
265	10 c. + 2 c. *Poinciana regia flamboyant*	15	10
266	25 c. + 5 c. Canna Lily	25	15
267	50 c. + 10 c. *Gardinia taitensis*	35	20
268	$1 + 10 c. Type **80**	60	40
	Set of 7	1·60	1·00
	First Day Cover		2·00

The surcharge on No. 268 is as T **99**, but with seriffed letters. On No. 264 silver blocking obliterates the design area around the lettering.

100 "Matavai Bay, Tahiti" (J. Barralet)

101 "*Resolution* and *Discovery*" (J. Webber)

(Des J. Berry)

1968 (12 Sept). *Bicentenary of Captain Cook's First Voyage of Discovery. Multicoloured. Invisible gum. P 13.*

(a) Postage. Vert. designs as T 100

269	½ c.	Type **100**	5	5
270	1 c.	"Island of Huaheine" (John Cleveley)	15	10
271	2 c.	"Town of St. Peter and St. Paul, Kamchatka" (J. Webber)	40	35
272	4 c.	"The Ice Islands" (Antarctica: W. Hodges)	40	35

(b) Air. Horiz designs as T 101

273	6 c.	Type **101**	90	65
274	10 c.	"The Island of Tahiti" (W. Hodges)	1·25	75
275	15 c.	"Karakakooa, Hawaii" (J. Webber)	1·50	90
276	25 c.	"The Landing at Middleburg" (J. Sherwin)	1·75	1·25
		Set of 8	6·00	4·00
		First Day Cover		4·50

Each value was issued in sheets of 10 stamps and 2 labels.

FLUORESCENT PAPER. From No. 277, *unless otherwise stated,* all issues are printed on paper treated with fluorescent security markings with invisible synthetic gum. These markings may be inverted or omitted in error.

COOK ISLANDS

102 Sailing

COOK ISLANDS 1c

103 "Madonna and Child" (Titian)

1968 (21 Oct). *Olympic Games, Mexico. T 102 and similar horiz designs. Multicoloured. P 13.*

277	1 c.	Type **102**	5	5
278	5 c.	Gymnastics	10	5
279	15 c.	High-jumping	15	5
280	20 c.	High-diving	15	5
281	30 c.	Cycling	15	10
282	50 c.	Hurdling	20	15
		Set of 6	70	30
		First Day Cover		85

Each value was issued in sheets of 10 stamps and 2 labels.

1968 (2 Dec). *Christmas. Paintings. T 103 and similar vert designs. Multicoloured. P 13½.*

283	1 c.	Type **103**	5	5
284	4 c.	"The Holy Family with Lamb" (Raphael)	10	5
285	10 c.	"The Virgin of the Rosary" (Murillo)	15	5
286	20 c.	"Adoration of the Kings" (Memling)	20	10
287	30 c.	"Adoration of the Magi" (Ghirlandaio)	25	15
		Set of 5	70	30
		First Day Cover		55
MS288	114 × 177 mm. Nos. 283/7 plus label		1·25	1·50
		First Day Cover		1·75

COOK ISLANDS

104 Camp-fire Cooking

1969 (6 Feb). *Diamond Jubilee of New Zealand Scout Movement and Fifth National (New Zealand) Jamboree. T 104 and similar square designs. Multicoloured. P 13½.*

289	½ c.	Type **104**	5	5
290	1 c.	Descent by rope	5	5
291	5 c.	Semaphore	10	5
292	10 c.	Tree-planting	15	5
293	20 c.	Constructing a shelter	25	10
294	30 c.	Lord Baden-Powell and island scene	40	15
		Set of 6	90	35
		First Day Cover		90

Each value was issued in sheets of 10 stamps and 2 labels.

105 High Jumping

1969 (7 July). *Third South Pacific Games, Port Moresby. T 105 and similar triangular designs. Multicoloured. Without fluorescent security markings. P 13 × 13½.*

295	½ c.	Type **105**	5	5
296	½ c.	Footballer	5	5
297	1 c.	Basketball	5	5
298	1 c.	Weightlifter	5	5
299	4 c.	Tennis-player	10	5
300	4 c.	Hurdler	10	5
301	10 c.	Javelin-thrower	30	20
302	10 c.	Runner	30	20
303	15 c.	Golfer	45	25
304	15 c.	Boxer	45	25
		Set of 10	1·50	1·00
		First Day Cover		1·25
MS305	174 × 129 mm. Nos. 295/304 plus two labels		1·60	1·75
		First Day Cover		2·00

Each value was issued in sheets containing 5 *se-tenant* pairs of both designs and 2 labels.

COOK ISLANDS

106 Flowers, Map and Captain Cook

1969 (8 Oct). *South Pacific Conference, Nouméa. T 106 and similar horiz designs. Multicoloured. Without fluorescent security markings. P 13.*

306	5 c.	Flowers, map and Premier Albert Henry	40	10
307	10 c.	Type **106**	80	40
308	25 c.	Flowers, map and N.Z. arms	85	60
309	30 c.	Queen Elizabeth II, map and flowers	95	65
		Set of 4	2·75	1·60
		First Day Cover		2·25

107 "Virgin and Child with Saints
Jerome and Dominic" (Lippi)

108 "The Resurrection
of Christ" (Raphael)

1969 (21 Nov). *Christmas. Paintings. T* **107** *and similar designs. Multicoloured. Without fluorescent security markings. P* 13.

310	1 c.	Type **107**	5	5
311	4 c.	"The Holy Family" (Fra Bartolomeo)	10	5
312	10 c.	"The Adoration of the Shepherds" (A. Mengs)	15	5
313	20 c.	"Madonna and Child with Saints" (R. Campin)	20	10
314	30 c.	"The Madonna of the Basket" (Correggio)	20	15
		Set of 5	60	30
		First Day Cover		60
MS315		132 × 9/ mm. Nos. 310/14	85	1·40
		First Day Cover		1·50

Each value was issued in sheets of 9 stamps and 1 label.

1970 (12 Mar). *Easter. Paintings. T* **108** *and similar vert designs showing "The Resurrection of Christ" by the artists named. Multicoloured. P* 13.

316	4 c.	Type **108**	10	5
317	8 c.	Dirk Bouts	10	5
318	20 c.	Altdorfer	15	10
319	25 c.	Murillo	20	10
		Set of 4	50	25
		First Day Cover		60
MS320		132 × 162 mm. Nos. 316/19	80	1·25
		First Day Cover		1·60

Each value was issued in sheets of 8 stamps and 1 label.

KIA ORANA

APOLLO 13

ASTRONAUTS

Te Atua to

Tatou Irinakianga

(109)

1970 (17–30 Apr). *Apollo 13. Nos. 233, 236, 239/40, 242 and 245/6 optd with T* **109** *(4 c. to $2) or with first three lines only in larger type ($4), by Govt Printer. A. Without fluorescent security markings. B. With fluorescent security markings.*

			A		B	
321	4 c.	Water Lily	5	5	†	
	a.	Opt albino	42·00	—	†	
322	8 c.	*Allamanda cathartica*	5	5	†	
323	15 c.	Frangipani	10	5	†	
324	20 c.	Thunbergia	15	15	†	
325	30 c.	*Euphorbia pulcherrima* poinsettia	20	20	†	
326	$2	Type **80**	75	1·25	†	
327	$4	Type **81** (30.4)	65·00	65·00	1·50	3·00
		Set of 7 (321/6A, 327B)	2·50	4·25		
		First Day Cover		5·50		

110 The Royal Family

(Des V. Whiteley (5 c.), J. Berry ($1))

1970 (12 June). *Royal Visit to New Zealand, T* **110** *and similar horiz designs. Multicoloured. P* 13.

328	5 c.	Type **110**	65	30
329	30 c.	Captain Cook and H.M.S. *Endeavour*	2·75	1·75
330	$1	Royal Visit commemorative coin	4·00	3·00
		Set of 3	6·75	4·50
		First Day Cover		6·00
MS331		145 × 97 mm. Nos. 328/30	8·00	9·00
		First Day Cover		10·00

Each value was issued in sheets of 8 stamps and 1 label.

FOUR

DOLLARS

FIFTH ANNIVERSARY SELF-GOVERNMENT AUGUST 1970	$4.00
(113)	(114)

1970 (27 Aug). *5th Anniv of Self-Government Nos. 328/30 optd with T* **113** *(30 c. and $1), or in single line in silver around frame of stamp (5 c.).*

332	5 c.	Type **110**	40	20
333	30 c.	Captain Cook and H.M.S. *Endeavour*	1·25	50
334	$1	Royal Visit commemorative coin	2·00	1·25
		Set of 3	3·25	1·75
		First Day Cover		3·00

1970 (11 Nov). *Nos. 247c and 248 surch with T* **114** *by Govt Printer, Rarotonga. A. Without fluorescent security markings. B. With fluorescent security markings.*

			A		B	
335	81	$4 on $8 multicoloured	30·00	30·00	5·50	4·00
336		$4 on $10 multicoloured	48·00	48·00	2·00	1·75
		Set of 2	75·00	75·00	7·50	5·75

There are variations in the setting of this surcharge and also in the rule.

PLUS 20c

UNITED
KINGDOM

SPECIAL
MAIL SERVICE

115 Mary, Joseph and Christ
in Manger

(116)

(Des from De Lisle Psalter)

1970 (30 Nov). *Christmas. T* **115** *and similar square designs. Multicoloured. P* 13.

337	1 c.	Type **115**	5	5
338	4 c.	Shepherds and Apparition of the Angel	10	5

339	10 c.	Mary showing Child to Joseph	15	5
340	20 c.	The Wise Men bearing Gifts	20	10
341	30 c.	Parents wrapping Child in swaddling clothes	25	15
		Set of 5	65	35
		First Day Cover		65
MS342	100 × 139 mm. Nos. 337/41 plus label	1·25	1·50
	First Day Cover		1·75

Each value was issued in sheets of 5 stamps and 1 label. Stamps from the miniature sheet are smaller, since they do not have the buff parchment border as on the stamps from the sheets.

1971.   *Nos. 242B and 243B surch as T* **116.**
343	30 c.+20 c. *Euphorbia pulcherrima poinsettia*		
	(25.2)	40	50
344	50 c.+20 c. *Gardinia taitensis* (8.3)	1·75	2·50
	Set of 2	2·10	3·00

The premium of 20 c. was to prepay a private delivery service fee in Great Britain during the postal strike. The mail was sent by air to a forwarding address in the Netherlands. No. 343 was intended for ordinary airmail ½ oz letters, and No. 344 included registration fee.

The postal strike ended on 8 March and both stamps were withdrawn on 12 March.

117 Wedding of Princess Elizabeth and Prince Philip

(Des from photographs. Litho Format)

1971 (11 Mar).   *Royal Visit of H.R.H. The Duke of Edinburgh. T* **117** *and similar horiz designs. Multicoloured. P* 13½.
345	1 c. Type **117**	30	50
346	4 c. Queen Elizabeth, Prince Philip, Princess Anne and Prince Charles at Windsor	75	1·10
347	10 c. Prince Philip sailing	1·00	1·25
348	15 c. Prince Philip in polo gear	1·00	1·25
349	25 c. Prince Philip in Naval uniform, and the Royal Yacht *Britannia*	1·50	2·00
	Set of 5	4·00	5·50
	First Day Cover		6·00
MS350	168 × 122 mm. No. 345/9 plus printed labels in positions 1,3,4, and 6	4·50	7·00
	First Day Cover		7·50

Each value was issued in sheets of 7 stamps and 2 labels.

(118)   (119)

1971 (8 Sept).   *Fourth South Pacific Games, Tahiti. Nos. 238B, 241B and 242B optd with T* **118** *in black, or surch as T* **119** *in blue.*
351	10 c. *Poinciana regia flamboyant*	10	5
352	10 c.+ 1 c. *Poinciana regia flamboyant*	10	5
353	10 c.+3 c. *Poinciana regia flamboyant*	10	5
354	25 c. Canna Lily	15	10
355	25 c.+1 c. Canna Lily	15	10
356	25 c.+3 c. Canna Lily	15	10
357	30 c. *Euphorbia pulcherrima poinsettia* . . .	15	10
358	30 c.+1 c. *Euphorbia pulcherrima poinsettia*	15	10
359	30 c.+3 c. *Euphorbia pulcherrima poinsettia* . . .	15	10
	Set of 9	1·10	65
	First Day Cover		1·40

The stamps additionally surcharged 1 c. or 3 c. helped to finance the Cook Islands' team at the games.

10c ≡
(120)

121 "Virgin and Child" (Bellini)

1971 (20 Oct).   *Nos. 230B, 233B, 236B/7B and 239B surch with T* **120.**
360	10 c. on 2½ c. *Clitoria ternatea*	15	25
361	10 c. on 4 c. Water Lily	15	25
362	10 c. on 8 c. *Allamanda cathartica*	15	25
	a. Surch inverted	£130	
363	10 c. on 9 c. Stephanotis	15	25
364	10 c. on 15 c. Frangipani	15	25
	a. Surch double	90·00	
	Set of 5	65	1·10

1971 (30 Nov).   *Christmas. T* **121** *and similar vert designs showing different paintings of the "Virgin and Child", by Bellini. P* 13.
365	1 c. multicoloured	8	5
366	4 c. multicoloured	8	5
367	10 c. multicoloured	25	5
368	20 c. multicoloured	50	10
369	30 c. multicoloured	50	25
	Set of 5	1·25	45
	First Day Cover		1·00
MS370	135 × 147 mm. Nos. 365/9	1·50	2·25
	First Day Cover		2·50
MS371	92 × 98 mm. 50 c. + 5 c. "The Holy Family in a Garland of Flowers (Jan Brueghel and Pieter van Avont) (41 × 41 *mm*)	75	1·40
	First Day Cover		1·60

Each value was issued in sheets of 8 stamps and 1 label.

**SOUTH PACIFIC COMMISSION
FEB. 1947 - 1972**
(122)

123 St. John

1972 (17 Feb).   *25th Anniv of South Pacific Commission. No. 244B optd with T* **122.**
| 372 | **80** | $1 multicoloured . . . . | 50 | 85 |
| | | First Day Cover . . . . | | 1·40 |

(Des from De Lisle Psalter)

1972 (6 Mar). *Easter. T* **123** *and similar vert designs. Multicoloured. P* 13.
373	5 c. Type **123**		5	5
374	10 c. Christ on the Cross		10	10
375	30 c. Mary, Mother of Jesus		25	25
	Set of 3		35	35
	First Day Cover			65
MS376	79 × 112 mm. Nos. 373/5 forming triptych of "The Crucifixion"		1·00	2·25
	First Day Cover			2·50

Stamps from the miniature sheet do not have a border around the perforations, and are therefore smaller than stamps from sheets.

HURRICANE RELIEF
P l u s 2c
(128)   129 High-jumping

HURRICANE RELIEF
P L U S 2c
(124)

Hurricane Relief
P l u s 5c
(125)

1972 (30 Mar). *Hurricane Relief. Nos. 373/5 surch as T* **124**, *and Nos. 239B, 241B and 243B surch as T* **125**, *by Govt Printer, Rarotonga.*
377	5 c. + 2 c. Type **123** (R.)		10	10
	a. Albino surch		45·00	
378	10 c. + 2 c. Christ on the Cross (R.)		15	15
379	15 c. + 5 c. Frangipani		20	20
380	25 c. + 5 c. Canna Lily		25	25
381	30 c. + 5 c. Mary, Mother of Jesus		30	30
	a. Albino surch			
382	50 c. + 10 c. Gardinia taitensis		35	35
	Set of 6		1·10	1·10
	First Day Cover			1·90

1972 (24 May). *Hurricane Relief. Nos. 383/91 surch as T* **128**.
392	5 c. + 2 c. Type **126**		10	10
393	5 c. + 2 c. Type **127**		10	10
394	10 c. + 2 c.	Astronauts on Moon	10	10
395	10 c. + 2 c.		10	10
396	25 c. + 2 c.	Moon Rover and astronauts	15	15
397	25 c. + 2 c.		15	15
398	30 c. + 2 c.	Splashdown and astronauts	20	15
399	30 c. + 2 c.		20	15
	Set of 8		1·00	1·00
	First Day Cover			1·75
MS400	83 × 205 mm. **MS391** surch 3 c. on each stamp		2·75	3·50
	First Day Cover			4·00

126 Rocket heading for Moon 127

1972 (17 Apr). *Apollo Moon Exploration Flights. T* **126/7** *and similar horiz designs. Multicoloured. P* 13.
383	5 c. Type **126**		15	10
384	5 c. Type **127**		15	10
385	10 c.	Astronauts on Moon	20	10
386	10 c.		20	10
387	25 c.	Moon Rover and astronauts working	25	15
388	25 c.		25	15
389	30 c.	Splashdown and helicopter	25	15
390	30 c.		25	15
	Set of 8		1·50	90
	First Day Cover			1·75
MS391	83 × 205 mm. Nos. 383/90		3·00	4·50
	First Day Cover			5·00

These were issued in horizontal *se-tenant* pairs of each value, forming one composite design.

1972 (26 June). *Olympic Games, Munich. T* **129** *and similar vert designs. Multicoloured. P* 13½.
401	10 c. Type **129**		15	5
402	25 c. Running		35	25
403	30 c. Boxing		40	25
	Set of 3		80	50
	First Day Cover			1·25
MS404	88 × 78 mm. 50 c. + 5 c. Pierre de Coubertin		1·40	2·50
	First Day Cover			3·25
MS405	84 × 133 mm. Nos. 401/3 plus se-tenant label		1·50	2·50
	First Day Cover			4·00

Each value was issued in sheets of 8 stamps and 1 label.

130 "The Rest on the Flight into Egypt"(Caravaggio) 131 Marriage Ceremony

1972 (11 Oct). *Christmas T* **130** *and similar vert designs. Multicoloured. P* 13.
406	1 c. Type **130**		5	5
407	5 c. "Madonna of the Swallow" (Guercino)		10	5
408	10 c. "Madonna of the Green Cushion" (Solario)		20	5
409	20 c. "Madonna and Child" (di Credi)		30	15
410	30 c. "Madonna and Child" (Bellini)		50	25
	Set of 5		1·00	45
	First Day Cover			1·00
MS411	141 × 152 mm. Nos. 406/10 plus se-tenant label in position 1		1·75	2·25
	First Day Cover			2·75
MS412	101 × 82 mm. 50 c. + 5 c. "The Holy Night" (Correggio) (31 × 43 mm)		75	1·75
	First Day Cover			2·25

Each value was issued in sheets of 9 stamps and 1 label.

MINIMUM PRICE

The minimum price quoted is 5p which represents a handling charge rather than a basis for valuing common stamps. For further notes about prices see introductory pages.

1972 (20 Nov). *Royal Silver Wedding. T **131** and similar black and silver designs. P* 13.

413	5 c.	Type **131**	25	15
414	10 c.	Leaving Westminster Abbey	60	40
415	15 c.	Bride and Bridegroom (40 × 41 *mm*)	75	50
416	30 c.	Family Group (67 × 40 *mm*)	1·10	80
		Set of 4	2·50	1·60
		First Day Cover		1·75

The 5, 10 and 15 c. values were each issued in sheets of 8 stamps and 1 label.

132 Taro Leaf

133 "Noli me Tangere" (Titian)

1973 (15 Mar). *Silver Wedding Coinage. T **132** and similar designs showing coins. P* 13.

417	1 c.	black, rosy carmine and gold	5	5
418	2 c.	black, bright blue and gold	5	5
419	5 c.	black, green and silver	12	5
420	10 c.	black, royal blue and silver	25	5
421	20 c.	black, deep blue-green and silver	35	10
422	50 c.	black, carmine and silver	65	20
423	$1	black, bright blue and silver	1·10	40
		Set of 7	2·25	70
		First Day Cover		1·40

Designs: *As T* **132**—2 c. Pineapple; 5 c. Hibiscus. 46 × 30 *mm*—10 c. Oranges; 20 c. White Tern; 50 c. Skipjack Tuna. 32 × 55 *mm*—$1 Tangaroa. Each value was issued in sheets of 20 stamps and 1 label.

1973 (9 Apr). *Easter. T **133** and similar vert designs. Multicoloured. P* 13.

424	5 c.	Type **133**	10	5
425	10 c.	"The Descent from the Cross" (Rubens)	15	5
426	30 c.	"The Lamentation of Christ" (Dürer)	20	10
		Set of 3	40	15
		First Day Cover		60
MS427	132 × 67 mm. Nos. 424/6		70	1·25
		First Day Cover		1·60

Each value was issued in sheets of 15 stamps and 1 label.

1973 (30 Apr). *Easter. Children's Charity. Designs as Nos. 424/6 in separate Miniature Sheets 67 × 87 mm, each with a face value of 50 c. + 5 c. P* 13 × 14.

MS428	As Nos. 424/6. Set of 3 sheets	1·90	2·75
	First Day Cover		3·50

134 Queen Elizabeth II in Coronation Regalia

TENTH ANNIVERSARY CESSATION OF NUCLEAR TESTING TREATY

(135)

1973 (1 June). *20th Anniv of Queen Elizabeth's Coronation. P* 14 × 13½.

429	**134**	10 c. multicoloured	90	1·75
		First Day Cover		2·25
MS430	64 × 89 mm. 50 c. as 10 c. P 13 × 14		3·50	4·50
		First Day Cover		6·50

The perforated portion of MS430 is similar to No. 429, but has no borders.

No. 429 was issued in sheets of 5 stamps and 1 label.

1973 (25 July). *Tenth Anniv of Treaty Banning Nuclear Testing. Nos. 234B, 236B, 238B, and 240B/242B optd with T **135**.

431	5 c.	*Bauhinia bi-pinnata rosea*	15	10
432	8 c.	*Allamanda cathartica*	15	10
433	10 c.	*Poinciana regia flamboyant*	15	10
434	20 c.	*Thunbergia*	20	20
435	25 c.	Canna Lily	25	25
436	30 c.	*Euphorbia pulcherrima poinsettia*	25	25
		Set of 6	1·00	90
		First Day Cover		1·50

136 Tipairua

1973 (17 Sept). *Maori Exploration of the Pacific. T **136** and similar horiz designs showing sailing craft. Multicoloured. P* 13.

437	½ c.	Type **136**	5	5
438	1 c.	Wa'a Kaulua	10	5
439	1½ c.	Tainui	15	5
440	5 c.	War canoe	40	10
441	10 c.	Pahi	60	15
442	15 c.	Amastasi	85	30
443	25 c.	Vaka	1·10	50
		Set of 7	3·00	1·10
		First Day Cover		1·75

137 The Annunciation

138 Princess Anne

1973 (30 Oct). *Christmas. T **137** and similar vert designs showing scenes from a 15th-century Flemish "Book of Hours". Multicoloured. P* 13.

444	1 c.	Type **137**	5	5
445	5 c.	The Visitation	5	5
446	10 c.	Annunciation to the Shepherds	5	5
447	20 c.	Epiphany	15	10
448	30 c.	The Slaughter of the Innocents	25	20
		Set of 5	50	40
		First Day Cover		90
MS449	121 × 128 mm. Nos. 444/8 plus *se-tenant* label		70	1·40
		First Day Cover		1·60

Each value was issued in sheets of 14 stamps and 1 label.
See also No. MS454.

1973 (14 Nov). *Royal Wedding. T* **138** *and similar vert designs. Multicoloured. P* 14 × 13½.

450	25 c. Type **138**	25	15
451	30 c. Capt. Mark Phillips	30	20
452	50 c. Princess Anne and Capt. Phillips	40	25
	Set of 3	85	55
	First Day Cover		65
MS453	119 × 100 mm. No. 450/2 plus *se-tenant* label.		
	P 13	1·00	75
	First Day Cover		1·25

Each value was issued in sheets of 8 stamps and 1 label.

1973 (3 Dec). *Christmas. Children's Charity. Designs as Nos.* 444/8 *in separate Miniature Sheets* 50 × 70 *mm, each with a face value of* 50 c. + 5 c.

MS454	As Nos. 444/8. Set of 5 sheets	1·00	1·50
	First Day Cover		3·75

139 Running

140 "Jesus carrying the Cross" (Raphael)

1974 (24 Jan). *Commonwealth Games, Christchurch. T* **139** *and similar multicoloured designs. P* 14 × 13½ (1 *and* 3 c.) *or* 13½ × 14 (*others*).

455	1 c. Diving (*vert*)	5	5
456	3 c. Boxing (*vert*)	5	5
457	5 c. Type **139**	5	5
458	10 c. Weightlifting	10	5
459	30 c. Cycling	30	35
	Set of 5	50	50
	First Day Cover		80
MS460	115 × 90 mm. 50 c. Discobolus	50	70
	First Day Cover		1·25

Each value was issued in sheets of 15 stamps and 1 label.

1974 (25 Mar). *Easter. T* **140** *and similar vert designs. Multicoloured. P* 13½.

461	5 c. Type **140**	5	5
462	10 c. "The Holy Trinity" (El Greco)	5	5
463	30 c. "The Deposition of Christ" (Caravaggio)	25	20
	Set of 3	30	25
	First Day Cover		65
MS464	130 × 70 mm. Nos. 461/3	60	65
	First Day Cover		1·40

Each value was issued in sheets of 20 stamps and 1 label.

1974 (22 Apr). *Easter. Children's Charity. Designs as Nos.* 461/3 *in separate Miniature Sheets* 59 × 87 *mm, each with a face value of* 50 c. + 5 c.

MS465	As Nos. 461/3. Set of 3 sheets	1·00	1·75
	First Day Cover		3·25

141 Helmet Shell

142 Queen Elizabeth II

1974 (17 May)–**75**. *Sea-shells. Horiz designs as T* **141** (½ *to* 60 c.) *T* **142** *or larger horiz design* ($4 *to* $10). *Multicoloured. P* 14 × 13½ ($4 *to* $10) *or* 13½ (*others*).

466	½ c. Type **141**	10	5
467	1 c. Vase shell	15	5
468	1½ c. Cockle shell	25	5
469	2 c. *Terebellum terebellum*	25	5
470	3 c. Bat volutes	30	5
471	4 c. Conch shell	30	5
472	5 c. Triton shell	30	5
473	6 c. Snake-head cowries	35	15
474	8 c. Helmet shell (*different*)	40	10
475	10 c. Auger shell	40	10
476	15 c. Metre shell	70	15
477	20 c. Naticacid shell	75	15
478	25 c. Scallop shell	80	25
479	30 c. Soldier cone shell	90	25
480	50 c. Cloth of Gold cone shell (26.8.74)	3·00	2·00
481	60 c. Olive shell (26.8.74)	3·00	2·25
482	$1 Type **142** (26.8.74)	2·50	2·75
483	$2 Type **142** (27.1.75)	2·50	2·10
484	$4 Queen Elizabeth II and seashells (17.3.75)	3·50	4·00
485	$6 As $4 (29.4.75)	10·00	7·00
486	$8 As $4 (30.5.75)	10·00	8·00
487	$10 As $4 (30.6.75)	10·00	9·00
	Set of 17 (Nos. 466/82)	13·00	7·50
	First Day Covers (7)		50·00

Nos. 484/7 are larger, 60 × 39 mm.

143 Footballer and Australasian Map

144 Obverse and Reverse of Commemorative $2·50 Silver Coin

1974 (5 July). *World Cup Football Championships. West Germany. T* **143** *and similar horiz designs. Multicoloured. P* 13.

488	25 c. Type **143**	20	20
489	50 c. Map and Munich Stadium	40	40
490	$1 Footballer, stadium and World Cup	65	65
	Set of 3	1·10	1·10
	First Day Cover		1·75
MS491	89 × 100 mm. Nos. 488/90	1·75	2·75
	First Day Cover		3·50

Each value was issued in sheets of 8 stamps and 1 label.

1974 (22 July). *Bicentenary of Capt. Cook's Second Voyage of Discovery. T* **144** *and similar vert design. P* 14.

492	$2·50, silver, black and violet	13·00	7·00
493	$7·50, silver, black and deep turquoise-green	25·00	15·00
	Set of 2	38·00	22·00
	First Day Cover		25·00
MS494	73 × 73 mm. Nos. 492/3	45·00	48·00
	First Day Cover		50·00

Design:—$7·50, As T **144** but showing $7·50 coin. Each value was issued in sheets of 5 stamps and 1 label.

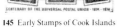

145 Early Stamps of Cook Islands   146 "Madonna of the
                                     Goldfinch" (Raphael)

1974 (16 Sept).   *Centenary of Universal Postal Union. T* **145** *and similar*
horiz designs. Multicoloured. P 13½ × 14.
495	10 c.	Type **145**	15	15
496	25 c.	Old landing strip, Rarotonga, and stamp of 1898	30	30
497	30 c.	Post Office, Rarotonga, and stamp of 1920	30	30
498	50 c.	U.P.U. emblem and stamps	40	40
		Set of 4	1·00	1·00
		First Day Cover		1·40
MS499	118 × 79 mm. Nos. 495/8. P 13		1·25	1·75
	First Day Cover			2·40

Each value was issued in sheets of 8 stamps and 1 label.

1974 (15 Oct).   *Christmas. T* **146** *and similar vert designs. Multicoloured.*
P 13.
500	1 c.	Type **146**	5	5
501	5 c.	"The Sacred Family" (Andrea del Sarto)	5	5
502	10 c.	"The Virgin adoring the Child" (Correggio)	10	5
503	20 c.	"The Holy Family" (Rembrandt)	20	20
504	30 c.	"The Virgin and Child" (Rogier Van Der Weyden)	30	30
		Set of 5	65	60
		First Day Cover		1·10
MS505	114 × 133 mm. Nos. 500/4 plus se-tenant label		75	1·25
	First Day Cover			1·75

Each value was issued in sheets of 15 stamps and 1 label.
See also No. **MS512**.

147 Churchill and Blenheim Palace

1974 (20 Nov).   *Birth Centenary of Sir Winston Churchill. T* **147** *and*
similar horiz designs. Multicoloured. P 13½ × 14.
506	5 c.	Type **147**	25	15
507	10 c.	Churchill and Houses of Parliament	40	25
508	25 c.	Churchill and Chartwell	80	50
509	30 c.	Churchill and Buckingham Palace	90	65
510	50 c.	Churchill and St. Paul's Cathedral	1·25	80
		Set of 5	3·25	2·10
		First Day Cover		2·75
MS511	108 × 114 mm. Nos. 506/10 plus se-tenant label		4·00	3·00
	First Day Cover			4·50

Each value was issued in sheets of 5 stamps and 1 label.

1974 (9 Dec).   *Christmas. Children's Charity. Designs as Nos.* 500/504
in separate miniature sheets 53 × 69 *mm, each with a face value of*
50 *c.* + 5 *c.*
MS512	As Nos. 500/4. Set of 5 sheets	1·50	2·25
	First Day Cover		4·00

148   Vasco Nuñez de Balboa and Discovery
                of Pacific Ocean (1513)

1975 (3 Feb).   *Pacific Explorers. T* **148** *and similar horiz designs.*
Multicoloured. P 13.
513	1 c.	Type **148**	10	10
514	5 c.	Fernando de Magellanes and map (1520)	35	20
515	10 c.	Juan Sebastian de Elcano and Vitoria (1520)	60	30
516	25 c.	Friar de Urdaneta and ship (1564–67)	1·50	1·00
517	30 c.	Miguel Lopez de Legazpi and ship (1564–67)	1·60	1·25
		Set of 5	3·75	2·50
		First Day Cover		3·25

149 "Apollo" Capsule

1975 (15 July).   *"Apollo-Soyuz" Space Project. T* **149** *and similar horiz*
designs. Multicoloured. P 13½.
518	25 c.	Type **149**	30	20
519	25 c.	"Soyuz" capsule	30	20
520	30 c.	"Soyuz" crew	35	25
521	30 c.	"Apollo" crew	35	25
522	50 c.	Cosmonaut within "Soyuz"	40	30
523	50 c.	Astronauts within "Apollo"	40	30
		Set of 6	1·90	1·40
		First Day Cover		1·75
MS524	119 × 119 mm. Nos. 518/23. P 13 × 14		2·50	3·00
	First Day Cover			4·00

Each value was issued in sheets containing 9 horizontal se-tenant pairs
of the two designs, together with 2 labels.

150 $100 Commemorative Gold Coin

1975 (8 Aug).   *Bicentenary of Captain Cook's Second Voyage. P* 13.
525	**150**	$2 brown, gold and bluish violet	6·50	3·00
		First Day Cover		4·00

No. 525 was issued in sheets of 5 stamps and 1 label.

151 Cook Islands' Flag and Map

1975 (8 Aug). *Tenth Anniv of Self-Government. T* **151** *and similar multicoloured designs. P* 13.

526	5 c. Type **151**	20	10
527	10 c. Premier Sir Albert Henry and flag (*vert*) . . .	30	10
528	25 c. Rarotonga and flag	70	40
	Set of 3	1·10	55
	First Day Cover		75

152 "Madonna by the Fireside" (R. Campin)   **153** "Entombment of Christ" (Raphael)

1975 (1 Dec). *Christmas. T* **152** *and similar vert designs. Multicoloured. P* 13½.

529	6 c. Type **152**	10	5
530	10 c. "Madonna in the Meadow" (Raphael)	10	5
531	15 c. "Madonna of the Oak" (attrib Raphael) . . .	15	10
532	20 c. "Adoration of the Shepherds" (J. B. Maino)	20	15
533	35 c. "The Annunciation" (Murillo)	30	25
	Set of 5	75	55
	First Day Cover		1·00
MS534	110 × 124 mm. Nos. 529/33	75	1·10
	First Day Cover		1·60

1975 (15 Dec). *Christmas. Children's Charity. Designs as Nos.* 529/33 *in separate miniature sheets* 53 × 71 *mm, each with a face value of* 75 c. + 5 c.

MS535	As Nos. 529/33. Set of 5 sheets	2·00	2·5C
	a. Error. Miniature sheet as No. 531 imperf . .	£250	
	First Day Cover		5·00

1976 (29 Mar). *Easter. T* **153** *and similar square designs. Multicoloured. P* 13.

536	7 c. Type **153**	15	10
537	15 c. "Pietà" (Veronese)	25	15
538	35 c. "Pietà" (El Greco)	40	35
	Set of 3	70	55
	First Day Cover		85
MS539	144 × 57 mm. Nos. 536/8	70	1·10
	First Day Cover		1·50

Each value was issued in sheets of 20 stamps and 1 label.

1976 (3 May). *Easter. Children's Charity. Designs as Nos.* 536/8 *in separate miniature sheets* 69 × 69 *mm, each with a face value of* 60 c. + 5 c.

MS540	As Nos. 536/8. Set of 3 sheets	1·75	2·00
	First Day Cover		3·75

154 Benjamin Franklin and H.M.S. *Resolution*

1976 (29 May). *Bicentenary of American Revolution. T* **154** *and similar horiz designs. Multicoloured. P* 13.

541	$1 Type **154**	6·00	2·00
542	$2 Captain Cook and H.M.S. *Resolution*	8·00	3·00
	Set of 2	14·00	5·00
	First Day Cover		9·00
MS543	118 × 58 mm. $3 Cook, Franklin and H.M.S. *Resolution* (74 × 31 mm)	14·00	9·00
	First Day Cover		14·00

Each value was issued in sheets of 5 stamps and 1 label.

Royal Visit July 1976

(155)

1976 (9 July). *Visit of Queen Elizabeth to the U.S.A. Nos.* 541/3 *optd with T* **155**.

544	$1 Type **154**	3·50	2·00
545	$2 Captain Cook and H.M.S. *Resolution*	5·50	3·00
	Set of 2	9·00	5·00
	First Day Cover		8·50
MS546	$3 Cook, Franklin and H.M.S. *Resolution*	10·00	8·50
	First Day Cover		11·00

156 Hurdling   **157** "The Visitation"

1976 (22 July). *Olympic Games, Montreal. T* **156** *and similar square designs. Multicoloured. P* 13.

547	7 c.	} Type **156**	10	10
548	7 c.		10	10
549	15 c.	} Hockey	15	10
550	15 c.		15	15
551	30 c.	} Fencing	25	25
552	30 c.		25	25
553	35 c.	} Football	30	30
554	35 c.		30	30
	Set of 8		1·40	1·40
	First Day Cover			1·75
MS555	104 × 146 mm. Nos. 547/54		1·40	2·00
	First Day Cover			3·00

Each value was issued in sheets containing 5 horizontal *se-tenant* pairs and 2 labels. In each pair the first stamp has the face-value on the right, the second has it on the left. Illustrated is the left-hand stamp of the 7 c. design.

1976 (12 Oct). *Christmas. T* **157** *and similar vert designs showing Renaissance sculptures. Multicoloured. P* 14 × 13½.

556	6 c. Type **157**	10	5
557	10 c. "Adoration of the Shepherds"	10	5
558	15 c. "Adoration of the Shepherds" (*different*) . .	15	10
559	20 c. "The Epiphany"	20	20
560	35 c. "The Holy Family"	25	25
	Set of 5	70	60
	First Day Cover		1·00
MS561	116 × 110 mm. Nos. 556/60. P 13	1·00	1·75
	First Day Cover		2·00

Each value was issued in sheets of 20 stamps and 1 label.

1976 (2 Nov). *Christmas. Children's Charity. Designs as Nos.* 556/60 *in separate miniature sheets* 66 × 80 *mm, each with a face value of* 75 c. + 5 c.

MS562	As Nos. 556/60. Set of 5 sheets	2·75	2·75
	First Day Cover		5·50

158 Obverse and Reverse of $5 Mangaia Kingfisher Coin

1976 (15 Nov). *National Wildlife and Conservation Day. P* 13

563	**158** $1 multicoloured	3·25	1·50
	First Day Cover		2·25

No. 563 was issued in sheets of 5 stamps and 1 label.

159 Imperial State Crown   **160** "Christ on the Cross"

1977 (7 Feb).   *Silver Jubilee. T* **159** *and similar vert designs. Multicoloured. P* 13.

564	25 c.	Type **159**	90	75
565	25 c.	Queen with regalia	90	75
566	50 c.	Westminster Abbey	2·00	1·75
567	50 c.	Coronation Coach	2·00	1·75
568	$1	Queen and Prince Philip	4·25	3·50
569	$1	Royal Visit, 1974	4·25	3·50
		Set of 6	13·00	11·00
		First Day Cover		12·00
MS570	130 × 136 mm. As Nos. 564/9 (borders and "COOK ISLANDS" in a different colour)		11·00	10·00
		First Day Cover		13·00

The two designs of each value are printed horizontally *se-tenant* throughout the sheet, and stamps from **MS570** have borders and "COOK ISLANDS" in a different colour.

1977 (28 Mar).   *Easter and 400th Birth Anniv of Rubens. T* **160** *and similar vert designs. Multicoloured. P* 14 × 13½.

571	7 c.	Type **160**	25	10
572	15 c.	"Christ on the Cross"	40	15
573	35 c.	"The Deposition of Christ"	80	40
		Set of 3	1·25	60
		First Day Cover		85
MS574	118 × 65 mm. Nos. 571/3. P 13		1·25	1·10
		First Day Cover		1·40

Each value was issued in sheets of 24 stamps and 1 label.

1977 (18 Apr).   *Easter. Children's Charity. Designs as Nos. 571/3 in separate miniature sheets* 60 × 79 *mm, each with a face value of* 60 c. + 5 c. P 13 × 14.

MS575	As Nos. 571/3. Set of 3 sheets	1·40	1·50
	First Day Cover		3·25

161 "Virgin and Child"   **162** Obverse and Reverse of
(Memling) $5 Cook Islands Swiftlet Coin

1977 (3 Oct).   *Christmas. T* **161** *and similar vert designs. Multicoloured. P* 14.

576	6 c.	Type **161**	10	5
577	10 c.	"Madonna and Child with Saints and Donors" (Memling)	10	5
578	15 c.	"Adoration of the Kings" (Geertgen)	20	10
579	20 c.	"Virgin and Child with Saints" (Crivelli)	25	15
580	35 c.	"Adoration of the Magi" (16th-cent Flemish School)	30	20
		Set of 5	85	50
		First Day Cover		85
MS581	118 × 111 mm. Nos. 576/80. P 13½		85	1·50
		First Day Cover		1·75

Each value was issued in sheets of 24 stamps and 1 label.

1977 (31 Oct).   *Christmas. Children's Charity. Designs as Nos.* 576/80 *in separate miniature sheets* 69 × 69 *mm, each with a face value of* 75 c. + 5 c.

MS582	As Nos. 576/80. Set of 5 sheets	1·90	2·00
	First Day Cover		4·50

1977 (15 Nov).   *National Wildlife and Conservation Day. P* 13.

583	**162**	$1 multicoloured	3·50	1·75
		First Day Cover		2·25

No. 583 was issued in sheets containing 10 stamps and 2 labels.

163 Captain Cook and H.M.S. *Resolution* (from paintings by N. Dance and H. Roberts)

1978 (20 Jan).   *Bicentenary of Discovery of Hawaii. T* **163** *and similar horiz designs. Multicoloured. P* 13½.

584	50 c.	Type **163**	1·50	60
585	$1	Earl of Sandwich, and Cook landing at Owhyhee (from paintings by Thomas Gainsborough and J. Cleveley)	2·00	1·00
586	$2	Obverse and reverse of $200 coin and Cook monument, Hawaii	3·25	1·75
		Set of 3	6·00	3·00
		First Day Cover		4·75
MS587	118 × 95 mm. Nos. 584/86		7·00	7·00
		First Day Cover		8·00

Each value was issued in sheets of 5 stamps and 1 label.

164 "Pieta" (Van der Weyden)   **165** Queen Elizabeth II

1978 (20 Mar).   *Easter. Paintings from National Gallery, London. T* **164** *and similar horiz designs. Multicoloured. P* 13.

588	15 c.	Type **164**	20	15
589	35 c.	"The Entombment" (Michelangelo)	35	30
590	75 c.	"The Supper at Emmaus" (Caravaggio)	65	55
		Set of 3	1·10	90
		First Day Cover		1·25
MS591	114 × 96 mm. Nos. 588/90		1·10	1·50
		First Day Cover		1·75

Each value was issued in sheets of 5 stamps and 1 label.

1978 (10 Apr).   *Easter. Children's Charity. Designs as Nos.* 588/90 *in separate miniature sheets,* 85 × 72 *mm, each with a face value of* 60 c. + 5 c. P 13½.

MS592	As Nos. 588/90. Set of 3 sheets	1·50	1·50
	First Day Cover		3·00

1978 (6 June).   *25th Anniv of Coronation. T* **165** *and similar vert designs. Multicoloured. P* 13.

593	50 c.	Type **165**	50	50
594	50 c.	The Lion of England	50	50
595	50 c.	Imperial State Crown	50	50
596	50 c.	Statue of Tangaroa (god)	50	50
597	70 c.	Type **165**	50	50
598	70 c.	Sceptre with Cross	50	50

599	70 c. St. Edward's Crown	. . . .	50	50
600	70 c. Rarotongan staff god	. . . .	50	50
	Set of 8	. . . .	3·75	3·75
	First Day Cover	. . . .		4·00
MS601	103 × 142 mm. Nos. 593/600*	. . . .	3·00	4·00
	First Day Cover	. . . .		4·50

Each value was issued in sheets containing the 4 designs and 2 labels.
* In No. MS601 the designs of Nos. 595 and 599 are transposed.

5c

(166)

1978 (10 Nov). *Nos. 466, 468, 473/4 and 478/81 surch as T* **166**.

602	5 c. on 1½ c. Cockle shell (Silver)	25	10
603	7 c. on ½ c. Type **141**	30	15
604	10 c. on 6 c. Snake-head cowries (Gold)	35	15
605	10 c. on 8 c. Helmet shell (Gold)	35	15
606	15 c. on ½ c. Type **141**	40	20
607	15 c. on 25 c. Scallop shell (Silver)	40	20
608	15 c. on 30 c. Soldier cone shell	40	20
609	15 c. on 50 c. Cloth of Gold cone shell (Silver) . .	40	20
610	15 c. on 60 c. Olive shell (Gold)	40	20
611	17 c. on ½ c. Type **141**	45	25
612	17 c. on 50 c. Cloth of Gold cone shell (Silver) . .	45	25
	Set of 11	3·75	1·75
	First Day Cover		2·75

(167)

1978 (13 Nov). *250th Birth Anniv of Captain Cook. Nos.* 584/7 *optd with T* **167** *on silver*.

613	50 c. Type **163**	1·50	75
614	$1 Earl of Sandwich, and Cook landing at Owhyhee (from paintings by Thomas Gainsborough and J. Cleveley)	2·00	1·00
615	$2 Obverse and reverse of $200 coin and Cook monument, Hawaii	3·00	2·00
	Set of 3	6·00	3·25
	First Day Cover		4·75
MS616	Nos. 613/15	9·00	9·00
	First Day Cover		9·50

168 Obverse and Reverse of
$5 Pitcairn Warblers Coin

1978 (15 Nov). *National Wildlife and Conservation Day. P* 13.

617	**168**	$1 multicoloured	1·75	1·00
		First Day Cover		1·50

169 "The Virgin and Child"
(Van der Weyden)

170 Virgin with Body
of Christ

1978 (8 Dec). *Christmas. Paintings. T* **169** *and similar vert designs. Multicoloured. P* 13.

618	15 c. Type **169**	20	10
619	17 c. "The Virgin and Child" (Crivelli)	25	15
620	35 c. "The Virgin and Child" (Murillo)	40	30
	Set of 3	75	50
	First Day Cover		80
MS621	107 × 70 mm. Nos. 618/20	90	1·25
	First Day Cover		1·50

1979 (12 Jan). *Christmas. Children's Charity. Designs as Nos.* 618/20 *in separate miniature sheets* 57 × 87 *mm, each with a face value of* 75 c. + 5 c. P 13½.

MS622	As Nos. 618/20. Set of 3 sheets	1·50	1·50
	First Day Cover		3·00

1979 (5 Apr). *Easter. Details of Painting "Descent" by Gaspar de Crayar. T* **170** *and similar vert designs. Multicoloured. P* 13.

623	10 c. Type **170**	10	10
624	12 c. St. John	15	15
625	15 c. Mary Magdalene	20	20
626	20 c. Weeping angels	20	20
	Set of 4	60	60
	First Day Cover		70
MS627	83 × 100 mm. As Nos. 623/6, but each with charity premium of 2 c.	65	75
	First Day Cover		1·10

Stamps from No. MS627 are slightly smaller, 32 × 40 mm, and are without borders.

171 "Captain Cook"
(James Weber).

172 Post-Rider

1979 (23 July). *Death Bicentenary of Captain Cook. T* **171** *and similar vert designs. Multicoloured. P* 14 × 13.

628	20 c. Type **171**	30	20
629	30 c. H.M.S. *Resolution*	50	35
630	35 c. H.M.S. *Endeavour*	60	45
631	50 c. "Death of Captain Cook" (George Carter) . . .	70	60
	Set of 4	1·90	1·40
	First Day Cover		1·75
MS632	78 × 112 mm. Nos. 628/31	1·90	2·00
	First Day Cover		2·50

Stamps from No. MS632 have black borders.

1979 (10 Sept). *Death Centenary of Sir Rowland Hill. History of Mail Transport. T* **172** *and similar square designs. Multicoloured. P* 14.

633	30 c. Type **172**	35	25
634	30 c. Mail coach	35	25
635	30 c. Automobile	35	25
636	30 c. Railway train	35	25
637	35 c. *Cap-Horniers* (sailing ship)	40	30
638	35 c. River steamer	40	30
639	35 c. *Deutschland* (liner)	40	30
640	35 c. *United States* (liner)	40	30
641	50 c. Balloon *Neptune*	50	40
642	50 c. Junkers "F 13" (aeroplane)	50	40
643	50 c. *Graf Zeppelin*	50	40
644	50 c. "Concorde"	50	40
	Set of 12	4·50	3·50
	First Day Cover		4·50
MS645	132 × 104 mm. Nos. 633/44	4·50	5·00
	First Day Cover		5·75

Nos. 633/6, 637/40 and 641/4 were each printed together, *se-tenant*, in blocks of 4 throughout the sheets.

6c　　≡

(173)

1979 (12 Sept). *Nos. 466, 468 and 481 surch as T* **173**.
646	6 c. on ½ c. Type **141** (Gold)		15	15
647	10 c. on 1½ c. Cockle shell (Silver)		20	20
648	15 c. on 60 c. Olive shell (Gold)		30	30
	Set of 3		60	60
	First Day Cover			1·10

174　Brother and Sister

175 "Apollo 11" Emblem

1979 (10 Oct). *International Year of the Child. T* **174** *and similar horiz designs. Multicoloured. P* 13.
649	30 c. Type **174**		25	25
650	50 c. Boy with tree drum		40	40
651	65 c. Children dancing		50	50
	Set of 3		1·00	1·00
	First Day Cover			1·40
MS652	102 × 75 mm. As Nos. 649/51, but each with charity premium of 5 c. P 13½ × 13		1·00	1·50
	First Day Cover			2·00

Designs for stamps from No. **MS**652 are as Nos. 649/51 but have I.Y.C. emblem in red.

1979 (7 Nov). *10th Anniv of Moon Landing. T* **175** *and similar vert designs. Multicoloured. P* 14.
653	30 c. Type **175**		30	35
654	50 c. Crew of "Apollo 11"		40	50
655	60 c. Astronaut on Moon		50	60
656	65 c. Command module after splashdown		55	65
	Set of 4		1·60	1·90
	First Day Cover			2·25
MS657	119 × 105 mm. Nos. 653/6. P 13½		1·75	2·00
	First Day Cover			2·50

COOK ISLANDS $1
176　Obverse and Reverse of $5 Rarotongan Fruit Dove Coin

177　Glass Christmas Tree Ornaments

1979 (15 Nov). *National Wildlife and Conservation Day. P* 13 × 14.
658	**176**	$1 multicoloured	2·00	1·90
		First Day Cover		2·25

1979 (14 Dec). *Christmas. T* **177** *and similar vert designs. Multicoloured. P* 13½. (*a*) *Postage.*
659	6 c. Type **177**		5	5
660	10 c. Hibiscus flower and star		10	10
661	12 c. Poinsettia flower, bells and candle		10	10
662	15 c. Poinsettia leaves and Tiki (god)		15	15

(*b*) *Air*
663	20 c. Type **177**		15	15
664	25 c. As 10 c.		20	20
665	30 c. As 12 c.		25	25
666	35 c. As 15 c.		30	30
	Set of 8		1·10	1·10
	First Day Cover			1·40

1980 (15 Jan). *Christmas. Children's Charity. Designs as Nos.* 659/66 *with additional premiums.* (*a*) *Postage.*
667	6 c. + 2 c. Type **177**		10	10
668	10 c. + 2 c. Hibiscus flower and star		15	15
669	12 c. + 2 c. Poinsettia flower, bells and candle		15	20
670	15 c. + 2 c. Poinsettia leaves and Tiki (god)		15	20

(*b*) *Air*
671	20 c. + 4 c. Type **177**		15	25
672	25 c. + 4 c. As 10 c.		20	30
673	30 c. + 4 c. As 12 c.		25	35
674	35 c. + 4 c. As 15 c.		30	40
	Set of 8		1·25	1·75
	First Day Cover			2·00

178 "Flagellation"

179　Dove with Olive Twig

1980 (31 Mar). *Easter. Illustrations by Gustave Doré. T* **178** *and similar vert designs in sepia and gold. P* 13.
675	20 c. Type **178**		15	20
676	20 c. "Crown of Thorns"		15	20
677	30 c. "Jesus Insulted"		25	30
678	30 c. "Jesus Falls"		25	30
679	35 c. "The Crucifixion"		25	30
680	35 c. "The Descent from the Cross"		25	30
	Set of 6		1·10	1·40
	First Day Cover			1·75
MS681	120 × 110 mm. As Nos. 675/80, but each with charity premium of 2 c.		1·10	1·50
	First Day Cover			2·00

Nos. 675/6, 677/8 and 679/80 were each printed together, *se-tenant*, in vertical pairs throughout the sheet.

1980 (23 Apr). *Easter. Children's Charity. Designs as Nos.* 675/80 *in separate miniature sheets* 60 × 71 *mm, each with a face value of* 75 *c.* + 5 *c. P* 13.
MS682	As Nos. 675/80. *Set of 6 sheets*		1·40	2·00
	First Day Cover			3·75

1980 (27 May). *75th Anniv of Rotary International. T* **179** *and similar horiz designs. Multicoloured. P* 14.
683	30 c. Type **179**		35	35
684	35 c. Hibiscus flower		40	40
685	50 c. Ribbons		50	50
	Set of 3		1·10	1·10
	First Day Cover			1·40
MS686	72 × 113 mm. Nos. 683/5 but each with premium of 3 c. P 13½		1·10	1·50
	First Day Cover			1·75

ZEAPEX STAMP EXHIBITION-AUCKLAND 1980

(180)   181 Queen Elizabeth
the Queen Mother

1980 (22 Aug). *"Zeapex 80" International Stamp Exhibition, Auckland. Nos. 633/45 optd with T **180** in black on silver background.*

687	30 c.	Type **172**	30	30
688	30 c.	Mail coach	30	30
689	30 c.	Automobile	30	30
690	30 c.	Railway train	30	30
691	35 c.	*Cap-Horniers* (sailing ship)	35	35
692	35 c.	River steamer	35	35
693	35 c.	*Deutschland* (liner)	35	35
694	35 c.	*United States* (liner)	35	35
695	50 c.	Balloon *Neptune*	65	45
696	50 c.	Junkers "F 13" (aeroplane)	65	45
697	50 c.	*Graf Zeppelin*	65	45
698	50 c.	"Concorde"	65	45
		Set of 12	4·75	4·00
		First Day Cover		4·50
MS699		132 × 104 mm. Nos. 687/98	5·00	5·00
		First Day Cover		5·50

1980 (22 Aug). *"Zeapex 80" International Stamp Exhibition, Auckland. As No. **MS681** but containing stamps without charity premium of 2 c. optd "Zeapex '80 Auckland + 10 c" in black on gold background.*

MS700	120 × 110 mm. Nos. 675/80 (*sold at* $1.80)		90	1·60
	First Day Cover			1·90

Stamps from No. **MS700** are unaffected by the overprint which appears on the sheet margin.

1980 (23 Sept). *80th Birthday of Queen Elizabeth the Queen Mother. P 13.*

701	**181**	50 c. multicoloured	1·40	90
		First Day Cover		1·10
MS702	64 × 78 mm. **181** $2 multicoloured		2·50	2·25
	First Day Cover			2·50

182 Satellites orbiting Moon   183 Scene from novel *From the Earth to the Moon*

1980 (7 Nov). *350th Death Anniv of Johannes Kepler (astronomer). T **182** and similar horiz designs. Multicoloured. P 13.*

703	12 c.	Type **182**	35	35
704	12 c.	Space-craft orbiting Moon	35	35
705	50 c.	Space-craft orbiting Moon (*different*)	80	80
706	50 c.	Astronaut and Moon vehicle	80	80
		Set of 4	2·10	2·10
		First Day Cover		2·40
MS707	122 × 122 mm. Nos. 703/6		2·10	2·40
	First Day Cover			2·75

Nos. 703/4 and 705/6 were each printed together, *se-tenant*, in horizontal pairs throughout the sheet.

1980 (7 Nov). *75th Death Anniv of Jules Verne (author). T **183** and similar vert designs showing scenes from the novel "From the Earth to the Moon". P 13.*

708	20 c.	multicoloured (green background)	35	35
709	20 c.	multicoloured (brown background)	35	35
710	30 c.	multicoloured (mauve background)	45	45
711	30 c.	multicoloured (blue background)	45	45
		Set of 4	1·40	1·40
		First Day Cover		1·60
MS712	121 × 122 mm. Nos. 708/11		1·50	1·75
	First Day Cover			2·00

Nos. 708/9 and 710/11 were each printed together, *se-tenant*, in horizontal pairs throughout the sheet.

COOK ISLANDS

184 *Siphonogorgia*   185 Annunciation

1980 (21 Nov)–**82**. *Corals (1st series). Multicoloured designs as T **184**. P 13 (1 c. to $1) or 14 × 13½ ($2 to $10).*

713	1 c.	Type **184**	10	5
714	1 c.	*Pavona praetorta*	10	5
715	1 c.	*Stylaster echinatus*	10	5
716	1 c.	*Tubastraea*	10	5
717	3 c.	*Millepora alcicornis*	15	5
718	3 c.	*Junceella gemmacea*	15	5
719	3 c.	*Fungia fungites*	15	5
720	3 c.	*Heliofungia actiniformis*	15	5
721	4 c.	*Distichopora violacea*	15	5
722	4 c.	*Stylaster*	15	5
723	4 c.	*Gonipora*	15	5
724	4 c.	*Caulastraea echinulata*	15	5
725	5 c.	*Ptilosarcus gurneyi*	20	5
726	5 c.	*Stylophora pistillata*	20	5
727	5 c.	*Melithaea squamata*	20	5
728	5 c.	*Porites andrewsi*	20	5
729	6 c.	*Lobophyllia bemprichii*	20	10
730	6 c.	*Palauastrea ramosa*	20	10
731	6 c.	*Bellonella indica*	20	10
732	6 c.	*Pectinia alcicornis*	20	10
733	8 c.	*Sarcophyton digitatum*	20	10
734	8 c.	*Melithaea albitincta*	20	10
735	8 c.	*Plerogyra sinuosa*	20	10
736	8 c.	*Dendrophyllia gracilis*	20	10
737	10 c.	Type **184** (19.12.80)	25	15
738	10 c.	As No. 714 (19.12.80)	25	15
739	10 c.	As No. 715 (19.12.80)	25	15
740	10 c.	As No. 716 (19.12.80)	25	15
741	12 c.	As No. 717 (19.12.80)	25	15
742	12 c.	As No. 718 (19.12.80)	25	15
743	12 c.	As No. 719 (19.12.80)	25	15
744	12 c.	As No. 720 (19.12.80)	25	15
745	15 c.	As No. 721 (19.12.80)	30	20
746	15 c.	As No. 722 (19.12.80)	30	20
747	15 c.	As No. 723 (19.12.80)	30	20
748	15 c.	As No. 724 (19.12.80)	30	20
749	20 c.	As No. 725 (19.12.80)	35	25
750	20 c.	As No. 726 (19.12.80)	35	25
751	20 c.	As No. 727 (19.12.80)	35	25
752	20 c.	As No. 728 (19.12.80)	35	25
753	25 c.	As No. 729 (19.12.80)	35	25
754	25 c.	As No. 730 (19.12.80)	35	25
755	25 c.	As No. 731 (19.12.80)	35	25
756	25 c.	As No. 732 (19.12.80)	35	25
757	30 c.	As No. 733 (19.12.80)	40	30
758	30 c.	As No. 734 (19.12.80)	40	30
759	30 c.	As No. 735 (19.12.80)	40	30
760	30 c.	As No. 736 (19.12.80)	40	30
761	35 c.	Type **184** (16.3.81)	45	35
762	35 c.	As No. 714 (16.3.81)	45	35
763	35 c.	As No. 715 (16.3.81)	45	35
764	35 c.	As No. 716 (16.3.81)	45	35
765	50 c.	As No. 717 (16.3.81)	65	55

766	50 c. As No. 718 (16.3.81)		65	55
767	50 c. As No. 719 (16.3.81)		65	55
768	50 c. As No. 720 (16.3.81)		65	55
769	60 c. As No. 721 (16.3.81)		75	65
770	60 c. As No. 722 (16.3.81)		75	65
771	60 c. As No. 723 (16.3.81)		75	65
772	60 c. As No. 724 (16.3.81)		75	65
773	70 c. As No. 725 (13.4.81)		1·00	75
774	70 c. As No. 726 (13.4.81)		1·00	75
775	70 c. As No. 727 (13.4.81)		1·00	75
776	70 c. As No. 728 (13.4.81)		1·00	75
777	80 c. As No. 729 (13.4.81)		1·25	80
778	80 c. As No. 730 (13.4.81)		1·25	80
779	80 c. As No. 731 (13.4.81)		1·25	80
780	80 c. As No. 732 (13.4.81)		1·25	80
781	$1 As No. 733 (20.5.81)		1·50	1·00
782	$1 As No. 734 (20.5.81)		1·50	1·00
783	$1 As No. 735 (20.5.81)		1·50	1·00
784	$1 As No. 736 (20.5.81)		1·50	1·00
785	$2 As No. 723 (27.11.81)		2·25	1·75
786	$3 As No. 720 (27.11.81)		3·00	2·40
787	$4 As No. 726 (11.1.82)		3·00	3·50
788	$6 As No. 715 (11.1.82)		4·00	4·50
789	$10 As No. 734 (5.3.82)		8·00	8·50
	Set of 77		48·00	38·00
	First Day Covers (8)			48·00

Nos. 761/84 are 30 × 40 mm and Nos. 785/9, which include a portrait of Queen Elizabeth II in each design, are 55 × 35 mm in size.

The four designs of each value to the $1 were printed together, *se-tenant*, in horizontal strips of 4 (Nos. 713/60) or in blocks of 4 (Nos. 761/84) throughout the sheet.

For similar designs with redrawn frames and inscriptions, see Nos. 966/92.

1980 (1 Dec). *Christmas. Illustrations from 13th-century French Prayer Book. T 185 and similar vert designs. Multicoloured. P 14 × 13½.*

801	15 c. Type **185**		15	15
802	30 c. Visitation		25	25
803	40 c. Nativity		30	30
804	50 c. Epiphany		40	40
	Set of 4		1·00	1·00
	First Day Cover			1·25
MS805	89 × 114 mm. Nos. 801/4. P 13½		1·25	1·50
	First Day Cover			1·75

1981 (9 Jan). *Christmas. Children's Charity. Designs as Nos. 801/4 in separate miniature sheets 55 × 68 mm, each with a face value of 75 c. + 5 c. Imperf.*

MS806	As Nos. 801/4. Set of 4 sheets		2·75	3·00
	First Day Cover			4·25

186 "The Crucifixion" (from book of Saint-Amand)

187 Prince Charles

1981 (10 Apr). *Easter. Illustrations from 12th-century French Prayer Books. T 186 and similar horiz designs. Multicoloured. P 13½ × 14.*

807	15 c. Type **186**		20	20
808	25 c. "Placing in Tomb" (from book of Ingeburge)		30	30
809	40 c. "Mourning at the Sepulchre" (from book of Ingeburge)		40	40
	Set of 3		80	80
	First Day Cover			1·00
MS810	72 × 116 mm. As Nos. 807/9 but each with charity premium of 2 c. P 13½		90	90
	First Day Cover			1·40

1981 (28 Apr). *Easter. Children's Charity. Designs as Nos. 807/9 in separate miniature sheets 64 × 53 mm, each with a face value of 75 c. + 5 c. Imperf.*

MS811	As Nos. 807/9. Set of 3 sheets		1·75	1·75
	First Day Cover			3·00

1981 (29 July). *Royal Wedding. T 187 and similar vert design. Multicoloured. P 14.*

812	$1 Type **187**		1·50	1·50
813	$2 Prince Charles and Lady Diana Spencer		2·75	2·75
	Set of 2		4·25	4·25
	Set of 2 optd "Specimen"		25·00	
	First Day Cover			4·50
MS814	106 × 59 mm. Nos. 812/13. P 13½		5·00	5·00
	Optd "Specimen"		25·00	
	First Day Cover			5·50

Nos. 812/13 were each printed in small sheets of 4.

188 Footballers   (189)

1981 (20 Oct). *World Cup Football Championship, Spain (1982). T 188 and similar horiz designs showing footballers. Multicoloured. P 13½ × 14.*

815	20 c. Type **188**		20	20
816	20 c. Figures to right of stamp		20	20
817	30 c. Figures to left		30	30
818	30 c. Figures to right		30	30
819	35 c. Figures to left		35	35
820	35 c. Figures to right		35	35
821	50 c. Figures to left		45	45
822	50 c. Figures to right		45	45
	Set of 8		2·40	2·40
	First Day Cover			2·75
MS823	180 × 94 mm. As Nos. 815/22, but each stamp with a charity premium of 3 c. P 13½		2·75	3·00
	First Day Cover			4·00

The two designs of each value were printed together, *se-tenant*, in horizontal pairs throughout the sheet, forming composite designs.

1981 (10 Nov). *International Year for Disabled Persons. Nos. 812/14 surch as T 189.*

824	$1 + 5 c. Type **187**		2·50	2·50
825	$2 + 5 c. Prince Charles and Lady Diana Spencer		4·50	5·00
	Set of 2		7·00	7·50
	First Day Cover			8·25
MS826	106 × 59 mm. $1 + 10 c., $2 + 10 c. As Nos. 824/5		7·00	9·00
	First Day Cover			10·00

Nos. 824/6 have commemorative inscriptions overprinted on the sheet margins.

190 "Holy Virgin with Child"

191 Princess of Wales (inscr "21st Birthday")

1981 (14 Dec). *Christmas. Details from Paintings by Rubens. T 190 and similar vert designs. Multicoloured. P 14 × 13½.*

827	8 c. Type **190**		20	10
828	15 c. "Coronation of St. Catherine"		25	15
829	40 c. "Adoration of the Shepherds"		45	35
830	50 c. "Adoration of the Magi"		55	40
	Set of 4		1·25	90
	First Day Cover			1·10
MS831	86 × 110 mm. As Nos. 827/30, but each with a charity premium of 3 c. P 13½		1·50	1·75
	First Day Cover			2·00

1982 (18 Jan). *Christmas. Children's Charity. Designs as Nos.* 827/30 *in separate miniature sheets* 62 × 78 *mm, each with a face value of* 75 c. + 5 c.

MS832	As Nos. 827/30. *Set of* 4 sheets	3·00	3·25
	First Day Cover		4·00

1982 (21 June). *21st Birthday of Princess of Wales. T* **191** *and similar horiz designs. Multicoloured.* P 14.

833	$1.25, Type **191**	1·25	1·25
	a. Pair. Nos. 833/4	2·50	2·50
834	$1.25, As Type **191**, but inscr "1 July 1982"	1·25	1·25
835	$2.50, Princess (*different*) (inscr "21st Birthday")	1·75	1·75
	a. Pair. Nos. 835/6	3·50	3·50
836	$2.50, As No. 835, but inscr "1 July 1982"	1·75	1·75
	Set of 4	5·50	5·50
	First Day Cover		6·00
MS837	92 × 72 mm. $1.25, Type **191**; $2.50, As No. 835. Both inscribed "21st Birthday 1 July 1982". P 13½.	2·75	2·75
	First Day Cover		3·25

The two designs for each value were printed together, *se-tenant*, in small sheets of 4.

(192)

1982 (12 July). *Birth of Prince William of Wales* (1st issue). *Nos.* 812/ 14 *optd as T* **192**.

838	$1 Type **187** (optd with T **192**)	3·50	2·25
	a. Pair. Nos. 838/9	7·00	4·50
839	$1 Type **187** (optd "PRINCE WILLIAM OF WALES")	3·50	2·25
840	$2 Prince Charles and Lady Diana Spencer (optd with T **192**)	6·00	5·00
	a. Pair. Nos. 840/1	12·00	10·00
841	$2 Prince Charles and Lady Diana Spencer (optd "PRINCE WILLIAM OF WALES")	6·00	5·00
	Set of 4	17·00	13·00
	First Day Cover		14·00
MS842	106 × 59 mm. Nos. 812/13 optd "21 JUNE 1982. ROYAL BIRTH".	9·00	8·50
	First Day Cover		9·50

1982 (3 Aug). *Birth of Prince William of Wales* (2nd issue). *Designs as Nos.* 833/7 *but with changed inscriptions. Multicoloured.* P 14.

843	$1.25, As Type **191** (inscr "Royal Birth")	1·25	1·25
	a. Pair. Nos. 843/4	2·50	2·50
844	$1.25, As Type **191** (inscr "21 June 1982")	1·25	1·25
845	$2.50, As No. 835 (inscr "Royal Birth")	1·75	1·75
	a. Pair. Nos. 845/6	3·50	3·50
846	$2.50, As No. 835 (inscr "21 June 1982")	1·75	1·75
	Set of 4	5·50	5·50
	First Day Cover		6·00
MS847	92 × 73 mm. $1.25, As Type **191**; $2.50, As No. 835. Both inscribed "Royal Birth 21 June 1982". P 13½.	2·75	2·75
	First Day Cover		3·25

193 "Serenade"   **194** Franklin D. Roosevelt

(Litho Format)

1982 (10 Sept). *Norman Rockwell* (*painter*) *Commemoration. T* **193** *and similar vert designs. Multicoloured.* P 13½ × 14.

848	5 c. Type **193**	15	10
849	10 c. "The Hikers"	15	15
850	20 c. "The Doctor and the Doll"	30	25
851	30 c. "Home from Camp"	35	30
	Set of 4	85	70
	First Day Cover		80

1982 (30 Sept). *Air. American Anniversaries. T* **194** *and similar vert designs. Multicoloured.* P 14.

852	60 c. Type **194**	80	70
853	80 c. Benjamin Franklin	90	80
854	$1.40, George Washington	1·40	1·25
	Set of 3	2·75	2·50
	First Day Cover		2·75
MS855	116 × 60 mm. Nos. 852/4. P 13½	2·75	3·00
	First Day Cover		3·25

Anniversaries:—60 c. Roosevelt birth centenary; 80 c. "Articles of Peace" negotiations bicentenary $1.40, Washington 250th birth anniv.

195 "Virgin with Garlands" (detail)   **196** Princess Diana
(Rubens) and Princess Diana   and Prince William
with Prince William

1982 (30 Nov). *Christmas. T* **195** *and similar horiz designs depicting different details from Rubens' painting "Virgin with Garlands". P* 13½ × 14.

856	35 c. multicoloured	45	35
857	48 c. multicoloured	60	50
858	60 c. multicoloured	75	60
859	$1.70, multicoloured	1·50	1·40
	Set of 4	3·00	2·50
	First Day Cover		2·75
MS860	104 × 83 mm. 60 c. × 4. Designs, each 27 × 32 mm, forming complete painting "Virgin with Garlands". P 13 × 13½	2·50	3·00
	First Day Cover		3·50

1982 (30 Nov). *Christmas. Birth of Prince William of Wales. Children's Charity. Sheet* 73 × 59 *mm.* P 13.

MS861	**196** 75 c. + 5 c. multicoloured.	95	1·10
	First Day Cover		1·40

No. **MS861** comes with 4 different background designs showing details from painting "Virgin with Garlands" (Rubens).

197 Statue of Tangaroa   **198** Scouts using
                                                    Map and Compass

1983 (14 Mar). *Commonwealth Day. T* **197** *and similar vert designs. Multicoloured.* P 14 × 13½.

862	60 c. Type **197**	55	60
863	60 c. Rarotonga oranges	55	60
864	60 c. Rarotonga airport	55	60
865	60 c. Prime Minister Sir Thomas Davis	55	60
	Set of 4	2·00	2·10
	First Day Cover		2·40

Nos. 862/5 were issued together, *se-tenant*, in blocks of four throughout the sheet.

1983 (5 Apr). *75th Anniv of Boy Scout Movement and 125th Birth Anniv of Lord Baden-Powell. T* **198** *and similar vert designs. Multicoloured. P* 13.

866	12 c.	Type **198**	30	20
867	12 c.	Hiking	30	20
868	36 c.	Campfire cooking	50	40
869	36 c.	Erecting tent	50	40
870	48 c.	Hauling on rope	70	55
871	48 c.	Using bos'n's chair	70	55
872	60 c.	Digging hole for sapling	90	70
873	60 c.	Planting sapling	90	70
		Set of 8	4·25	3·25
		First Day Cover		3·75
MS874		161 × 132 mm. As Nos. 866/73, but each with a premium of 2 c.	4·25	4·25
		First Day Cover		4·75

The two designs of each value were printed together, *se-tenant*, in horizontal pairs throughout the sheets.

XV WORLD JAMBOREE
(199)

1983 (4 July). *15th World Scout Jamboree, Alberta, Canada. Nos. 866/74 optd with T* **199** *(Nos. 875, 877, 879, 881) or with* "ALBERTA, CANADA 1983" *(others)*.

875	12 c.	Type **198**	20	20
876	12 c.	Hiking	20	20
877	36 c.	Campfire cooking	40	40
878	36 c.	Erecting tent	40	40
879	48 c.	Hauling on rope	55	55
880	48 c.	Using bos'n's chair	55	55
881	60 c.	Digging hole for sapling	70	70
882	60 c.	Planting sapling	70	70
		Set of 8	3·25	3·25
		First Day Cover		3·75
MS883		161 × 132 mm. As Nos. 875/82, but each with a premium of 2 c.	3·25	3·75
		First Day Cover		4·75

The two designs of each value were printed together, *se-tenant*, in horizontal pairs throughout the sheet. In each such pair the left-hand design is overprinted with Type **199** and the right-hand with "ALBERTA, CANADA 1983".

18c
(200)

$5.60
(201)

1983 (12–30 Aug). *Various stamps surch.* (*a*) *Nos. 733/6, 745/8, 753/64 and 773/6 as T* **200**.

884	18 c. on 8 c. multicoloured (No. 733)	20	20
885	18 c. on 8 c. multicoloured (No. 734)	20	20
886	18 c. on 8 c. multicoloured (No. 735)	20	20
887	18 c. on 8 c. multicoloured (No. 736)	20	20
888	36 c. on 15 c. multicoloured (No. 745)	40	40
889	36 c. on 15 c. multicoloured (No. 746)	40	40
890	36 c. on 15 c. multicoloured (No. 747)	40	40
891	36 c. on 15 c. multicoloured (No. 748)	40	40
892	36 c. on 30 c. multicoloured (No. 757)	40	40
893	36 c. on 30 c. multicoloured (No. 758)	40	40
894	36 c. on 30 c. multicoloured (No. 759)	40	40
895	36 c. on 30 c. multicoloured (No. 760)	40	40
896	36 c. on 35 c. mult (No. 761) (30.8.83)	40	40
897	36 c. on 35 c. mult (No. 762) (30.8.83)	40	40
898	36 c. on 35 c. mult (No. 763) (30.8.83)	40	40
899	36 c. on 35 c. mult (No. 764) (30.8.83)	40	40
900	48 c. on 25 c. multicoloured (No. 753)	55	55
901	48 c. on 25 c. multicoloured (No. 754)	55	55
902	48 c. on 25 c. multicoloured (No. 755)	55	55
903	48 c. on 25 c. multicoloured (No. 756)	55	55
904	72 c. on 70 c. multicoloured (No. 773)	80	80
905	72 c. on 70 c. multicoloured (No. 774)	80	80
906	72 c. on 70 c. multicoloured (No. 775)	80	80
907	72 c. on 70 c. multicoloured (No. 776)	80	80

(*b*) *Nos. 788/9, 813, 835/6 and 854 as T* **201** *in gold*

908	96 c. on $1.40, George Washington	1·25	1·25
909	96 c. on $2 Prince Charles and Lady Diana Spencer	7·50	5·00
	a. Surch double	£125	
	b. Error. Surch on No. 840	16·00	
	ba. Pair. Nos. 909b/c	32·00	
	c. Error. Surch on No. 841	16·00	
910	96 c. on $2.50, Princess Diana (inscr "21st Birthday") (30.8.83)	2·50	2·50
911	96 c. on $2.50, As No. 910 but inscr "1 July 1982" (30.8.83)	2·50	2·50
912	$5.60 on $6 *Stylaster echinatus*	7·50	6·50
913	$5.60 on $10 *Melithaea albitincta* (30.8.83)	6·00	6·00
	Set of 30	35·00	30·00
	First Day Covers (2)		35·00

The surcharge on No. 908 is printed in gold, on a black background, over the old value.

202 Union Flag

203 Dish Aerial, Satellite Earth Station

1983 (9 Sept). *Cook Islands Flags and Ensigns. T* **202** *and similar horiz designs. Multicoloured. P* 13½ × 14. (*a*) *Postage. Gold frames.*

914	6 c.	Type **202**	5	5
915	6 c.	Group Federal flag	5	5
916	12 c.	Raratonga ensign	10	10
917	12 c.	Flag of New Zealand	10	10
918	15 c.	Cook Islands' flag (1973–79)	15	15
919	15 c.	Cook Islands' National flag	15	15

(*b*) *Air. Silver frames and backgrounds changed*

920	20 c.	Type **202**	20	25
921	20 c.	Group Federal flag	20	25
922	30 c.	Raratonga ensign	25	30
923	30 c.	Flag of New Zealand	25	30
924	35 c.	Cook Islands' flag (1973–79)	30	35
925	35 c.	Cook Islands' National flag	30	35
		Set of 12	1·75	2·00
		First Day Cover		2·40
MS926		Two sheets, each 132 × 120 mm. (a) Nos. 914/19; (b) Nos. 920/5. P 13	1·90	2·50
		First Day Cover		3·00

The two designs of each value were issued as *se-tenant* horizontal pairs within the sheets.

1983 (10 Oct). *World Communications Year. T* **203** *and similar vert designs showing satellites. P* 13.

927	36 c. multicoloured	30	35
928	48 c. multicoloured	45	45
929	60 c. multicoloured	55	60
930	96 c. multicoloured	85	90
	Set of 4	1·90	2·10
	First Day Cover		2·40
MS931	90 × 65 mm. $2 multicoloured	1·75	2·00
	First Day Cover		2·25

204 "La Belle Jardinière"   205 Montgolfier Balloon, 1783

1983 (14 Nov). *Christmas. 500th Birth Anniv of Raphael. T* **204** *and similar vert designs. Multicoloured. P* 14 × 13½.

932	12 c. Type **204**	10	10
933	18 c. "Madonna and Child with Five Saints"	20	25
934	36 c. "Madonna and Child with St. John"	30	35
935	48 c. "Madonna of the Fish"	40	45
936	60 c. "The Madonna of the Baldacchino"	55	60
	Set of 5	1·40	1·60
	First Day Cover		1·90
MS937	139 × 113 mm. As Nos. 932/6 but each with a premium of 3 c.	1·60	1·75
	First Day Cover		2·10

Nos. 932/6 were each printed in small sheets of 5 stamps and 1 label.

1983 (9 Dec). *Christmas. 500th Birth Anniv of Raphael. Children's Charity. Designs as Nos.* 932/6 *in separate miniature sheets* 66 × 82 *mm, each with a face value of* 85 *c.* + 5 *c. P* 13.

MS938	As Nos. 932/6. Set of 5 sheets	4·00	4·25
	First Day Cover		5·00

1984 (16 Jan). *Bicentenary of Manned Flight* (1983). *T* **205** *and similar vert designs. Multicoloured. P* 13.

939	36 c. Type **205**	30	35
940	48 c. Ascent of Adorne, Strasbourg, 1784	40	45
941	60 c. Balloon driven by sails, 1785	55	60
942	72 c. Ascent of man on horse, 1798	70	75
943	96 c. Aerial acrobatics by Godard, 1850	85	90
	Set of 5	2·50	2·75
	First Day Cover		3·25
MS944	104 × 85 mm. $2.50, Blanchard and Jeffries crossing Channel, 1785	2·25	2·75
	First Day Cover		3·25
MS945	122 × 132 mm. As Nos. 939/43 but each with a premium of 5 c.	3·00	3·00
	First Day Cover		3·75

Nos. 939/43 were each printed in small sheets of 5 stamps and 1 label.

206 Cuvier's Beaked Whale   207 Athens, 1896

1984 (10 Feb). *Save the Whales. T* **206** *and similar horiz designs. Multicoloured. P* 13.

946	10 c. Type **206**	20	15
947	18 c. Risso's Dolphin	35	30
948	20 c. True's Beaked Whale	35	30
949	24 c. Long-finned Pilot Whale	40	30
950	30 c. Narwhal	45	35
951	36 c. White Whale	55	45
952	42 c. Common Dolphin	65	50

953	48 c. Commerson's Dolphin	75	60
954	60 c. Bottle-nosed Dolphin	95	70
955	72 c. Sowerby's Beaked Whale	1·10	85
956	96 c. Common Porpoise	1·25	1·10
957	$2 Boutu	2·00	1·90
	Set of 12	8·00	6·50
	First Day Cover		8·50

1984 (8 Mar). *Olympic Games, Los Angeles. T* **207** *and similar vert designs showing official posters of earlier Games. Multicoloured. P* 13½.

958	18 c. Type **207**	15	20
959	24 c. Paris, 1900	20	25
960	36 c. St. Louis, 1904	30	35
961	48 c. London, 1948	40	45
962	60 c. Tokyo, 1964	45	50
963	72 c. Berlin, 1936	55	60
964	96 c. Rome, 1960	75	80
965	$1.20, Los Angeles, 1930	90	95
	Set of 8	3·50	3·75
	First Day Cover		4·25

208 *Siphonogorgia*

$3.60

(209)

1984 (23 Mar–10 Aug). *Corals* (2nd series). (*a*) *Designs as No.* 713 *etc, but with redrawn frames and inscriptions as in T* **208**. *Multicoloured. P* 13.

966	1 c. Type **208**	5	5
967	2 c. *Millepora alcicornis*	5	5
968	3 c. *Distichopora violacea*	5	5
969	5 c. *Ptilosarcus gurneyi*	5	5
970	10 c. *Lobophyllia bemprichii*	5	5
971	12 c. *Sarcophyton digitatum*	10	10
972	14 c. *Pavona praetorta*	10	10
973	18 c. *Junceella gemmacea*	15	15
974	20 c. *Stylaster*	15	15
975	24 c. *Stylophora pistillata*	15	20
976	30 c. *Palauastrea ramosa*	20	25
977	36 c. *Melithaea albitincta*	25	30
978	40 c. *Stylaster echinatus*	25	30
979	42 c. *Fungia fungites*	25	30
980	48 c. *Goniopora*	30	35
981	50 c. *Melithaea squamata* (15 May)	30	35
982	52 c. *Bellonella indica* (15 May)	35	40
983	55 c. *Plerogyra sinuosa* (15 May)	35	40
984	60 c. *Tubastraea* (15 May)	40	45
985	70 c. *Heliofungia actiniformis* (15 May)	45	50
986	85 c. *Caulastraea echinulata* (15 May)	55	60
987	96 c. *Porites andrewsi* (15 May)	65	70
988	$1.10, *Pectinia alcicornis* (15 May)	70	75
989	$1.20, *Dendrophyllia gracilis* (15 May)	80	85

(b) Nos. 785/9 surch as T **209** in gold on black

990	$3.60 on $2 Gonipora (28 June)	2·40	2·50
991	$4.20 on $3 Heliofungia actiniformis (28 June)	2·75	3·00
992	$5 on $4 Stylophora pistillata (28 June)	3·25	3·40
993	$7.20 on $6 Stylaster echinatus (20 July)	5·00	5·25
994	$9.60 on $10 Melithaea albitincta (10 Aug) . .	6·50	6·75
	Set of 29	23·00	25·00
	First Day Covers (5)		30·00

Equestrian
Team Dressage
Germany

COOK ISLANDS

(**210**)

211 Capt. Cook's Cottage, Melbourne

1984 (24 Aug). Olympic Gold Medal Winners. Nos. 963/5 optd as T **210**.

995	72 c. Berlin, 1936 (optd T **210**)	60	65
996	96 c. Rome, 1960 (optd "Decathlon Daley Thompson Great Britain")	80	85
997	$1.20, Los Angeles, 1930 (optd "Four Gold Medals Carl Lewis U.S.A.")	1·00	1·10
	Set of 3	2·25	2·40
	First Day Cover		2·75

1984 (20 Sept). "Ausipex" International Stamp Exhibition, Melbourne. T **211** and similar horiz designs. Multicoloured. P 13.

998	36 c. Type **211**	55	55
999	48 c. "H.M.S. Endeavour careened for Repairs" (Sydney Parkinson)	75	75
1000	60 c. "Cook's landing at Botany Bay" (E. Phillips Fox)	85	85
1001	$2 "Capt. James Cook" (John Webber) . . .	2·50	2·50
	Set of 4	4·25	4·25
	First Day Cover		4·50
MS1002	140 × 100 mm. As Nos. 998/1001, but each with a face value of 90 c.	4·50	4·75
	First Day Cover		5·50

Commemorating-
15 Sept. 1984

COOK ISLANDS

(**212**)

213 "Virgin on Throne with Child" (Giovanni Bellini)

1984 (15 Oct). Birth of Prince Henry. Nos. 812 and 833/6 optd or surch (No. 1007) as T **212**.

1003	$1.25, Type **191** (optd with T **212**) (Gold)	1·75	1·10
	a. Pair. Nos. 1003/4	3·00	2·25
1004	$1.25, As Type **191**, but inscr "1 July 1982' (optd "Birth H.R.H. Prince Henry") (Gold)	1·75	1·10
1005	$2.50, Princess Diana (inscr "21st Birthday") (optd with T **212**) (Gold)	3·00	2·00
	a. Pair. Nos. 1005/6	6·00	4·00
1006	$2.50, As No. 835, but inscr "1 July 1982" (optd "Birth H.R.H. Prince Henry") (Gold)	3·00	2·00
1007	$3 on $1 Type **187** (surch "Royal Birth Prince Henry 15 Sept. 1984") (Sil.)	6·00	4·00
	Set of 5	13·50	9·25
	First Day Cover		10·50

1984 (21 Nov). Christmas. T **213** and similar vert designs. Multicoloured. P 14.

1008	36 c. Type **213**	30	35
1009	48 c. "Virgin and Child" (anonymous, 15th century)	40	45
1010	60 c. "Virgin and Child with Saints" (Alvise Vivarini)	45	50
1011	96 c. "Virgin and Child with Angels" (H. Memling)	75	80
1012	$1.20, "Adoration of Magi" (G. Tiepolo)	90	95
	Set of 5	2·50	2·75
	First Day Cover		3·25
MS1013	120 × 113 mm. As Nos. 1008/12, but each with a premium of 5 c. P 13½	2·75	3·00
	First Day Cover		3·75

1984 (10 Dec). Christmas. Designs as Nos. 1008/12 in separate miniature sheets, 62 × 76 mm, each with a face value of 95 c. + 5 c. P 13½.

MS1014	As Nos. 1008/12. Set of 5 sheets	3·75	4·00
	First Day Cover		5·00

214 Downy Woodpecker

1985 (23 Apr). Birth Bicentenary of John J. Audubon (ornithologist). T **214** and similar vert designs showing original paintings. Multicoloured. P 13 × 13½.

1015	30 c. Type **214**	55	30
1016	55 c. Black-throated Blue Warbler	75	50
1017	65 c. Yellow-throated Warbler	85	55
1018	75 c. Chestnut-sided Warbler	1·00	65
1019	95 c. Dickcissel	1·25	80
1020	$1.15, White-crowned Sparrow	1·50	95
	Set of 6	5·50	3·25
	First Day Cover		3·75
MS1021	Three sheets, each 76 × 75 mm. (a) $1.30, Red-cockaded Woodpecker; (b) $2.80, Seaside Sparrow; (c) $5.30, Zenaida Dove. Set of 3 sheets	8·50	8·50
	First Day Cover		10·00

COOK ISLANDS **20**ᶜ

'Kingston Flyer'   NEW ZEALAND

215 "The Kingston Flyer" (New Zealand)

(Des and litho Format)

1985 (14 May). Famous Trains. T **215** and similar horiz designs. Multicoloured. Ordinary paper. P 14 × 13½.

1022	20 c. Type **215**.	45	20
1023	55 c. Class "640" (Italy).	75	50
1024	65 c. "Gotthard" type (Switzerland)	90	55
1025	75 c. Union Pacific No. 6900 (U.S.A)	1·00	65
1026	95 c. "Super Continental" type (Canada)	1·25	80
1027	$1.15, "TGV" type (France)	1·50	95
1028	$2.20, "The Flying Scotsman" (Great Britain)	2·50	1·75
1029	$3.40, "The Orient Express"	2·75	2·25
	Set of 8	10·00	7·00
	First Day Cover		8·50

216 "Helena Fourment"   217 "Lady Elizabeth,
(Peter Paul Rubens)   1908" (Mabel Hankey)

1985 (6 June). *International Youth Year.* T **216** *and similar vert designs. Multicoloured.* P 13.
1030	55 c. Type **216**	60	50
1031	65 c. "Vigee-Lebrun and Daughter" (E. Vigee-Lebrun)	65	55
1032	75 c. "On the Terrace" (P. Renoir)	75	65
1033	$1.30, "Young Mother Sewing" (M. Cassatt)	1·10	1·10
	Set of 4	2·75	2·50
	First Day Cover		3·00
MS1034	103 × 106 mm. As Nos. 1030/3, but each with a premium of 10 c.	2·75	3·25
	First Day Cover		4·00

1985 (28 June). *Life and Times of Queen Elizabeth the Queen Mother.* T **217** *and similar vert designs showing paintings. Multicoloured.* P 13.
1035	65 c. Type **217**	50	55
1036	75 c. "Duchess of York, 1923" (Savely Sorine)	60	65
1037	$1.15, "Duchess of York, 1925" (Philip de Laszlo)	90	95
1038	$2.80, "Queen Elizabeth, 1938" (Sir Gerald Kelly)	2·10	2·25
	Set of 4	3·75	4·00
	First Day Cover		4·50
MS1039	69 × 81 mm. $5.30, As $2.80.	4·00	4·25
	First Day Cover		4·75

Nos. 1035/8 were each printed in small sheets of 4 stamps.
For these designs in a miniature sheet, each with a face value of 55 c., see No. **MS**1079.

218 Albert Henry   219 Golf
(Prime Minister,
1965–78).

1985 (29 July). *20th Anniv of Self-Government.* T **218** *and similar vert designs. Multicoloured.* P 13.
1040	30 c. Type **218**	25	30
1041	50 c. Sir Thomas Davis (Prime Minister, 1978–Apr. 1983 and from Nov. 1983)	40	45
1042	65 c. Geoffrey Henry (Prime Minister, Apr.–Nov. 1983)	50	55
	Set of 3	1·00	1·10
	First Day Cover		1·40
MS 1043	134 × 70 mm. As Nos. 1040/2, but each with a face value of 55 c.	1·25	1·40
	First Day Cover		1·75

1985 (29 July). *South Pacific Mini Games, Rarotonga.* T **219** *and similar vert designs. Multicoloured.* P 14.
1044	55 c. Type **219**	75	75
1045	65 c. Rugby	85	85
1046	75 c. Tennis	95	95
	Set of 3	2·25	2·25
	First Day Cover		2·50
MS1047	126 × 70 mm. Nos. 1044/6, but each with a premium of 10 c. P 13½.	2·50	2·75
	First Day Cover		3·25

220 Sea Horse,   221 "Madonna of
Gearwheel and Leaves   the Magnificat"

1985 (29 July). *Pacific Conferences, Rarotonga.* P 13.
1048	**220**	55 c. black, gold and rosine	45	50
1049		65 c. black, gold and violet	50	55
1050		75 c. black, gold and blue-green	60	65
		Set of 3	1·40	1·50
		First Day Cover		1·75
MS1051	126 × 81 mm. As Nos. 1048/50, but each with a face value of 50 c.		1·25	1·40
	First Day Cover			2·00

No. 1048 shows the South Pacific Bureau for Economic Co-operation logo and is inscribed "S.P.E.C. Meeting, 30 July–1 Aug 1985, Rarotonga". No. 1049 also shows the S.P.E.C. logo, but is inscribed "South Pacific Forum, 4–6 Aug 1985, Rarotonga". No. 1050 shows the Pacific Islands Conference logo and the inscription "Pacific Islands Conference, 7–10 Aug 1985, Rarotonga".

1985 (18 Nov). *Christmas. Virgin and Child Paintings by Botticelli.* T **221** *and similar vert designs. Multicoloured.* P 14.
1052	55 c. Type **221**	50	50
1053	65 c. "Madonna with Pomegranate"	55	55
1054	75 c. "Madonna and Child with Six Angels"	65	65
1055	95 c. "Madonna and Child with St. John"	80	80
	Set of 4	2·25	2·25
	First Day Cover		2·75
MS1056	90 × 104 mm. As Nos. 1052/5, but each stamp with a face value of 50 c. P 13½	1·75	2·00
	First Day Cover		2·50

1985 (9 Dec). *Christmas. Virgin and Child Paintings by Botticelli. Square designs (46 × 46 mm) as Nos. 1052/5 in separate miniature sheets, 50 × 51 mm, with face values of $1.20, $1.45, $2.20 and $2.75. Imperf.*
MS1057	As Nos. 1052/5. Set of 4 sheets	6·50	7·00
	First Day Cover		7·50

222 "The Eve of the Deluge"   223 Queen Elizabeth II
(John Martin)

1986 (13 Mar). *Appearance of Halley's Comet. Paintings. T* **222** *and similar vert designs. Multicoloured. P* 14.

1058	55 c. Type **222**.....................	60	60
1059	65 c. "Lot and his Daughters" (Lucas van Ley-den)	70	70
1060	75 c. "Auspicious Comet" (from treatise *c* 1587)	80	80
1061	$1.25, "Events following Charles I" (Herman Saftleven)	1·25	1·25
1062	$2 "Ossian receiving Napoleonic Officers" (Anne Louis Girodet-Trioson)	2·00	2·00
	Set of 5	4·75	4·75
	First Day Cover		4·25
MS1063	130 × 100 mm. As Nos. 1058/62, but each with a face value of 70 c. P 13½	2·75	3·25
	First Day Cover		3·75
MS1064	84 × 63 mm. $4 "Halley's Comet of 1759 over the Thames" (Samuel Scott). P 13½	3·25	3·75
	First Day Cover		4·50

1986 (21 Apr). *60th Birthday of Queen Elizabeth II. T* **223** *and similar vert designs showing formal portraits. P* 13 × 13½.

1065	95 c. multicoloured	1·00	1·00
1066	$1.25, multicoloured	1·25	1·25
1067	$1.50, multicoloured	1·50	1·50
	Set of 3	3·25	3·25
	First Day Cover		3·50
MS1068	Three sheets, each 44 × 75 mm. As Nos. 1065/7, but with face values of $1.10, $1.95 and $2.45. Set of 3 sheets	5·50	6·50
	First Day Cover		7·00

224 U.S.A. 1847 Franklin 5 c.
Stamp and H.M.S. *Resolution*
at Rarotonga

225 Head of Statue
of Liberty

1986 (21 May). *"Ameripex '86" International Stamp Exhibition, Chicago. T* **224** *and similar horiz designs. Multicoloured. P* 14.

1069	$1 Type **224**	1·25	1·25
1070	$1.50, Chicago	1·60	1·60
1071	$2 1975 definitive $2, Benjamin Franklin and H.M.S. *Resolution*	2·25	2·25
	Set of 3	4·50	4·50
	First Day Cover		5·00

1986 (4 July). *Centenary of Statue of Liberty. T* **225** *and similar vert designs. Multicoloured. P* 14.

1072	$1 Type **225**	75	75
1073	$1.25, Hand and torch of Statue	90	90
1074	$2.75, Statue of Liberty	2·00	2·00
	Set of 3	3·25	3·25
	First Day Cover		3·75

226 Miss Sarah Ferguson   (227)

Stampex 86

Adelaide

1986 (23 July). *Royal Wedding. T* **226** *and similar multicoloured designs. P* 14 ($1, $2) *or* 13½ × 13 ($3).

1075	$1 Type **226**	85	85
1076	$2 Prince Andrew	1·60	1·75
1077	$3 Prince Andrew and Miss Sarah Ferguson (57 × 31 mm).....................	2·40	2·50
	Set of 3	4·25	4·50
	First Day Cover		5·00

Nos. 1075/7 were each printed in small sheets of 4 stamps.

1986 (4 Aug). *"Stampex '86" Stamp Exhibition, Adelaide. No.* MS1002 optd with T **227** in gold (circle) and black (inscr) only on design as No. 1001.

MS1078	90 c. × 4 multicoloured	3·50	4·00
	First Day Cover		4·75

The "Stampex '86" exhibition emblem is also overprinted on the sheet margin.

1986 (4 Aug). *86th Birthday of Queen Elizabeth the Queen Mother. Designs as Nos. 1035/8 in miniature sheet,* 91 × 116 *mm, each stamp with a face value of* 55 c. *Multicoloured. P* 13 × 13½.

MS1079	55 c. × 4. As Nos. 1035/8	2·00	2·50
	First Day Cover		2·75

55c

+10c

CHRISTMAS 1986

228 "The Holy Family with St. John   (229)
the Baptist and St. Elizabeth"

POPE JOHN PAUL II
* NOV 21-24 1986 *
FIRST PAPAL VISIT TO SOUTH PACIFIC

1986 (17 Nov). *Christmas. Paintings by Rubens. T* **228** *and similar vert designs. Multicoloured. P* 13½.

1080	55 c. Type **228**....................	40	45
1081	$1.30, "Virgin with the Garland"	90	95
1082	$2.75, "The Adoration of the Magi" (detail) ..	1·90	2·00
	Set of 3	3·00	3·00
	First Day Cover		3·50
MS1083	140 × 100 mm. As Nos. 1080/2, but each size 36 × 46 mm with a face value of $2.40	5·50	6·50
	First Day Cover		7·50
MS1084	80 × 70 mm. $6.40 As No. 1081 but size 32 × 50 mm	5·50	6·50
	First Day Cover		7·50

1986 (21 Nov). *Visit of Pope John Paul II to South Pacific. Nos.* 1080/4 such as T **229** in silver.

1085	55 c. + 10 c. Type **228**	60	60
1086	$1 30 + 10 c. "Virgin with the Garland"	1·25	1·25
1087	$2.75 + 10 c. "The Adoration of the Magi" (detail)	2·50	2·50
	Set of 3	4·00	4·00
	First Day Cover		4·50
MS1088	140 × 100 mm. As Nos. 1085/7, but each size 36 × 46 mm with a face value of $2.40 + 10 c.	6·50	7·50
	First Day Cover		8·50
MS1089	80 × 70 mm. $6.40 + 50 c. As No. 1086 but size 32 × 50 mm	6·50	7·50
	First Day Cover		8·50

THE WORLD CENTRE FOR
FINE STAMPS IS 399 STRAND

HURRICANE RELIEF

10c   +50c

(230)   (231)

1987 (10–12 Feb). *Various stamps surch as T* **230** *by N.Z. Govt Printer.*

(a) On Nos. 741/56, 761/76 and 787/8

1090	10 c. on 15 c. *Distichopora violacea* (11.2)	10	10
1091	10 c. on 15 c. *Stylaster* (11.2)	10	10
1092	10 c. on 15 c. *Gonipora* (11.2)	10	10
1093	10 c. on 15 c. *Caulastraea echinulata* (11.2)	10	10
1094	10 c. on 25 c. *Lobophyllia bemprichii* (11.2)	10	10
1095	10 c. on 25 c. *Palauastrea ramosa* (11.2)	10	10
1096	10 c. on 25 c. *Bellonella indica* (11.2)	10	10
1097	10 c. on 25 c. *Pectinia alcicornis* (11.2)	10	10
1098	18 c. on 12 c. *Millepora alcicornis* (11.2)	15	15
1099	18 c. on 12 c. *Junceella gemmacea* (11.2)	15	15
1100	18 c. on 12 c. *Fungia fungites* (11.2)	15	15
1101	18 c. on 12 c. *Heliofungia actiniformis* (11.2) . . .	15	15
1102	18 c. on 20 c. *Ptilosarcus gurneyi* (11.2)	15	15
1103	18 c. on 20 c. *Stylophora pistillata* (11.2)	15	15
1104	18 c. on 20 c. *Melithaea squamata* (11.2)	15	15
1105	18 c. on 20 c. *Porites andrewsi* (11.2)	15	15
1106	55 c. on 35 c. Type **184** (11.2)	40	45
1107	55 c. on 35 c. *Pavona praetorta* (11.2)	40	45
1108	55 c. on 35 c. *Stylaster echinatus* (11.2)	40	45
1109	55 c. on 35 c. *Tubastraea* (11.2)	40	45
1110	65 c. on 50 c. As No. 1098 (11.2)	45	50
1111	65 c. on 50 c. As No. 1099 (11.2)	45	50
1112	65 c. on 50 c. As No. 1100 (11.2)	45	50
1113	65 c. on 50 c. As No. 1101 (11.2)	45	50
1114	65 c. on 60 c. As No. 1090 (11.2)	45	50
1115	65 c. on 60 c. As No. 1091 (11.2)	45	50
1116	65 c. on 60 c. As No. 1092 (11.2)	45	50
1117	65 c. on 60 c. As No. 1093 (11.2)	45	50
1118	75 c. on 70 c. As No. 1102 (11.2)	55	60
1119	75 c. on 70 c. As No. 1103 (11.2)	55	60
1120	75 c. on 70 c. As No. 1104 (11.2)	55	60
1121	75 c. on 70 c. As No. 1105 (11.2)	55	60
1122	$6.40 on $4 *Stylophora pistillata*	4·50	4·75
1123	$7.20 on $6 *Stylaster echinatus*	5·00	5·25

(b) On Nos. 812/13 in gold (12 Feb)

1124	$9.40 on $1 Type **187**	15·00	16·00
1125	$9.40 on $2 Prince Charles and Lady Diana Spencer	15·00	16·00

(c) On Nos. 835/6 in gold (12 Feb)

1126	$9.40 on $2.50 Princess of Wales (inscr "21st Birthday")	15·00	16·00
1127	$9.40 on $2.50 As No. 1126, but inscr "1 July 1982"	15·00	16·00

(d) On Nos. 966/8, 971/2, 975, 979/80, 982 and 987/9

1128	5 c. on 1 c. Type **208**	5	5
1129	5 c. on 2 c. *Millepora alcicornis*	5	5
1130	5 c. on 3 c. *Distichopora violacea*	5	5
1131	5 c. on 12 c. *Sarcophyton digitatum*	5	5
1132	5 c. on 14 c. *Pavona praetorta*	5	5
1133	18 c. on 24 c. *Stylophora pistillata*	15	15
1134	55 c. on 36 c. *Bellonella indica*	40	45
1135	65 c. on 42 c. *Fungia fungites*	45	50
1136	75 c. on 48 c. *Gonipora*	55	60
1137	95 c. on 96 c. *Porites andrewsi*	70	75
1138	95 c. on $1.10 *Pectinia alcicornis*	70	75
1139	95 c. on $1.20 *Dendrophyllia gracilis*	70	75

(e) On Nos. 998/1001 in gold (No. 143) or gold (value) and black (bars) (others) (12 Feb)

1140	$1.30 on 36 c. Type **211**	1·40	1·50
1141	$1.30 on 48 c. "The *Endeavour* careened for Repairs" (Sydney Parkinson)	1·40	1·50
1142	$1.30 on 60 c. "Cook's landing at Botany Bay" (E. Phillips Fox)	1·40	1·50
1143	$1.30 on $2 "Capt. James Cook" (John Webber)	1·40	1·50

(f) On Nos. 1065/7 in gold (12 Feb)

1144	**223** $2.80 on 95 c. multicoloured	7·00	7·50
1145	– $2.80 on $1.25 multicoloured	7·00	7·50
1146	– $2.80 on $1.50 multicoloured	7·00	7·50

(g) On Nos. 1075/7 in gold (value) and black (bars) (12 Feb)

1147	$2.80 on $1 Type **226**	6·00	6·50
1148	$2.80 on $2 Prince Andrew	6·00	6·50
1149	$2.80 on $3 Prince Andrew and Miss Sarah Ferguson (57 × 31 mm)	6·00	6·50
	Set of 60	£100	£120
	First Day Covers (3)		£130

1987 (17 June). *Various stamps surch as T* **230**.

(a) On Nos. 785/6 and 789

1150	$2.80 on $2 *Gonipora*	2·10	2·25
1151	$5 on $3 *Heliofungia actiniformis*	4·00	4·25
1152	$9.40 on $10 *Melithaea albitincta*	7·50	7·75

(b) On Nos. 838/42 (in gold on Nos. 1153/6)

1153	$9.40 on $1 Type **187** (No. 838).	7·50	7·75
	a. Pair. Nos. 1153/4	15·00	15·50
1154	$9.40 on $1 Type **187** (No. 839).	7·50	7·75
1155	$9.40 on $2 Prince Charles and Lady Diana Spencer (No. 840)	7·50	7·75
	a. Pair. Nos. 1155/6	15·00	15·50
1156	$9.40 on $2 Prince Charles and Lady Diana Spencer (No. 841)	7·50	7·75
	Set of 7	40·00	40·00
	First Day Cover		45·00
MS1157	106 × 59 mm. $9.20 on $1 Type **187**; $9.20 on $2 Prince Charles and Lady Diana Spencer	14·50	15·00
	First Day Cover		20·00

1987 (30 June–31 July). *Hurricane Relief Fund. Various stamps surch as T* **231**.

(a) On Nos. 1035/9 in silver

1158	65 c. + 50 c. Type **217**	80	85
1159	75 c. + 50 c. "Duchess of York, 1923". (Savely Sorine)	85	90
1160	$1.15 + 50 c. "Duchess of York, 1925" (Philip de Laszlo)	1·10	1·25
1161	$2.80 + 50 c. "Queen Elizabeth, 1938" (Sir Gerald Kelly)	2·25	2·40
MS1162	69 × 81 mm. $5.30 + 50 c. As $2.80 + 50 c. . . .	4·00	4·25

(b) On Nos. 1058/62 (in silver on Nos. 1164/6)

1163	55 c. + 50 c. Type **222**	75	80
1164	65 c. + 50 c. "Lot and his Daughters" (Lucas van Leyden)	80	85
1165	75 c. + 50 c. "Auspicious Comet" (from treatise c 1587)	85	90
1166	$1.25 + 50 c. "Events following Charles I" (Herman Saftleven)	1·25	1·40
1167	$2 + 50 c. "Ossian receiving Napoleonic Offi- cers" (Anne Louis Girodet-Trioson)	1·75	2·00

(c) On Nos. 1065/8 (in silver on No. 1169) (31 July)

1168	**223** 95 c. + 50 c. multicoloured	1·00	1·10
1169	– $1.25 + 50 c. multicoloured	1·25	1·40
1170	– $1.50 + 50 c. multicoloured	1·40	1·50
MS1171	Three sheets, each 44 × 75 mm. As Nos. 1168/70, but with face values of $1.10 + 50 c., $1.95 + 50 c., $2.45 + 50 c. . . . . *Set of 3 sheets*	5·00	5·25

(d) On Nos. 1069/71 (in silver on No. 1172)

1172	$1 + 50 c. Type **224**	1·00	1·10
1173	$1.50 + 50 c. Chicago	1·40	1·50
1174	$2 + 50 c. 1975 definitive $2, Benjamin Franklin and H.M.S. *Resolution*	1·75	1·90

(e) On Nos. 1072/4 (in silver on Nos. 1175 and 1177)

1175	$1 + 50 c. Type **225**	1·00	1·10
1176	$1.25 + 50 c. Hand and torch of Statue	1·25	1·40
1177	$2.75 + 50 c. Statue of Liberty	2·25	2·40

(f) On Nos. 1075/7 in silver (31 July)

1178	$1 + 50 c. Type **226**	1·00	1·25
1179	$2 + 50 c. Prince Andrew	1·75	1·90
1180	$3 + 50 c. Prince Andrew and Miss Sarah Ferguson (57 × 31 mm)	2·40	2·50

(g) On Nos. 1080/4 in silver

1181	55 c. + 50 c. Type **226**	75	80
1182	$1.30 + 50 c. "Virgin with the Garland"	1·25	1·40
1183	$2.75 + 50 c. "The Adoration of the Magi" (detail)	2·25	2·40
MS1184	140 × 100 mm. As No. 1181/3, but each size 36 × 46 mm with a face value of $2.40 + 50 c.	6·00	6·25
MS1185	80 × 70 mm. $6.40 + 50 c. As No. 1182, but size 32 × 50 mm.	4·75	5·00

(h) On Nos. 1122, 1134/7 *and* 1150/1

1186	55 c. + 25 c. on 52 c. *Bellonella indica*	55	60
1187	65 c. + 25 c. on 42 c. *Fungia fungites*	65	70
1188	75 c. + 25 c. on 48 c. *Goniopora*	70	75
1189	95 c. + 25 c. on 96 c. *Porites andrewsi*	85	90
1190	$2.80 + 50 c. on $2 *Goniopora*	2·25	2·40
1191	$5 + 50 c. on $3 *Heliofungia actiniformis*	3·75	4·00
1192	$6.40 + 50 c. on $4 *Stylophora pistillata*	4·75	5·00
	Set of 31	40·00	45·00

ROYAL WEDDING FORTIETH ANNIVERSARY

(232)

1987 (20 Nov). *Royal Ruby Wedding. Nos.* 484 *and* 787 *optd with T* **232** *in black on gold.*

1193	$4 Queen Elizabeth II and seashells	2·75	3·00
1194	$4 Queen Elizabeth II and *Stylophora pistillata*	2·75	3·00
	Set of 2	5·50	6·00
	First Day Cover		6·50

233 "The Holy Family" (Rembrandt)

1987 (7 Dec). *Christmas. T* **233** *and similar horiz designs showing different paintings of the Holy Family by Rembrandt.* P 13½.

1195	$1.25, multicoloured.	85	90
1196	$1.50, multicoloured.	1·00	1·10
1197	$1.95, multicoloured.	1·40	1·50
	Set of 3	3·00	3·25
	First Day Cover		3·75
MS1198	100 × 140 mm. As Nos. 1195/7, but each size 47 × 36 mm with a face value of $1.15	2·40	2·75
MS1199	70 × 80 mm. $6 As No. 1196, but size 40 × 31 mm. P 13 × 13½	4·25	4·75
	First Day Covers (2)		8·50

234 Olympic Commemorative $50 Coin

(Des G. Vasarhelyi)

1988 (26 Apr). *Olympic Games, Seoul. T* **234** *and similar vert designs. Multicoloured.* P 13½ × 14.

1200	$1.50, Type **234**	1·10	1·25
	a. Horiz strip of 3. Nos. 1200/2	3·00	
1201	$1.50, Olympic torch and Seoul Olympic Park . .	1·10	1·25

1202	$1.50, Steffi Graf playing tennis and Olympic medal	1·10	1·25
	Set of 3	3·00	3·50
	First Day Cover		4·00
MS1203	131 × 81 mm. $10 Combined design as Nos. 1200/2, but measuring 114 × 47 mm. P 13½	8·50	9·00
	First Day Cover		11·00

Nos. 1200/2 were printed together, *se-tenant,* in horizontal strips of 3 throughout the sheet, each strip forming a composite design.

MILOSLAV MECIR CZECHOSLOVAKIA GOLD MEDAL WINNER MEN'S TENNIS

(235)

1988 (12 Oct). *Olympic Tennis Medal Winners, Seoul. Nos.* 1200/3 *optd as T* **235**.

1204	$1.50, Type **234** (optd with T **235**)	1·10	1·25
	a. Horiz strip of 3. Nos. 1204/6	3·00	
1205	$1.50, Olympic torch and Seoul Olympic Park (optd "TIM MAYOTTE UNITED STATES GABRIELA SABATINI ARGENTINA SILVER MEDAL WINNERS")	1·10	1·25
1206	$1.50, Steffi Graf playing tennis and Olympic medal (optd "GOLD MEDAL WINNER STEFFI GRAF WEST GERMANY")	1·10	1·25
	Set of 3	3·00	3·50
	First Day Cover		4·00
MS1207	131 × 81 mm. $10 Combined design as Nos. 1200/2, but measuring 114 × 47 mm. (optd "GOLD MEDAL WINNER SEOUL OLYMPIC GAMES STEFFI GRAF-WEST GERMANY")	7·00	7·50
	First Day Cover		9·00

236 "Virgin and Child"   237 "Apollo 11" leaving Earth

1988 (11 Nov). *Christmas. T* **236** *and similar vert designs showing paintings of "The Nativity" ($6.40) or different versions of "Virgin and Child" by Dürer.* P 13½.

1208	70 c. multicoloured	50	55
1209	85 c. multicoloured	60	65
1210	95 c. multicoloured	65	70
1211	$1.25, multicoloured	90	95
	Set of 4	2·40	2·50
	First Day Cover		3·25
MS1212	80 × 100 mm. $6.40, multicoloured (45 × 60 mm)	4·50	4·75
	First Day Cover		6·00

(Des G. Vasarhelyi)

1989 (14 July). *20th Anniv of First Manned Landing on Moon. T* **237** *and similar horiz designs. Multicoloured.* P 13.

1213	40 c. Type **237**	30	35
	a. Horiz pair. Nos. 1213/14	60	70
1214	40 c. Lunar module over Moon	30	35
1215	55 c. Armstrong stepping onto Moon	40	45
	a. Horiz pair. Nos. 1215/16	80	90
1216	55 c. Astronaut on Moon	40	45
1217	65 c. Working on lunar surface	50	55
	a. Horiz pair. Nos. 1217/18	1·00	1·10
1218	65 c. Conducting experiment	50	55

1219	75 c. "Apollo 11" leaving Moon	55	60
	a. Horiz pair. Nos. 1219/20	1·10	1·25
1220	75 c. Splashdown in South Pacific	55	60
	Set of 8	3·25	3·50
	First Day Cover		4·00
MS1221	108 × 91 mm. $4.20, Astronauts on Moon . . .	3·25	3·50
	First Day Cover		4·00

Nos. 1213/14, 1215/16, 1217/18 and 1219/20 were each printed together, horizontally se-tenant, in sheets of 12.

238 Raratonga Flycatcher

(Des G. Drummond)

1989 (4 Oct). *Endangered Birds of the Cook Islands.* T **328** *and similar horiz designs. Multicoloured.* (*a*) *Postage.* P 13½ × 13

1222	15 c. Type **238**	10	15
1223	20 c. Pair of Raratonga Flycatchers	15	20
1224	65 c. Pair of Rarotongan Fruit Doves	50	55
1225	70 c. Rarotongan Fruit Dove	50	55
	Set of 4	1·10	1·25
	First Day Cover		1·75

(*b*) *Air.* P 13½

MS1226	Four sheets, each 70 × 53 mm. As Nos. 1222/5, but with face values of $1, $1.25, $1.50, $1.75 and each size 50 × 32 mm. *Set of 4 sheets*	4·00	4·25
	First Day Cover		4·75

STAMP BOOKLET

PRICE given is for complete booklet.

1982 (June). *Royal Wedding. Multicoloured cover, 130 × 74 mm, showing Prince and Princess of Wales. Stitched.*
B1 $6 booklet containing Nos. 812/13 × 2 . . . . 12·00

OFFICIAL STAMPS

(O 1)

O.H.M.S.
(O 2)

1975 (17 Mar–19 May). *Nos. 228/31, 233, 235/7, 239/40, 243/5 and 246c/7 optd with Type O **1** (5, 10, 18, 25 and 30 c. surch also), in black and silver.*
O 1	1 c. *Hibiscus syriacus*	
O 2	2 c. Frangipani	
O 3	3 c. "Suva Queen"	
O 4	4 c. Water Lily	
O 5	5 c. on 2½ c. *Clitoria ternatea*	
O 6	8 c. *Allamanda cathartica*	
O 7	10 c. on 6 c. Hibiscus	
O 8	18 c. on 20 c. Thunbergia	
O 9	25 c. on 9 c. Stephanotis	
O10	30 c. on 15 c. Frangipani	
O11	50 c. *Gardinia taitensis*	
O12	$1 Type **80**	
O13	$2 Type **80**	
O14	$4 Type **81** (19 May)	
O15	$6 Type **81** (19 May)	
	Set of 15.	† 30·00

These stamps were only sold to the public cancelled-to-order and not in unused condition.

1978 (19 Oct)–**79**. *Nos. 466/7, 474, 478/81, 484/5, 542 and 568/9 optd or surch (2, 5, 10, 15, 18 and 35 c.) as Type O **2**.*
O16	1 c. Vase shell (Silver)	10	5
O17	2 c. on ½ c. Type **141**	10	5
O18	5 c. on ½ c. Type **141**	15	5
O19	10 c. on 8 c. Helmet shell (Silver)	20	10
O20	15 c. on 50 c. Cloth of Gold cone shell (Silver) . .	25	10
O21	18 c. on 60 c. Olive shell (Silver)	25	15
O22	25 c. Scallop shell	35	20
O23	30 c. Soldier cone shell (Silver)	35	25
O24	35 c. on 60 c. Olive shell (Silver)	40	30
O25	50 c. Cloth of Gold cone shell (Silver)	65	35
O26	60 c. Olive shell (Silver)	75	45
O27	$1 Queen and Prince Philip (Silver)	2·75	1·25

O28	$1 Royal Visit, 1974 (Silver)	2·75	1·25
O29	$2 Captain Cook and H.M.S. *Resolution*	4·50	3·00
O30	$4 Queen Elizabeth II and seashells (15.2.79)	4·00	3·25
O31	$6 As $4 (15.2.79)	6·50	6·00
	Set of 16	21·00	15·00

These stamps were originally only sold to the public cancelled-to-order and not in unused condition. They were made available to overseas collectors in mint condition during 1980.

75c

O.H.M.S.
(O 3)

O.H.M.S.
(O 4)

O.H.M.S.
(O 5)

1985 (10 July)–**89**. (a) *Nos. 969/74, 976, 978, 981, 984/6 and 988/9 optd or surch as Type O **3** by silver foil embossing.*
O32	5 c. *Ptilosarcus gurneyi*	5	5
O33	10 c. *Lobophyllia bemprichii*	5	10
	a. Opt double, one albino	50·00	
O34	12 c. *Sarcophyton digitatum* (5.5.86)	10	10
O35	14 c. *Pavona praetorta* (5.5.86)	10	10
O36	18 c. *Junceella gemmacea* (5.5.86)	15	15
O37	20 c. *Stylaster*	15	15
O38	30 c. *Palauastrea ramosa*	20	25
O39	40 c. *Stylaster echinatus*	25	30
O40	50 c. *Melithaea squamata* (5.5.86)	30	35
O41	55 c. on 85 c. *Caulastraea echinulata*	35	40
	a. "O.H.M.S." albino	†	—
O42	60 c. *Tubastraea*	40	45
O43	70 c. *Heliofungia actiniformis* (5.5.86)	45	50
O44	$1.10, *Pectinia alcicornis*	70	75
O45	$2 on $1.20, *Dendrophyllia gracilis*	1·40	1·50

(b) *Nos. 862/5 surch with Type O **4** by gold foil embossing*
O46	75 c. on 60 c. Type **197** (5.5.86)	50	55
O47	75 c. on 60 c. Rarotonga oranges (5.5.86)	50	55
O48	75 c. on 60 c. Rarotonga airport (5.5.86)	50	55
O49	75 c. on 60 c. Prime Minister Sir Thomas Davis (5.5.86)	50	55

(c) *Nos. 786/8 surch as T **209** in silver and black further optd with Type O **5** by silver foil embossing*
O50	$5 on $3 *Heliofungia actiniformis* (5.5.86)	3·25	3·50
O51	$9 on $4 *Stylophora pistillata* (30.5.89)	6·00	6·25
O52	$14 on $6 *Stylaster echinatus* (12.7.89)	9·00	9·25
	Set of 21	23·00	24·00

AITUTAKI

Stamps of COOK ISLANDS were used in Aitutaki from 1892 until 1903.

PRICES FOR STAMPS ON COVER TO 1945

Nos. 1/8	from × 4
Nos. 9/14	from × 3
Nos. 15/29	from × 4
Nos. 30/2	from × 6

PRICES

Edward VII and George V issues (1903–1927)

First column = Mounted Mint
Second column = Used

NEW ZEALAND DEPENDENCY

The island of Aitutaki, previously under British protection, was annexed by New Zealand on 11 June 1901.

Stamps of New Zealand overprinted or surcharged.

AITUTAKI.
(1)

Ava Pene.
(2) ½d.

Tai Pene.
(3) 1d.

Rua Pene Ma Te Ava.
(4) 2½d.

Toru Pene.
(5) 3d.

Ono Pene.
(6) 6d.

Tai Tiringi.
(7) 1s.

1903 (June)–**11.** 1902 *issue surch with T* **1** *at top, and T* **2** *to* **7** *at foot.* W 43. (a) P 14.

1	23	½d. green (R.)	3·25	6·50
2	42	1d. carmine (B.)	4·00	5·50
3	27	2½d. deep blue (R.) (9.11)	6·00	15·00
		a. "Ava" without stop	£130	£160
		Set of 3	12·00	24·00

(b) P 11

4	27	2½d. blue (R.)	6·50	11·00
5	28	3d. yellow-brown (B.)	6·50	15·00
6	31	6d. rose-red (B.)	16·00	25·00
7	34	1s. bright red (B.)	55·00	75·00
		a. "Tiringi" without stop	£300	£400
8		1s. orange-red (B.)	65·00	85·00
		a. "Tiringi" without stop	£400	£500
		b. *Orange-brown*	£140	£160
		c. Do. "Tiringi" without stop	£850	£1000
		Set of 4	75·00	£110

With the exception of No. 3, the above were issued in Auckland on 12 June and in Aitutaki on 29 June 1903.

AITUTAKI.

Ono Pene.
(8)

1911–16. ½d. and 1d. surch as on Nos. 1/2, 6d. and 1s. as T **8**.

9	50	½d. green (R.) 9.11)	55	2·50
10	52	1d. carmine (B.) (2.13)	2·00	6·50
11	51	6d. carmine (B.) (p 14 × 14½) (23.5.16)	35·00	60·00
12		1s. vermilion (B.) (p 14 × 14½) (9.14)	55·00	£100
		Set of 4	80·00	£150

1916–17. *King George V stamps surch as T* **8**. P 14 × 14½.

13	60	6d. carmine (B.) (6.6.16)	7·50	18·00
		a. Perf 14 × 13½	14·00	35·00
		b. Vert pair. Nos. 13/13a	48·00	75·00
14		1s. vermilion (B.) (3.17)	30·00	60·00
		a. Perf 14 × 13½	28·00	60·00
		b. Vert pair. Nos. 14/14a	£140	£200
		c. "Tai" without dot	£200	£275
		d. "Tiringi" no dot on second "i"	£250	£300
		e. "Tiringi" no dot on third "i"	£300	£350
		Set of 2	35·00	75·00

1917–18. *King George V stamps optd* "AITUTAKI", *only, as in T* **8**. W **43**. P 14 × 14½.

15	60	2½d. deep blue (R.) (12.18)	1·40	8·50
		a. Perf 14 × 13½	2·00	8·50
		b. Vert pair. Nos. 15/15a	70·00	95·00
16		3d. chocolate (B.) (1.18)	1·25	9·00
		a. Perf 14 × 13½	1·75	10·00
		b. Vert pair. Nos. 16/16a	65·00	90·00
17		6d. carmine (B.) (11.17)	4·50	9·00
		a. Perf 14 × 13½	7·00	17·00
		b. Vert pair. Nos. 17/17a	70·00	95·00
18		1s. vermilion (B.) (11.17)	10·00	18·00
		a. Perf 14 × 13½	14·00	25·00
		b. Vert pair. Nos. 18/18a	80·00	£110
		Set of 4	15·00	38·00

1917–20. *Optd* "AITUTAKI" *as in T* **8**. *Typo.* W **43**. P 14 × 15.

19	61	½d. green (R.) (2.20)	1·00	3·25
20	52	1d. carmine (B.) (5.20)	1·75	6·00
21	61	1½d. slate (R.) (11.17)	3·25	14·00
22		1½d. orange-brown (R.) (2.19)	80	5·50
23		3d. chocolate (B.) (6.19)	3·50	10·00
		Set of 5	9·25	35·00

(Des and recess Perkins, Bacon & Co)

1920 (23 Aug). *As Types of Cook Islands, but inscr* "AITUTAKI". *No wmk.* P 14.

24	9	½d. black and green	2·75	8·50
25	10	1d. black and dull carmine	2·25	5·00
26	11	1½d. black and sepia	5·50	9·00
27	12	3d. black and deep blue	1·75	9·00
28	13	6d. red-brown and slate	5·00	14·00
29	14	1s. black and purple	7·50	16·00
		Set of 6	22·00	55·00

(Recess Govt Printing Office, Wellington)

1924–27. *As Types of Cook Islands, but inscr* "AITUTAKI". W **43** *of New Zealand.* P 14.

30	9	½d. black and green (5.27)	2·00	7·50
31	10	1d. black and deep carmine (10.24)	2·50	6·50
32	16	2½d. black and dull blue (10.27)	6·00	27·00
		Set of 3	9·50	38·00

Cook Islands stamps superseded those of Aitutaki on 15 March 1932. Separate issues were resumed in 1972.

PUZZLED ?

Then you need
PHILATELIC TERMS ILLUSTRATED
to tell you all you need to know about printing methods, papers, errors, varieties, watermarks, perforations, etc. 192 pages, some in full colour, soft cover. Third Edition.

PART OF COOK ISLANDS

On 9 August 1972, Aitutaki became a Port of Entry into the Cook Islands, and at the close of business on the previous day, Cook Islands stamps were withdrawn from sale there. Whilst remaining part of the Cook Islands, Aitutaki has a separate postal service.

PRINTERS. Stamps of Aitutaki were printed in photogravure by Heraclio Fournier, Spain, *unless otherwise stated.* All issues are on paper treated with fluorescent security markings, and with synthetic gum. The fluorescent markings can be found inverted or omitted.

```
                    PRICES
            Elizabeth II issues (from 1953)

        First column = Unmounted Mint
        Second column = Used
```

Aĭtutaki

(9)　　　　　　(10)

(Optd by Govt Printer, Wellington)

1972 (9 Aug). *Nos. 227B etc. of Cook Is. optd with T* **9** (applied horizontally on $1), by New Zealand Govt Printer.

33	½ c. Type **79**	30	80
34	1 c. *Hibiscus syriacus*	70	1·40
35	2½ c. *Clitoria ternatea*	3·50	8·00
36	4 c. Water Lily (No. 233B)	70	85
37	5 c. *Bauhinia bi-pinnata rosea*	4·50	8·50
38	10 c. *Poinciana regia flamboyant*	4·50	6·50
39	20 c. Thunbergia	70	1·00
40	25 c. Canna Lily	70	1·00
41	50 c. *Gardinia taitensis*	3·75	3·25
42	$1 Type **80**	6·50	6·50
	a. Shade*		
	Set of 10	23·00	35·00
	First Day Cover		38·00

* No. 42a has the border flowers predominantly in a carmine colour instead of scarlet, and may be due to a missing yellow colour.

1972 (27 Oct). *Christmas. Nos. 406/8 of Cook Is. optd in silver with* T **10**.

43	**130**	1 c. multicoloured	5	5
44	–	5 c. multicoloured	10	15
45	–	10 c. multicoloured	10	25
		Set of 3	20	40
		First Day Cover		55

1972 (20 Nov). *Royal Silver Wedding. As Nos. 413 and 415 of Cook Is., but inscr* "COOK ISLANDS Aitutaki".

46	**131**	5 c. black and silver	4·75	2·75
47	–	15 c. black and silver	2·75	1·50
		Set of 2	7·50	7·25
		First Day Cover		7·50

AITUTAKI

(11)　　　　　　(12)

1972 (24 Nov). *No. 245B of Cook Is. optd with T* **11** *by Govt Printer, Rarotonga.*

48	**80**	$2. multicoloured	60	1·00
		a. Optd "AJTUTAKI" for "AITUTAKI" (R. 2/4)	25·00	
		b. On No. 245A (gum arabic printing)	50·00	
		ba. Optd "AJTUTAKI" for "AITUTAKI" (R. 2/4)		
		First Day Cover		1·75

1972 (11 Dec). *Nos. 227B etc of Cook Is. optd with T* **12**, *by Heraclio Fournier.*

49	½ c. Type **79**	5	5
50	1 c. *Hibiscus syriacus*	10	10
51	2½ c. *Clitoria ternatea*	10	10
52	4 c. Water Lily (No. 233B)	15	15

53	5 c. *Bauhinia bi-pinnata rosea*	15	15
54	10 c. *Poinciana regia flamboyant*	25	25
55	20 c. Thunbergia	45	50
56	25 c. Canna Lily	50	55
57	50 c. *Gardinia taitensis*	80	90
58	$1 Type **80**	1·50	1·75
	Set of 10	3·50	4·00
	First Day Cover		5·50

AITUTAKI

13 "Christ Mocked"　　　　(14)
(Grünewald)

1973 (6 Apr). *Easter. T* **13** *and similar vert designs. Multicoloured. P* 13.

59	1 c. Type **13**	5	5
60	1 c. "St. Veronica" (Van der Weyden)	5	5
61	1 c. "The Crucified Christ with Virgin Mary, Saints and Angels" (Raphael)	5	5
62	1 c. "Resurrection" (Piero della Francesca)	5	5
63	5 c. "The Last Supper" (Master of Amiens)	15	15
64	5 c. "Condemnation" (Holbein)	15	15
65	5 c. "Christ on the Cross" (Rubens)	15	15
66	5 c. "Resurrection" (El Greco)	15	15
67	10 c. "Disrobing of Christ" (El Greco)	15	15
68	10 c. "St. Veronica" (Van Oostsanen)	15	15
69	10 c. "Christ on the Cross" (Rubens)	15	15
70	10 c. "Resurrection" (Bouts)	15	15
	Set of 12	1·25	1·25
	First Day Cover		1·60

Nos. 59/62, 63/6 and 67/70 were each printed together, *se-tenant,* in blocks of 4 throughout the sheet.

1973 (14 May). *Silver Wedding Coinage. Nos. 417/23 of Cook Is. optd in silver and black as T* **14**.

71	1 c. black, rosy carmine and gold	5	5
72	2 c. black, bright blue and gold	5	5
73	5 c. black, green and silver	10	10
74	10 c. black, royal blue and silver	15	15
75	20 c. black, deep blue-green and silver	25	20
76	50 c. black, carmine and silver	50	40
77	$1 black, bright blue and silver	80	60
	Set of 7	1·60	1·40
	First Day Cover		2·00

TENTH ANNIVERSARY
CESSATION
OF
NUCLEAR TESTING
TREATY

(15)

16 Red Hibiscus and Princess Anne

1973 (13 Aug). *Tenth Anniv of Treaty Banning Nuclear Testing. Nos. 236B, 238B, 240B and 243B of Cook Is. optd with T* **15** *and T* **12** *together.*

78	8 c. *Allamanda cathartica*	20	15
79	10 c. *Poinciana regia flamboyant*	20	15
80	20 c. Thunbergia	40	25
81	50 c. *Gardinia taitensis*	80	60
	Set of 4	1·40	1·00
	First Day Cover		1·50

1973 (14 Nov). *Royal Wedding. T* **16** *and similar horiz design. Multicoloured. P* 13½ × 14.

82	25 c. Type **16**		25	10
83	30 c. Capt. Phillips and Blue Hibiscus		25	10
	Set of 2		50	20
	First Day Cover			55
MS84	114 × 65 mm. Nos. 82/3. P 13		65	55
	First Day Cover			75

17 "Virgin and Child"
(Montagna)

18 *Murex ramosus*

1973 (10 Dec). *Christmas. T* **17** *and similar vert designs showing "The Virgin and Child" by the artists listed. Multicoloured. P* 13½.

85	1 c. Type **17**		5	5
86	1 c. Crivelli		5	5
87	1 c. Van Dyck		5	5
88	1 c. Perugino		5	5
89	5 c. Veronese (child at shoulder)		10	10
90	5 c. Veronese (child on lap)		10	10
91	5 c. Cima		10	10
92	5 c. Memling		10	10
93	10 c. Memling		10	10
94	10 c. Del Colle		10	10
95	10 c. Raphael		10	10
96	10 c. Lotto		10	10
	Set of 12		80	80
	First Day Cover			1·40

Nos. 85/8, 89/92 and 93/6 were each printed together, *se-tenant*, in blocks of 4 throughout the sheet.

1974 (31 Jan)–**75**. *T* **18** *and similar horiz designs showing sea-shells. Multicoloured. P* 13.

97	½ c. Type **18**		10	10
98	1 c. *Nautilus macromphallus*		15	10
99	2 c. *Harpa major*		20	10
100	3 c. *Phalium strigatum*		20	10
101	4 c. *Cypraea talpa*		20	10
102	5 c. *Mitra stictica*		20	10
103	8 c. *Charonia tritonis*		25	10
104	10 c. *Murex triremis*		25	10
105	20 c. *Oliva sericea*		60	10
106	25 c. *Tritonalia rubeta*		70	25
107	60 c. *Strombus latissimus*		1·40	70
108	$1 *Biplex perca*		1·75	1·10
109	$2 Queen Elizabeth II and *Terebra maculata* (20.1.75)		5·00	4·75
110	$5 Queen Elizabeth II and *Cypraea hesitata* (28.2.75)		12·00	9·50
	Set of 14		21·00	16·00
	First Day Covers (3)			22·00

Nos 109/110 are larger, 53 × 25 mm.

19 Bligh and H.M.S. *Bounty*

(Des G. Vasarhelyi)

1974 (11 Apr). *William Bligh's Discovery of Aitutaki. T* **19** *and similar horiz designs. Multicoloured. P* 13½.

114	1 c. Type **19**		20	10
115	1 c. H.M.S. *Bounty*		20	10
116	5 c. Bligh, and H.M.S. *Bounty* at Aitutaki		40	15

117	5 c. Aitutaki chart of 1856		40	15
118	8 c. Capt. Cook and H.M.S. *Resolution*		50	15
119	8 c. Map of Aitutaki and inset location map		50	15
	Set of 6		2·00	70
	First Day Cover			1·50

Nos. 114/15, 116/17 and 118/19 were each printed together, *se-tenant*, in horizontal and vertical pairs throughout the sheet.
See also Nos. 123/8.

20 Aitutaki Stamps of 1903,
and Map

21 "Virgin and Child"
(Hugo van der Goes)

1974 (15 July). *Centenary of Universal Postal Union. T* **20** *and similar horiz design. Multicoloured. P* 13½ × 14.

120	25 c. Type **20**		40	40
121	50 c. Stamps of 1903 and 1920, and map		60	60
	Set of 2		1·00	1·00
	First Day Cover			1·25
MS122	66 × 75 mm. Nos. 120/1. P 13		1·00	2·00
	First Day Cover			2·25

Each value was issued in sheets of 5 stamps and 1 label.

1974 (9 Sept). *Air. As Nos.* 114/119 *but larger* (46 × 26 *mm*), *denominations changed, and inscr* "AIR MAIL".

123	10 c. Type **19**		50	15
124	10 c. H.M.S. *Bounty*		50	15
125	25 c. Bligh, and H.M.S. *Bounty* at Aitutaki		65	25
126	25 c. Aitutaki chart of 1856		65	25
127	30 c. Capt Cook and H.M.S. *Resolution*		65	25
128	30 c. Map of Aitutaki and inset location map		65	25
	Set of 6		3·25	1·10
	First Day Cover			2·50

Nos. 123/4, 125/6 and 127/8 were each printed together, *se-tenant*, in horizontal and vertical pairs throughout the sheet.

1974 (11 Oct). *Christmas. T* **21** *and similar vert designs showing "Virgin and Child" by the artists listed. Multicoloured. P* 13.

129	1 c. Type **21**		5	5
130	5 c. Bellini		10	10
131	8 c. Gerard David		10	10
132	10 c. Antonello da Messina		10	10
133	25 c. Joos van Cleve		20	20
134	30 c. Master of the Life of St. Catherine		20	20
	Set of 6		65	65
	First Day Cover			1·00
MS135	127 × 134 mm. Nos. 129/34		1·25	1·60
	First Day Cover			1·90

Each value was issued in sheets of 15 stamps and 1 label.

22 Churchill as Schoolboy

(23)

1974 (29 Nov). *Birth Centenary of Sir Winston Churchill. T* **22** *and similar vert designs. Multicoloured. P* 13½.

136	10 c.	Type **22**	30	25
137	25 c.	Churchill as young man	60	50
138	30 c.	Churchill with troops	75	60
139	50 c.	Churchill painting	1·10	80
140	$1	Giving "V" sign	2·00	1·50
		Set of 5	4·25	3·25
		First Day Cover		3·75

MS141 115 × 108 mm. Nos. 136/40 plus *se-tenant*
label. P 13 .... 5·00 4·00
First Day Cover .... 4·75
Each value was issued in sheets of 5 stamps and 1 label.

1974 (2 Dec.). *Children's Christmas Fund. Nos.* 129/34 *surch with T* **23**.

142	1 c. + 1 c. multicoloured		5	5
143	5 c. + 1 c. multicoloured		5	5
144	8 c. + 1 c. multicoloured		10	10
145	10 c. + 1 c. multicoloured		10	10
146	25 c. + 1 c. multicoloured		20	20
147	30 c. + 1 c. multicoloured		20	20
	Set of 6		55	55
	First Day Cover			1·25

24 Soviet and U.S. Flags

25 "Madonna and Child with Saints Francis and John" (Lorenzetti)

1975 (24 July). *"Apollo-Soyuz" Space Project. T* **24** *and similar horiz design. Multicoloured. P* 13 × 14.

148	25 c.	Type **24**	35	25
149	50 c.	Daedalus and space capsule	55	40
		Set of 2	90	65
		First Day Cover		1·00

MS150 123 × 61 mm. Nos. 148/9 .... 1·25 1·40
First Day Cover .... 1·75
Each value was issued in sheets of 8 stamps and 1 label.

1975 (24 Nov). *Christmas. T* **25** *and similar vert designs. Multicoloured. P* 13½.

151	6 c.	⎫	10	10
152	6 c.	⎬ Type **25**	10	10
153	6 c.	⎭	10	10
154	7 c.	⎫	10	10
155	7 c.	⎬ "Adoration of the Kings" (Van der	10	10
156	7 c.	⎭ Weyden)	10	10
157	15 c.	⎫ "Madonna and Child Enthroneth with	15	15
158	15 c.	⎬ Saints Onufrius and John the Baptist"	15	15
159	15 c.	⎭ (Montagna)	15	15
160	20 c.	⎫	20	15
161	20 c.	⎬ "Adoration of the Shepherds" (Reni)	20	15
162	20 c.	⎭	20	15
		Set of 12	1·50	1·40
		First Day Cover		1·75

MS163 104 × 201 mm. Nos. 151/62. P 13 .... 2·25 2·50
First Day Cover .... 2·75
Nos. 151/3, 154/6, 157/9 and 160/2 were each printed together, *se-tenant*, in horizontal strips of 3 throughout the sheet, forming composite designs. Type **25** shows the left-hand stamp of the 6 c. design.

1975 (19 Dec). *Children's Christmas Fund. Nos.* 151/62 *surch as T* **23**, *in silver.*

164	6 c. + 1 c.	⎫	15	10
165	6 c. + 1 c.	⎬ Type **25**	15	10
166	6 c. + 1 c.	⎭	15	10
167	7 c. + 1 c.	⎫	15	10
168	7 c. + 1 c.	⎬ "Adoration of the Kings" (Van der	15	10
169	7 c. + 1 c.	⎭ Weyden)	15	10
170	15 c. + 1 c.	⎫	20	15
171	15 c. + 1 c.	⎬ "Madonna and Child"	20	15
172	15 c. + 1 c.	⎭ (Montagna)	20	15
173	20 c. + 1 c.	⎫	25	20
174	20 c. + 1 c.	⎬ "Adoration of the Shepherds"	25	20
175	20 c. + 1 c.	⎭ (Reni)	25	20
		Set of 12	2·00	1·50
		First Day Cover		2·00

26 "The Descent" (detail, 15th-cent Flemish School)

27 "The Declaration of Independence" (detail)

1976 (5 Apr). *Easter. Various vert designs showing portions of "The Descent" as in T* **26**. *P* 13.

176	**26**	15 c. multicoloured	15	15
177	–	30 c. multicoloured	20	20
178	–	35 c. multicoloured	25	25
		Set of 3	55	55
		First Day Cover		1·00

MS179 87 × 67 mm. Nos. 176/8 forming a complete
picture of "The Descent". P 12½ × 13 .... 1·00 1·25
First Day Cover .... 1·60
Stamps from No. **MS**179 have no borders and are therefore smaller than stamps from the sheets.
Each value was issued in sheets of 8 stamps and 1 label.

1976 (1 June). *Bicentenary of American Revolution. T* **27** *and similar vert designs showing paintings by John Trumbull. Multicoloured. P* 13.

180	30 c.	⎫	60	30
181	30 c.	⎬ Type **27**	60	30
182	30 c.	⎭	60	30
183	35 c.	⎫	70	40
184	35 c.	⎬ "The Surrender of Lord Cornwallis at	70	40
185	35 c.	⎭ Yorktown"	70	40
186	50 c.	⎫	80	45
187	50 c.	⎬ "The Resignation of General	80	45
188	50 c.	⎭ Washington"	80	45
		Set of 9	5·75	3·00
		First Day Cover		5·50

MS189 132 × 120 mm. Nos. 180/8. P 13 .... 5·50 5·00
First Day Cover .... 6·50
Nos. 180/2, 183/5 and 186/8 were each printed together, *se-tenant*, in horizontal strips of 3 throughout the sheet, forming composite designs. Each sheet includes 3 stamp-size labels. Type **27** shows the left-hand stamp of the 30 c. design.
Stamps from No. **MS**189 have their borders in a different colour and come with a different inscription.

28 Cycling

1976 (15 July).   *Olympic Games, Montreal. T* **28** *and similar horiz designs. Multicoloured. P* 13 × 14.

190	15 c.	Type **28**	25	15
191	35 c.	Sailing	50	25
192	60 c.	Hockey	70	30
193	70 c.	Sprinting	75	35
		Set of 4	2·00	95
		First Day Cover		1·50
MS194	107 × 97 mm. Nos. 190/3		2·00	2·00
		First Day Cover		2·50

Stamps from No. **MS**194 have borders of a different colour.
Each value was issued in sheets of 5 stamps and 1 label.

ROYAL VISIT JULY 1976

(29)   30 "The Visitation"

1976 (30 July).   *Visit of Queen Elizabeth to the U.S.A. Nos.* 190/**MS**194 *optd with T* **29**.

195	15 c.	Type **28**	30	20
196	35 c.	Sailing	55	35
197	60 c.	Hockey	75	50
198	70 c.	Sprinting	80	55
		Set of 4	2·25	1·40
		First Day Cover		2·00
MS199	107 × 97 mm. Nos. 195/8		2·25	2·75
		First Day Cover		3·25

1976 (18 Oct).   *Christmas. T* **30** *and similar vert designs. Figures in gold; background colours given. P* 13.

200	6 c.	} deep bluish green	5	5
201	6 c.		5	5
202	7 c.	} dull brown-purple	10	10
203	7 c.		10	10
204	15 c.	} deep blue	10	10
205	15 c.		10	10
206	20 c.	} reddish violet	15	15
207	20 c.		15	15
		Set of 8	70	70
		First Day Cover		1·25
MS208	128 × 96 mm. As Nos. 200/207 but with borders on three sides		1·00	1·40
		First Day Cover		1·75

Designs:—No. 201, Angel; No. 202, Angel; No. 203, Shepherds; No. 204, Joseph; No. 205, Mary and the Child; No. 206, Wise Man; No. 207, Two Wise Men.
Nos. 200/1, 202/3, 204/5 and 206/7 were each printed together, *se-tenant*, in horizontal pairs throughout the sheet, forming composite designs. Type **30** shows the left-hand stamp of the 6 c. design.

+1c

(31)

32 Alexander Graham Bell and First Telephone

1976 (19 Nov).   *Children's Christmas Fund. Nos.* 200/**MS**208 *surch in silver as T* **31**.

209	6 c. + 1 c.	} "The Visitation"	10	10
210	6 c. + 1 c.		10	10
211	7 c. + 1 c.	} "Angel and Shepherds"	10	10
212	7 c. + 1 c.		10	10
213	15 c. + 1 c.	} "The Holy Family"	15	15
214	15 c. + 1 c.		15	15

215	20 c. + 1 c.	} "The Magi"	15	15
216	20 c. + 1 c.		15	15
		Set of 8	85	85
		First Day Cover		1·25
MS217	128 × 96 mm. As Nos. 209/216 but with a premium of " + 2 c." and borders on three sides		1·00	1·40
		First Day Cover		1·75

1977 (3 Mar).   *Telephone Centenary* (1976). *T* **32** *and similar horiz design. P* 13.

218	25 c.	black, gold and dull scarlet	25	15
219	70 c.	black, gold and lilac	55	40
		Set of 2	80	55
		First Day Cover		85
MS220	116 × 59 mm. As Nos. 218/19 but with different colours		90	1·25
		First Day Cover		1·50

Design:—70 c. Earth Station and satellite.

33 "Christ on the Cross" (detail)

1977 (31 Mar).   *Easter and 400th Birth Anniv of Rubens. T* **33** *and similar horiz designs. Multicoloured. P* 13½ × 14.

221	15 c.	Type **33**	30	15
222	20 c.	"Lamentation for Christ"	35	20
223	35 c.	"Christ with Straw"	45	25
		Set of 3	1·00	55
		First Day Cover		90
MS224	115 × 57 mm. Nos. 221/3. P 13 × 12½		1·00	1·25
		First Day Cover		1·50

Each value was issued in sheets of 8 stamps and 1 label.

34 Capt. Bligh, George III and H.M.S. *Bounty*

1977 (21 Apr).   *Silver Jubilee. T* **34** *and similar horiz designs. Multicoloured. P* 13.

225	25 c.	Type **34**	65	45
226	35 c.	Rev. Williams, George IV and Aitutaki Church	75	50
227	50 c.	Union Jack, Queen Victoria and island map	90	75
228	$1	Balcony scene, 1953	1·50	1·25
		Set of 4	3·50	2·75
		First Day Cover		3·00
MS229	130 × 87 mm. Nos. 225/8 but with gold borders. P 13½ × 13		3·50	2·75
		First Day Cover		3·25

Each value was issued in sheets of 5 stamps and 1 label.

+1c

35 The Shepherds   (36)

1977 (14 Oct). *Christmas. T* **35** *and similar vert designs. Multicoloured. P* 13½ × 14.

230	6 c. Type **35**		5	5
231	6 c. Angel		5	5
232	7 c. Mary, Jesus and ox		5	5
233	7 c. Joseph and donkey		5	5
234	15 c. Three Wise Men		10	10
235	15 c. Virgin and Child		10	10
236	20 c. Joseph		10	10
237	20 c. Mary and Jesus on donkey		10	10
	Set of 8		55	55
	First Day Cover			1·00
MS238	130 × 95 mm. Nos. 230/7		80	1·50
	First Day Cover			1·75

Each design covers two stamps; Type **35** shows the left-hand stamp of the 6 c. design.

1977 (15 Nov). *Children's Christmas Fund. Nos.* 230/7 *surch with T* **36**.

239	6 c. + 1 c. ⎫	Type **35**	5	5
240	6 c. + 1 c. ⎭		5	5
241	7 c. + 1 c. ⎫	The Holy Family	5	5
242	7 c. + 1 c. ⎭		5	5
243	15 c. + 1 c.	The Three Kings with Virgin and	10	10
244	15 c. + 1 c.	Child	10	10
245	20 c. + 1 c. ⎫	Flight into Egypt	10	10
246	20 c. + 1 c. ⎭		10	10
	Set of 8		55	55
	First Day Cover			1·00
MS247	130 × 95 mm. As Nos. 239/46 but each with premium of "+ 2 c."		85	1·10
	First Day Cover			2·00

37 Hawaiian Goddess

38 "Christ on the Way to Calvary" (Martini)

1978 (19 Jan). *Bicentenary of Discovery of Hawaii. T* **37** *and similar multicoloured designs. P* 13½.

248	35 c. Type **37**		45	35
249	50 c. Figurehead of H.M.S. *Resolution* (*horiz*)		75	55
250	$1 Hawaiian temple figure		1·00	80
	Set of 3		2·00	1·50
	First Day Cover			2·50
MS251	168 × 75 mm. Nos. 248/50		2·50	2·75
	First Day Cover			3·50

1978 (17 Mar). *Easter. Details of Paintings from Louvre, Paris. T* **38** *and similar horiz designs. Multicoloured. P* 13½ × 14.

252	15 c. Type **38**		10	10
253	20 c. "Piéta of Avignon" (E. Quarton)		15	10
254	35 c. "Pilgrims at Emmaus" (Rembrandt)		20	15
	Set of 3		40	30
	First Day Cover			70
MS255	108 × 83 mm. Nos. 252/4		55	70
	First Day Cover			1·25

Each value was printed in two panes of 9 within the sheet, both panes including one *se-tenant* stamp-size label.

1978 (17 Mar). *Easter. Children's Charity. Designs as Nos.* 252/4, *but smaller* (34 × 26 *mm*) *and without margins, in separate miniature sheets* 75 × 58 *mm, each with a face value of* 50 c. + 5 c. *P* 14.

MS256	As Nos. 252/4 *Set of 3 sheets*		1·25	1·40
	First Day Cover			2·25

39 Yale of Beaufort

40 "Adoration of the Infant Jesus"

1978 (15 June). *25th Anniv of Coronation. T* **39** *and similar vert designs. Multicoloured. P* 13½ × 13.

257	$1 Type **39**		75	85
258	$1 Queen Elizabeth II		75	85
259	$1 Aitutaki ancestral statue		75	85
	Set of 3		2·00	2·25
	First Day Cover			2·50
MS260	98 × 127 mm. Nos. 257/9 × 2		3·25	3·50
	First Day Cover			4·50

Stamps from No. **MS260** have coloured borders, the upper row in lavender and the lower in apple-green.

Nos. 257/9 were printed together, *se-tenant*, in small sheets of 6, containing two horizontal strips of 3.

1978 (4 Dec). *Christmas. 450th Death Anniv of Dürer. T* **40** *and similar vert designs. Multicoloured. P* 13 × 14.

261	15 c. Type **40**		25	15
262	17 c. "The Madonna with Child"		30	15
263	30 c. "The Madonna with the Iris"		40	20
264	35 c. "The Madonna of the Siskin"		45	25
	Set of 4		1·25	65
	First Day Cover			1·10
MS265	101 × 109 mm. As Nos. 261/4 but each with premium of "+ 2 c."		1·25	1·50
	First Day Cover			1·75

Nos. 261/4 were each printed in small sheets of 6, including 1 *se-tenant* stamp-size label.

41 "Captain Cook" (Nathaniel Dance)

42 Girl with Flowers

1979 (20 July). *Death Bicentenary of Captain Cook. Paintings. T* **41** *and similar vert design. Multicoloured. P* 14 × 13½.

266	50 c. Type **41**		90	80
267	75 c. "H.M.S. *Resolution* and *Adventure* at Matavai Bay" (William Hodges)		1·10	95
	Set of 2		2·00	1·75
	First Day Cover			2·25
MS268	94 × 58 mm. Nos. 266/7. P 13½		2·00	2·75
	First Day Cover			3·25

1979 (1 Oct). *International Year of the Child. T* **42** *and similar vert designs. Multicoloured. P* 14 × 13½.

269	30 c. Type **42**		15	15
270	50 c. Boy playing guitar		20	20
271	65 c. Children in canoe		30	30
	Set of 3		60	60
	First Day Cover			1·25
MS272	104 × 80 mm. As Nos. 269/71, but each with a premium of "+ 3 c."		1·00	1·25
	First Day Cover			1·75

43 "Man writing a Letter"   **44** "The Burial of Christ"
(painting by G. Metsu)   (detail, Quentin Metsys)

1979 (14 Nov).   *Death Centenary of Sir Rowland Hill. T* **43** *and similar horiz designs. Multicoloured. P* 13.

273	50 c.	Type **43**	70	70
274	50 c.	Sir Rowland Hill with Penny Black, 1903 ½d. and 1911 1d. stamps	70	70
275	50 c.	"Girl in Blue reading a Letter" (painting by J. Vermeer)	70	70
276	65 c.	"Woman writing a Letter" (painting by G. Terborch)	75	75
277	65 c.	Sir Rowland Hill with Penny Black, 1903 3d. and 1920 ½d. stamps	75	75
278	65 c.	"Lady reading a Letter" (painting by J. Vermeer)	75	75
		Set of 6	4·00	4·00
		First Day Cover		4·50
MS279		151 × 85 mm. 30 c. × 6. As Nos. 273/8	2·50	3·00
		First Day Cover		3·25

Nos. 273/5 and 276/8 were printed together, *se-tenant*, in horizontal strips of 3, the sheet having two panes separated by margin, one containing 273/5 × 3, the other containing 276/8 × 3.

1980 (3 Apr).   *Easter. T* **44** *and similar vert designs showing different details of painting "The Burial of Christ" by Quentin Metsys. P* 13.

280	20 c.	multicoloured	20	15
281	30 c.	multicoloured	30	25
282	35 c.	multicoloured	35	30
		Set of 3	75	60
		First Day Cover		80
MS283		93 × 71 mm. As Nos. 280/2, but each with premium of " + 2 c."	75	90
		First Day Cover		1·25

45 Einstein as Young Man   **46** Ancestor Figure, Aitutaki

1980 (21 July).   *25th Death Anniv of Albert Einstein (physicist). T* **45** *and similar vert designs. Multicoloured. P* 14 × 13½.

284	12 c.	Type **45**	20	20
285	12 c.	Atom and "E = mc²" equation	20	20
286	15 c.	Einstein as middle-aged man	25	25
287	15 c.	Cross over nuclear explosion (Nuclear Test Ban Treaty, 1963)	25	25
288	20 c.	Einstein as old man	30	30
289	20 c.	Hand over bomb explosion (Nuclear Test Ban Treaty, 1963)	30	30
		Set of 6	1·40	1·40
		First Day Cover		1·60
MS290		113 × 118 mm. Nos. 284/9. P 13½	1·40	1·60
		First Day Cover		1·90

Nos. 284/5, 286/7 and 288/9 were each printed together, *se-tenant*, in horizontal pairs throughout the sheet.

1980 (26 Sept).   *South Pacific Festival of Arts. T* **46** *and similar vert designs. Multicoloured. P* 13¾.

291	6 c.	Type **46**	5	5
292	6 c.	Staff god image, Rarotonga	5	5
293	6 c.	Trade adze, Mangaia	5	5
294	6 c.	Carved image of Tangaroa, Rarotonga	5	5
295	12 c.	Wooden image, Aitutaki	10	10
296	12 c.	Hand club, Rarotonga	10	10
297	12 c.	Carved mace "god", Mangaia	10	10
298	12 c.	Fisherman's god, Rarotonga	10	10
299	15 c.	Ti'i image, Aitutaki	15	15
300	15 c.	Fisherman's god, Rarotonga (*different*)	15	15
301	15 c.	Carved mace "god", Cook Islands	15	15
302	15 c.	Carved image of Tangaroa, Rarotonga (*different*)	15	15
303	20 c.	Chief's headdress, Aitutaki	15	15
304	20 c.	Carved "mace" god, Rarotonga (*different*)	15	15
305	20 c.	Staff god image, Rarotonga (*different*)	15	15
306	20 c.	Carved image of Tangaroa, Rarotonga (*different*)	15	15
		Set of 16	1·60	1·60
		First Day Cover		1·75
MS307		134 × 194 mm. Nos. 291/306	1·60	1·75
		First Day Cover		2·00

The four designs of each value were printed together, *se-tenant*, in blocks of 4 throughout the sheet.

47 Virgin and Child   **48** "Mourning Virgin"
(13th-century)

1980 (21 Nov).   *Christmas. Sculptures. T* **47** *and similar vert designs showing various Virgin and Child works from the periods given. Multicoloured. P* 13.

308	15 c.	Type **47**	15	15
309	20 c.	14th-century	15	15
310	25 c.	15th-century	15	15
311	35 c.	15th-century (*different*)	20	20
		Set of 4	60	60
		First Day Cover		80
MS312		82 × 120 mm. As Nos. 308/11 but each with premium of 2 c.	80	95
		First Day Cover		1·25

1981 (31 Mar).   *Easter. Details of Sculpture "Burial of Christ" by Pedro Roldan. T* **48** *and similar vert designs. P* 14.

313	30 c.	gold and myrtle-green	25	25
314	40 c.	gold and deep reddish lilac	30	30
315	50 c.	gold and Prussian blue	30	30
		Set of 3	75	75
		First Day Cover		1·25
MS316		107 × 60 mm. As Nos. 313/15 but each with premium of 2 c.	1·10	1·25
		First Day Cover		1·50

Designs:—40 c. "Christ"; 50 c. "Saint John".

MINIMUM PRICE

The minimum price quoted is 5p which represents a handling charge rather than a basis for valuing common stamps. For further notes about prices see introductory pages.

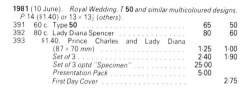

49 Gouldian Finch   50 Prince Charles
(*Poephila gouldiae*)

1981 (6 Apr)–**82**. *Birds* (1st series). *Multicoloured designs as T* 49.
P 14 × 13½ (1 c. to 10 c.), 13½ × 14 (15 c. to 70 c.) or 13 ($1 to $4).

317	1 c.	Type **49**	15	5
318	1 c.	Common Starling (*Sturnus vulgaris*)	15	5
319	2 c.	Golden Whistler (*Pachycephala pectoralis*)	15	5
320	2 c.	Scarlet Robin (*Petroica multicolor*)	15	5
321	3 c.	Rufous Fantail (*Rhipidura rufifrous*)	20	10
322	3 c.	Peregrine Falcon (*Falco peregrinus*)	20	10
323	4 c.	Java Sparrow (*Padda oryzivora*)	20	10
324	4 c.	Barn Owl (*Tyto alba*)	20	10
325	5 c.	Tahitian Lory (*Vini peruviana*)	20	10
326	5 c.	White-breasted Wood Swallow (*Artamus leucorhynchus*)	20	10
327	6 c.	Purple Swamphen (*Porphyrio porphyrio*)	25	10
328	6 c.	Rock Dove (*Columba livia*)	25	10
329	10 c.	Chestnut-breasted Mannikin (*Lonchura castaneothorax*)	40	10
330	10 c.	Zebra Dove (*Geopelia striata*)	40	10
331	12 c.	Eastern Reef Heron (*Egretta sacra*)	40	15
332	12 c.	Common Mynah (*Acridotheres tristis*)	40	15
333	15 c.	Whimbrel (*Numenius phaeopus*) (*horiz*) (8.5.81)	50	15
334	15 c.	Black-browed Albatross (*Diomeda melanophris*) (*horiz*) (8.5.81)	50	15
335	20 c.	American Golden Plover (*Pluvialis dominica*) (*horiz*) (8.5.81)	60	20
336	20 c.	White Tern (*Gygis alba*) (*horiz*) (8.5.81)	60	20
337	25 c.	Spotbill Duck (*Anas superciliosa*) (*horiz*) (8.5.81)	70	25
338	25 c.	Brown Booby (*Sula leucogaster*) (*horiz*) (8.5.81)	70	25
339	30 c.	Great Frigate Bird (*Fregata minor*) (*horiz*) (8.5.81)	90	30
340	30 c.	Pintail (*Anas acuta*) (*horiz*) (8.5.81)	90	30
341	35 c.	Long-billed Reed Warbler (*Conopoderas caffra caffra*) (14.1.82)	1·00	35
342	35 c.	Pomarine Skua (*Stercorarius pomarinus*) (14.1.82)	1·00	35
343	40 c.	Banded Rail (*Gallirallus philippensis goodsoni*) (14.1.82)	1·25	40
344	40 c.	Spotted Triller (*Lalage maculosa pumila*) (14.1.82)	1·25	40
345	50 c.	Royal Albatross (*Diomedea epomophora*) (14.1.82)	1·40	60
346	50 c.	Stephen's Lory (*Vini stepheni*) (14.1.82)	1·40	60
347	70 c.	Red-headed Parrot Finch (*Erythrura cyaneovirens*) (14.1.82)	2·00	1·00
348	70 c.	Orange Dove (*Ptilinopus victor victor*) (14.1.82)	2·00	1·00
349	$1	Blue-headed Flycatcher (*Myiagra azureocapilla whitneyi*) (15.2.82)	2·50	1·75
350	$2	Red-bellied Flycatcher (*Myiagra vanikorensis rufiventris*) (15.2.82)	4·75	3·00
351	$4	Red Munia (*Amandava amandava*) (19.3.82)	6·50	5·00
352	$5	Flat-billed Kingfisher (*Halcyon recurvirostris*) (19.3.82)	8·50	7·50
		Set of 36	38·00	22·00
		First Day Covers (5)		28·00

The two designs of each value (1 c. to 70 c.) were printed together, *se-tenant*, in horizontal and vertical pairs throughout the sheet.
Nos. 341/8 are 35 × 27 mm and Nos. 349/52, which include a portrait of Queen Elizabeth II, 35 × 48 mm in size.
See also Nos. 475/94 for redrawn designs as Type **65**.
Nos. 353/90 are vacant.

THE WORLD CENTRE FOR
FINE STAMPS IS 399 STRAND

1981 (10 June). *Royal Wedding. T* **50** *and similar multicoloured designs.*
P 14 ($1.40) or 13 × 13½ (*others*).

391	60 c.	Type **50**	65	50
392	80 c.	Lady Diana Spencer	80	60
393	$1.40,	Prince Charles and Lady Diana (87 × 70 mm)	1·25	1·00
		Set of 3	2·40	1·90
		Set of 3 optd "Specimen"	25·00	
		Presentation Pack	5·00	
		First Day Cover		2·75

+5c   AITUTAKI COOK ISLANDS

(51)   52 Footballers   53 "The Holy Family"

1981 (23 Nov). *International Year for Disabled Persons. Nos.* 391/3
surch with T **51** *on gold background.*

394	60 c. + 5 c. Type **50**	1·25	1·25
395	80 c. + 5 c. Lady Diana Spencer	1·75	1·75
396	$1.40 + 5 c. Prince Charles and Lady Diana	3·25	3·25
	Set of 3	5·50	5·50
	First Day Cover		6·00

Nos. 394/6 have commemorative inscriptions overprinted on the sheet margins.

1981 (30 Nov). *World Cup Football Championship, Spain* (1982). *T* **52**
and similar horiz designs showing footballers. Multicoloured. P 14.

397	12 c.	Ball to left of stamp	15	15
398	12 c.	Ball to right	15	15
399	15 c.	Ball to right	20	20
400	15 c.	Ball to left	20	20
401	20 c.	Ball to left	25	25
402	20 c.	Ball to right	25	25
403	25 c.	Type **52**	30	30
404	25 c.	"ESPANA 82" inscr on printed background	30	30
		Set of 8	1·60	1·60
		First Day Cover		1·75
MS405	100 × 137 mm. 12 c. + 2 c., 15 c. + 2 c., 20 c. + 2 c., 25 c. + 2 c., each × 2. As Nos. 397/404	1·75	2·00
		First Day Cover		2·50

The two designs of each value were printed together, *se-tenant*, in horizontal pairs throughout the sheet.

1981 (10 Dec). *Christmas. Details from Etchings by Rembrandt. T* **53** *and similar designs in purple-brown and gold. P* 14.

406	15 c.	Type **53**	20	15
407	30 c.	"Virgin with Child"	35	30
408	40 c.	"Adoration of the Shepherds" (*horiz*)	50	45
409	50 c.	"The Holy Family" (*horiz*)	60	50
		Set of 4	1·50	1·25
		First Day Cover		1·50
MS410	Designs as Nos. 406/9 in separate miniature sheets, 65 × 82 mm or 82 × 65 mm, each with a face value of 80 c. + 5 c. P 14 × 13½. Set of 4 sheets	2·75	3·00
		First Day Cover		3·50

54 Princess of Wales   (55)

1982 (24 June). *21st Birthday of Princess of Wales. T* **54** *and similar vert designs. Multicoloured. P* 14.

411	70 c.	Type **54**	70	70
412	$1	Prince and Princess of Wales	85	85
413	$2	Princess Diana (*different*)	1·60	1·75
		Set of 3	2·75	3·00
		First Day Cover		3·00
MS414	82 × 91 mm. Nos. 411/13		2·75	2·75
		First Day Cover		3·00

Nos. 411/13 were each printed in small sheets of 6 including two *se-tenant* stamp-size labels. The silver markings in the margins of the individual stamps differ for each position in the sheetlet.

1982 (13 July). *Birth of Prince William of Wales* (1st issue). *Nos. 391/3 optd as T* **55**.

415	60 c.	Type **50** (optd with T **55**)	2·00	1·50
	a.	Pair. Nos. 415/16	4·00	3·00
416	60 c.	Type **50** (optd "COMMEMORATING THE ROYAL BIRTH")	2·00	1·50
417	80 c.	Lady Diana Spencer (optd with T **55**)	2·50	1·75
	a.	Pair. Nos. 417/18	5·00	3·50
418	80 c.	Lady Diana Spencer (optd "COMMEMO-RATING THE ROYAL BIRTH")	2·50	1·75
419	$1.40,	Prince Charles and Lady Diana (87 × 70 mm) (optd as T **55**)	4·50	3·00
	a.	Pair. Nos. 419/20	9·00	6·00
420	$1.40,	Prince Charles and Lady Diana (87 × 70 mm) (optd "COMMEMORATING THE ROYAL BIRTH")	4·50	3·00
		Set of 6	16·00	11·00
		First Day Cover		12·00

Nos. 415/16, 417/18 and 419/20 were each printed together in *se-tenant* pairs, horiz and vert, throughout the sheets.

1982 (5 Aug). *Birth of Prince William of Wales* (2nd issue). *As Nos.* 411/14, *but inscr* "ROYAL BIRTH 21 JUNE 1982 PRINCE WILLIAM OF WALES". *Multicoloured. P* 14.

421	70 c.	Type **54**	70	70
422	$1	Prince and Princess of Wales	85	85
423	$2	Princess Diana (*different*)	1·60	1·60
		Set of 3	2·75	2·75
		First Day Cover		3·00
MS424	81 × 91 mm. Nos. 421/3		2·75	3·00
				3·50

56 "Virgin and Child"   57 Aitutaki Bananas
(12th-century sculpture)

1982 (10 Dec). *Christmas. Religious Sculptures. T* **56** *and similar vert designs. Multicoloured. P* 13.

425	18 c.	Type **56**	20	20
426	36 c.	"Virgin and Child" (12th-century)	30	30
427	48 c.	"Virgin and Child" (13th-century)	45	45
428	60 c.	"Virgin and Child" (15th-century)	65	65
		Set of 4	1·40	1·40
		First Day Cover		1·75
MS429	99 × 115 mm. As Nos. 425/8 but each with 2 c. charity premium		1·40	1·75
		First Day Cover		2·25

Nos. 425/8 were each printed in small sheets of 6 including one *se-tenant*, stamp size, label, depicting the Prince and Princess of Wales with Prince William.

1983 (14 Mar). *Commonwealth Day. T* **57** *and similar horiz designs. Multicoloured. P* 13.

430	48 c.	Type **57**	65	50
431	48 c.	Ancient Ti'i image	65	50
432	48 c.	Tourist canoeing	65	50
433	48 c.	Captain William Bligh and chart	65	50
		Set of 4	2·40	1·75
		First Day Cover		2·00

Nos. 430/3 were issued together, *se-tenant*, in blocks of four throughout the sheet.

15th WORLD SCOUT JAMBOREE

58 Scouts around Campfire   (59)

1983 (18 Apr). *75th Anniv of Boy Scout Movement. T* **58** *and similar horiz designs. Multicoloured. P* 13½ × 14.

434	36 c.	Type **58**	65	45
435	48 c.	Scout saluting	80	55
436	60 c.	Scouts hiking	95	75
		Set of 3	2·25	1·60
		First Day Cover		2·00
MS437	78 × 107 mm. As Nos. 434/6 but each with premium of 3 c. P 13		2·25	2·50
		First Day Cover		3·00

1983 (11 July). *15th World Scout Jamboree, Alberta, Canada. Nos. 434/7 optd with T* **59**.

438	36 c.	Type **58**	65	45
439	48 c.	Scout saluting	80	55
440	60 c.	Scouts hiking	95	75
		Set of 3	2·25	1·60
		First Day Cover		2·00
MS441	78 × 107 mm. As Nos. 438/40 but each with a premium of 3 c.		2·25	2·50
		First Day Cover		3·00

60 Modern Sport Balloon   (61)   (62)

1983 (22 July). *Bicentenary of Manned Flight. T* **60** *and similar vert designs showing different modern sport balloons. P* 14 × 13.

442	18 c.	multicoloured	15	15
443	36 c.	multicoloured	35	30
444	48 c.	multicoloured	40	35
445	60 c.	multicoloured	55	45
		Set of 4	1·25	1·10
		First Day Cover		1·40
MS446	64 × 80 mm. $2.50, multicoloured (48½ × 28½ mm)		1·90	2·50
		First Day Cover		3·00

Nos. 442/5 were each issued in small sheets of 4 stamps.

1983 (22 Sept). *Various stamps surch.*

       (a) *Nos. 335/48 and 352 as T* **61**

447	18 c.	on 20 c. American Golden Plover (*Pluvialis dominica*)	20	15
448	18 c.	on 20 c. White Tern (*Gygis alba*)	20	15
449	36 c.	on 25 c. Spotbill Duck (*Anas superciliosa*)	35	30
450	36 c.	on 25 c. Brown Booby (*Sula leucogaster*)	35	30

451	36 c. on 30 c. Great Frigate Bird (*Fregata minor*)	35	30
452	36 c. on 30 c. Pintail (*Anas acuta*)	35	30
453	36 c. on 35 c. Long-billed Reed Warbler (*Cono-poderas caffra caffra*)	35	30
454	36 c. on 35 c. Pomarine Skua (*Stercorarius po-marinus*)	35	30
455	48 c. on 40 c. Banded Rail (*Gallirallus philippensis goodsoni*)	50	40
456	48 c. on 40 c. Spotted Triller (*Lalage maculosa pumila*)	50	40
457	48 c. on 50 c. Royal Albatross (*Diomedea epom-ophora*)	50	40
458	48 c. on 50 c. Stephen's Lory (*Vini stepheni*) . . .	50	40
459	72 c. on 70 c. Red-headed Parrot Finch (*Erythrura cyaneovirens*)	75	60
460	72 c. on 70 c. Orange Dove (*Ptilinopus victor victor*)	75	60
461	$5.60 on $5 Flat-billed Kingfisher (*Halcyon recurvirostris*)	6·00	4·75

(*b*) *Nos. 392/3 and 412/13 as T* **62**

462	96 c. on 80 c. Lady Diana Spencer (Gold)	4·50	2·50
	a. Error. Surch on No. 417	12·00	
	ab. Pair. Nos. 462a/b	25·00	
	b. Error. Surch on No. 418	12·00	
463	96 c. on $1 Prince and Princess of Wales	4·00	2·00
464	$1.20 on $1.40, Prince Charles and Lady Diana (Gold)	4·50	2·50
	a. Error. Surch on No. 419	12·00	
	ab. Pair. Nos. 464a/b	25·00	
	b. Error. Surch on No. 420	12·00	
465	$1.20 on $2 Princess Diana	4·00	2·00
	Set of 19	26·00	17·00
	First Day Cover		23·00

On Nos. 462 and 464 the gold surcharge is printed on a black obliterating panel over the original face value.

63 International Mail

64 "Madonna of the Chair"

1983 (29 Sept). *World Communications Year. T* **63** *and similar vert designs. Multicoloured. P* 14 × 13½.

466	48 c. Type **63**	45	45
467	60 c. Telecommunications	60	60
468	96 c. Space satellites	90	90
	Set of 3	1·75	1·75
	First Day Cover		2·25
MS469	126 × 53 mm. As Nos. 466/8. P 13	1·90	2·25
	First Day Cover		2·75

1983 (21 Nov). *Christmas. 500th Birth Anniv of Raphael. T* **64** *and similar horiz designs. Multicoloured. P* 13½ × 14.

470	36 c. Type **64**	25	30
471	48 c. "The Alba Madonna"	35	40
472	60 c. "Conestabile Madonna"	50	55
	Set of 3	1·00	1·10
	First Day Cover		1·40
MS473	95 × 116 mm. As Nos. 470/2, but each with a premium of 3 c. P 13	1·25	1·40
	First Day Cover		2·00

1983 (15 Dec). *Christmas. 500th Birth Anniv of Raphael. Children's Charity. Designs as Nos. 470/2 in separate miniature sheets,* 46 × 47 mm, *each with different frames and a face value of* 85 c. + 5 c. *Imperf.*

MS474	As Nos. 470/2. *Set of 3 sheets*	2·75	2·75
	First Day Cover		3·50

65 Gouldian Finch   **66** Javelin-throwing

1984 (13 Feb–2 July). *Birds (2nd series). Designs as Nos. 317 etc, but with redrawn frames and inscriptions as in T* **65**. *Multicoloured. P* 13 × 13½ ($3 *to* $9.60) *or* 14 (*others*).

475	2 c. Type **65**	5	5
476	3 c. Common Starling	5	5
477	5 c. Scarlet Robin	5	5
478	10 c. Golden Whistler	5	5
479	12 c. Rufous Fantail	10	10
480	18 c. Peregrine Falcon	15	15
481	24 c. Barn Owl	15	20
482	30 c. Java Sparrow	20	25
483	36 c. White-breasted Wood Swallow	25	30
484	48 c. Tahitian Lory	30	35
485	50 c. Rock Dove (26 Mar)	30	35
486	60 c. Purple Swamphen (26 Mar)	40	45
487	72 c. Zebra Dove (26 Mar)	50	55
488	96 c. Chestnut-breasted Mannikin (26 Mar)	65	70
489	$1.20, Common Mynah (26 Mar)	80	85
490	$2.10, Eastern Reef Heron (30 Apr)	1·40	1·50
491	$3 Blue-headed Flycatcher (30 × 42 *mm*) (30 Apr)	2·00	2·25
492	$4.20, Red-bellied Flycatcher (30 × 42 *mm*) (5 June)	2·75	3·00
493	$5.60, Red Munia (30 × 42 *mm*) (5 June)	3·75	4·00
494	$9.60, Flat-billed Kingfisher (30 × 42 *mm*) (2 July)	6·50	6·75
	Set of 20	18·00	19·00
	First Day Covers (5)		25·00

1984 (24 July). *Olympic Games, Los Angeles. T* **66** *and similar vert designs showing Memorial Coliseum and various events. Multicoloured. P* 13 × 13½.

495	36 c. Type **66**	30	35
496	48 c. Shot-putting	40	45
497	60 c. Hurdling	45	55
498	$2 Basketball	1·10	1·50
	Set of 4	2·00	2·50
	First Day Cover		3·00
MS499	88 × 117 mm. As Nos. 495/8, but each with a charity premium of 5 c.	2·25	3·00
	First Day Cover		3·50

1984 (21 Aug). *Olympic Gold Medal Winners. Nos.* 495/8 *optd as T* **210** *of Cook Islands in gold on black background.*

500	36 c. Type **66** (optd "Javelin Throw Tessa Sanderson Great Britain")	30	35
501	48 c. Shot-putting (optd "Shot Put Claudia Losch Germany")	40	45
502	60 c. Hurdling (optd "Heptathlon Glynis Nunn Australia")	45	55
503	$2 Basketball (optd "Team Basketball United States")	1·10	1·50
	Set of 4	2·00	2·50
	First Day Cover		3·00

STANLEY GIBBONS
STAMP COLLECTING SERIES

Introductory booklets on *How to Start, How to Identify Stamps* and *Collecting by Theme*. A series of well illustrated guides at a low price. Write for details.

67 Capt. William Bligh and Chart   (**68**)

71 Grey Kingbird   **72** The Queen Mother, aged Seven

1984 (14 Sept). *"Ausipex" International Stamp Exhibition, Melbourne.*
T 67 and similar horiz designs. Multicoloured. P 14.

504	60 c. Type **67**		50	55
505	96 c. H.M.S. *Bounty* and map		80	85
506	$1.40, Aitutaki stamps of 1974, 1979 and 1981			
	with map		1·25	1·40
	Set of 3		2·25	2·50
	First Day Cover			2·75
MS507	85 × 113 mm. As Nos. 504/6, but each with a			
	premium of 5 c. P 13½		2·40	3·00
	First Day Cover			3·25

1985 (22 Mar). *Birth Bicentenary of John J. Audubon (ornithologist).*
T 71 and similar vert designs showing original paintings. Multicoloured.
P 13.

518	55 c. Type **71**		60	60
519	65 c. Bohemian Waxwing		65	65
520	75 c. Summer Tanager		75	75
521	95 c. Common Cardinal		90	90
522	$1.15, White-winged Crossbill		1·10	1·10
	Set of 5		3·50	3·50
	First Day Cover			4·00

1984 (10 Oct). *Birth of Prince Henry (1st issue). No. 391 surch with T 68*
in gold.

508	$3 on 60 c. Type **50**		4·00	3·00

On No. 508 the gold surcharge is printed on a black obliterating panel
over the original face value.

1985 (14 June). *Life and Times of Queen Elizabeth the Queen Mother.*
T 72 and similar horiz designs. Multicoloured. P 13.

523	55 c. Type **72**		45	50
524	65 c. Engagement photograph, 1922		50	55
525	75 c. With young Princess Elizabeth		60	65
526	$1.30, With baby Prince Charles		1·00	1·10
	Set of 4		2·25	2·50
	First Day Cover			2·75
MS527	75 × 49 mm. $3 Queen Mother on her 63rd			
	birthday		2·25	2·40
	First Day Cover			2·75

Nos. 523/6 were each printed in sheetlets of 4 stamps.
For these stamps in a miniature sheet see No. **MS550**.

69 The Annunciation   **70** Princess Diana with
                                        Prince Henry

73 "The Calmady Children"
(T. Lawrence)

1984 (16 Nov). *Christmas. Details from Altarpiece, St. Paul's Church,*
Palencia, Spain. T 69 and similar vert designs. Multicoloured. P 13½ × 13.

509	36 c. Type **69**		30	35
510	48 c. The Nativity		40	45
511	60 c. The Epiphany		45	50
512	96 c. The Flight into Egypt		75	80
	Set of 4		1·75	1·90
	First Day Cover			2·40
MS513	Designs as Nos. 509/12 in separate miniature			
	sheets, each 45 × 53 mm and with a face value of			
	90 c.+7 c. Imperf. *Set of 4 sheets*		3·00	3·25
	First Day Cover			4·00

1985 (16 Sept). *International Youth Year. T 73 and similar horiz designs.*
Multicoloured. P 13.

528	75 c. Type **73**		50	55
529	90 c. "Madame Charpentier's Children" (Renoir)		60	65
530	$1.40, "Young Girls at Piano" (Renoir)		95	1·00
	Set of 3		1·90	2·00
	First Day Cover			2·40
MS531	103 × 104 mm. As Nos. 528/30, but each with a			
	premium of 10 c.		2·25	2·50
	First Day Cover			3·00

1984 (10 Dec). *Birth of Prince Henry (2nd issue). T 70 and similar vert*
designs. Multicoloured. P 14.

514	48 c. Type **70**		45	45
515	60 c. Prince William with Prince Henry		50	50
516	$2.10, Prince and Princess of Wales with chil-			
	dren		1·60	1·60
	Set of 3		2·25	2·25
	First Day Cover			2·50
MS517	113 × 65 mm. As Nos. 514/16, but each with a			
	face value of 96 c.+7 c. P 13½		2·25	2·40
	First Day Cover			2·75

74 "Adoration of the Magi" (Giotto)
and *Giotto* Spacecraft

1985 (15 Nov). *Christmas. Appearance of Halley's Comet* (1st issue). *Multicoloured. P* 13.

532	95 c. Type **74**		75	80
533	95 c. Type **74** but showing *Planet A* spacecraft		75	80
534	$1.15, Type **74**		90	95
535	$1.15, As No. 533		90	95
	Set of 4		3·00	3·25
	First Day Cover			3·75
MS536	52 × 55 mm. $6.40, As Type **74** but without spacecraft (30 × 31 mm). Imperf		5·50	6·00
	First Day Cover			6·50

Nos. 532/3 and 534/5 were each printed together, *se-tenant*, in horizontal pairs throughout the sheets.

75 Halley's Comet, A.D. 684 (from "Nuremberg Chronicle")

76 Queen Elizabeth II on Coronation Day (from photo by Cecil Beaton)

1986 (25 Feb). *Appearance of Halley's Comet* (2nd issue). *T* **75** *and similar multicoloured designs. P* 13½ × 13.

537	90 c. Type **75**		65	70
538	$1.25, Halley's Comet, 1066 (from Bayeux Tapestry)		85	90
539	$1.75, Halley's Comet, 1456 (from "Lucerne Chronicles")		1·25	1·40
	Set of 3		2·50	2·75
	First Day Cover			3·25
MS540	107 × 82 mm. As Nos. 537/9, but each with a face value of 95 c.		1·90	2·50
	First Day Cover			3·00
MS541	65 × 80 mm. $4.20, "Melencolia I" (Albrecht Dürer woodcut) (61 × 76 mm). Imperf		2·75	3·25
	First Day Cover			3·75

1986 (21 Apr). *60th Birthday of Queen Elizabeth II. Multicoloured. P* 14.

542	95 c. Type **76**		65	70
	First Day Cover			95
MS543	58 × 68 mm. $4.20, As Type **76**, but showing more of the portrait without oval frame. P 13½		3·00	3·50
	First Day Cover			4·00

No. 542 was printed in sheetlets of five stamps and one stamp-size label at top left.

77 Head of Statue of Liberty

78 Prince Andrew and Miss Sarah Ferguson

1986 (27 June). *Centenary of Statue of Liberty. T* **77** *and similar horiz design. Multicoloured. P* 14.

544	$1 Type **77**		70	75
545	$2.75, Statue of Liberty at sunset		1·90	2·00
	Set of 2		2·50	2·75
	First Day Cover			3·25
MS546	91 × 79 mm. As Nos. 544/5, but each with a face value of $1.25. P 13½		1·90	2·25
	First Day Cover			3·00

1986 (23 July). *Royal Wedding. P* 14.

547	**78** $2 multicoloured		1·50	1·60
	First Day Cover			2·00
MS548	85 × 70 mm. **78** $5 multicoloured. P 13½		3·75	4·25
	First Day Cover			4·75

No. 547 was printed in sheetlets of 5 stamps and one stamp-size label at top left.

1986 (4 Aug). *"Stampex '86" Stamp Exhibition, Adelaide. No.* **MS**507 *with "Ausipex" emblems obliterated in gold.*

MS549	As Nos. 504/6, but each with a premium of 5 c.		2·50	3·00
	First Day Cover			3·50

The "Stampex '86" exhibition emblem is overprinted on the sheet margin.

1986 (4 Aug). *86th Birthday of Queen Elizabeth the Queen Mother. Nos.* 523/6 *in miniature sheet,* 132 × 82 *mm. P* 13½ × 13.

MS550	Nos. 523/6		2·50	3·00
	First Day Cover			3·50

79 "St. Anne with Virgin and Child"   (**80**)

1986 (21 Nov). *Christmas. Paintings by Dürer. T* **79** *and similar vert designs. Multicoloured. P* 13½.

551	75 c. Type **79**		55	60
552	$1.35, "Virgin and Child"		90	95
553	$1.95, "The Adoration of the Magi"		1·50	1·60
554	$2.75, "Madonna of the Rosary"		1·90	2·00
	Set of 4		4·25	4·75
	First Day Cover			6·00
MS555	88 × 125 mm. As Nos. 551/4, but each stamp with a face value of $1.65		4·50	5·50
	First Day Cover			6·50

1986 (25 Nov). *Visit of Pope John Paul II to South Pacific. Nos.* 551/5 *surch with T* **80** *in silver.*

556	75 c. + 10 c. Type **79**		75	75
557	$1.35 + 10 c. "Virgin and Child"		1·25	1·25
558	$1.95 + 10 c. "The Adoration of the Magi"		1·75	1·75
559	$2.75 + 10 c. "Madonna of the Rosary"		2·25	2·25
	Set of 4		5·50	5·50
	First Day Cover			7·00
MS560	88 × 125 mm. As Nos. 556/9, but each stamp with a face value of $1.65 + 10 c.		6·00	6·50
	First Day Cover			8·00

(**81**)   (**82**)

1987 (29 Apr). *Hurricane Relief Fund. Nos. 544/5, 547, 551/4 and 556/9 surch with T **81** in black (Nos. 563, 569) or silver (others).*

561	75 c. + 50 c. Type **79**	1·10	1·10
562	75 c. + 10 c. + 50 c. Type **79**	1·25	1·25
563	$1 + 50 c. Type **77**	1·40	1·40
564	$1.35 + 50 c. "Virgin and Child" (Dürer)	1·60	1·60
565	$1.35 + 10 c. + 50 c. "Virgin and Child" (Dürer).	1·75	1·75
566	$1.95 + 50 c. "The Adoration of the Magi" (Dürer)	2·10	2·10
567	$1.95 + 10 c. + 50 c. "The Adoration of the Magi" (Dürer)	2·10	2·10
568	$2 + 50 c. Type **78**	2·10	2·10
569	$2.75 + 50 c. Statue of Liberty at sunset	2·75	2·75
570	$2.75 + 50 c. "Madonna of the Rosary" (Dürer)	2·75	2·75
571	$2.75 + 10 c. + 50 c. "Madonna of the Rosary" (Dürer)	3·00	3·00
	Set of 11	20·00	20·00
	First Day Cover		24·00

1987 (20 Nov). *Royal Ruby Wedding. Nos. 391/3 surch as T **82**.*

572	$2.50 on 60 c. Type **50**	2·25	2·25
573	$2.50 on 80 c. Lady Diana Spencer	2·25	2·25
574	$2.50 on $1.40, Prince Charles and Lady Diana (87 × 70 mm)	2·25	2·25
	Set of 3	6·00	6·00
	First Day Cover		6·50

On Nos. 572/4 the original values are obliterated in gold.

83 "Angels" (detail from "Virgin with Garland")

1987 (10 Dec). *Christmas. T **83** and similar designs showing different details of angels from "Virgin with Garland" by Rubens. P 13 × 13½.*

575	70 c. multicoloured	50	55
576	85 c. multicoloured	60	65
577	$1.50, multicoloured	1·00	1·10
578	$1.85, multicoloured	1·25	1·40
	Set of 4	3·00	3·25
	First Day Cover		3·75
MS579	92 × 120 mm. As Nos. 575/8, but each with a face value of 95 c.	2·75	3·25
MS580	96 × 85 mm. $6 "Virgin with Garland" (diamond, 56 × 56 mm). P 13	4·75	5·50
	First Day Covers (2)		10·00

84 Chariot Racing and Athletics

(Des G. Vasarhelyi. Litho Questa)

1988 (22 Aug). *Olympic Games, Seoul. T **84** and similar horiz designs showing ancient and modern Olympic sports. Multicoloured. P 14½.*

581	70 c. Type **84**	50	55
582	85 c. Greek runners and football	60	65
583	95 c. Greek wrestling and handball	65	70
584	$1.40, Greek hoplites and tennis	1·00	1·10
	Set of 4	2·50	2·75
	First Day Cover		3·00
MS585	103 × 101 mm. As Nos. 581 and 584, but each with face value of $2	2·75	3·00
	First Day Cover		3·50

1988 (10 Oct). *Olympic Medal Winners, Los Angeles. Nos. 581/4 optd as T **235** of Cook Islands.*

586	70 c. Type **84** (optd "FLORENCE GRIFFTH JOYNER UNITED STATES 100 M AND 200 M")	50	55
587	85 c. Greek runners and football (optd "GELINDO BORDIN ITALY MARATHON")	60	65
588	95 c. Greek wrestling and handball (optd "HITO-SHI SAITO JAPAN JUDO")	65	70
589	$1.40, Greek hoplites and tennis (optd "STEFFI GRAF WEST GERMANY WOMEN'S TENNIS)	1·00	1·10
	Set of 4	2·50	2·75
	First Day Cover		3·25

85 "Adoration of the Shepherds" (detail)

1988 (2 Nov). *Christmas. T **85** and similar multicoloured designs showing paintings by Rembrandt. P 13½.*

590	55 c. Type **85**	40	45
591	70 c. "The Holy Family"	50	55
592	85 c. "Presentation in the Temple"	60	65
593	95 c. "The Holy Family" (different)	65	70
594	$1.15, "Presentation in the Temple" (different)	80	85
	Set of 5	2·75	3·00
	First Day Cover		3·50
MS595	85 × 101 mm. $4.50, As Type **85** but 52 × 34 mm. P 14	3·25	3·50
	First Day Cover		4·25

86 H.M.S. *Bounty* leaving Spithead and King George III

(Des Jennifer Toombs)

1989 (3 July). *Bicentenary of Discovery of Aitutaki by Capt. Bligh. T **86** and similar horiz designs. Multicoloured. P 13½ × 13.*

596	55 c. Type **86**	40	45
597	65 c. Breadfruit plants	50	55
598	75 c. Old chart showing Aitutaki and Capt. Bligh	55	60
599	95 c. Native outrigger and H.M.S. *Bounty* off Aitutaki	70	75
600	$1.65, Fletcher Christian confronting Bligh	1·25	1·40
	Set of 5	3·00	3·50
	First Day Cover		4·25
MS601	94 × 72 mm. $4.20, "Mutineers casting Bligh adrift" (Robert Dodd) (60 × 45 mm). P 13½	3·25	3·50
	First Day Cover		4·50

THE WORLD CENTRE FOR FINE STAMPS IS 399 STRAND

87 "Apollo 11" Astronaut on Moon

1989 (28 July).   *20th Anniv of First Manned Landing on Moon. T* **87** *and similar horiz designs. Multicoloured. P* 13½ × 13.

602	75 c. Type **87**	55	60
603	$1.15, Conducting experiment on Moon	85	90
604	$1.80, Astronaut on Moon carrying equip-		
	ment	1·40	1·50
	Set of 3	2·50	2·75
	First Day Cover		3·50
MS605	105 × 86 mm. $6.40, Astronaut on Moon with		
	U.S. flag (40 × 27 *mm*). P 13½	4·75	5·00
	First Day Cover		5·50

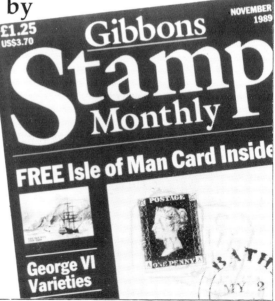

STAMP BOOKLET

PRICE given is for complete booklet.

1982 (June). *Royal Wedding. Cover as No. B1 of Cook Islands but inscr "Aitutaki".*

B1 $5.60, booklet containing Nos. 391/2 × 4 . . . .   12·00

75c ▬

O.H.M.S.   O.H.M.S.

(O 2)   (O 3)

OFFICIAL STAMPS

O H.M.S.

(O 1)

1978 (3 Nov)–**79.** *Nos. 98/105, 107/10 and 227/8 optd or surch (Nos. O8/9 and O15) as Type O 1.*

O 1	1 c. *Nautilus macromphallus*	25	5
O 2	2 c. *Harpa major*	35	5
O 3	3 c. *Phalium strigatum*	35	5
O 4	4 c. *Cypraea talpa* (Gold)	35	5
O 5	5 c. *Mitra stictica*	35	5
O 6	8 c. *Charonia tritonis*	40	10
O 7	10 c. *Murex triremis*	50	15
O 8	15 c. on 60 c. *Strombus latissimus*	75	20
O 9	18 c. on 60 c. *Strombus latissimus*	75	20
O10	20 c. *Oliva sericea* (Gold)	75	20
O11	50 c. Union Jack, Queen Victoria and island map	1·50	70
O12	60 c. *Strombus latissimus*	2·00	85
O13	$1 *Biplex perca*	2·25	1·50
O14	$2 Queen Elizabeth II and *Terebra maculata* (20.2.79)	3·50	2·00
O15	$4 on $1 Balcony scene, 1953 (Sil.) (20.2.79)	6·00	3·00
O16	$5 Queen Elizabeth II and *Cypraea hesitata* (20.2.79)	7·00	4·00
	Set of 16	25·00	12·00

These stamps were originally only sold to the public cancelled-to-order and not in unused condition.

They were made available to overseas collectors in mint condition during 1980.

1985 (9 Aug)–**88.** (a) *Nos. 351, 475, 477/88 and 489/94 optd or surch as Type O 2 by foil embossing in blue ($14) or emerald (others).*

O17	2 c. Type **65**	5	5
O18	5 c. Scarlet Robin	5	5
O19	10 c. Golden Whistler	5	8
O20	12 c. Rufous Fantail	8	10
O21	18 c. Peregrine Falcon	12	15
O22	20 c. on 24 c. Barn Owl	12	15
O23	30 c. Java Sparrow	20	25
O24	40 c. on 36 c. White-breasted Wood Swallow . . .	25	30
O25	50 c. Rock Dove	30	35
O26	55 c. on 48 c. Tahitian Lory	35	40
O27	60 c. Purple Swamphen	40	45
O28	65 c. on 72 c. Zebra Dove	45	50
O29	80 c. on 96 c. Chestnut-breasted Mannikin . . .	55	60
O30	$1.20, Common Mynah (15.6.88)	80	85
O31	$2.10, Eastern Reef Heron (15.6.88)	1·40	1·50
O32	$3 Blue-headed Flycatcher (30 × 42 mm) (1.10.86)	2·00	2·25
O33	$4.20, Red-bellied Flycatcher (30 × 42 mm) (1.10.86)	2·75	3·00
O34	$5.60, Red Munia (30 × 42 mm) (1.10.86)	3·75	4·00
O35	$9.60, Flat-billed Kingfisher (30 × 42 mm) (1.10.86)	6·50	6·75
O36	$14 on $4 Red Munia (35 × 48 mm) (15.6.88). . .	9·00	9·50

(b) *Nos. 430/3 surch as Type O 3 by gold foil embossing*

O37	75 c. on 48 c. Type **57**	50	55
O38	75 c. on 48 c. Ancient Ti'i image	50	55
O39	75 c. on 48 c. Tourist canoeing	50	55
O40	75 c. on 48 c. Captain William Bligh and chart . .	50	55
	Set of 24	28·00	30·00

PENRHYN ISLAND

Stamps of COOK ISLANDS were used on Penrhyn Island from late
1901 until the issue of the surcharged stamps in May 1902.

PRICES FOR STAMPS ON COVER TO 1945

Nos. 1/8	from × 4
Nos. 9/10	from × 50
Nos. 11/13	—
Nos. 14/18	from × 3
Nos. 19/23	from × 2
Nos. 24/37	from × 3
Nos. 38/40	from × 5

PRICES
Edward VII and George V issues (1902–1929)

First column = Mounted Mint
Second column = Used

NEW ZEALAND DEPENDENCY

The island of Penrhyn, previously under British protection, was annexed
by New Zealand on 11 June 1901.

Stamps of New Zealand overprinted or surcharged

PENRHYN ISLAND.

$\frac{1}{2}$ PENI.

(1)

PENRHYN ISLAND.
TAI PENI.
(2) 1d.

PENRHYN ISLAND.
$2\frac{1}{2}$ PENI.
(3)

1902 (5 May).   1902 *issue surch with T* **1**, **2** *and* **3**.

(a) Thick, white Pirie paper. No wmk. P 11
1	**27**	2½d. blue (R.)	1·25	3·50
		a. "½" and "P" spaced	12·00	22·00

(b) Thin, hard Basted Mills paper. W **38** *of New Zealand.* (i) *P* 11
3	**42**	1d. carmine (Br.)	£100	£110

(ii) *P* 14
4	**23**	½d. green (R.)	80	3·25
		a. No stop after "ISLAND"	85·00	90·00
5	**42**	1d. carmine (Br.)	3·00	6·50
		a. Pale carmine	3·00	6·50

(iii) *P* 11 × 14
7	**42**	1d. carmine (Br.)	£150	£150

(iv) *Mixed perfs*
8	**42**	1d. carmine (Br.)	£225	

(c) Thin, hard Cowan paper. W **43** *of New Zealand.* (i) *P* 14
9	**23**	½d. green (R.)	90	3·50
		a. No stop after "ISLAND"	60·00	65·00
10	**42**	1d. carmine (B.)	90	2·75
		a. No stop after "ISLAND"	40·00	55·00

(ii) *P* 11 × 14
11	**42**	1d. carmine (B.)		

(iii) *Mixed perfs*
12	**23**	½d. green (R.)	£175	£200
13	**42**	1d. carmine (B.)	60·00	75·00

THE WORLD CENTRE FOR
FINE STAMPS IS 399 STRAND

PENRHYN ISLAND.
(4)

Toru Pene.
(5) 3d.

Ono Pene.
(6) 6d.

Tahi Silingi.
(7) 1s.

1903 (28 Feb).   1902 *issue surch with name at top. T* **4**, *and values at foot.*
T **5**/7. *W* **43** *of New Zealand. P* 11.
14	**28**	3d. yellow-brown (B.)	9·00	14·00
15	**31**	6d. rose-red (B.)	15·00	24·00
16	**34**	1s. brown-red (B.)	38·00	48·00
17		1s. bright red (B.)	38·00	48·00
18		1s. orange-red (B.)	45·00	45·00
		Set of 3	55·00	75·00

1914–15.   Surch with T **1** (½d.) or optd with T **4** at top and surch with T **6**/7
at foot.
19	**50**	½d. yellow-green (C.) (5.14)	90	3·25
		a. No stop after "ISLAND"	32·00	55·00
		b. No stop after "PENI"	70·00	95·00
20		½d. yellow-green (Verm.) (1.15)	65	3·25
		a. No stop after "ISLAND"	15·00	30·00
		b. No stop after "PENI"	35·00	55·00
22	**51**	6d. carmine (B.) (8.14)	27·00	48·00
23		1s. vermilion (B.) (8.14)	45·00	70·00
		Set of 4	65·00	£110

1917–20.   King George V stamps optd with name only. T **4**. W **43** of New
Zealand. P 14 × 14½.
24	**60**	2½d. blue (R.) (10.20)	1·25	3·75
		a. No stop after "ISLAND"	70·00	£100
		b. Perf 14 × 13½	3·00	7·00
		c. Vert pair. Nos. 24/4b	50·00	60·00
25		3d. chocolate (B.) (6.18)	9·00	25·00
		a. Perf 14 × 13½	9·50	27·00
		b. Vert pair. Nos. 25/5a	70·00	90·00
26		6d. carmine (B.) (1.18)	5·00	12·00
		a. No stop after "ISLAND"	£120	£170
		b. Perf 14 × 13½	7·00	16·00
		c. Vert pair. Nos. 26/6b	55·00	75·00
27		1s. vermilion (B.) (12.17)	12·00	25·00
		a. No stop after "ISLAND"	£170	£225
		b. Perf 14 × 13½	15·00	30·00
		c. Vert pair. Nos. 27/7b	£110	£140
		Set of 4	24·00	60·00

1917–20.   Optd as T **4**. Typo. W **43** of New Zealand. P 14 × 15.
28	**61**	½d. green (R.) (2.20)	65	1·25
		a. No stop after "ISLAND"	45·00	60·00
		b. Narrow spacing	5·00	7·50
29		1½d. slate (R.) (11.17)	4·00	7·50
		a. Narrow spacing	17·00	28·00
30		1½d. orange-brown (R.) (2.19)	60	5·50
		a. Narrow spacing	5·00	17·00
31		3d. chocolate (B.) (6.19)	3·00	8·00
		a. Narrow spacing	14·00	28·00
		Set of 4	7·50	20·00

The overprint was applied in a setting of 30 (6 × 5) in which positions 22
to 24 had "PENRHYN ISLAND" spaced approximately ½ mm apart instead
of 1¼ mm.

(Recess P.B.)

1920 (23 Aug).   As Types of Cook Islands but inscr "PENRHYN". No wmk.
P 14.
32	**9**	½d. black and emerald	90	4·00
		a. Imperf between (vert pair)*	£550	
		b. Imperf vert (horiz pair)*	£550	
33	**10**	1d. black and deep red	1·25	4·00
34	**11**	1½d. black and deep violet	6·50	9·00
35	**12**	3d. black and red	2·00	5·00
36	**13**	6d. red-brown and sepia	3·25	13·00
37	**14**	1s. black and slate-blue	9·00	17·00
		Set of 6	20·00	45·00

*Nos. 32a/b occur from a sheet on which the top two rows were imperf
between horizontally and the second row additionally imperf vertically.

(Recess Govt Printing Office, Wellington)

As Types of Cook Islands, but inscr "PENRHYN". W **43**. P 14.

38	**9**	½d. black and green (5.29)	2·00	7·50
39	**10**	1d. black and deep carmine (14.3.28)	2·00	6·50
40	**16**	2½d. red-brown and dull blue (10.27)	1·75	10·00
		Set of 3	5·25	22·00

> Cook Islands stamps superseded those of Penrhyn Island on 15 March 1932. Separate issues were resumed in 1973.

PART OF COOK ISLANDS

PRICES

Elizabeth II issues (from 1953)

First column = Unmounted Mint
Second column = Used

PRINTERS. Stamps of Penrhyn were printed in photogravure by Heraclio Fournier, Spain, unless otherwise stated. All issues except Nos. 41A/52A and **MS**412 are on paper treated with fluorescent security markings and with synthetic gum. The fluorescent markings can be found inverted or omitted.

PENRHYN

NORTHERN
(8)

PENRHYN
NORTHERN
(9)

1973 (24 Oct–14 Nov). Nos. 228/45 of Cook Is optd with T **8** (without "NORTHERN" on $1, $2).

A. Without fluorescent security markings. Gum arabic
B. With fluorescent security markings. PVA gum

			A		B	
41	1 c.	multicoloured	60	—	5	10
42	2 c.	multicoloured	90	—	5	10
43	3 c.	multicoloured	1·25	—	10	10
44	4 c.	multicoloured (No. 233) . .	1·50	—	10	10
a.		Optd on Cook Is No. 232 .	60·00	—	†	
45	5 c.	multicoloured	1·75	—	10	10
46	6 c.	multicoloured	2·00	—	20	30
47	8 c.	multicoloured	2·25	—	30	40
48	15 c.	multicoloured	4·25	—	45	50
49	20 c.	multicoloured	†		75	80
50	50 c.	multicoloured	15·00	—	1·75	1·75
51	$1	multicoloured	28·00	—	2·25	2·25
52	$2	multicoloured (14.11) . . .	55·00	—	2·50	2·50
		Set of 11	£100	—		
		Set of 12	†		7·50	7·50
		First Day Covers (2)				10·00

1973 (14 Nov). Royal Wedding. Nos. 450/2 of Cook Is optd as T **9**, in silver.

53	**138**	25 c. multicoloured	85	25
54	–	30 c. multicoloured	85	25
55	–	50 c. multicoloured	85	25
		Set of 3	2·25	65
		First Day Cover		85

10 Ostracion sp

11 Penrhyn Stamps of 1902

1974 (15 Aug)-**75**. Fishes. T **10** and similar horiz designs. Multicoloured. P 13½ (½ c. to $1) or 13 × 12½ ($2, $5).

56	½ c.	Type **10**	15	5
57	1 c.	Monodactylus argenteus	30	5
58	2 c.	Pomacanthus imperator	40	5
59	3 c.	Chelmon rostratus	40	5
60	4 c.	Chaetodon ornatissimus	40	5
61	5 c.	Chaetodon melanotus	40	5
62	8 c.	Chaetodon raffessi	45	10
63	10 c.	Chaetodon ephippium	50	10
64	20 c.	Pygoplites diacanthus	1·25	25
65	25 c.	Heniochus acuminatus	1·25	25
66	60 c.	Plectorhynchus chaetodonoides	2·50	90
67	$1	Balistapus undulatus	2·75	1·25
68	$2	Birds-eye view of Penrhyn (12.2.75)	4·50	5·00
69	$5	Satellite view of Australasia (12.3.75) . . .	6·50	5·50
		Set of 14	20·00	12·00
		First Day Covers (3)		17·00

Nos. 68/9 are larger, 63 × 25 mm.

1974 (27 Sept). Centenary of Universal Postal Union. T **11** and similar vert design. Multicoloured. P 13.

70	25 c.	Type **11**	25	25
71	50 c.	Stamps of 1920	40	40
		Set of 2	65	65
		First Day Cover		80

Each value was issued in sheets of 8 stamps and 1 label.

12 "Adoration of the Kings" (Memling)

1974 (30 Oct). Christmas. T **12** and similar horiz designs. Multicoloured. P 13.

72	5 c.	Type **12**	15	10
73	10 c.	"Adoration of the Shepherds" (Hugo van der Goes)	20	15
74	25 c.	"Adoration of the Magi" (Rubens)	35	25
75	30 c.	"The Holy Family" (Borgianni)	45	35
		Set of 4	1·00	80
		First Day Cover		90

13 Churchill giving "V" Sign

(**14**)

1974 (30 Nov). Birth Centenary of Sir Winston Churchill. T **13** and similar vert design. P 13.

76	30 c.	agate and gold	90	70
77	50 c.	myrtle-green and gold	1·10	80
		Set of 2	2·00	1·50
		First Day Cover		1·75

Design:—50 c. Full-face portrait.

1975 (24 July). "Apollo-Soyuz" Space Project. No. 69 optd with T **14**.

78	$5	Satellite view of Australasia	4·50	5·00
		First Day Cover		5·50

15 "Virgin and Child"   16 "Pietà"
(Bouts)

19 "The Flight into Egypt"   20 The Queen in
                                   Coronation Robes

1975 (21 Nov). *Christmas. T* **15** *and similar vert designs showing the "Virgin and Child". Multicoloured. P* 14 × 13.

79	7 c.	Type **15**	25	15
80	15 c.	Leonardo da Vinci	50	25
81	35 c.	Raphael	85	45
		Set of 3	1·50	75
		First Day Cover		1·00

1976 (19 Mar). *Easter and 500th Birth Anniv of Michelangelo. T* **16** *and similar vert designs. P* 14 × 13.

82	15 c.	sepia and gold	25	15
83	20 c.	blackish purple and gold	30	20
84	35 c.	myrtle-green and gold	40	25
		Set of 3	85	55
		First Day Cover		75
MS85	112 × 72 mm. Nos. 82/4		95	1·40
		First Day Cover		2·00

Each value was issued in sheets of 8 stamps and 1 label.

1976 (20 Oct). *Christmas. Dürer Engravings. T* **19** *and similar horiz designs. P* 13.

97	7 c.	black and silver	10	10
98	15 c.	steel blue and silver	20	15
99	35 c.	violet and silver	30	25
		Set of 3	55	45
		First Day Cover		75

Designs:— 15 c. "Adoration of the Magi"; 35 c. "The Nativity".

1977 (24 Mar). *Silver Jubilee. T* **20** *and similar vert designs. Multicoloured. P* 13.

100	50 c.	Type **20**	85	75
101	$1	Queen and Prince Philip	1·10	90
102	$2	Queen Elizabeth II	1·50	1·25
		Set of 3	3·00	2·50
		First Day Cover		2·75
MS103	128 × 87 mm. Nos. 100/2. P 13		4·25	3·75
		First Day Cover		4·50

Stamps from the miniature sheet have silver borders.

17 "Washington crossing the   18 Running
Delaware" (E. Leutze)

21 "The Annunciation"   22 Iiwi

1976 (20 May). *Bicentenary of American Revolution. T* **17** *and similar vert designs. Multicoloured. P* 13.

86	30 c.		60	20
87	30 c. ⎫ Type **17**		60	20
88	30 c. ⎭		60	20
89	50 c. ⎫		70	30
90	50 c. ⎬ "The Spirit of '76" (A. M. Willard)		70	30
91	50 c. ⎭		70	30
		Set of 6	3·50	1·40
		First Day Cover		2·25
MS92	103 × 103 mm. Nos. 86/91. P 13		3·50	3·75
		First Day Cover		4·50

Nos. 86/8 and 89/91 were each printed together, *se-tenant*, in horizontal strips of 3 throughout the sheet, forming composite designs. Each sheet includes 3 stamp-size labels. Type **17** shows the left-hand stamp of the 30 c. design.

1976 (9 July). *Olympic Games, Montreal. T* **18** *and similar horiz designs. Multicoloured. P* 14.

93	25 c.	Type **18**	30	15
94	30 c.	Long Jumping	40	20
95	75 c.	Throwing the Javelin	70	35
		Set of 3	1·25	65
		First Day Cover		95
MS96	86 × 128 mm. Nos. 93/5. P 14 × 13		1·60	2·25
		First Day Cover		2·75

1977 (23 Sept). *Christmas. T* **21** *and similar designs showing illustrations by J. S. von Carolsfeld. P* 13.

104	7 c.	light stone, purple-brown and gold	25	15
105	15 c.	pale rose, deep maroon and gold	40	25
106	35 c.	blackish green, pale green and gold	70	40
		Set of 3	1·25	70
		First Day Cover		1·10

Designs:— 15 c. "The Announcement to the Shepherds"; 35 c. "The Nativity".

1978 (19 Jan). *Bicentenary of Discovery of Hawaii. T* **22** *and similar vert designs showing extinct Hawaiian birds or artefacts. Multicoloured. P* 13.

107	20 c.	Type **22**	50	30
108	20 c.	Elgin cloak	50	30
109	30 c.	Apapane	60	40
110	30 c.	Feather image of a god	60	40
111	35 c.	Moorhen	70	45
112	35 c.	Feather cape, helmet and staff	70	45
113	75 c.	Hawaii O-o	1·25	80
114	75 c.	Feather image and cloak	1·25	80
		Set of 8	5·50	3·50
		First Day Cover		3·75
MS115	Two sheets each 78 × 119 mm containing (a) Nos. 107, 109, 111, 113; (b) Nos. 108, 110, 112, 114		6·50	6·50
		First Day Cover		7·00

Nos. 107/8, 109/10, 111/12 and 113/14 were each printed together, *se-tenant*, in horizontal and vertical pairs throughout the sheet.

23 "The Road to   **24** Royal Coat of Arms
Calvary"

1978 (10 Mar). *Easter and 400th Birth Anniv of Rubens. T* **23** *and similar vert designs. Multicoloured. P 13.*

116	10 c. Type **23**	10	10
117	15 c. "Christ on the Cross"	15	15
118	35 c. "Christ with Straw"	25	25
	Set of 3	45	45
	First Day Cover		75
MS119	87 × 138 mm. Nos. 116/18	75	1·2F
	First Day Cover		1·50

Stamps from No. **MS**119 are slightly larger (28 × 36 mm).

1978 (17 Apr). *Easter. Children's Charity. Designs as Nos. 116/18 in separate miniature sheets, 49 × 68 mm, each with a face value of 60 c.+5 c. P 12½–13.*

MS120	As Nos. 116/18. Set of 3 sheets	1·50	2·25
	First Day Cover		2·75

1978 (24 May). *25th Anniv of Coronation. T* **24** *and similar vert designs. P 13.*

121	90 c. black, gold and deep lilac	55	75
122	90 c. multicoloured	55	75
123	90 c. black, gold and deep bluish green	55	75
	Set of 3	1·50	2·00
	First Day Cover		2·50
MS124	75 × 122 mm. Nos. 121/3	1·50	2·25
	First Day Cover		2·75

Designs:—No. 122, Queen Elizabeth II; No. 123, New Zealand coat of arms.

Nos. 121/3 were printed together in small sheets of 6, containing two *se-tenant* strips of 3, with horizontal gutter margin between.

25 "Madonna of the   **26** Sir Rowland Hill and G.B.
Pear"   Penny Black Stamp

1978 (29 Nov). *Christmas. 450th Death Anniv of Dürer. T* **25** *and similar vert design. Multicoloured. P 14.*

125	30 c. Type **25**	35	25
126	35 c. "The Virgin and Child with St. Anne"	35	25
	Set of 2	70	50
	First Day Cover		75
MS127	101 × 60 mm. Nos. 125/6. P 13½	70	1·25
	First Day Cover		1·50

Nos. 125/6 were each printed in small sheets of 6.

1979 (26 Sept). *Death Centenary of Sir Rowland Hill. T* **26** *and similar vert designs. Multicoloured. P 13½ × 14.*

128	75 c. Type **26**	75	65
129	75 c. 1974 Centenary of Universal Postal Union 25 c. and 50 c. commemoratives	75	65
130	90 c. Sir Rowland Hill	90	80

131	90 c. 1978 25th anniv of Coronation 90 c. (Queen Elizabeth II) commemorative	90	80
	Set of 4	3·00	2·75
	First Day Cover		3·25
MS132	116 × 58 mm. Nos. 128/31	3·00	3·50
	First Day Cover		3·75

Stamps from No. **MS**132 have cream backgrounds.

Nos. 128/9 and 130/1 were each printed together, *se-tenant*, in horizontal and vertical pairs throughout small sheets of 8.

27 Max and Moritz   **28** "Christ carrying Cross"
(Book of Ferdinand II)

1979 (20 Nov). *International Year of the Child. Illustrations from Max and Moritz stories by Wilhelm Busch. T* **27** *and similar horiz designs. Multicoloured. P 13.*

133	12 c. Type **27**	20	10
134	12 c. Max and Moritz looking down chimney ...	20	10
135	12 c. Max and Moritz making off with food	20	10
136	12 c. Cook about to beat dog	20	10
137	15 c. Max sawing through bridge	25	10
138	15 c. Pursuer approaching bridge	25	10
139	15 c. Bridge collapsing under pursuer	25	10
140	15 c. Pursuer in river	25	10
141	20 c. Baker locking shop	30	20
142	20 c. Max and Moritz coming out of hiding	30	20
143	20 c. Max and Moritz falling in dough	30	20
144	20 c. Max and Moritz after being rolled into buns by baker	30	20
	Set of 12	2·75	1·50
	First Day Cover		1·75

Nos. 133/6, 137/40 and 141/4 were each printed together, *se-tenant*, in sheets of 4, either with or without labels containing extracts from the books on the top and bottom selvedge.

1980 (28 Mar). *Easter. Scenes from 15th-century Prayer Books. T* **28** *and similar vert designs. Multicoloured. P 13.*

145	12 c. Type **28**	10	10
146	20 c. "The Crucifixion" (William Vrelant, Book of Duke of Burgundy)	15	15
147	35 c. "Descent from the Cross" (Book of Ferdinand II)	25	25
	Set of 3	45	45
	First Day Cover		60
MS148	111 × 65 mm. Nos. 145/7	45	70
	First Day Cover		90

Stamps from No. **MS**148 have cream borders.

1980 (28 Mar). *Easter. Children's Charity. Designs as Nos. 145/7 in separate miniature sheets 54 × 85 mm, each with a face value of 70 c. + 5 c.*

MS149	As Nos. 145/7. Set of 3 sheets	1·00	1·75
	First Day Cover		2·75

MINIMUM PRICE

The minimum price quoted is 5p which represents a handling charge rather than a basis for valuing common stamps. For further notes about prices see introductory pages.

29 Queen Elizabeth the   **30** Falk Hoffman, D.D.R.
Queen Mother in 1937   (platform diving) (gold)

1980 (17 Sept). *80th Birthday of Queen Elizabeth the Queen Mother.*
P 13.

150	**29**	$1 multicoloured.	2·50	1·50
		First Day Cover		1·75
MS151	55 × 84 mm. **29** $2.50, multicoloured	3·00	2·75
		First Day Cover		3·00

1980 (14 Nov). *Olympic Games, Moscow. Medal Winners. T* **30** *and similar vert designs. Multicoloured. P* 13½.

152	10 c.	Type **30**	10	10
153	10 c.	Martina Jaschke, D.D.R. (platform diving) (gold)	10	10
154	20 c.	Tomi Polkolainen, Finland (archery) (gold)	15	15
155	20 c.	Kete Losaberidse, U.S.S.R. (archery) (gold)	15	15
156	30 c.	Czechoslovakia (football) (gold)	20	20
157	30 c.	D.D.R. (football) (silver)	20	20
158	50 c.	Barbel Wockel, D.D.R. (200-metre dash) (gold)	30	30
159	50 c.	Pietro Mennea, Italy (200-metre dash) (gold)	30	30
		Set of 8	1·40	1·40
		First Day Cover		1·75
MS160	150 × 106 mm. Nos. 152/9. P 13	1·40	1·75
		First Day Cover		2·00

Stamps from No. **MS**160 have gold borders.
Nos. 152/3, 154/5, 156/7 and 158/9 were each printed together, *se-tenant*, in horizontal pairs throughout the sheet.

31 "The Virgin of Counsellors"   **32** Amatasi
(Luis Dalmau)

1980 (5 Dec). *Christmas. Paintings. T* **31** *and similar vert designs.*
Multicoloured. P 13.

161	20 c.	Type **31**	15	15
162	35 c.	"Virgin and Child" (Serra brothers)	20	20
163	50 c.	"The Virgin of Albocacer" (Master of the Porciuncula)	30	30
		Set of 3	60	60
		First Day Cover		80
MS164	135 × 75 mm. Nos. 161/3	90	1·25
		First Day Cover		1·50

1980 (5 Dec). *Christmas. Children's Charity. Designs as Nos.* 161/3 *in separate miniature sheets,* 54 × 77 *mm., each with a face value of* 70 c. + 5 c.

MS165	As Nos. 161/3. *Set of* 3 *sheets*	2·50	2·75
	First Day Cover		3·25

1981 (16 Feb–21 Sept). *Sailing Craft and Ships* (*1st series*). *Multicoloured designs as T* **32**. *P* 14 (*Nos.* 166/85), 13 × 14½ (*Nos.* 186/205) *or* 13½ (*Nos.* 206/8).

166	1 c.	Type **32**	10	10
167	1 c.	Ndrua	10	10
168	1 c.	Waka	10	10
169	1 c.	Tongiaki	10	10
170	3 c.	Va'a Teu'ua	20	10
171	3 c.	Victoria, 1500	20	10
172	3 c.	Golden Hind, 1560	20	10
173	3 c.	Boudeuse, 1760	20	10
174	4 c.	H.M.S. Bounty, 1787	20	10
175	4 c.	L'Astrolabe, 1811	20	10
176	4 c.	Star of India, 1861	20	10
177	4 c.	Great Republic, 1853	20	10
178	6 c.	Balcutha, 1886	25	10
179	6 c.	Coonatto, 1863	25	10
180	6 c.	Antiope, 1866	25	10
181	6 c.	Teaping, 1863	25	10
182	10 c.	Preussen, 1902	25	10
183	10 c.	Pamir, 1921	25	10
184	10 c.	Cap Hornier, 1910	25	10
185	10 c.	Patriarch, 1869	25	10
186	15 c.	As Type **32** (16 Mar)	30	30
187	15 c.	As No. 167 (16 Mar)	30	30
188	15 c.	As No. 168 (16 Mar)	30	30
189	15 c.	As No. 169 (16 Mar)	30	30
190	15 c.	As No. 170 (16 Mar)	30	30
191	20 c.	As No. 171 (16 Mar)	30	30
192	20 c.	As No. 172 (16 Mar)	30	30
193	20 c.	As No. 173 (16 Mar)	30	30
194	30 c.	As No. 174 (16 Mar)	45	45
195	30 c.	As No. 175 (16 Mar)	45	45
196	30 c.	As No. 176 (16 Mar)	45	45
197	30 c.	As No. 177 (16 Mar)	45	45
198	50 c.	As No. 178 (16 Mar)	75	75
199	50 c.	As No. 179 (16 Mar)	75	75
200	50 c.	As No. 180 (16 Mar)	75	75
201	50 c.	As No. 181 (16 Mar)	75	75
202	$1	As No. 182 (15 May)	1·25	95
203	$1	As No. 183 (15 May)	1·25	95
204	$1	As No. 184 (15 May)	1·25	95
205	$1	As No. 185 (15 May)	1·25	95
206	$2	Cutty Sark, 1869 (26 June)	3·00	2·25
207	$4	Mermerus, 1872 (26 June)	5·00	4·00
208	$6	H.M.S Resolution and Discovery, 1776–80 (21 Sept)	6·50	5·50
		Set of 43	27·00	23·00
		First Day Covers (5)		28·00

Nos. 186/205 are 41 × 25 mm and Nos. 206/8 47 × 33 mm in size.
On Nos. 166/205 the four designs of each value were printed together, *se-tenant*, in blocks of 4 throughout the sheet.
For redrawn versions of these designs in other face values see Nos. 337/55.

33 "Jesus at the Grove"   **34** Prince Charles as
(Veronese)   Young Child

1981 (5 Apr). *Easter. Paintings. T* **33** *and similar vert designs. Multicoloured. P* 14.

218	30 c.	Type **33**	25	20
219	40 c.	"Christ with Crown of Thorns" (Titian) . . .	30	25
220	50 c.	"Pietà" (Van Dyck)	40	30
		Set of 3	85	65
		First Day Cover		1·00
MS221	110 × 68 mm. Nos. 218/20. P 13½	1·00	1·50
		First Day Cover		1·75

1981 (5 Apr). *Easter. Children's Charity. Designs as Nos.* 218/20 *in separate miniature sheets* 70 × 86 *mm., each with a face value of* 70 c. + 5 c. *P* 13½.

MS222	As Nos. 218/20. *Set of* 3 *sheets*	2·00	2·50
	First Day Cover		3·00

1981 (10 July). *Royal Wedding. T **34** and similar vert designs. Multicoloured. P* 14.

223	40 c.	Type **34**	45	45
224	50 c.	Prince Charles as schoolboy	55	55
225	60 c.	Prince Charles as young man	60	60
226	70 c.	Prince Charles in ceremonial Naval uniform	65	65
227	80 c.	Prince Charles as Colonel-in-Chief, Royal Regiment of Wales	70	70
		Set of 5	2·75	2·75
		Set of 5 optd "Specimen"	25·00	
		First Day Cover		3·00
MS228	99 × 89 mm. Nos. 223/7		2·75	3·25
		Optd "Specimen"	25·00	
		First Day Cover		3·50

Nos. 223/7 were each printed in small sheets of 6 including one *se-tenant* stamp-size label.

1981 (30 Nov). *International Year for Disabled Persons. Nos. 223/8 surch as T **51** of Aitutaki.*

229	40 c. + 5 c. Type **34**		60	75
230	50 c. + 5 c. Prince Charles as schoolboy		70	85
231	60 c. + 5 c. Prince Charles as young man		80	95
232	70 c. + 5 c. Prince Charles in ceremonial Naval uniform		85	1·10
233	80 c. + 5 c. Prince Charles as Colonel-in-Chief, Royal Regiment of Wales		90	1·40
	Set of 5		3·50	4·50
	First Day Cover			6·00
MS234	99 × 89 mm. As Nos. 229/33, but 10 c. premium on each stamp		4·50	5·00
	First Day Cover			6·50

Nos. 229/34 have commemorative inscriptions overprinted on the sheet margins.

35 Footballer 36 "The Virgin on a Crescent"

1981 (7 Dec). *World Cup Football Championship, Spain (1982). T **35** and similar vert designs showing footballers. Multicoloured. P* 13.

235	15 c.	Type **35**	15	15
236	15 c.	Footballer wearing orange jersey with black and mauve stripes	15	15
237	15 c.	Player in blue jersey	15	15
238	35 c.	Player in blue jersey	25	25
239	35 c.	Player in red jersey	25	25
240	35 c.	Player in yellow jersey with green stripes	25	25
241	50 c.	Player in orange jersey	35	35
242	50 c.	Player in mauve jersey	35	35
243	50 c.	Player in black jersey	35	35
		Set of 9	2·00	2·00
		First Day Cover		2·25
MS244	113 × 151 mm. As Nos. 235/43, but each stamp with a premium of 3 c.		2·75	2·75
		First Day Cover		3·25

The three designs of each value were printed together, *se-tenant*, in horizontal strips of 3 throughout the sheet.

1981 (15 Dec). *Christmas. Details from Engravings by Dürer. T **36** and similar vert designs in violet, deep reddish purple and stone. P* 13 × 13½.

245	30 c.	Type **36**	45	35
246	40 c.	"The Virgin at the Fence"	55	45
247	50 c.	"The Holy Virgin and Child"	65	55
		Set of 3	1·50	1·25
		First Day Cover		1·50
MS248	134 × 75 mm. As Nos. 245/7, but each stamp with a premium of 2 c.		1·50	1·50
		First Day Cover		1·75
MS249	Designs as Nos. 245/7 in separate miniature sheets, 58 × 85 mm, each with a face value of 70 c. + 5 c. P 14 × 13½. Set of 3 sheets		2·25	2·25
		First Day Cover		2·75

37 Lady Diana Spencer (38)
as Baby

1982 (1 July). *21st Birthday of Princess of Wales. T **37** and similar vert designs. Multicoloured. P* 14.

250	30 c.	Type **37**	30	30
251	50 c.	As young child	45	45
252	70 c.	As schoolgirl	60	60
253	80 c.	As teenager	80	80
254	$1.40, As young lady	1·25	1·25
		Set of 5	3·00	3·00
		First Day Cover		3·25
MS255	87 × 110 mm. Nos. 250/4		3·00	3·25
		First Day Cover		3·50

1982 (30 July). *Birth of Prince William of Wales. Nos. 223/8 optd with T **38**.*

256	40 c.	Type **34**	90	80
257	50 c.	Prince Charles as schoolboy	1·25	90
258	60 c.	Prince Charles as young man	1·40	1·00
259	70 c.	Prince Charles in ceremonial Naval uniform	1·60	1·25
260	80 c.	Prince Charles as Colonel-in-Chief, Royal Regiment of Wales	2·00	1·60
		Set of 5	6·50	5·00
		First Day Cover		5·50
MS261	99 × 89 mm. Nos. 256/60		8·50	7·00
		First Day Cover		8·00

1982 (6 Sept). *Birth of Prince William of Wales. As Nos. 250/5 but with changed inscriptions. Multicoloured. P* 13½ × 14.

262	30 c.	As Type **37** (inscr "21 JUNE 1982. BIRTH OF PRINCE WILLIAM OF WALES")	25	30
263	30 c.	As Type **37** (inscr "COMMEMORATING THE BIRTH OF PRINCE WILLIAM OF WALES")	25	30
264	50 c.	As No. 251 (inscr "21 JUNE 1982. BIRTH OF PRINCE WILLIAM OF WALES")	40	45
265	50 c.	As No. 251 (inscr "COMMEMORATING THE BIRTH OF PRINCE WILLIAM OF WALES")	40	45
266	70 c.	As No. 252 (inscr "21 JUNE 1982. BIRTH OF PRINCE WILLIAM OF WALES")	60	65
267	70 c.	As No. 252 (inscr "COMMEMORATING THE BIRTH OF PRINCE WILLIAM OF WALES")	60	65
268	80 c.	As No. 253 (inscr "21 JUNE 1982. BIRTH OF PRINCE WILLIAM OF WALES")	60	65
269	80 c.	As No. 253 (inscr "COMMEMORATING THE BIRTH OF PRINCE WILLIAM OF WALES")	60	65
270	$1.40, As No. 254 (inscr "21 JUNE 1982. BIRTH OF PRINCE WILLIAM OF WALES")	1·10	1·25
271	$1.40, As No. 254 (inscr "COMMEMORATING THE BIRTH OF PRINCE WILLIAM OF WALES")	1·10	1·25
		Set of 10	5·50	6·00
		First Day Cover		6·50
MS272	88 × 109 mm. As MS255 (stamps inscr "21 JUNE 1982. ROYAL BIRTH PRINCE WILLIAM OF WALES")		2·75	2·75
		First Day Cover		3·00

Nos. 262/3, 264/5, 266/7, 268/9 and 270/1 were each printed together, *se-tenant*; there being three examples of the "21 JUNE 1982 . . ." and two of "COMMEMORATING . . ." in each sheet of 5 stamps and 1 label.

THE WORLD CENTRE FOR FINE STAMPS IS 399 STRAND

39 "Virgin and Child" (detail, Joos Van Cleve)	40 Red Coral	43 School of Sperm Whales	44 *Mercury* (cableship)

1982 (10 Dec). *Christmas. Details from Renaissance Paintings of "Virgin and Child". T* **39** *and similar vert designs. Multicoloured. P* 14 × 13½.

273	35 c.	Type **39**	30	30
274	48 c.	"Virgin and Child" (Filippino Lippi)	45	45
275	60 c.	"Virgin and Child" (Cima da Conegliano)	60	60
		Set of 3	1·25	1·25
		First Day Cover		1·50
MS276		134 × 73 mm. As Nos. 273/5 but each with 2 c. charity premium. P 13	1·60	2·00
		First Day Cover		2·50

Nos. 273/5 were each printed in small sheets of 6 including one *se-tenant*, stamp size, label, depicting the Prince and Princess of Wales with Prince William.

1982 (10 Dec). *Christmas. Children's Charity. Designs as Nos. 273/5, but without frames, in separate miniature sheets,* 60 × 85 *mm, each with a face value of* 70 *c.* + 5 *c. P* 13.

MS277		As Nos. 273/5. Set of 3 sheets	1·75	1·90
		First Day Cover		2·50

1983 (14 Mar). *Commonwealth Day. T* **40** *and similar vert designs. Multicoloured. P* 13.

278	60 c.	Type **40**	55	60
279	60 c.	Aerial view of Penrhyn atoll	55	60
280	60 c.	Eleanor Roosevelt on Penrhyn during Second World War	55	60
281	60 c.	Map of South Pacific	55	60
		Set of 4	2·00	2·10
		First Day Cover		2·40

Nos. 278/81 were issued together, *se-tenant*, in blocks of four throughout the sheet.

41 Scout Emblem and Blue Tropical Flower	(42)

1983 (5 Apr). *75th Anniv of Boy Scout Movement. T* **41** *and similar horiz designs. Multicoloured. P* 13 × 14.

282	36 c.	Type **41**	55	45
283	48 c.	Emblem and pink flower	70	55
284	60 c.	Emblem and orange flower	85	75
		Set of 3	1·90	1·60
		First Day Cover		2·00
MS285		86 × 46 mm. $2. As 48 c., but with elements of design reversed	2·40	2·75
		First Day Cover		3·50

1983 (8 July). *15th World Scout Jamboree, Alberta, Canada. Nos.* 282/5 *optd with T* **42**.

286	36 c.	Type **41**	55	45
287	48 c.	Emblem and pink flower	70	55
288	60 c.	Emblem and orange flower	85	75
		Set of 3	1·90	1·60
		First Day Cover		2·00
MS289		86 × 46 mm. $2 As 48 c., but with elements of design reversed	2·40	2·75
		First Day Cover		3·50

1983 (29 July). *Whale Conservation. T* **43** *and similar vert designs. Multicoloured. P* 13.

290	8 c.	Type **43**	25	15
291	15 c.	Harpooner preparing to strike	45	25
292	35 c.	Whale attacking boat	80	55
293	60 c.	Dead whales marked with flags	1·40	85
294	$1	Dead Blue Whales on slipway	1·75	1·75
		Set of 5	4·25	2·75
		First Day Cover		3·25

1983 (23 Sept). *World Communications Year. T* **44** *and similar horiz designs. Multicoloured. P* 13.

295	36 c.	Type **44**	40	35
296	48 c.	Men watching cable being laid	50	45
297	60 c.	*Mercury* (different)	70	60
		Set of 3	1·40	1·25
		First Day Cover		1·75
MS298		115 × 90 mm. As Nos. 295/7 but each with charity premium of 3 c.	1·50	1·60
		First Day Cover		2·00

On No. **MS**298 the values are printed in black and have been transposed with the World Communications Year logo.

1983 (26 Sept). *Various stamps surch as T* **200** *of Cook Islands.*

(a) Nos. 182/5, 190/7 and 206

299	18 c.	on 10 c. *Preussen*, 1902	15	20
300	18 c.	on 10 c. *Pamir*, 1921	15	20
301	18 c.	on 10 c. *Cap Hornier*, 1910	15	20
302	18 c.	on 10 c. *Patriarch*, 1869	15	20
303	36 c.	on 20 c. Va'a Teu'ua	30	35
304	36 c.	on 20 c. *Victoria*, 1500	30	35
305	36 c.	on 20 c. *Golden Hind*, 1560	30	35
306	36 c.	on 20 c. *Boudeuse*, 1760	30	35
307	36 c.	on 30 c. H.M.S. *Bounty*, 1787	30	35
308	36 c.	on 30 c. *L'Astrolabe*, 1811	30	35
309	36 c.	on 30 c. *Star of India*, 1861	30	35
310	36 c.	on 30 c. *Great Republic*, 1853	30	35
311	$1.20	on $2 *Cutty Sark*, 1869	1·25	1·40

(b) Nos. 252/3

312	72 c.	on 70 c. Princess Diana as schoolgirl	2·00	1·50
313	96 c.	on 80 c. Princess Diana as teenager	2·25	1·75
		Set of 15	8·00	7·00
		First Day Cover		11·00

1983 (28 Oct). *Nos. 208, 225/6, 254 and 268/9 surch as T* **200** *of Cook Islands.*

314	48 c.	on 60 c. Prince Charles as young man (Gold)	2·50	1·50
	a.	Error. Surch on No. 258	4·50	4·50
315	72 c.	on 70 c. Prince Charles in ceremonial Naval uniform	3·00	1·75
	a.	Error. Surch on No. 259	4·50	4·50
316	96 c.	on 80 c. As No. 253 (inscr "21 JUNE 1982 . . .")	2·00	1·00
	a.	Error. Surch on No. 260	5·00	5·00
317	96 c.	on 80 c. As No. 253 (inscr "COMMEMO-RATING . . .")	1·25	1·00
318	$1.20	on $1.40, Princess Diana as young lady	2·50	1·50
319	$5.60	on $6 H.M.S. *Resolution* and *Discovery*, 1776–80	5·50	4·50
		Set of 6	15·00	10·00

45 George Cayley's Airship Design, 1837

1983 (31 Oct). *Bicentenary of Manned Flight. T* **45** *and similar horiz designs. Multicoloured. P* 13. A. *Inscr* "NORTHERN COOK ISLANS". B. *Corrected spelling optd in black on silver over original inscription.*

		A		B	
320	36 c. Type **45**	75	60	30	35
321	48 c. Dupuy De Lome's man-powered airship, 1872	1·00	70	40	45
322	60 c. Santos Dumont's sixth airship, 1901	1·25	1·00	45	50
323	96 c. Lebaudy's practical airship, 1902	2·00	1·50	75	80
324	$1.32, LZ 127 Graf Zeppelin, 1929	3·00	2·00	1·00	1·10
	Set of 5	7·25	5·50	2·75	3·00
	First Day Cover		6·50		3·50
MS325	113 × 138 mm. Nos. 320/4	8·00	9·00	2·75	3·50
	First Day Cover		10·00		4·00

46 "Madonna in the Meadow"

47 Waka

1983 (30 Nov). *Christmas. 500th Birth Anniv of Raphael. T* **46** *and similar vert designs. Multicoloured. P* 13.

326	36 c. Type **46**	35	40
327	42 c. "Tempi Madonna"	35	40
328	48 c. "The Smaller Cowper Madonna"	45	50
329	60 c. "Madonna della Tenda"	55	60
	Set of 4	1·60	1·75
	First Day Cover		2·25
MS330	87 × 115 mm. As Nos. 326/9 but each with a charity premium of 3 c.	1·75	2·00
	First Day Cover		2·50

1983 (1 Dec). *Nos. 227, 266/7 and 270/1 surch as T* **200** *of Cook Islands.*

331	72 c. on 70 c. As No. 252 (inscr "21 JUNE 1982...")	2·00	1·25
332	72 c. on 70 c. As No. 252 (inscr "COMMEMORATING...")	1·25	90
333	96 c. on 80 c. Prince Charles as Colonel-in-Chief, Royal Regiment of Wales	2·00	1·00
334	$1.20 on $1.40, As No. 254 (inscr "21 JUNE 1982...")	2·25	1·25
335	$1.20 on $1.40, As No. 254 (inscr "COMMEMORATING...")	1·75	1·00
	Set of 5	8·50	5·00
	First Day Cover		6·50

1983 (28 Dec). *Christmas. 500th Birth Anniv of Raphael. Children's Charity. Designs as Nos.* 326/9 *in separate miniature sheets,* 65 × 84 *mm, each with a face value of* 75 *c.* + 5 *c. P* 13.

MS336	As Nos. 326/9. Set of 4 sheets	3·00	3·50
	First Day Cover		4·25

1984 (8 Feb–15 June). *Sailing Craft and Ships* (2nd series). *Designs as Nos.* 166, *etc. but with redrawn frames, inscriptions and compass rose at top right as in T* **47**. *Multicoloured. P* 13 × 13½ ($9.60), 13 ($3, $5) *or* 11 (*others*).

337	2 c. Type **47**	5	5
338	4 c. Amatasi	5	5
339	5 c. Ndrua	5	5
340	8 c. Tongiaki	5	5
341	10 c. Victoria	5	5
342	18 c. Golden Hind	15	15
343	20 c. Boudeuse	15	15
344	30 c. H.M.S. Bounty	20	25
345	36 c. L'Astrolabe	25	30
346	48 c. Great Republic	30	35
347	50 c. Star of India (21 Mar)	30	35
348	60 c. Coonatta (21 Mar)	40	45
349	72 c. Antiope (21 Mar)	50	55
350	80 c. Balcutha (21 Mar)	55	60
351	96 c. Cap Hornier (21 Mar)	65	70
352	$1.20, Pamir (21 Mar)	80	85
353	$3 Mermerus (41 × 31 mm) (4 May)	2·00	2·25
354	$5 Cutty Sark (41 × 31 mm) (4 May)	3·25	3·50
355	$9.60, H.M.S. Resolution and Discovery (41 × 31 mm) (15 June)	6·50	6·75
	Set of 19	14·00	15·00
	First Day Covers (4)		22·00

48 Olympic Flag

1984 (20 July). *Olympic Games, Los Angeles. T* **48** *and similar horiz designs. Multicoloured. P* 13½ × 13.

356	35 c. Type **48**	30	35
357	60 c. Olympic torch and flags	50	55
358	$1.80, Ancient athletes and Coliseum	1·50	1·60
	Set of 3	2·10	2·25
	First Day Cover		2·50
MS359	103 × 86 mm. As Nos. 356/8 but each with a charity premium of 5 c.	2·40	2·50
	First Day Cover		3·00

$2

Birth of
Prince Henry
15 Sept. 1984

(50)

49 Penrhyn Stamps of 1978, 1979 and 1981

1984 (20 Sept). *"Ausipex" International Stamp Exhibition, Melbourne. T* **49** *and similar horiz design. Multicoloured. P* 13½ × 13.

360	60 c. Type **49**	50	55
361	$1.20, Location map of Penrhyn	1·00	1·10
	Set of 2	1·50	1·60
	First Day Cover		1·75
MS362	90 × 90 mm. As Nos. 360/1, but each with a face value of 96 c.	1·75	2·00
	First Day Cover		2·50

1984 (18 Oct). *Birth of Prince Henry. Nos.* 223/4 *and* 250/1 *surch as T* **50**.

363	$2 on 30 c. Type **37**	2·25	1·50
364	$2 on 40 c. Type **34**	2·75	1·50
365	$2 on 50 c. Prince Charles as schoolboy	2·75	1·75
366	$2 on 50 c. Lady Diana as young child (Gold)	2·25	1·50
	Set of 4	9·00	6·00
	First Day Cover		7·50

51 "Virgin and Child"   **52** Harlequin Ducks
(Giovanni Bellini)

1984 (15 Nov).   *Christmas. Paintings of the Virgin and Child by different artists. T* **51** *and similar vert designs. Multicoloured.* P 13 × 13½.

367	36 c. Type **51**	. . . .	30	35
368	48 c. Lorenzo di Credi	. . . .	40	45
369	60 c. Palma the Older	. . . .	45	50
370	96 c. Raphael	. . . .	75	80
	Set of 4	. . . .	1·75	1·90
	First Day Cover	. . . .		2·50
MS371	93 × 118 mm. As Nos. 367/70, but each with a			
	charity premium of 5 c.	. . . .	2·00	2·50
	First Day Cover	. . . .		3·00

1984 (10 Dec).   *Christmas. Children's Charity. Designs as Nos. 367/70, but without frames, in separate miniature sheets 67 × 81 mm, each with a face value of 96 c. + 10 c.* P 13½.

MS372	As Nos. 367/70. Set of 4 sheets	. . . .	3·00	3·25
	First Day Cover	. . . .		3·75

1985 (9 Apr).   *Birth Bicentenary of John J. Audubon (ornithologist). T* **52** *and similar horiz designs showing original paintings. Multicoloured.* P 13.

373	20 c. Type **52**	. . . .	40	25
374	55 c. Sage Grouse	. . . .	80	60
375	65 c. Solitary Sandpiper	. . . .	95	65
376	75 c. Dunlin	. . . .	1·25	75
	Set of 4	. . . .	3·00	2·00
	First Day Cover	. . . .		2·50
MS377	Four sheets, each 70 × 53 mm. As Nos. 373/6,			
	but each with a face value of 95 c. Set of 4 sheets	. .	3·50	4·50
	First Day Cover	. . . .		5·50

53 Lady Elizabeth   **54** "The House in the Wood"
Bowes-Lyon, 1921

1985 (24 June).   *Life and Times of Queen Elizabeth the Queen Mother. T* **53** *and similar vert designs, each deep bluish violet, silver and yellow.* P 13.

378	75 c. Type **53**	. . . .	60	65
379	95 c. With baby Princess Elizabeth, 1926	. . . . . .	75	80
380	$1.20, Coronation Day, 1937	. . . .	95	1·00
381	$2.80, On her 70th birthday	. . . .	2·10	2·25
	Set of 4	. . . .	4·00	4·50
	First Day Cover	. . . .		4·50
MS382	66 × 90 mm. $5 The Queen Mother	. . . .	3·75	4·00
	First Day Cover	. . . .		4·50

Nos. 378/81 were each printed in small sheets of 4 stamps.
For these stamps in a miniature sheet see No. **MS**403.

1985 (10 Sept).   *International Youth Year and Birth Centenary of Jacob Grimm (folklorist). T* **54** *and similar vert designs. Multicoloured.* P 13 × 13½.

383	75 c. Type **54**	. . . .	60	55
384	95 c. "Snow-White and Rose-Red"	. . . .	75	70
385	$1.15, "The Goose Girl"	. . . .	95	85
	Set of 3	. . . .	2·10	1·90
	First Day Cover	. . . .		2·40

55 "The Annunciation"

1985 (25 Nov).   *Christmas. Paintings by Murillo. T* **55** *and similar horiz designs. Multicoloured.* P 14.

386	75 c. Type **55**	. . . .	60	65
387	$1.15, "Adoration of the Shepherds"	. . . .	85	90
388	$1.80, "The Holy Family"	. . . .	1·40	1·50
	Set of 3	. . . .	2·50	2·75
	First Day Cover	. . . .		3·25
MS389	66 × 131 mm. As Nos. 386/8, but each with a			
	face value of 95 c. P 13½	. . . .	2·25	2·50
	First Day Cover	. . . .		3·00
MS390	Three sheets, each 66 × 72 mm. As Nos. 386/8			
	but with face values of $1.20, $1.45 and $2.75. P 13½			
	Set of 3 sheets	. . . .	4·00	4·25
	First Day Cover	. . . .		4·75

56 Halley's Comet

1986 (4 Feb).   *Appearance of Halley's Comet. T* **56** *and similar horiz design showing details of the painting "Fire and Ice" by Camille Rendal. Multicoloured.* P 13½ × 13.

391	$1.50, Type **56**	. . . .	1·10	1·25
392	$1.50, Stylised *Giotto* spacecraft	. . . .	1·10	1·25
	Set of 2	. . . .	2·25	2·50
	First Day Cover	. . . .		3·00
MS393	108 × 43 mm. $3 As Nos. 391/2 (104 × 39 mm).			
	Imperf	. . . .	2·25	2·50
	First Day Cover	. . . .		3·00

Nos. 391/2 were printed together, *se-tenant*, in horizontal pairs throughout the sheets, forming a composite design of the complete painting.

57 Princess Elizabeth aged Three,   **58** Statue of Liberty
1929, and Bouquet   under Construction, Paris

1986 (21 Apr). *60th Birthday of Queen Elizabeth II. T* **57** *and similar horiz designs. Multicoloured. P* 13½ × 13 ($2.50) *or* 14 (*others*).

394	95 c. Type **57**	80	80
395	$1.45, Profile of Queen Elizabeth and St. Edward's Crown	1·25	1·25
396	$2.50, Queen Elizabeth aged three and in profile with Imperial State Crown (56 × 30 mm)	2·00	2·00
	Set of 3	3·50	3·50
	First Day Cover		4·00

1986 (27 June). *Centenary of Statue of Liberty* (1st *issue*). *T* **58** *and similar vert designs, each black, gold and yellow-green. P* 13 × 13½.

397	95 c. Type **58**	65	70
398	$1.75, Erection of Statue, New York	1·10	1·25
399	$3 Artist's impression of Statue, 1876	2·10	2·25
	Set of 3	3·50	3·75
	First Day Cover		4·25

See also No. **MS412**.

$2.00

(60)

59 Prince Andrew and Miss Sarah Ferguson

1986 (23 July). *Royal Wedding. T* **59** *and similar vert design. Multi-coloured. P* 13.

400	$2.50, Type **59**	1·75	1·90
401	$3.50, Profiles of Prince Andrew and Miss Sarah Ferguson	2·40	2·50
	Set of 2	4·25	4·50
	First Day Cover		5·00

Nos. 400/1 were each printed in sheetlets of 4 stamps and 2 stamp-size labels.

1986 (4 Aug). *"Stampex '86" Stamp Exhibition, Adelaide. No.* **MS362** *surch with T* **60** *in black on gold.*

MS402	$2 on 96 c. × 2	3·25	3·75
	First Day Cover		4·25

The "Stampex '86" exhibition emblem is overprinted on the sheet margin.

1986 (4 Aug). *86th Birthday of Queen Elizabeth the Queen Mother. Nos.* 378/81 *in miniature sheet*, 90 × 120 *mm. P* 13 × 13½.

MS403	Nos. 378/81	4·50	5·00
	First Day Cover		5·50

1986 (20 Nov). *Christmas. Engravings by Rembrandt. T* **61** *and similar vert designs, each red-brown, yellow-ochre and gold. P* 13.

404	65 c. Type **61**	45	50
405	$1.75 "Virgin and Child"	1·25	1·40
406	$2.50 "The Holy Family"	1·75	2·00
	Set of 3	3·00	3·50
	First Day Cover		4·00
MS407	120 × 87 mm. As Nos. 404/6, but each size 31 × 39 mm with a face value of $1.50. P 13½ × 13	3·00	3·25
	First Day Cover		4·00

1986 (24 Nov). *Visit of Pope John Paul II to South Pacific. Nos.* 404/7 *surch as T* **62** *in greenish blue.*

408	65 c. + 10 c. Type **61**	75	75
409	$1.75 + 10 c. "Virgin and Child"	1·75	1·75
410	$2.50 + 10 c. "The Holy Family"	2·25	2·25
	Set of 3	4·25	4·25
	First Day Cover		5·00
MS411	120 × 87 mm. As Nos. 408/10, but each size 31 × 39 mm with a face value of $1.50 + 10 c.	4·25	4·50
	First Day Cover		5·50

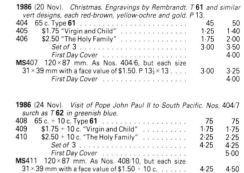

63 Head and Torch of Statue of Liberty

Fortieth Royal Wedding Anniversary 1947-87

(64)

1987 (15 Apr). *Centenary of Statue of Liberty* (1986) (2nd *issue*). *Two sheets, each* 122 × 122 *mm, containing T* **63** *and similar multicoloured designs. Litho. P* 14 × 13½ (*vert*) *or* 13½ × 14 (*horiz*).

MS412 Two sheets (a) 65 c. Type **63**; 65 c. Torch at sunset; 65 c. Restoration workers with flag; 65 c. Statue and Manhattan skyline; 65 c. Workers and scaffolding. (b) 65 c. Workers on Statue crown (*horiz*); 65 c. Aerial view of Ellis Island (*horiz*); 65 c. Ellis Island Immigration Centre (*horiz*); 65 c. View from Statue to Ellis Island and Manhattan (*horiz*); 65 c. Restoration workers (*horiz*). *Set of 2 sheets* .... 6·00 / 6·50

First Day Covers (2) .... 7·00

1987 (20 Nov). *Royal Ruby Wedding. Nos.* 68/9 *optd with T* **64** *in magenta.*

413	$2 Birds-eye view of Penrhyn	1·40	1·50
414	$5 Satellite view of Australasia	3·50	3·75
	Set of 2	4·75	5·25
	First Day Cover		5·75

61 "The Adoration of the Shepherds"   (62)   65 "The Garvagh Madonna"   66 Athletics

1987 (11 Dec).   *Christmas. Religious Paintings by Raphael. T* **65** *and similar vert designs. Multicoloured. P* 13½.

415	95 c. Type **65**	65	70
416	$1.60, "The Alba Madonna"	1·10	1·25
417	$2.25, "The Madonna of the Fish"	1·60	1·75
	Set of 3	3·00	3·25
	First Day Cover		3·75
MS418	91 × 126 mm. As Nos. 415/17, but each with a face value of $1.15	2·75	3·25
MS419	70 × 86 mm. $4.80, As No. 417, but size 36 × 39 mm	4·25	4·75
	First Day Cover		9·50

1988 (29 July).   *Olympic Games, Seoul. T* **66** *and similar horiz designs. Multicoloured. P* 13½ × 13 *(horiz) or* 13 × 13½ *(vert).*

420	55 c. Type **66**	40	45
421	95 c. Pole vaulting (*vert*)	65	70
422	$1.25, Shotputting	90	95
423	$1.50, Lawn Tennis (*vert*)	1·10	1·25
	Set of 4	2·75	3·00
	First Day Cover		3·25
MS424	110 × 70 mm. As Nos. 421 and 423, but each with a face value of $2.50	3·50	3·75
	First Day Cover		4·25

1988 (14 Oct).   *Olympic Gold Medal Winners, Seoul. Nos.* 420/4 *optd as* T **235** *of Cook Islands.*

425	55 c. Type **66** (optd "CARL LEWIS UNITED STATES 100 METERS")	40	45
426	95 c. Pole vaulting (optd "LOUISE RITTER UNITED STATES HIGH JUMP")	65	70
427	$1.25, Shot putting (optd "ULF TIMMERMANN EAST GERMANY SHOT-PUT")	90	95
428	$1.50, Lawn Tennis (optd "STEFFI GRAF WEST GERMANY WOMEN'S TENNIS")	1·10	1·25
	Set of 4	2·75	3·00
	First Day Cover		3·25
MS429	110 × 70 mm. $2.50, As No. 421 (optd. "JACKIE JOYNER-KERSEE United States Heptathlon"); $2.50, As No. 423 (optd "STEFFI GRAF West Germany Women's Tennis MILOSLAV MECIR Czechoslovakia Men's Tennis")	3·50	3·75
	First Day Cover		4·25

67 "Virgin and Child"   68 Neil Armstrong
                               stepping onto Moon

1988 (9 Nov).   *Christmas. T* **67** *and similar designs showing different "Virgin and Child" paintings by Titian. P* 13 × 13½.

430	70 c. multicoloured	50	55
431	85 c. multicoloured	60	65
432	95 c. multicoloured	65	70
433	$1.25, multicoloured	90	95
	Set of 4	2·40	2·50
	First Day Cover		3·00
MS434	100 × 80 mm. $6.40, As Type **67**, but diamond-shaped (57 × 57 mm). P 13	4·50	4·75
	First Day Cover		5·25

(Des G. Vasarhelyi)

1989 (24 July).   *20th Anniv of First Manned Landing on Moon. T* **68** *and similar horiz designs. Multicoloured. P* 14.

435	55 c. Type **68**	40	45
436	75 c. Astronaut on Moon carrying equipment . . .	55	60
437	95 c. Conducting experiment on Moon	70	75
438	$1.25, Crew of "Apollo 11"	95	1·00
439	$1.75, Crew inside "Apollo 11"	1·40	1·50
	Set of 5	3·50	3·75
	First Day Cover		4·25

STAMP BOOKLET

PRICE given is for complete booklet.

1982 (June).   *Royal Wedding. Cover as No. B1 of Cook Islands, but inscr "Penrhyn".*
B1 $4.50, booklet containing Nos. 223/4 × 5 . . . .   10·00

OFFICIAL STAMPS

O.H.M.S.

(O 1)

1978 (14 Nov).   *Nos. 57/66, 89/91 and 101/2 optd or surch (Nos. O8/9 and O12) as Type O 1.*

O 1	1 c.	*Monodactylus argenteus*	15	5
O 2	2 c.	*Pomacanthus imperator*	15	5
O 3	3 c.	*Chelmon rostratus*	25	10
O 4	4 c.	*Chaetodon ornatissimus*	25	10
O 5	5 c.	*Chaetodon melanotus*	30	10
O 6	8 c.	*Chaetodon raffessi*	35	15
O 7	10 c.	*Chaetodon ephippium*	40	15
O 8	15 c.	on 60 c. *Plectorhynchus chaetodonoides* .	45	25
O 9	18 c.	on 60 c. *Plectorhynchus chaetodonoides* .	50	25
O10	20 c.	*Pygoplites diacanthus*	50	25
O11	25 c.	*Heniochus acuminatus* (Silver)	55	30
O12	30 c.	on 60 c. *Plectorhynchus chaetodonoides* .	55	35
O13	50 c.	⎫ "The Spirit of '76" (A. M. Willard)	70	55
O14	50 c.	⎬	70	55
O15	50 c.	⎭ (Gold)	70	55
O16	$1	Queen and Prince Philip (Silver)	2·25	1·40
O17	$2	Queen Elizabeth II (Gold)	4·50	2·75
		Set of 17	12·00	7·00

These stamps were originally only sold to the public cancelled-to-order and not in unused condition. They were made available to overseas collectors in mint condition during 1980.

65c

O.H.M.S.

O.ℋ.ℳ.S.

(O 2)

O.H.M.S.

(O 3)

1985 (15 Aug)–**87**.   (a) *Nos. 206/8, 337/47 and 349/55 optd or surch as Type O 2 by foil embossing in red ($2, $4, $6) or silver (others).*

O18	2 c.	Type **47**	5	5
O19	4 c.	Amatasi	5	5
O20	5 c.	Ndrua	5	5
O21	8 c.	Tongiaki	5	5
O22	10 c.	Victoria	5	5
O23	18 c.	Golden Hind	15	15
O24	20 c.	Boudeuse	15	15
O25	30 c.	H.M.S. *Bounty*	20	25
O26	40 c.	on 36 c. L'*Astrolabe*	25	30
O27	50 c.	*Star of India*	30	35
O28	55 c.	on 48 c. *Great Republic*	35	40
O29	75 c.	on 72 c. *Antiope* (29.4.86)	50	55
O30	75 c.	on 96 c. *Cap Hornier* (29.4.86)	50	55
O31	80 c.	*Balcutha* (29.4.86)	55	60
O32	$1.20,	*Pamir* (29.4.86)	80	85
O33	$2	*Cutty Sark* (29.4.86)	1·40	1·50
O34	$3	*Mermerus* (29.4.86)	2·00	2·25
O35	$4	*Mermerus* (29.4.86)	2·75	3·00
O36	$5	*Cutty Sark* (2.11.87)	3·25	3·50
O37	$6	H.M.S. *Resolution* and *Discovery* (2.11.87)	4·00	4·25
O38	$9.60,	H.M.S. *Resolution* and *Discovery* (2.11.87)	6·50	6·75

(b) *Nos. 278/81 surch as Type O 3 by silver foil embossing*

O39	65 c.	on 60 c. Type **40**	40	45
O40	65 c.	on 60 c. Aerial view of Penrhyn atoll	40	45
O41	65 c.	on 60 c. Eleanor Roosevelt on Penrhyn during Second World War	40	45
O42	65 c.	on 60 c. Map of South Pacific	40	45
		Set of 25	22·00	24·00

Niue

1902 12 Pence = 1 Shilling
       20 Shillings = 1 Pound
1967 100 Cents = 1 New Zealand Dollar

One of the Cook Is. Group, in the South Pacific. A former dependency of New Zealand, Niue became self-governing in 1974.

NEW ZEALAND DEPENDENCY

Stamps of New Zealand overprinted

NIUE
(1)

1902 (4 Jan). Handstamped with T **1**, in green or bluish green. Pirie paper. Wmk double-lined "N Z" and Star, W **38** of New Zealand. P 11.
1 **42** 1d. carmine £375 £375
A few overprints were made with a greenish violet ink. These occurred only in the first vertical row and part of the second row of the first sheet overprinted owing to violet ink having been applied to the pad (Price £1400 un).

NIUE.
½ PENI.
(2)

NIUE.
TAHA PENI.
3 1d.

NIUE.
2½ PENI.
(4)

1902 (4 Apr). Type-set surcharges. T **2**, **3**, and **4**.

(i) Pirie paper. No wmk. P 11
2 **27** 2½d. blue (R.) . . . . 1·25 2·75
   a. No stop after "PENI" . . . . 24·00 35·00
   b. Surch double . . . .

(ii) Basted Mills paper. Wmk double-lined "N Z" and Star, W **38** of New Zealand.

(a) Perf 14
3 **23** ½d. green (R.) . . . . 75 2·25
   a. Spaced "U" and "E" . . . . 4·00 7·50
   b. Surch inverted £275 £350
   c. Surch double . . . .
4 **42** 1d. carmine (B.) . . . . 5·00 7·50
   a. Spaced "U" and "E" . . . . 26·00 32·00
   b. No stop after "PENI" . . . . 60·00 65·00
   c. Varieties a. and b. on same stamp £100 £100

(b) P 11 and 14 compound
5 **42** 1d. carmine (B.) . . . . 75 1·40
   a. Spaced "U" and "E" . . . . 5·50 7·50
   b. No stop after "PENI" . . . . 13·00 17·00
   c. Varieties a. and b. on same stamp . . . . . . 55·00 60·00

(c) Mixed perfs
6 **23** ½d. green (R.) £250
7 **42** 1d. carmine (B.) £250

1902 (2 May). Type-set surcharges, T **2**, **3**. Cowan paper. Wmk single-lined "N Z" and Star, W **43** of New Zealand. (a) P 14.
8 **23** ½d. green (R.) 65 80
   a. Spaced "U" and "E" . . . . 4·25 5·00
9 **42** 1d. carmine (B.) 50 65
   a. Surch double £600
   b. Spaced "U" and "E" . . . . 14·00 16·00
   c. No stop after "PENI" . . . . 14·00 16·00
   d. Varieties b. and c. on same stamp . . . . . . 42·00 55·00

(b) Perf 11 and 14 compound
10 **23** ½d. green (R.) . . . .

(c) Mixed perfs
11 **23** ½d. green (R.) . . . .
12 **42** 1d. carmine (B.) £250
   a. Space "U" and "E" £150

NIUE.
(5)

Tolu e Pene.
6 3d.

Ono e Pene.
7 6d.

Taha e Sileni.
8 1s.

1903 (2 July). Optd with name at top, T **5**, and values at foot, T **6/8**, in blue. W **43** of New Zealand. P 11.
13 **28** 3d. yellow-brown . . . . 5·00 5·00
14 **31** 6d. rose-red . . . . 4·75 9·00
15 **34** 1s. brown-red ("Tahae" joined) £750
16   1s. bright red . . . . 20·00 24·00
   a. Orange-red . . . . 25·00 32·00
   Set of 3 . . . . 27·00 35·00

NIUE.
½ PENI.
(9)

NIUE.
(10)

1911 (30 Nov). ½d. surch with T **9**, others optd at top as T **5** and values at foot as T **7**, **8**. W **43** of New Zealand. P 14 × 14½.
17 **50** ½d. green (C.) 45 40
18 **51** 6d. carmine (B.) . . . . 2·00 7·00
19   1s. vermilion (B.) . . . . 6·50 28·00
   Set of 3 . . . . 8·00 32·00

1915 (Sept). Surch as T **4**. W **43** of New Zealand. P 14.
20 **27** 2½d. deep blue (C.) . . . . 8·00 15·00

1917 (Aug). 1d. surch as T **3**, 3d. optd as T **5** with value as T **6**. W **43** of New Zealand.
21 **52** 1d. carmine (p 14 × 15) (Br.) . . . . 5·00 5·50
   a. No stop after "PENI" £100
22 **60** 3d. chocolate (p 14 × 14½) (B.) . . . . 45·00 70·00
   a. No stop after "Pene" £450
   b. Perf 14 × 13½ . . . . 60·00 85·00
   c. Vert pair, Nos. 22/2b £180

1917–21. Optd with T **10**. W **43** of New Zealand. (a) P 14 × 15.

23	**61**	½d. green (R.) (2.20)	50	70
24	**52**	1d. carmine (B.) (10.17)	1·75	2·50
25	**61**	1½d. slate (R.) (11.17)	80	1·75
26		1½d. orange-brown (R.) (2.19)	70	2·00
27		3d. chocolate (B.) (6.19)	1·40	9·00

(b) P 14 × 14½

28	**60**	2½d. deep blue (R.) (10.20)	90	2·50
		a. Perf 14 × 13½	1·60	3·75
		b. Vert pair, Nos. 28/a	15·00	22·00
29		3d. chocolate (B.) (10.17)	1·25	1·50
		a. Perf 14 × 13½	1·60	2·50
		b. Vert pair, Nos. 29/a	25·00	32·00
30		6d. carmine (B.) (8.21)	4·25	13·00
		a. Perf 14 × 13½	4·75	13·00
		b. Vert pair, Nos. 30/a	30·00	45·00
31		1s. vermilion (B.) (10.18)	4·75	13·00
		a. Perf 14 × 13½	7·50	13·00
		b. Vert pair, Nos. 31/a	30·00	45·00
		Set of 9	14·50	40·00

1918–29. Postal Fiscal stamps as Type F **4** of New Zealand optd with T **10**. W **43** of New Zealand (sideways).

(i) Chalk-surfaced "De La Rue" paper. (a) P 14

32	5s. yellow-green (R.) (7.18)	65·00	80·00

(b) P 14½ × 14, comb

33	2s. deep blue (R.) (9.18)	15·00	32·00
34	2s. 6d. grey-brown (B.) (2.23)	17·00	32·00
35	5s. yellow-green (R.) (10.18)	20·00	45·00
36	10s. maroon (B.) (2.23)	70·00	90·00
37	£1 rose-carmine (B.) (2.23)	£130	£150
	Set of 5	£225	£300

(ii) Thick, opaque, white chalk-surfaced "Cowan" paper. P 14½ × 14

37a	5s. yellow-green (R.) (10.29)	20·00	45·00
37b	10s. brown-red (B.) (2.27)	70·00	90·00
37c	£1 rose-pink (B.) (2.28)	£130	£150
	Set of 3	£200	£250

(Des, eng and recess by P.B.)

1920 (23 Aug). As T **9** to **14** of Cook Islands but inscr "NIUE". No wmk. P 14.

38	½d. black and green	2·00	3·25
39	1d. black and dull carmine	1·75	1·25
40	1½d. black and red	2·25	3·25
41	3d. black and blue	60	3·75
42	6d. red-brown and green	80	7·00
43	1s. black and sepia	1·50	8·50
	Set of 6	8·00	24·00

1925–27. Pictorial stamps as 1920 and new values as T **16/17** of Cook Islands, but inscr "NIUE". W **43** of New Zealand. P 14.

44	½d. black and green (1927)	1·00	3·75
45	1d. black and deep carmine (1925)	65	75
46	2½d. black and blue (10.27)	1·00	4·75
47	4d. black and violet (10.27)	2·00	7·00
	Set of 4	4·25	14·50

1927–28. Admiral type of New Zealand optd as T **10**. W **43** of New Zealand. P 14.

(a) Jones paper

48	**72**	2s. deep blue (2.27) (R.)	15·00	42·00
	Wi. Wmk inverted		

(b) Cowan paper

49	**72**	2s. light blue (R.) (2.28)	14·00	30·00

1931 (Apr). No. 40 surch as T **18** of Cook Is.

50	2d. on 1½d. black and red	1·00	90

1931 (12 Nov). Postal Fiscal stamps as Type F **6** of New Zealand optd as T **10**. W **43** of New Zealand, Thick, opaque, chalk-surfaced "Cowan" paper. P 14.

51	2s. 6d.deep brown (B.)	5·50	11·00
52	5s. green (R.)	24·00	45·00
53	10s. carmine-lake (B.)	35·00	65·00
54	£1 pink (B.)	55·00	90·00
	Set of 4	£110	£190

See also Nos. 79/82 for different type of overprint.

(Des L. C. Mitchell. Recess P.B.)

1932 (16 Mar). As T **20** to **26** of Cook Is, but frames include "NIUE" as well as "COOK ISLANDS." No wmk. P 13.

55	½d. black and emerald	2·75	7·00
	a. Perf 14 × 13	70·00	
56	1d. black and deep lake	1·00	25
57	2d. black and red-brown	75	2·25
	a. Perf 13 and 14 mixed	80·00	£125
58	2½d. black and slate-blue	3·50	16·00
59	4d. black and greenish blue	6·00	16·00
	a. Perf 14	6·00	13·00
60	6d. black and orange-vermilion	2·00	2·25
61	1s. black and purple (p 14)	2·00	5·00
	Set of 7	16·00	40·00

(Recess from Perkins, Bacon's plates at Govt Ptg Office, Wellington, N.Z.)

1932–36. Pictorial types as 1932, but W **43** of New Zealand. P 14.

62	½d. black and emerald	50	75
63	1d. black and deep lake	50	30
	Wi. Wmk inverted	45·00	
64	2d. black and yellow-brown (1.4.36)	40	70
	Wi. Wmk inverted		
65	2½d. black and slate-blue	40	2·00
	Wi. Wmk inverted	45·00	
66	4d. black and greenish blue	70	1·25
	Wi. Wmk inverted		
67	6d. black and red-orange (1.4.36)	70	65
68	1s. black and purple (1.4.36)	4·00	11·00
	Set of 7	6·50	15·00

Imperforate proofs of No. 65 are known used on registered mail from Niue postmarked 30 August 1945 or 29 October 1945.

See also Nos. 89/97.

1935 (7 May). Silver Jubilee. Designs as Nos. 63, 65 and 67 (colours changed) optd as T **27** of Cook Is (wider vertical spacing on 6d.). W **43** of New Zealand. P 14.

69	1d. red-brown and lake	60	1·50
	a. Narrow "K" in "KING"	2·75	8·00
	b. Narrow "B" in JUBILEE	2·75	8·00
70	2½d. dull and deep blue (R.)	3·00	2·50
	a. Narrow first "E" in "GEORGE"	4·00	12·00
71	6d. green and orange	3·00	5·00
	a. Narrow "N" in "KING"	12·00	32·00
	Set of 3	6·00	8·00
	First Day Cover		16·00

For illustrations of varieties, see Cook Islands.

Examples of No. 70 imperforate horizontally are from proof sheets not issued through the Post and Telegraph Department (Price £400 for vert pair).

NIUE   NIUE.

   (13)   (14)

1937 (13 May). Coronation Issue. Nos. 599/601 of New Zealand optd with T **13**.

72	1d. carmine	40	15	15
73	2½d. Prussian blue	45	20	25
74	6d. red-orange	55	25	15
	Set of 3	1·25	55	50

1938 (2 May). As T **29** to **31** of Cook Is., but frames inscr. "NIUE COOK ISLANDS". W **43** of New Zealand. P 14.

75	1s. black and violet	3·25	1·50	4·00
76	2s. black and red-brown	6·50	2·50	9·00
77	3s. light blue and emerald-green	13·00	5·00	9·00
	Set of 3	21·00	8·00	18·00

1940 (2 Sept). As T **32** of Cook Islands, but additionally inscr "NIUE". W **98** of New Zealand. P 13½ × 14.

78	3d. on 1½d. black and purple	10	5	5

1941-67. *Postal Fiscal stamps as Type* F **6** *of New Zealand with thin opt,* T **14**. P 14.

(i) *Thin, hard, chalk-surfaced "Wiggins Teape" paper with vertical mesh* (1941–43). (a) W **43** *of New Zealand*

79	2s. 6d. deep brown (B.) (4.41)	23·00	10·00	20·00
80	5s. green (R.) (4.41)	£170	75·00	£140
81	10s. pale carmine-lake (B.) (6.42)	£100	65·00	£140
82	£1 pink (B.) (2.43?)	£170	80·00	£200
	Set of 4	£425	£200	£450

(b) W **98** *of New Zealand* (1944–45)

83	2s. 6d. deep brown (B.) (3.45)	3·00	1·50	6·50
	Wi. Wmk inverted (11.51)	3·00	1·50	7·50
84	5s. green (R.) (11.44)	5·50	3·50	9·00
	Wi. Wmk inverted (19.5.54)	6·50	3·25	8·00
85	10s. carmine-lake (B.) (11.45).	40·00	15·00	35·00
	Wi. Wmk inverted	35·00	12·00	45·00
86	£1 pink (B.) (6.42)	28·00	14·00	40·00
	Set of 4	65·00	26·00	90·00

(ii) *Unsurfaced "Wiggins Teape" paper with horizontal mesh.* W **98** *of New Zealand*

87	2s. 6d. deep brown (p. 14 × 13½) (1.11.57)	3·25	1·60	3·00
88	5s. pale yellowish green (*wmk sideways*) (6.67)	48·00	25·00	70·00
	Ea. Comb perf 14 × 13.8	80·00	40·00	£100

No. 88 is line perf 14 × 13.9. Nos. 88 and 88Ea were only on sale at Wellington as no supplies were sent to Niue.

1944-46. *As T* **20** *to* **25** *and* **29** *to* **31** *of Cook Is. but additionally inscr* "NIUE". W **98** *of New Zealand (sideways on* ½d., 1d., 1s. *and* 2s.)

89	½d. black and emerald	50	30	60
90	1d. black and deep lake	50	30	60
91	2d. black and red-brown	1·50	35	1·50
92	2½d. black and slate-blue (1946)	60	30	85
93	4d. black and greenish blue	60	30	90
	Wi. Wmk inverted and reversed	12·00	7·50	
94	6d. black and red-orange	70	40	1·40
95	1s. black and violet	1·25	60	1·25
96	2s. black and red-brown (1945)	4·00	1·75	3·50
97	3s. light blue and emerald-green (1945)	8·50	4·50	6·50
	Set of 9	16·00	8·00	15·00

1946 (1 June). *Peace. Nos. 668, 670, 674/5 of New Zealand optd as* T **14**, *but without stop* (twice, reading up and down on 2d.).

98	1d. green (Blk.)	10	5	5
99	2d. purple (B.)	10	5	5
100	6d. chocolate and vermilion (Blk.)	10	5	10
	a. Opt double, one albino			
101	8d. black and carmine (B.)	10	5	10
	Set of 4	35	15	20
	First Day Cover			60

Nos. 102/112 are no longer used.

15 Map of Niue

16 H.M.S. *Resolution*

17 Alofi Landing

18 Native Hut

19 Arch at Hikutavake

20 Alofi Bay

21 Spearing Fish

22 Cave, Makefu

23 Bananas

24 Matapa Chasm

(Des J. Berry. Recess B.W.)

1950 (3 July). W **98** *of New Zealand (sideways inverted on* 1d., 2d., 3d., 4d., 6d. *and* 1s.). P 13½ × 14 (*horiz*), 14 × 13½ (*vert*).

113	**15**	½d. orange and blue	5	5	5
114	**16**	1d. brown and blue-green	1·25	70	20
115	**17**	2d. black and carmine	10	5	10
116	**18**	3d. blue and violet-blue	5	5	10
117	**19**	4d. olive-green and purple-brown	5	5	10
118	**20**	6d. green and brown-orange	20	10	15
119	**21**	9d. orange and brown	10	5	15
120	**22**	1s. purple and black	10	5	5
121	**23**	2s. brown-orange and dull green . .	1·00	50	2·00
122	**24**	3s. blue and black	3·50	1·50	3·75
		Set of 10	5·75	2·75	6·00

PRICES
Elizabeth II issues (from 1953)

First column = Unmounted Mint
Second column = Used

1953 (25 May). *Coronation. As Nos.* 715 *and* 717 *of New Zealand, but inscr* "NIUE".

123	3d. brown	65	30
124	6d. slate-grey	95	30
	Set of 2	1·60	30
	First Day Cover		1·50

(New Currency. 100 cents = 1 dollar)

(25)

26

1967 (10 July–7 Aug). *Decimal currency.* (a) *Nos.* 113/22 *surch as* T **25**.

125	**15**	½ c. on ½d.	5	5
126	**16**	1 c. on 1d.	80	15
127	**17**	2 c. on 2d.	5	5
128	**18**	2½ c. on 3d.	5	5
129	**19**	3 c. on 4d.	5	5
130	**20**	5 c. on 6d.	5	5
131	**21**	8 c. on 9d.	5	5
132	**22**	10 c. on 1s.	5	5
133	**23**	20 c. on 2s.	60	1·25
134	**24**	30 c. on 3s.	1·50	1·75
		Set of 10	2·75	3·00

(b) Arms type of New Zealand without value, surch as in T **26**. W **98** of New Zealand (sideways). P 14 (line.)

135	**26**	25 c.	deep yellow-brown	65	65
		a.	Rough perf 11	8·00	13·00
		Eb.	Comb perf 14 (7 Aug)	65	65
136		50 c.	pale yellowish green (comb perf 14)	1·00	1·00
		a.	Rough perf 11	9·00	15·00
137		$1	magenta	80	1·50
		a.	Rough perf 11	13·00	15·00
		Eb.	Comb perf 14	80	1·50
138		$2	light pink	1·40	2·50
		a.	Rough perf 11	15·00	20·00
		Eb.	Comb perf 14	1·40	2·50
			Set of 4	3·50	5·00
			Set of 4 (Nos. 135a/8a)	40·00	55·00

The line perf measures 14 × 13.9 and the comb perf is 14 × 13.8. The 50 c. is only known in the comb perf. The perf 11 stamps were done on an old hand machine as an emergency and only 2500 sets were produced.

1967 (3 Oct). Christmas. As T **278** of New Zealand, but inscr "NIUE".

139	2½ c. multicoloured	5	5
	Wi. Wmk sideways inverted	15	
	First Day Cover		20

1969 (1 Oct). Christmas. As T **301** of New Zealand, but inscr "NIUE". W **98** of New Zealand. P 13½ × 14½.

140	2½ c. multicoloured	5	5
	First Day Cover		20

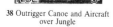

27 "Pua"　　　　37 Kalahimu

(Des Mrs. K. W. Billings. Litho Enschedé)

1969 (27 Nov). T **27** and similar vert designs. Multicoloured. P 12½ × 13½.

141	½ c. Type **27**	5	5
142	1 c. "Golden Shower"	5	5
143	2 c. Flamboyant	5	5
144	2½ c. Frangipani	5	5
145	3 c. Niue Crocus	5	5
146	5 c. Hibiscus	10	5
147	8 c. "Passion Fruit"	10	5
148	10 c. "Kampui"	10	5
149	20 c. Queen Elizabeth II (after Anthony Buckley)	1·00	1·25
150	30 c. Tapeu Orchid	1·75	1·75
	Set of 10	3·00	3·00

(Des G. F. Fuller. Photo Enschedé)

1970 (19 Aug). Indigenous Edible Crabs. T **37** and similar horiz designs. Multicoloured. P 13½ × 12½.

151	3 c. Type **37**	10	10
152	5 c. Kalavi	10	10
153	30 c. Unga	30	25
	Set of 3	45	40
	First Day Cover		55

1970 (1 Oct). Christmas. As T **314** of New Zealand, but inscr "NIUE".

154	2½ c. multicoloured	5	5
	Ea. Green (inscr and face value) printed double	£130	
	First Day Cover		20

38 Outrigger Canoe and Aircraft　　39 Spotted Triller
over Jungle

(Des L. C. Mitchell. Litho B.W.)

1970 (9 Dec). Opening of Niue Airport. T **38** and similar horiz designs. Multicoloured. P 13½.

155	3 c. Type **38**	10	10
156	5 c. Cargo liner and aircraft over harbour	15	10
157	8 c. Aircraft over Airport	15	20
	Set of 3	35	35
	First Day Cover		50

(Des A. G. Mitchell. Litho B.W.)

1971 (23 June). Birds. T **39** and similar horiz designs. Multicoloured. P 13½.

158	5 c. Type **39**	15	10
159	10 c. Purple-capped Fruit Dove	70	15
160	20 c. Blue-crowned Lory	80	20
	Set of 3	1·50	40
	First Day Cover		80

1971 (6 Oct). Christmas. As T **325** of New Zealand, but inscr "NIUE".

161	3 c. multicoloured	5	5
	First Day Cover		20

40 Niuean Boy　　　　41 Octopus Lure

(Des L. C. Mitchell. Litho Harrison)

1971 (17 Nov). Niuean Portraits. T **40** and similar vert designs. Multicoloured. P 13 × 14.

162	4 c. Type **40**	5	5
163	6 c. Girl with garland	8	5
164	9 c. Man	10	10
165	14 c. Woman with garland	15	20
	Set of 4	35	35
	First Day Cover		50

(Des A. G. Mitchell. Litho B.W.)

1972 (3 May). South Pacific Arts Festival, Fiji. T **41** and similar multicoloured designs. P 13½.

166	3 c. Type **41**	10	5
167	5 c. War weapons	15	10
168	10 c. Sika throwing (horiz)	20	10
169	25 c. Vivi dance (horiz)	30	20
	Set of 4	65	40
	First Day Cover		65

42 Alofi Wharf

(Des A. G. Mitchell. Litho Questa)

1972 (6 Sept). 25th Anniversary of South Pacific Commission. T **42** and similar horiz designs. Multicoloured. P 14.

170	4 c. Type **42**	10	5
171	5 c. Medical Services	15	10
172	6 c. Schoolchildren	15	10
173	18 c. Dairy cattle	25	20
	Set of 4	60	40
	First Day Cover		55

1972 (4 Oct). *Christmas. As T* **332** *of New Zealand but inscr* "NIUE".
174   3 c. multicoloured   5   5
         First Day Cover   20

43 Kokio

CHRISTMAS 1973
44 "Large Flower Piece"
(Jan Brueghel)

(Des G. F. Fuller. Litho Harrison)

1973 (27 June). *Fishes. T* **43** *and similar horiz designs. Multicoloured. P* 14 × 13½.
175   8 c. Type **43**   25   25
176   10 c. Loi   30   30
177   15 c. Malau   40   40
178   20 c. Palu   45   45
         Set of 4 . . . .   1·25   1·25
         First Day Cover . . . .   1·50

(Des and litho Enschedé)

1973 (21 Nov). *Christmas. T* **44** *and similar vert designs showing flower studies by the artists listed. Multicoloured. P* 14 × 13½.
179   4 c. Type **44**   5   5
180   5 c. Bollongier   10   5
181   10 c. Ruysch   15   15
         Set of 3   25   20
         First Day Cover   40

45 Capt. Cook and Bowsprit   **46** King Fataaiki

(Des A. G. Mitchell. Litho Questa)

1974 (20 June). *Bicentenary of Capt. Cook's Visit. T* **45** *and similar horiz designs each showing Cook's portrait. Multicoloured. P* 13½ × 14.
182   2 c. Type **45**   30   20
183   3 c. Niue landing place   30   25
184   8 c. Map of Niue   50   40
185   20 c. Ensign of 1774 and Administration
         Building   70   80
         Set of 4 . . . .   1·60   1·50
         First Day Cover . . . .   2·00

SELF-GOVERNMENT

(Des A. G. Mitchell. Litho Questa)

1974 (19 Oct). *Self-Government. T* **46** *and similar multicoloured designs. P* 14 × 13½ (4 *and* 8 c.) *or* 13½ × 14 (*others*).
186   4 c. Type **46**   5   5
187   8 c. Annexation Ceremony, 1900   10   10
188   10 c. Legislative Assembly Chambers (*horiz*) . . .   10   10
189   20 c. Village meeting (*horiz*)   15   15
         Set of 4   35   30
         First Day Cover   60

47 Decorated Bicycles   **48** Children going to Church

(Des B. C. Strong. Litho D.L.R.)

1974 (13 Nov). *Christmas. T* **47** *and similar vert designs. P* 12½.
190   3 c. multicoloured   5   5
191   10 c. multicoloured   10   5
192   20 c. dull red-brown, slate and black   20   15
         Set of 3   30   20
         First Day Cover   45
Designs:— 10 c. Decorated motorcycles; 20 c. Motor transport to church.

(Des Enid Hunter. Litho Questa)

1975 (29 Oct). *Christmas. T* **48** *and similar horiz designs. Multicoloured. P* 14.
193   4 c. Type **48**   5   5
194   5 c. Child with balloons on bicycle   10   5
195   10 c. Balloons and gifts on tree   15   15
         Set of 3   25   20
         First Day Cover   45

49 Hotel Buildings   **50** Preparing Ground for Taro

(Des B. C. Strong. Litho Harrison)

1975 (19 Nov). *Opening of Tourist Hotel. T* **49** *and similar horiz design. Multicoloured. P* 13½ × 13.
196   8 c. Type **49**   10   5
197   20 c. Ground-plan and buildings   15   15
         Set of 2   25   20
         First Day Cover   45

(Des A. G. Mitchell. Litho Questa)

1976 (3 Mar). *T* **50** *and similar horiz designs showing food gathering. Multicoloured. P* 13½ × 14.
198   1 c. Type **50**   5   5
199   2 c. Planting taro   8   5
200   3 c. Banana gathering   8   5
201   4 c. Harvesting taro   10   5
202   5 c. Gathering shell fish   15   5
203   10 c. Reef fishing   15   5
204   20 c. Luku gathering   20   15
205   50 c. Canoe fishing   40   60
206    $1 Coconut husking   60   80
207    $2 Uga gathering . . . .   1·00   1·40
         Set of 10 . . . .   2·50   2·75
         First Day Cover . . . .   4·00
See also Nos. 249/58 and 264/73.

A regular new issue supplement to this
catalogue appears each month in

GIBBONS STAMP MONTHLY

—from your newsagent or by postal subscription
—sample copy and details on request.

51 Water   52 Christmas Tree, Alofi

(Des A. G. Mitchell. Litho Questa)

1976 (7 July). *Utilities. T 51 and similar vert designs. Multicoloured. P 14.*

208	10 c. Type **51**	5	5
209	15 c. Power	15	15
210	20 c. Telecommunications	15	15
	Set of 3	30	30
	First Day Cover		55

(Des A. G. Mitchell. Litho Questa)

1976 (15 Sept). *Christmas. T 52 and similar horiz design. Multicoloured. P 14.*

211	9 c. Type **52**	10	10
212	15 c. Church Service, Avatele	15	15
	Set of 2	25	25
	First Day Cover		45

53 Queen Elizabeth II and Westminster Abbey

(Des and photo Heraclio Fournier)

1977 (7 June). *Silver Jubilee. T 53 and similar horiz design. Multicoloured. P 13½.*

213	$1 Type **53**	1·50	75
214	$2 Coronation regalia	2·00	1·00
	Set of 2	3·50	1·75
	First Day Cover		2·75
MS215	72 × 104 mm. Nos. 213/14.	3·50	2·50
	First Day Cover		3·50

Stamps from the miniature sheet have a blue border.

54 Child Care   55 "The Annunciation"

(Des R. M. Conly. Litho Questa)

1977 (29 June). *Personal Services. T 54 and similar horiz designs. Multicoloured. P 14½.*

216	10 c. Type **54**	15	10
217	15 c. School dental clinic	20	20
218	20 c. Care of the aged	20	20
	Set of 3	50	45
	First Day Cover		60

(Des and photo Heraclio Fournier)

1977 (15 Nov). *Christmas. T 55 and similar vert designs showing paintings by Rubens. Multicoloured. P 13.*

219	10 c. Type **55**	15	10
220	12 c. "Adoration of the Magi"	15	10
221	20 c. "Virgin in a Garland"	25	20
222	35 c. "The Holy Family"	45	35
	Set of 4	90	65
	First Day Cover		90
MS223	82 × 129 mm. Nos. 219/22	1·50	1·75
	First Day Cover		2·00

12c

(56)

1977 (15 Nov). *Nos. 198 etc., 214, 216 and 218 surch as T 56 by New Zealand Govt Printer.*

224	12 c. on 1 c. Type **50**	25	25
225	16 c. on 2 c. Planting taro	30	30
226	30 c. on 3 c. Banana gathering	50	40
227	35 c. on 4 c. Harvesting taro	55	45
228	40 c. on 5 c. Gathering shell fish	60	50
229	60 c. on 20 c. Luku gathering	85	65
230	70 c. on $1 Coconut husking	95	70
231	85 c. on $2 Uga gathering	1·00	70
232	$1.10 on 10 c. Type **54**	1·00	75
233	$2.60 on 20 c. Care of the aged	1·75	1·25
234	$3.20 on $2 Coronation regalia (Gold)	2·00	1·50
	Set of 11	8·50	6·50
	First Day Cover		10·00

57 "An Island View in Atooi"

(Photo Heraclio Fournier)

1978 (18 Jan). *Bicentenary of Discovery of Hawaii. T 57 and similar horiz designs showing paintings by John Webber. Multicoloured. P 13.*

235	12 c. Type **57**	55	30
236	16 c. "View of Karakaooa, in Owhyhee"	65	40
237	20 c. "Offering before Capt. Cook in the Sandwich Islands"	70	45
238	30 c. "Tereoboo, King of Owhyhee bringing presents to Capt. Cook"	90	50
239	35 c. "Canoe in the Sandwich Islands, the rowers masked"	1·00	55
	Set of 5	3·50	2·00
	First Day Cover		2·75
MS240	121 × 121 mm. Nos. 235/9	4·25	4·25
	First Day Cover		4·75

Nos. 235/9 were each printed in small sheets of 6, including 1 *se-tenant* stamp-size label.

58 "The Deposition of   59 Flags of Niue and U.K.
Christ" (Caravaggio)

(Photo Heraclio Fournier)

1978 (15 Mar). *Easter. Paintings from the Vatican Galleries. T* **58** *and similar vert design. Multicoloured. P* 13.

241	10 c. Type **58**	10	10
242	20 c. "The Burial of Christ" (Bellini)	25	25
	Set of 2	35	35
	First Day Cover		45
MS243	102 × 68 mm. Nos. 241/2...............	45	60
	First Day Cover		75

1978 (15 Mar). *Easter. Children's Charity. Designs as Nos. 241/2 in separate miniature sheets* 64 × 78 *mm, each with a face value of* 70 c.+5 c. *P* 13.

MS244	As Nos. 241/2. Set of 2 sheets	1·75	2·00
	First Day Cover		3·00

(Photo Heraclio Fournier)

1978 (26 June). *25th Anniv of Coronation. T* **59** *and similar horiz designs. Multicoloured.* A. *White border.* B. *Turquoise-green border. P* 13.

		A		B	
245	$1.10 Type **59**	1·25	1·00	1·25	1·00
246	$1 10 Coronation portrait by Cecil Beaton	1·25	1·00	1·25	1·00
247	$1.10 Queen's personal flag for New Zealand	1·25	1·00	1·25	1·00
	Set of 3	3·25	2·75	3·25	2·75
	First Day Cover		3·00		3·00
MS248	87 × 98 mm. Nos. 245/7....	4·25	3·50	†	
	First Day Cover		4·75		

Nos. 245/7 were printed together in small sheets of 6, containing two *se-tenant* strips of 3, with horizontal gutter margin between. The upper strip has white borders, the lower turquoise-green.

(Litho Questa)

1978 (27 Oct). *Designs as Nos. 198/207 but margin colours changed and silver frame. P* 13½ × 14.

249	12 c. Type **50**	20	20
250	16 c. Planting taro	20	20
251	30 c. Banana gathering	30	25
252	35 c. Harvesting taro	30	30
253	40 c. Gathering shell fish	40	30
254	60 c. Reef fishing	45	35
255	75 c. Luku gathering	50	40
256	$1.10, Canoe fishing	1·10	80
257	$3.20, Coconut husking	1·25	1·25
258	$4.20, Uga gathering	1·40	1·40
	Set of 10	5·50	5·00
	First Day Cover		10·00

See also Nos. 264/73.

60 "Festival of the Rosary"

(Des and photo Heraclio Fournier)

1978 (30 Nov). *Christmas. 450th Death Anniv of Dürer. T* **60** *and similar horiz designs. Multicoloured. P* 13.

259	20 c. Type **60**	30	20
260	30 c. "The Nativity"	35	30
261	35 c. "Adoration of the Magi"	35	35
	Set of 3	90	75
	First Day Cover		1·00
MS262	143 × 82 mm. Nos. 259/61	1·25	1·50
	First Day Cover		1·75

Nos. 259/61 were each printed in small sheets of 6.

1978 (30 Nov). *Christmas. Children's Charity. Designs as Nos. 259/61 in separate miniature sheets* 74 × 66 *mm, each with a face value of* 60 c. + 5 c. *P* 13.

MS263	As Nos. 259/61. Set of 3 sheets	2·00	2·00
	First Day Cover		3·00

(Litho Questa)

1979 (26 Feb–28 May). *Air. Designs as Nos. 249/58 but gold frames and additionally inscr* "AIRMAIL". *P* 13½ × 14.

264	15 c. Planting taro	20	15
265	20 c. Banana gathering	25	15
266	23 c. Harvesting taro	30	15
267	50 c. Canoe fishing	70	20
268	90 c. Reef fishing	85	35
269	$1.35, Type **50** (30.3)	1·25	1·50
270	$2.10, Gathering shell fish (30.3)	2·00	2·25
271	$2.60, Luku gathering (30.3)	2·00	2·50
272	$5.10, Coconut husking (28.5)	2·25	3·50
273	$6.35, Uga gathering (28.5)	2·50	4·50
	Set of 10	11·00	14·00
	First Day Cover		20·00

PRINTERS. The following stamps were printed in photogravure by Heraclio Fournier, Spain, *except where otherwise stated.*

61 "Pietà" (Gregorio Fernandez) **62** "The Nurse and Child" (Franz Hals)

1979 (2 Apr). *Easter. Paintings. T* **61** *and similar horiz design. Multicoloured. P* 13.

274	30 c. Type **61**	30	25
275	35 c. "Burial of Christ" (Pedro Roldan)	35	25
	Set of 2	65	50
	First Day Cover		65
MS276	82 × 82 mm. Nos. 274/5	90	1·00
	First Day Cover		1·40

1979 (2 Apr). *Easter. Children's Charity. Designs as Nos. 274/5 in separate miniature sheets* 86 × 69 *mm, each with a face value of* 70 c.+5 c. *P* 13.

MS277	As Nos. 274/5. Set of 2 sheets	1·75	1·75
	First Day Cover		3·00

1979 (31 May). *International Year of the Child. Details of Paintings. T* **62** *and similar vert designs. Multicoloured. P* 14 × 13½.

278	16 c. Type **62**	20	15
279	20 c. "Child of the Duke of Osuna" (Goya)	25	20
280	30 c. "Daughter of Robert Strozzi" (Titian) ...	40	35
281	35 c. "Children eating Fruit" (Murillo)	40	40
	Set of 4	1·10	1·00
	First Day Cover		1·10
MS282	80 × 115 mm. Nos. 278/81. P 13	1·25	1·50
	First Day Cover		1·75

1979 (31 May). *International Year of the Child. Children's Charity. Designs as Nos. 278/81 in separate miniature sheets* 99 × 119 *mm, each with a face value of* 70 c. + 5 c. *P* 13.

MS283	As Nos. 278/81. Set of 4 sheets	3·00	2·50
	First Day Cover		3·50

63 Penny Black Stamp   **64** Cook's Landing at Botany Bay

1979 (3 July).   *Death Centenary of Sir Rowland Hill. T* **63** *and similar vert designs. Multicoloured. P* 14 × 13½.

284	20 c. Type **63**	20	15
285	20 c. Sir Rowland Hill and original Bath mail coach	20	15
286	30 c. Basel 1845 2½ r. stamp	30	20
287	30 c. Sir Rowland Hill and Alpine village coach	30	20
288	35 c. U.S.A. 1847 5 c. stamp	35	25
289	35 c. Sir Rowland Hill and first Transatlantic U.S.A. mail vessel	35	25
290	50 c. France 1849 20 c. stamp	50	35
291	50 c. Sir Rowland Hill and French Post Office railway van, 1849	50	35
292	60 c. Bavaria 1849 1 k. stamp	55	40
293	60 c. Sir Rowland Hill and Bavarian coach with mail	55	40
	Set of 10	3·50	2·50
	First Day Cover		3·25
MS294	143 × 149 mm. Nos. 284/93	3·50	3·75
	First Day Cover		4·25

Nos. 284/5, 286/7, 288/9, 290/1 and 292/3 were each printed together, *se-tenant*, in horizontal pairs throughout the sheet forming composite designs.

1979 (30 July).   *Death Bicentenary of Captain Cook. T* **64** *and similar horiz designs. Multicoloured. P* 14.

295	20 c. Type **64**	35	30
296	30 c. Cook's men during a landing on Erromanga	50	40
297	35 c. H.M.S. *Resolution* and H.M.S. *Discovery* in Queen Charlotte's Sound	55	45
298	75 c. Death of Captain Cook, Hawaii	95	70
	Set of 4	2·10	1·75
	First Day Cover		2·25
MS299	104 × 80 mm. Nos. 295/8. P 13½	2·50	3·00
	First Day Cover		3·50

65 Launch of "Apollo 11"   **66** "Virgin of Tortosa"
(P. Serra)

1979 (27 Sept).   *10th Anniv of Moon Landing. T* **65** *and similar vert designs. Multicoloured. P* 13½.

300	30 c. Type **65**	25	20
301	35 c. Lunar module on Moon	30	25
302	60 c. Helicopter, recovery ship and command module after splashdown	40	40
	Set of 3	85	75
	First Day Cover		1·00
MS303	120 × 82 mm. Nos. 300/2	1·00	1·40
	First Day Cover		1·75

Stamps from No. **MS303** have the inscription in gold on a blue panel.

1979 (29 Nov).   *Christmas. Paintings. T* **66** *and similar vert designs. Multicoloured. P* 13.

304	20 c. Type **66**	10	10
305	25 c. "Virgin with Milk" (R. di Mur)	15	15
306	30 c. "Virgin and Child" (S. di G. Sassetta)	20	20
307	50 c. "Virgin and Child" (J. Huguet)	25	25
	Set of 4	60	60
	First Day Cover		95
MS308	95 × 113 mm. Nos. 304/7	75	1·25
	First Day Cover		1·60

1979 (29 Nov).   *Christmas. Children's Charity. Designs as Nos.* 304/7 *in separate miniature sheets,* 49 × 84 *mm, each with a face value of* 85 *c.*+5 *c. P* 13.

MS309	As Nos. 304/7. *Set of 4 sheets*	1·50	2·00
	First Day Cover		3·00

**HURRICANE
RELIEF
Plus 2c**

(67)   **68** "Pietà" (Bellini)

1980 (25 Jan).   *Hurricane Relief. Various stamps surch as T* **67** *in black* (Nos. 310/19) *or silver* (320/30).

(a) *Nos. 284/93* (Death Centenary of Sir Rowland Hill)

310	20 c. + 2 c. Type **63**	20	25
311	20 c. + 2 c. Sir Rowland Hill and original Bath coach	20	25
312	30 c. + 2 c. Basel 1845 2½ r. stamp	30	35
313	30 c. + 2 c. Sir Rowland Hill and Alpine village coach	30	35
314	35 c. + 2 c. U.S.A. 1847 5 c. stamp	35	40
315	35 c. + 2 c. Sir Rowland Hill and first Transatlantic U.S.A. mail vessel	35	40
316	50 c. + 2 c. France 1849 20 c. stamp	50	55
317	50 c. + 2 c. Sir Rowland Hill and French Post Office railway van, 1849	50	55
318	60 c. + 2 c. Bavaria 1849 1 k. stamp	60	65
319	60 c. + 2 c. Sir Rowland Hill and Bavarian coach with mail	60	65

(b) *Nos. 295/8* (Death Bicentenary of Captain Cook)

320	20 c. + 2 c. Type **64**	20	25
321	30 c. + 2 c. Cook's men during a landing on Erromanga	30	35
322	35 c. + 2 c. H.M.S. *Resolution* and H.M.S. *Discovery* in Queen Charlotte's Sound	35	40
323	75 c. + 2 c. Death of Captain Cook, Hawaii	75	80

(c) *Nos. 300/2* (10th Anniv of Moon Landing)

324	30 c. + 2 c. Type **65**	30	35
325	35 c. + 2 c. Lunar module on Moon	35	40
326	60 c. + 2 c. Helicopter, recovery ship and command module after splashdown	60	65

(d) *Nos. 304/7* (Christmas)

327	20 c. + 2 c. Type **66**	20	25
328	25 c. + 2 c. "Virgin with Milk" (R. de Mur)	25	30
329	30 c. + 2 c. "Virgin and Child" (S. di G. Sassetta)	30	35
330	50 c. + 2 c. "Virgin and Child" (J. Huguet)	50	55
	Set of 21	7·50	8·00
	First Day Cover		9·00

On Nos. 310/19 "HURRICANE RELIEF" covers the two designs of each value.

1980 (2 Apr).   *Easter. Paintings. T* **68** *and similar horiz designs showing* "Pietà" *paintings by various artists. Multicoloured. P* 13½ × 13.

331	25 c. Type **68**	15	15
332	30 c. Botticelli	20	20
333	35 c. Antony van Dyck	20	20
	Set of 3	50	50
	First Day Cover		75
MS334	75 × 104 mm. As Nos. 331/3, but each with additional premium of "+ 2 c."	55	90
	First Day Cover		1·25

The premiums on No. **MS334** were used to support Hurricane Relief.

1980 (2 Apr). *Easter. Hurricane Relief. Designs as Nos. 331/3 in separate miniature sheets, 75 × 52 mm, each with a face value of 85 c. + 5 c. P 13 × 14.*

MS335	As Nos. 331/3. Set of 3 sheets	1·25	1·75
	First Day Cover		3·00

69 Ceremonial Stool, New Guinea

1980 (30 July). *South Pacific Festival of Arts, New Guinea. T **69** and similar vert designs. Multicoloured. P 13.*

336	20 c.	Type **69**	20	20
337	20 c.	Ku-Tagwa plaque, New Guinea	20	20
338	20 c.	Suspension hook, New Guinea	20	20
339	20 c.	Ancestral board, New Guinea	20	20
340	25 c.	Platform post, New Hebrides	25	25
341	25 c.	Canoe ornament, New Ireland	25	25
342	25 c.	Carved figure, Admiralty Islands	25	25
343	25 c.	Female with child, Admiralty Islands	25	25
344	30 c.	The God A'a, Rurutu (Austral Islands)	25	30
345	30 c.	Statue of Tangaroa, Cook Islands	25	30
346	30 c.	Ivory pendant, Tonga	25	30
347	30 c.	Tapa (Hiapo) cloth, Niue	25	30
348	35 c.	Feather box (Waka), New Zealand	30	35
349	35 c.	Hei-Tiki amulet, New Zealand	30	35
350	35 c.	House post, New Zealand	30	35
351	35 c.	Feather image of god Ku, Hawaii	30	35
		Set of 16	3·75	4·00
		First Day Cover		4·50

MS352 Four sheets, each 86 × 124 mm. (a) Nos. 336, 340, 344, 348; (b) Nos. 337, 341, 345, 349; (c) Nos. 338, 342, 346, 350; (d) Nos. 339, 343, 347, 351. Each stamp with an additional premium of 2 c. *Set of 4 sheets* .... 4·00 4·25

First Day Cover .... 4·75

Nos. 336/9, 340/3, 344/7 and 348/51 were each printed together, *se-tenant*, in horizontal strips of 4 throughout the sheet.

NEW ZEALAND STAMP EXHIBITION

ZEAPEX '80 AUCKLAND

(**70**)   (**71**)

1980 (22 Aug). *"Zeapex '80" International Stamp Exhibition, Auckland. Nos. 284, 286, 288, 290 and 292 optd with T **70** and Nos. 285, 287, 289, 291 and 293 optd with T **71**, both in black on silver background.*

353	20 c.	Type **63**	20	20
354	20 c.	Sir Rowland Hill and original Bath mail coach	20	20
355	30 c.	Basel 1845 2½ r. stamp	30	25
356	30 c.	Sir Rowland Hill and Alpine village coach	30	25
357	35 c.	U.S.A. 1847 5 c. stamp	35	25
358	35 c.	Sir Rowland Hill and first Transatlantic U.S.A. mail vessel	35	25
359	50 c.	France 1849 20 c. stamp	45	30
360	50 c.	Sir Rowland Hill and French Post Office railway van, 1849	45	30
361	60 c.	Bavaria 1849 1 k. stamp	55	35

362	60 c.	Sir Rowland Hill and Bavarian coach with mail	55	35
		Set of 10	3·50	2·50
		First Day Cover		3·00

MS363 143 × 149 mm. Nos. 353/62, each additionally surcharged '' + 2 c.'' .... 3·75 3·25

First Day Cover .... 3·75

72 Queen Elizabeth the   **73** 100 Metre Dash
Queen Mother

1980 (15 Sept). *80th Birthday of Queen Elizabeth the Queen Mother. P 13.*

364	**72**	$1.10, multicoloured	1·75	1·75
		First Day Cover		2·00
MS365	55 × 80 mm. **72** $3 multicoloured		3·00	3·00
		First Day Cover		3·50

No. 364 was printed in small sheets of 6 including one *se-tenant* stamp-size label.

1980 (30 Oct). *Olympic Games, Moscow. T **73** and similar horiz designs. Multicoloured. P 14 × 13½.*

366	20 c.	Type **73**	15	15
367	20 c.	Allen Wells, Great Britain (winner of 100 metre dash)	15	15
368	25 c.	⎫ 400 metre freestyle (winner, Ines	15	20
369	25 c.	⎬ Diers, D.D.R.)	15	20
370	30 c.	⎫ "Soling" Class Yachting (winner, Den-	20	20
371	30 c.	⎬ mark)	20	20
372	35 c.	⎫ Football (winner, Czechoslovakia)	20	25
373	35 c.	⎬	20	25
		Set of 8	1·25	1·40
		First Day Cover		1·75

MS374 119 × 128 mm. Nos. 366/73, each stamp including premium of 2 c. .... 1·60 2·00

First Day Cover .... 2·40

Nos. 366/7, 368/9, 370/1 and 372/3 were each printed together, *se-tenant*, in horizontal pairs throughout the sheet, forming composite designs. On the 25 c. and 35 c. stamps the face value is at right on the first design and at left on the second in each pair. For the 30 c. No. 370 has a yacht with a green sail at left and on No. 371 one with a red sail.

74 "The Virgin and Child"   **75** *Phalaenopsis sp.*

1980 (28 Nov). *Christmas and 450th Death Anniv of Andrea del Sarto (painter). T **74** and similar vert designs showing different "The Virgin and Child" works. P 13.*

375	20 c.	multicoloured	15	15
376	25 c.	multicoloured	15	15
377	30 c.	multicoloured	20	20
378	35 c.	multicoloured	20	20
		Set of 4	60	60
		First Day Cover		90
MS379	87 × 112 mm. Nos. 375/8		85	95
		First Day Cover		1·25

1980 (28 Nov). *Christmas. Children's Charity. Designs as Nos. 375/8 in separate miniature sheets 62 × 84 mm, each with a face value of 80 c. + 5 c. P 13.*

MS380	As Nos. 375/8. Set of 4 sheets	2·75	3·00
	First Day Cover		3·50

1981 (2 Apr)–**82**. *Flowers (1st series). Horiz designs as T 75. Multicoloured. P 13.*

381	2 c. Type **75**	5	5
382	2 c. Moth Orchid	5	5
383	5 c. *Euphorbia pulcherrima*	5	5
384	5 c. Poinsettia	5	5
385	10 c. *Thunbergia alata*	10	10
386	10 c. Black-eyed Susan	10	10
387	15 c. *Cochlospermum hibiscoides*	15	15
388	15 c. Buttercup Tree	15	15
389	20 c. *Begonia sp.*	20	20
390	20 c. Begonia	20	20
391	25 c. *Plumeria sp.*	25	25
392	25 c. Frangipani	25	25
393	30 c. *Strelitzia reginae* (26 May)	30	30
394	30 c. Bird of Paradise (26 May)	30	30
395	35 c. *Hibiscus syriacus* (26 May)	30	30
396	35 c. Rose of Sharon (26 May)	30	30
397	40 c. *Nymphaea sp.* (26 May)	35	35
398	40 c. Water Lily (26 May)	35	35
399	50 c. *Tibouchina sp.* (26 May)	45	45
400	50 c. Princess Flower (26 May)	45	45
401	60 c. *Nelumbo sp.* (26 May)	55	55
402	60 c. Lotus (26 May)	55	55
403	80 c. *Hybrid hibiscus* (26 May)	65	65
404	80 c. Yellow Hibiscus (26 May)	65	65
405	$1 Golden Shower Tree (*Cassia fistula*) (9.12.81)	85	85
406	$2 *Orchid var.* (9.12.81)	1·75	1·75
407	$3 *Orchid sp.* (9.12.81)	2·50	2·50
408	$4 *Euphorbia pulcherrima poinsettia* (15.1.82)	3·50	3·50
409	$6 *Hybrid hibiscus* (15.1.82)	5·00	5·00
410	$10 Scarlet Hibiscus (*Hibiscus rosasinensis*) (12.3.82)	8·50	8·50
	Set of 30	26·00	26·00
	First Day Covers (5)		32·00

The two designs of the 2 c. to 80 c. show different drawings of the same flower, one inscribed with its name in Latin, the other giving the common name. These were printed together, *se-tenant*, in horizontal and vertical pairs throughout the sheet.

Nos. 405/10 are larger, 47 × 33 mm.

See also Nos. 527/36.

76 "Jesus Defiled" (El Greco)   77 Prince Charles

1981 (10 Apr). *Easter. Details of Paintings. T 76 and similar horiz designs. Multicoloured. P 14.*

425	35 c. Type **76**	30	30
426	50 c. "Pietà" (Fernando Gallego)	50	50
427	60 c. "The Supper of Emmaus" (Jacopo da Pontormo)	55	55
	Set of 3	1·25	1·25
	First Day Cover		1·40
MS428	69 × 111 mm. As Nos. 425/7, but each with charity premium of 2 c. P 13½	1·40	1·60
	First Day Cover		1·90

1981 (10 Apr). *Easter. Children's Charity. Designs as Nos. 425/7 in separate miniature sheets 78 × 86 mm, each with a face value of 80 c. + 5 c. P 13½ × 14.*

MS429	As Nos. 425/7. Set of 3 sheets	2·50	2·75
	First Day Cover		3·50

1981 (26 June). *Royal Wedding. T 77 and similar vert designs. Multicoloured. P 14.*

430	75 c. Type **77**	1·25	1·00
431	95 c. Lady Diana Spencer	1·50	1·25
432	$1.20, Prince Charles and Lady Diana	1·75	1·50
	Set of 3	4·00	3·25
	Set of 3 optd "Specimen"	25·00	
	First Day Cover		3·75
MS433	78 × 85 mm. Nos. 430/2	4·00	3·50
	Optd "Specimen"	25·00	
	First Day Cover		4·25

Nos. 430/2 were each printed in small sheets of 6, including one *se-tenant* stamp-size label.

NIUE   +5c

78 Footballer Silhouettes   (79)

1981 (16 Oct). *World Cup Football Championship, Spain (1982). T 78 and similar horiz designs showing footballer silhouettes. P 13.*

434	30 c. blue-green, gold & new blue (Type **78**)	20	20
435	30 c. blue-green, gold and new blue (gold figure 3rd from left of stamp)	20	20
436	30 c. blue-green, gold and new blue (gold figure 4th from left)	20	20
437	35 c. new blue, gold and reddish orange (gold figure 3rd from left)	25	25
438	35 c. new blue, gold and reddish orange (gold figure 4th from left)	25	25
439	35 c. new blue, gold and reddish orange (gold figure 2nd from left)	25	25
440	40 c. reddish orange, gold and blue-green (gold figure 3rd from left, displaying close control)	25	25
441	40 c. reddish orange, gold and blue-green (gold figure 2nd from left)	25	25
442	40 c. reddish orange, gold and blue-green (gold figure 3rd from left, heading)	25	25
	Set of 9	1·90	1·90
	First Day Cover		2·50
MS443	162 × 122 mm. 30 c. + 3 c., 35 c. + 3 c., 40 c. + 3 c. (each × 3). As Nos. 434/42	2·00	2·50
	First Day Cover		3·25

The three designs of each value were printed together, *se-tenant*, in horizontal strips of 3 throughout the sheets.

1981 (3 Nov). *International Year for Disabled Persons. Nos. 430/3 surch as T 79.*

444	75 c. + 5 c. Type **77**	2·25	1·50
445	95 c. + 5 c. Lady Diana Spencer	2·75	1·75
446	$1.20 + 5 c. Prince Charles and Lady Diana	3·75	2·00
	Set of 3	8·00	4·75
	First Day Cover		5·25
MS447	78 × 85 mm. As Nos. 444/6, each surcharged "+ 10 c."	8·00	5·25
	First Day Cover		5·75

Nos. 444/6 have commemorative inscription overprinted on the sheet margins.

80 "The Holy Family   81 Prince of Wales
with Angels"

1981 (11 Dec). *Christmas and 375th Birth Anniv of Rembrandt. T* **80** *and similar vert designs. Multicoloured. P* 14 × 13.

448	20 c.	Type **79**	25	20
449	35 c.	"Presentation in the Temple"	35	30
450	50 c.	"Virgin and Child in Temple"	45	40
451	60 c.	"The Holy Family"	50	45
		Set of 4	1·40	1·25
		First Day Cover		1·40
MS452		79 × 112 mm. Nos. 448/51	1·40	1·50
		First Day Cover		1·75

1982 (22 Jan). *Christmas. Children's Charity. Designs as Nos.* 448/51 *in separate miniature sheets* 66 × 80 *mm, each with a face value of* 80 *c.*+5 *c. P* 14 × 13.

MS453	As Nos. 448/51. Set of 4 sheets	2·50	2·75
	First Day Cover		3·75

1982 (1 July). *21st Birthday of Princess of Wales. T* **81** *and similar horiz designs. Multicoloured. P* 14.

454	50 c.	Type **81**	55	55
455	$1.25, Prince and Princess of Wales		1·25	1·25
456	$2.50, Princess of Wales		2·00	2·00
		Set of 3	3·50	3·50
		First Day Cover		3·75
MS457	81 × 101 mm. Nos. 454/6		3·75	4·00
		First Day Cover		4·50

Nos. 454/6 were each printed in small sheets of 6 including one *se-tenant* stamp-size label.
The stamps from No. **MS457** are without white borders.

(82)   83 Infant

1982 (23 July). *Birth of Prince William of Wales* (1st issue). *Nos.* 430/3 *optd as T* **82**.

458	75 c.	Type **77** (optd with T **82**)	2·25	1·75
		a. Pair. Nos. 458/9	4·50	3·50
459	75 c.	Type **77** (optd "BIRTH OF PRINCE WIL-LIAM OF WALES 21 JUNE 1982")	2·25	1·75
460	95 c.	Lady Diana Spencer (optd with T **82**)	3·25	2·25
		a. Pair. Nos. 460/1	6·50	4·50
461	95 c.	Lady Diana Spencer (optd "BIRTH OF PRINCE WILLIAM OF WALES 21 JUNE 1982")	3·25	2·25
462	$1.20, Prince Charles and Lady Diana Spencer (optd with T **82**)		4·25	2·75
		a. Pair. Nos. 462/3	8·50	5·50
463	$1.20, Prince Charles and Lady Diana Spencer (optd "BIRTH OF PRINCE WILLIAM OF WALES 21 JUNE 1982")		4·25	2·75
		Set of 6	18·00	12·00
		First Day Cover		13·00
MS464	78 × 85 mm. Nos. 430/2 each optd "PRINCE WILLIAM OF WALES 21 JUNE 1982"		8·50	6·00
		First Day Cover		7·00

Nos. 458/9, 460/1 and 462/3 were each printed *se-tenant* in small sheets of 6, containing three stamps overprinted with Type **82**, two with "BIRTH OF PRINCE WILLIAM OF WALES 21 JUNE 1982" and one stamp-size label.

1982 (10 Sept). *Birth of Prince William of Wales* (2nd issue). *Designs as Nos.* 454/7 *but with changed inscriptions. Multicoloured. P* 14.

465	50 c.	Type **81**	55	55
466	$1.25, Prince and Princess of Wales		1·25	1·25
467	$2.50, Princess of Wales		2·00	2·00
		Set of 3	3·50	3·50
		First Day Cover		3·75
MS468	81 × 101 mm. As Nos. 465/7		3·75	4·00
		First Day Cover		4·50

Nos. 465/7 were each printed in small sheets of 6 including one *se-tenant*, stamp-size, label.

1982 (3 Dec). *Christmas. Paintings of Infants by Bronzino, Murillo and Boucher. T* **83** *and similar horiz designs. P* 13 × 14½.

469	40 c.	multicoloured	45	35
470	52 c.	multicoloured	55	45
471	83 c.	multicoloured	90	80
472	$1.05, multicoloured		1·10	95
		Set of 4	2·75	2·25
		First Day Cover		2·75
MS473	110 × 76 mm. Designs as Nos. 469/72 (each 31 × 27 mm), but without portrait of Princess and Prince William. P 13½		2·50	2·75
		First Day Cover		3·50

84   Prince and Princess of   85   Prime Minister Robert Rex
Wales with Prince William

1982 (3 Dec). *Christmas. Children's Charity. Sheet* 72 × 58 *mm. P* 13 × 13½.

MS474	**84**	80 c.+5 c. multicoloured	85	90
		First Day Cover		1·40

No. **MS474** occurs with four different designs in the sheet margin.

1983 (14 Mar). *Commonwealth Day. T* **85** *and similar horiz designs. Multicoloured. P* 13.

475	70 c.	Type **85**	65	70
476	70 c.	H.M.S. *Resolution* and H.M.S. *Adventure* off Niue, 1774	65	70
477	70 c.	Passion flower	65	70
478	70 c.	Limes	65	70
		Set of 4	2·40	2·50
		First Day Cover		2·75

Nos. 475/8 were issued together, *se-tenant*, in blocks of four throughout the sheet.

86 Scouts signalling   (87)

1983 (28 Apr). *75th Anniv of Boy Scout Movement and 125th Birth Anniv of Lord Baden-Powell. T* **86** *and similar vert designs. Multicoloured. P* 13.

479	40 c.	Type **86**	35	40
480	50 c.	Planting sapling	45	50
481	83 c.	Map-reading	85	90
		Set of 3	1·50	1·60
		First Day Cover		2·00
MS482	137 × 90 mm. As Nos. 479/81, but each with premium of 3 c.		1·60	1·75
		First Day Cover		2·25

1983 (14 July). *15th World Scout Jamboree, Alberta, Canada. Nos. 479/82 optd with T* **87**, *in black on silver background.*

483	40 c. Type **86**	35	40
484	50 c. Planting sapling	45	50
485	83 c. Map-reading	85	90
	Set of 3	1·50	1·60
	First Day Cover		2·00
MS486	137 × 90 mm. As Nos. 483/5, but each with premium of 3 c.	1·60	1·75
	First Day Cover		2·00

88 Black Right Whale

1983 (15 Aug). *Protect the Whales. T* **88** *and similar horiz. designs. Multicoloured. P 13 × 14.*

487	12 c. Type **88**	25	15
488	25 c. Fin Whale	35	30
489	35 c. Sei Whale	50	40
490	40 c. Blue Whale	55	50
491	58 c. Bowhead Whale	75	60
492	70 c. Sperm Whale	95	80
493	83 c. Humpback Whale	1·25	95
494	$1.05, Minke Whale ("Lesser Rorqual")	1·50	1·25
495	$2.50, Grey Whale	2·75	2·50
	Set of 9	8·00	6·50
	First Day Cover		8·50

89 Montgolfier Balloon, 1783

1983 (14 Oct). *Bicentenary of Manned Flight. T* **89** *and similar horiz designs. Multicoloured.* (a) *Postage. P* 13½.

496	25 c. Type **89**	20	20
497	40 c. Wright Brothers' *Flyer*, 1903	35	35
498	58 c. *Graf Zeppelin*, 1928	50	50
499	70 c. Boeing "247", 1933	65	65
500	83 c. "Apollo 8", 1968	80	80
501	$1.05, Space shuttle *Columbia*, 1982	95	95
	Set of 6	3·00	3·00
	First Day Cover		3·50

(b) *Air. Inscr* "AIRMAIL"

MS502	118 × 130 mm. Nos. 496/501. P 13.	3·00	3·25
	First Day Cover		3·75

90 "The Garvagh Madonna"

91 Morse Key Transmitter

1983 (25 Nov). *Christmas. 500th Birth Anniv of Raphael. T* **90** *and similar vert designs. Multicoloured. P* 14 × 13½.

503	30 c. Type **90**	25	30
504	40 c. "Madonna of the Granduca"	30	35
505	58 c. "Madonna of the Goldfinch"	45	50
506	70 c. "The Holy Family of Francis I"	55	60
507	83 c. "The Holy Family with Saints"	65	70
	Set of 5	2·00	2·25
	First Day Cover		2·75
MS508	120 × 114 mm. As Nos. 503/7 but each with a premium of 3 c.	2·25	2·50
	First Day Cover		3·00

1983 (30 Nov). *Various stamps surch as T* **200** *of Cook Islands.*

(a) *Nos. 393/4, 399/404 and 407*

509	52 c. on 30 c. *Strelitzia reginae*	40	45
510	52 c. on 30 c. Bird of Paradise	40	45
511	58 c. on 50 c. *Tibouchina sp.*	50	55
512	58 c. on 50 c. Princess Flower	50	55
513	70 c. on 60 c. *Nelumbo sp.*	55	60
514	70 c. on 60 c. Lotus	55	60
515	83 c. on 80 c. *Hybrid hibiscus*	70	75
516	83 c. on 80 c. Yellow Hibiscus	70	75
517	$3.70 on $3 *Orchid sp.*	3·00	3·25

(b) *Nos. 431/2 and 455/6*

518	$1.10 on 95 c. Lady Diana Spencer	3·00	2·25
	a. Error. Surch on No. 458	6·00	6·00
	ab. Pair. Nos. 518a/b	15·00	15·00
	b. Error. Surch on No. 459	9·00	9·00
519	$1.10 on $1.25, Prince and Princess of Wales	2·25	2·00
520	$2.60 on $1.20, Prince Charles and Lady Diana	5·50	3·50
	a. Error. Surch on No. 462	6·00	6·00
	ab. Pair. Nos. 520a/b	15·00	15·00
	b. Error. Surch on No. 463	9·00	9·00
521	$2.60 on $2.50, Princess of Wales	3·50	3·25
	Set of 13	19·00	17·00
	First Day Cover		24·00

1983 (29 Dec). *Christmas. 500th Birth Anniv of Raphael. Children's Charity. Designs as Nos. 503/7 in separate miniature sheets, 65 × 80 mm, each with face value of 85 c. + 5 c. P* 13½.

MS522	As Nos. 503/7. *Set of 5 sheets*	3·25	3·50
	First Day Cover		4·50

1984 (23 Jan). *World Communications Year. T* **91** *and similar vert designs. Multicoloured. P* 13 × 13½.

523	40 c. Type **91**	30	35
524	52 c. Wall-mounted phone	40	45
525	83 c. Communications satellite	60	65
	Set of 3	1·10	1·25
	First Day Cover		1·50
MS526	114 × 90 mm. Nos. 523/5	1·10	1·25
	First Day Cover		1·75

92 *Phalaenopsis sp.*

93 Discus-throwing

1984 (20 Feb–23 July). *Flowers (2nd series). Designs as Nos. 381 etc., but with gold frames and redrawn inscr as in T* **92**. *Multicoloured. P* 13 (*Nos. 537/42) or 13 × 13½ (others).*

527	12 c. Type **92**	10	10
528	25 c. *Euphorbia pulcherrima*	15	20
529	30 c. *Cochlospermum hibiscoides*	20	25
530	35 c. *Begonia sp.*	25	30
531	40 c. *Plumeria sp.*	25	30
532	52 c. *Strelitzia reginae*	35	40
533	58 c. *Hibiscus syriacus*	35	40
534	70 c. *Tibouchina sp.*	45	50
535	83 c. *Nelumbo sp.*	55	60

536	$1.05, *Hybrid hibiscus*	70	75
537	$1.75, *Cassia fistula* (39 × 31 *mm*) (10.5)	1·10	1·25
538	$2.30, *Orchid var.* (39 × 31 *mm*) (10.5)	1·50	1·60
539	$3.90, *Orchid sp.* (39 × 31 *mm*) (10.5)	2·50	2·75
540	$5 *Euphorbia pulcherrima poinsettia* (39 × 31 *mm*) (18.6)	3·25	3·50
541	$6.60, *Hybrid hibiscus* (39 × 31 *mm*) (18.6) . .	4·25	4·50
542	$8.30, *Hibiscus rosasinensis* (39 × 31 *mm*) (23.7)	5·50	5·75
	Set of 16	19·00	20·00
	First Day Covers (4)		26·00

1984 (15 Mar). *Olympic Games, Los Angeles. T* **93** *and similar multicoloured designs showing ancient Greek sports. P* 14.

547	30 c. Type **93**	25	30
548	35 c. Sprinting (*horiz*)	30	35
549	40 c. Horse racing (*horiz*)	35	40
550	58 c. Boxing (*horiz*)	50	55
551	70 c. Javelin-throwing	60	65
	Set of 5	1·75	2·00
	First Day Cover		2·25

Discus Throw
Rolf Danneberg
Germany

94 Koala   (95)

1984 (24 Aug). *"Ausipex" International Stamp Exhibition, Melbourne* (1*st issue*). *P* 14. (*a*) *Postage Vert designs as T* **94** *showing Koala Bears.*

552	25 c. multicoloured	30	30
553	35 c. multicoloured	35	35
554	40 c. multicoloured	40	40
555	58 c. multicoloured	55	55
556	70 c. multicoloured	65	65

(*b*) *Air. Vert designs showing Red Kangaroos*

557	83 c. multicoloured	75	75
558	$1.05, multicoloured	95	95
559	$2.50, multicoloured	2·25	2·25
	Set of 8	5·50	5·50
	First Day Cover		6·00
MS560	110 × 64 mm. $1.75, Wallaby; $1.75, Koala Bear. P 13½	3·25	3·50
	First Day Cover		4·00

See also Nos. **MS** 566/7.

1984 (7 Sept). *Olympic Gold Medal Winners, Los Angeles. Nos.* 547/51 *optd as T* **95** *in red* (35 *c.*) *or gold* (*others*).

561	30 c. Type **93** (opt T **95**)	25	30
562	35 c. Sprinting (optd "1,500 Metres Sebastian Coe Great Britain")	30	35
563	40 c. Horse racing (optd "Equestrian Mark Todd New Zealand")	30	35
564	58 c. Boxing (optd "Boxing Tyrell Biggs United States")	45	50
565	70 c. Javelin throwing (optd "Javelin Throw Arto Haerkoenen Finland")	55	30
	Set of 5	1·75	1·90
	First Day Cover		2·40

1984 (20 Sept). *"Ausipex" International Stamp Exhibition, Melbourne* (2*nd issue*). *Designs as Nos.* 552/60 *in miniature sheets of six or four. Multicoloured. P* 13½.

MS566	109 × 105 mm. Nos. 552/6 and $1.75, Koala (as No. **MS**560)	3·00	3·25
	First Day Cover		3·75
MS567	80 × 105 mm. Nos. 557/9 and $1.75, Wallaby (as No. **MS**560)	4·50	4·75
	First Day Cover		6·00

$2
Prince Henry

|||| ||||

15. 9. 84

96 Niue National Flag and Premier
Sir Robert Rex   (97)

1984 (19 Oct). *10th Anniv of Self-Government. T* **96** *and similar horiz designs. Multicoloured. P* 13.

568	40 c. Type **96**	30	35
569	58 c. Map of Niue and Premier Rex	45	50
570	70 c. Premier Rex receiving proclamation of self-government	55	60
	Set of 3	1·10	1·25
	First Day Cover		1·50
MS571	110 × 83 mm. Nos. 568/70	1·25	1·40
	First Day Cover		1·75
MS572	100 × 74 mm. $2.50, As 70 c. (50 × 30 *mm*) . . .	1·75	1·90
	First Day Cover		2·40

1984 (22 Oct). *Birth of Prince Henry. Nos.* 430 *and* 454 *optd as T* **97**.

573	$2 on 50 c. Type **81** (Sil.)	2·50	1·75
574	$2 on 75 c. Type **77** (R.)	2·50	1·75
	Set of 2	5·00	3·50
	First Day Cover		3·75

98 "The Nativity"   99 House Wren
(A. Vaccaro)

1984 (23 Nov). *Christmas. T* **98** *and similar vert designs. Multicoloured. P* 13 × 13½.

575	40 c. Type **98**	30	35
576	58 c. "Virgin with Fly" (anon, 16th-century)	45	50
577	70 c. "The Adoration of the Shepherds" (B. Murillo)	55	60
578	83 c. "Flight into Egypt" (B. Murillo)	65	70
	Set of 4	1·75	1·90
	First Day Cover		2·40
MS579	115 × 111 mm. As Nos. 575/8 but each stamp with a 5 c. premium	2·00	2·25
	First Day Cover		2·75
MS580	Four sheets, each 66 × 98 mm. As Nos. 575/8, but each stamp 30 × 42 mm. with a face value of 95 c. + 10 c. P 13½. Set of 4 sheets	3·00	3·25
	First Day Cover		4·00

1985 (15 Apr). *Birth Bicentenary of John J. Audubon* (*ornithologist*). *T* **99** *and similar horiz designs showing original paintings. Multicoloured. P* 14.

581	40 c. Type **99**	60	35
582	70 c. Veery	85	60
583	83 c. Grasshopper Sparrow	1·00	70
584	$1.05, Henslow's Sparrow	1·25	85
585	$2.50, Vesper Sparrow	2·25	2·00
	Set of 5	5·50	4·00
	First Day Cover		5·00
MS586	Five sheets, each 54 × 60 mm. As Nos. 581/5 (34 × 46 *mm*) but without commemorative inscription and each with a face value of $1.75. Set of 5 sheets	7·50	8·50
	First Day Cover		11·00

100 The Queen Mother in Garter
Robes

1985 (14 June). *Life and Times of Queen Elizabeth the Queen Mother.
T* **100** *and similar horiz designs. Multicoloured. P* 13.
587 70 c. Type **100** 55   60
588 $1.15, In open carriage with the Queen 90   95
589 $1.50, With Prince Charles during 80th birthday
      celebrations .... 1·10 1·25
      Set of 3 .... 2·25 2·50
      First Day Cover ....   2·75
MS590 70 × 70 mm. $3 At her desk in Clarence House
  (38 × 35 mm) .... 2·25 2·50
      First Day Cover ....   2·75
Nos. 587/9 were each issued in sheetlets of five stamps and one
stamp-size label at top left, showing the Queen Mother's arms.
For Nos. 587/9 in miniature sheet see No. **MS**627.

MINI SOUTH PACIFIC GAMES.RAROTONGA

52
c

(**101**)

1985 (26 July). *South Pacific Mini Games, Rarotonga. Nos.* 547/8 *and*
550/1 *surch as T* **101** *in black and gold.*
591 52 c. on 70 c. Javelin-throwing 40   45
592 83 c. on 58 c. Boxing 65   70
593 95 c. on 35 c. Sprinting 75   80
594 $2 on 30 c. Type **93** .... 1·50 1·60
      Set of 4 .... 3·00 3·25
      First Day Cover ....   3·75

PACIFIC ISLANDS CONFERENCE.RAROTONGA

(**102**)

1985 (26 July). *Pacific Islands Conference, Rarotonga. Nos* 475/8 *optd
with T* **102** *in black on silver.*
595 70 c. Type **85** 55   60
596 70 c. *Resolution* and *Adventure* off Niue, 1774 .. 55   60
597 70 c. Passion flower 55   60
598 70 c. Limes 55   60
      Set of 4 .... 2·00 2·25
      First Day Cover ....   2·75
No. 595 also shows an overprinted amendment to the caption which
now reads "Premier Sir Robert Rex K.B.E.".

103 "R. Strozzi's Daughter"   104 "Virgin and Child"
      (Titian)

1985 (11 Oct). *International Youth Year. T* **103** *and similar vert designs.
Multicoloured. P* 13.
599 58 c. Type **103** 55   50
600 70 c. "The Fifer" (E. Manet) 70   60
601 $1.15, "Portrait of a Young Girl" (Renoir) .... 1·10   95
602 $1.50, "Portrait of M. Berard" (Renoir) ...... 1·40 1·25
      Set of 4 .... 3·25 3·00
      First Day Cover ....   3·50
MS603 Four sheets, each 63 × 79 mm. As Nos. 599/602
but each with face value of $1.75 + 10 c.
      Set of 4 sheets .... 6·00 6·50
      First Day Cover ....   8·00

1985 (29 Nov). *Christmas. Details of Paintings by Correggio. T* **104** *and
similar vert designs. Multicoloured. P* 13 × 13½.
604 58 c. Type **104** 45   50
605 85 c. "Adoration of the Magi" 65   70
606 $1.05, "Virgin with Child and St. John" 80   85
607 $1.45, "Virgin and Child with St. Catherine" .. 1·10 1·25
      Set of 4 .... 2·75 3·00
      First Day Cover ....   3·50
MS608 83 × 123 mm. As Nos. 604/7, but each stamp
with a face value of 60 c. + 10 c. .... 2·10 2·25
      First Day Cover ....   2·75
MS609 Four sheets, each 80 × 90 mm. 65 c. Type **104**;
95 c. As No. 605; $1.20, As No. 606; $1.75, As No. 607
(each stamp 49 × 59 mm). Imperf. Set of 4 sheets .. 3·50 3·75
      First Day Cover ....   4·50

105 "The Constellations" (detail)

1986 (24 Jan). *Appearance of Halley's Comet. T* **105** *and similar horiz
designs showing details from ceiling painting "The Constellations" by
Giovanni De Vecchi. Nos.* 611/13 *show different spacecraft at top left.
P* 13½.
610 60 c. multicoloured 45   50
611 75 c. multicoloured (*Vega* spacecraft) 60   65
612 $1.10, multicoloured (*Planet A* spacecraft) ... 85   90
613 $1.50, multicoloured (*Giotto* spacecraft) ..... 1·10 1·25
      Set of 4 .... 2·75 3·00
      First Day Cover ....   3·50
MS614 125 × 91 mm. As Nos. 610/13 but each stamp
with a face value of 95 c. .... 2·75 3·00
      First Day Cover ....   3·50
Stamps from No. **MS**614 are without borders.

106 Queen Elizabeth II and Prince Philip

107 U.S.A. 1847 Franklin 5 c. Stamp and Washington Sculpture, Mt. Rushmore, U.S.A.

1986 (28 Apr). *60th Birthday of Queen Elizabeth II. T* **106** *and similar vert designs. Multicoloured. P* 14½ × 13.

615	$1.10, Type **106**	85	85
616	$1.50, Queen and Prince Philip at Balmoral	1·10	1·10
617	$2 Queen at Buckingham Palace	1·60	1·60
	Set of 3	3·25	3·25
	First Day Cover		3·50
MS618	110 × 70 mm. As Nos. 615/17, but each stamp with a face value of 75 c.	1·60	1·75
	First Day Cover		2·00
MS619	58 × 89 mm. $3 Queen and Prince Phillip at Windsor Castle	2·10	2·25
	First Day Cover		2·50

1986 (22 May). *"Ameripex '86" International Stamp Exhibition, Chicago. T* **107** *and similar vert design. Multicoloured. P* 14.

620	$1 Type **107**	90	90
	a. Horiz pair. Nos. 620/1	1·75	1·75
621	$1 Flags of Niue and U.S.A. and Mt. Rushmore sculptures	90	90
	Set of 2	1·75	1·75
	First Day Cover		2·00

Nos. 620/1 were printed together, *se-tenant*, in horizontal pairs, within sheetlets of 8 stamps, each pair forming a composite design.

108 "Statue under Construction, Paris, 1883" (Victor Dargaud)

1986 (4 July). *Centenary of Statue of Liberty (1st issue). T* **108** *and similar vert design. Multicoloured. P* 13 × 13½.

622	$1 Type **108**	90	90
623	$2.50, "Unveiling of the Statue of Liberty" (Edmund Morand)	2·00	2·00
	Set of 2	2·75	2·75
	First Day Cover		3·25
MS624	107 × 73 mm. As Nos. 622/3, but each stamp with a face value of $1.25	2·00	2·50
	First Day Cover		3·00

See also No. **MS648**.

109 Prince Andrew, Miss Sarah Ferguson and Westminster Abbey

1986 (23 July). *Royal Wedding. T* **109** *and similar horiz design. Multicoloured. P* 13½ × 13.

625	$2.50, Type **109**	2·00	2·25
	First Day Cover		2·75
MS626	106 × 68 mm. $5 Prince Andrew and Miss Sarah Ferguson (43 × 30 mm)	4·00	4·25
	First Day Cover		4·75

1986 (4 Aug). *86th Birthday of Queen Elizabeth the Queen Mother. Nos.* 587/9 *in miniature sheet,* 109 × 83 *mm. P* 13.

MS627	Nos. 587/9	2·75	3·00
	First Day Cover		3·50

110 Great Egret

111 "Virgin and Child" (Perugino)

1986 (4 Aug). *"Stampex '86" Stamp Exhibition, Adelaide. Australian Birds. T* **110** *and similar multicoloured designs. P* 13 × 13½ (40, 75 c., $1, $2.20) *or* 13½ × 13 (*others*).

628	40 c. Type **110**	50	40
629	60 c. Painted Finch (*horiz*)	60	50
630	75 c. Australian King Parrot	80	70
631	80 c. Variegated Wren (*horiz*)	95	75
632	$1 Peregrine Falcon	1·25	1·00
633	$1.65, Azure Kingfisher (*horiz*)	1·75	1·50
634	$2.20 Budgerigars	1·90	1·90
635	$4.25, Emu (*horiz*)	3·25	3·50
	Set of 8	10·00	9·25
	First Day Cover		12·00

1986 (14 Nov). *Christmas. Paintings from the Vatican Museum. T* **111** *and similar vert designs. Multicoloured. P* 14.

636	80 c. Type **111**	60	65
637	$1.15, "Virgin of St. N. dei Frari" (Titian)	80	85
638	$1.80, "Virgin with Milk" (Lorenzo di Credi)	1·25	1·40
639	$2.60, "Madonna of Foligno" (Raphael)	1·75	1·90
	Set of 4	4·00	4·25
	First Day Cover		4·75
MS640	87 × 110 mm. As Nos. 636/9, but each stamp with a face value of $1.50. P 13½	4·00	4·25
	First Day Cover		4·75
MS641	70 × 100 mm. $7.50 As No. 639, but 27 × 43 mm. P 14½ × 13	5·50	5·75
	First Day Cover		6·50

+10c

40TH WEDDING ANNIV.

4.85

(112)

(114)   115 "The Nativity"

1986 (21 Nov). *Visit of Pope John Paul II to South Pacific. Nos.* 636/41 *surch as T* **112** *in black on silver.*

642	80 c. + 10 c. Type **111**		80	80
643	$1.15 + 10 c. "Virgin of St. N. dei Frari" (Titian)		1·00	1·00
644	$1.80 + 10 c. "Virgin with Milk" (Lorenzo di Credi)		1·75	1·75
645	$2.60 + 10 c. "Madonna of Foligno" (Raphael)		2·25	2·25
	Set of 4		5·25	5·25
	First Day Cover			6·50
MS646	87 × 110 mm. As No. 642/5, but each stamp with a face value of $1.50 + 10 c.		5·00	6·00
	First Day Cover			7·50
MS647	70 × 100 mm. $7.50 + 50 c. As No. 645, but 27 × 43 mm		6·50	7·00
	First Day Cover			8·50

1987 (20 May). *Centenary of Statue of Liberty* (1986) *(2nd issue). Two sheets, each* 122 × 122 *mm, containing multicoloured designs as T* **63** *of Cook Islands (Penrhyn). Litho. P* 13½ × 14 *(horiz) or* 14 × 13½ *(vert).*

MS648	Two sheets (a) 75 c. Sailing ship under Brooklyn Bridge; 75 c. Restoring Statue's flame; 75 c. Steam-cleaning Statue's torch; 75 c. *Esmeralda* (Chilean cadet ship) off Manhattan; 75 c. Cadet barque at dusk. (b) 75 c. Statue of Liberty at night (*vert*); 75 c. Statue at night (side view) (*vert*); 75 c. Cleaning Statue's crown (*vert*); 75 c. Statue at night (rear view) (*vert*); 75 c. Cleaning a finial (*vert*). *Set of 2 sheets*	4·25	4·50
	First Day Covers (2)		6·00

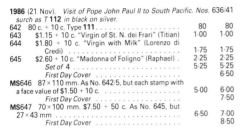

113 Boris Becker, Olympic Rings and Commemorative Coin

(Des G. Vasarhelyi. Litho Questa)

1987 (25 Sept). *Olympic Games, Seoul* (1988). *Tennis* (1st issue). *T* **113** *and similar horiz designs showing Boris Becker in play. P* 13½ × 14.

649	80 c. multicoloured	75	75
650	$1.15, multicoloured	1·00	1·00
651	$1.40, multicoloured	1·25	1·25
652	$1.80, multicoloured	1·50	1·50
	Set of 4	4·00	4·00
	First Day Cover		4·50

(Des G. Vasarhelyi. Litho Questa)

1987 (20 Oct). *Olympic Games. Seoul* (1988). *Tennis* (2nd issue). *Horiz designs as T* **113**, *but showing Steffi Graf. P* 13½ × 14.

653	85 c. multicoloured	75	75
654	$1.05, multicoloured	1·00	1·00
655	$1.30, multicoloured	1·25	1·25
656	$1.75, multicoloured	1·50	1·50
	Set of 4	4·00	4·00
	First Day Cover		4·50

1987 (20 Nov). *Royal Ruby Wedding. Nos* 616/17 *optd with T* **114**.

657	$4.85 on $1.50, Queen and Prince Philip at Balmoral	3·50	3·75
658	$4.85 on $2 Queen at Buckingham Palace	3·50	3·75
	Set of 2	7·00	7·50
	First Day Cover		8·50

On Nos. 657/8 the original values are obliterated in gold.

1987 (4 Dec). *Christmas. Religious Paintings by Dürer. T* **115** *and similar horiz designs. Multicoloured. P* 13½.

659	80 c. Type **115**	55	60
660	$1.05, "Adoration of the Magi"	75	80
661	$2.80, "Celebration of the Rosary"	2·00	2·10
	Set of 3	3·00	3·25
	First Day Cover		3·75
MS662	100 × 140 mm. As Nos. 659/61, but each size 48 × 37 mm with a face value of $1.30	2·75	3·00
MS663	90 × 80 mm. $7.50, As No. 661, but size 51 × 33 mm	5·25	5·50
	First Day Covers (2)		10·00

Nos. 659/61 each include a detail of an angel with lute as in T **115**. Stamps from the miniature sheets are without this feature.

116 Franz Beckenbauer in Action

(Des G. Vasarhelyi. Litho Questa)

1988 (20 June). *European Cup Football Championship, West Germany. T* **116** *and similar horiz designs. Multicoloured. P* 13½ × 14.

664	20 c. Type **116**	15	20
665	40 c. German "All Star" team in action	30	35
666	60 c. Bayern Munich team with European Cup, 1974	40	45
667	80 c. World Cup match, England, 1966	55	60
668	$1.05, World Cup match, Mexico, 1970	75	80
669	$1.30, Beckenbauer with pennant, 1974	90	95
670	$1.80, Beckenbauer and European Cup, 1974	1·25	4·25
	Set of 7	3·75	4·25
	First Day Cover		4·75

Australia 24 Jan 88
French Open 4 June 88

(117)   118 Angels

1988 (14 Oct). *Steffi Graf's Tennis Victories. Nos.653/6 optd as T 117.*
671   85 c. multicoloured (optd with T 117)   60   65
672   $1.05, multicoloured (optd "Wimbledon 2 July
          88 U S Open 10 Sept. 88")   75   80
673   $1.30, multicoloured (optd "Women's Tennis
          Grand Slam: 10 September 88")   90   95
674   $1.75, multicoloured (optd "Seoul Olympic
          Games Gold Medal Winner") . . . .   1·25   1·40
          Set of 4 . . . .   3·25   3·50
          First Day Cover . . . .   4·00

1988 (28 Oct). *Christmas. T 118 and similar vert designs showing details
from "The Adoration of the Shepherds" by Rubens. Multicoloured.
P 13½.*
675   60 c. Type **118**   40   45
676   80 c. Shepherds   55   60
677   $1.05, Virgin Mary   75   80
678   $1.30, Holy Child   90   95
          Set of 4 . . . .   2·40   2·50
          First Day Cover . . . .   3·00
MS679   83 × 103 mm. $7.20, The Nativity (38 × 49 mm).   5·00   5·50
          First Day Cover . . . .   6·50

119 Astronaut and "Apollo 11" Emblem

(Des G. Vasarhelyi)

1989 (20 July). *20th Anniv of First Manned Landing on Moon. T 119 and
similar horiz designs. Multicoloured. P 14.*
680   $1.50, Type **119** . . . .   1·10   1·25
          a. Horiz strip of 3. Nos. 680/2 . . . .   3·00
681   $1.50, Earth and Moon . . . .   1·10   1·25
682   $1.50, Astronaut and "Apollo 1" emblem . . . . . .   1·10   1·25
          Set of 3 . . . .   3·00   3·50
          First Day Cover . . . .   4·00

MS683   160 × 64 mm. As Nos. 680/2, but each stamp
          with a face value of $1.15. P 13 . . . .   2·50   2·75
          First Day Cover . . . .   3·50
Nos. 680/2 were printed together, *se-tenant*, in horizontal strips of 3
throughout the sheet.

STAMP BOOKLET

PRICE given is for a complete booklet.

1982 (June). *Royal Wedding. Multicoloured cover, 129 × 74 mm, showing Prince and Princess of Wales. Stitched.*
B1 $8.50, booklet containing Nos. 430/1 × 5 . . . .   15·00

OFFICIAL STAMPS

O.H.M.S.   O.H.M.S.

(O 1)   (O 2)

1985 (1 July)–**87**. *Nos. 408/10 optd with Type O 2 in gold and Nos. 527/42
optd with Type O 1 in blue, all by foil embossing.*
O 1   12 c. Type **92**   10   10
O 2   25 c. *Euphorbia pulcherrima*   15   20
O 3   30 c. *Cochlospermum hibiscoides*   20   25
O 4   35 c. *Begonia sp.*   25   30
O 5   40 c. *Plumeria sp.*   25   30
O 6   52 c. *Strelitzia reginae*   35   40
O 7   58 c. *Hibiscus syriacus*   35   40
O 8   70 c. *Tibouchina sp.*   45   50
O 9   83 c. *Nelumbo sp.*   55   60
O10 $1.05, *Hybrid hibiscus*   70   75
O11 $1.75, *Cassia fistula* . . . .   1·10   1·25
O12 $2.30, *Orchid var.* (29.11.85) . . . .   1·50   1·60
O13 $3.90, *Orchid sp.* (29.11.85) . . . .   2·50   2·75
O14 $4 *Euphorbia pulcherrima poinsettia* (1.4.86) .   2·75   3·00
O15 $5 *Euphorbia pulcherrima poinsettia* (1.4.86) .   3·25   3·50
O16 $6 *Hybrid hibiscus* (29.4.87) . . . .   4·00   4·25
O17 $6.60, *Hybrid hibiscus* (15.9.86) . . . .   4·25   4·50
O18 $8.30 *Hibiscus rosasinensis* (15.9.86) . . . .   5·50   5·75
O19 $10 *Scarlet hibiscus* (29.4.87) . . . .   6·00   6·25
          Set of 19 . . . .   30·00   32·00

Ross Dependency

1957 12 Pence = 1 Shilling
          20 Shillings = 1 Pound
1967 100 Cents = 1 New Zealand Dollar

A dependency of New Zealand in the Antarctic on the Ross Sea.

1 H.M.S. *Erebus*

2 Shackleton and Scott

3 Map of Ross Dependency and New Zealand

4 Queen Elizabeth II

(Des E. M. Taylor (3d.), L. C. Mitchell (4d.), R. Smith (8d.), J. Berry (1s. 6d.). Recess D.L.R.)

1957 (11 Jan). *W* **98** *of New Zealand (Mult* N Z *and Star*). *P* 13 (1s. 6d.) *or* 14 (*others*).

1	1	3d. indigo	2·50	75
2	2	4d. carmine-red	2·50	75
3	3	8d. bright carmine-red & ultram (*shades*) . . .	2·50	1·00
		Ea. Bright carmine-red and blue	6·50	4·00
4	4	1s. 6d. slate-purple	2·50	1·25
		Set of 4	9·00	3·25

(New Currency. 100 cents = 1 dollar)

5 H.M.S. *Erebus*

1967 (10 July). *Decimal currency. As Nos. 1/4 but with values inscr in decimal currency as T* **5**. *Chalky paper (except* 15 c.*). W* **98** *of New Zealand* (*sideways on* 7 c.). *P* 13 (15 c.) *or* 14 (*others*).

5	5	2 c. indigo (*shades*)	8·00	4·75
		Ea. Deep blue		
6	2	3 c. carmine-red	7·00	4·75
		Wi. Wmk inverted	75·00	
7	3	7 c. bright carmine-red and ultramarine	9·00	7·50
8	4	15 c. slate-purple	12·00	12·00
		Wi. Wmk inverted	75·00	
		Set of 4	32·00	26·00

6 Great Skua

7 Scott Base

(Des M. Cleverley. Litho B.W.)

1972 (18 Jan)-**79**. *Horiz design as T* **6** (3 *to* 8 c.) *or* **7** (10, 18 c.). *Ordinary paper. P* 14½ × 14 (10, 18 c.) *or* 13 (*others*).

9		3 c. black, brownish grey and pale blue	1·10	1·10
		a. Chalk-surfaced paper (2.79)	65	75
10		4 c. black, royal blue and violet	70	85
		a. Chalk-surfaced paper (2.79)	40	60
11		5 c. black, brownish grey and rose-lilac	70	85
		a. Chalk-surfaced paper (2.79)	30	60
12		8 c. black, yellow-brown and brownish grey . . .	70	1·00
		a. Chalk-surfaced paper (2.79)	40	70
13		10 c. black, turquoise-green and slate-green	1·00	1·50
		a. Perf 13½ × 13. Chalk-surfaced paper (2.79) .	40	80
		Eab. Black printed double	†	20·00
14		18 c. black, violet and bright violet	2·25	2·50
		a. Perf 13½ × 13. Chalk-surfaced paper (2.79) .	50	1·25
		Set of 6	5·75	7·00
		Set of 6 (Nos. 9a/14a)	2·40	4·25
		First Day Cover		8·50

Designs:—4 c. "Hercules" aeroplane at Williams Field; 5 c. Shackleton's Hut; 8 c. Supply ship H.M.N.Z.S. *Endeavour*; 18 c. Tabular ice floe.

Ross Dependency   5ᶜ

8 Adelie Penguins

(Des R. Conly. Litho Asher and Co, Melbourne)

1982 (20 Jan). *Horiz designs as T* **8**. *Multicoloured. P* 15½.

15	5	5 c. Type **8**	15	10
16		10 c. Tracked vehicles	10	10
17		20 c. Scott Base	15	20
18		30 c. Field party	25	30
19		40 c. Vanda Station	30	30
20		50 c. Scott's hut, Cape Evans	30	35
		Set of 6	1·10	1·25
		Presentation Pack	2·00	
		First Day Cover		2·00

The post office at Scott Base closed on 30 September 1987 and Nos. 15/20 were withdrawn from sale at philatelic counters in New Zealand on 31 December 1987.

Tokelau

1948 12 Pence = 1 Shilling
20 Shillings = 1 Pound
1967 100 Cents (or sene) = 1 New Zealand Dollar

Three islands N. of Samoa, previously known as the Union Islands. Formerly part of the Gilbert and Ellice Islands, they were declared part of New Zealand as from 1 January 1949.

PRICES
George VI issues (1937–1952)

First column = Unmounted Mint
Second column = Mounted Mint
Third column = Used

1 Atafu Village and Map

2 Nukunonu Hut and Map

3 Fakaofo Village and Map

(Des J. Berry from photographs by T. T. C. Humphrey. Recess B.W.)

1948 (22 June). *W* **98** *of New Zealand* (*Mult N* Z *and Star*). P 13½.
1	1	½d. red-brown and purple	15	10	25
2	2	1d. chestnut and green	20	10	25
		Wi. Wmk inverted	£275	£170	
3	3	2d. green and ultramarine	25	10	30
		Set of 3	55	25	70

PRICES
Elizabeth II issues (from 1953)

First column = Unmounted Mint
Second column = Used

1953 (15 June*). *Coronation. As No. 715 of New Zealand, but inscr* "TOKELAU ISLANDS".
4		3d. brown	3·50	3·75
		First Day Cover		8·00

* This is the date of issue in Tokelau. The stamps were released in New Zealand on 25 May.

THE WORLD CENTRE FOR FINE STAMPS IS 399 STRAND

ONE SHILLING

6D

TOKELAU
ISLANDS

    (4)   (5)

1956 (27 Mar). *No. 1 surch with T* **4** *by Govt Printer, Wellington.*
5	1	1s. on ½d. red-brown and purple	4·00	3·50

1966 (8 Nov.). *Postal fiscal stamps of New Zealand (Type F* **6**), *but without value, surch as T* **5** *by Govt Printer, Wellington. W* **98** *of New Zealand. P* 14.
6		6d. light blue	65	1·00
7		8d. light emerald	75	1·00
8		2s. light pink	85	1·40
		Set of 3	2·00	3·00

(New Currency. 100 cents = 1 dollar (New Zealand))

5c

   **1**c   TOKELAU
ISLANDS

    (6)   (7)

1967 (4 Sept*). *Decimal currency.*

(a) *Nos.* 1/3 *surch in decimal currency as T* **6** *by Govt Printer, Wellington*
9	2	1 c. on 1d.	60	60
10	3	2 c. on 2d.	1·00	1·00
11	1	10 c. on ½d.	2·00	2·00

(b) *Postal Fiscal stamps of New Zealand (Type F* **6**), *but without value, surch as T* **7** *by Govt Printer, Wellington. W* **98** *of New Zealand* (*sideways*). P 14 (*line*)
12	F **6**	3 c. reddish lilac	50	30
		Ea. Comb perf	80	60
13		5 c. light blue	50	30
		Ea. Comb perf	80	60
14		7 c. light emerald	50	30
		Ea. Comb perf	90	60
15		20 c. light pink	65	40
		Ea. Comb perf	1·50	1·25
		Set of 7	5·25	4·50

* This is the date of issue in Tokelau. The stamps were released in New Zealand on 10 July.
The line perf measures 14 × 13.9 and the comb perf is 14 × 13.8.

8 British Protectorate   12 H.M.S. *Dolphin*, 1765
(1877)

(Des New Zealand P.O. artists from suggestions by Tokelau Administration.
Litho B.W.)

1969 (8 Aug). *History of Tokelau. T **8** and similar horiz designs.
W **98** of New Zealand. P* 13 × 12½.

16	5 c.	ultramarine, yellow and black	25	15
17	10 c.	vermilion, yellow and black	30	15
18	15 c.	green, yellow and black	35	15
19	20 c.	yellow-brown, yellow and black	40	20
		Set of 4	1·10	60
		First Day Cover		1·50

Designs:— 10 c. Annexed to Gilbert and Ellice Islands, 1916; 15 c. New
Zealand Administration, 1925; 20 c. New Zealand Territory, 1948.

1969 (1 Oct). *Christmas. As T **301** of New Zealand, but inscr* "TOKELAU
ISLANDS". *W **98** of New Zealand. P* 13½ × 14½.

20	2 c.	multicoloured	10	15
		First Day Cover		50

1970 (1 Oct). *Christmas. As T **314** of New Zealand but inscr* "TOKELAU
ISLANDS". *P* 12½.

21	2 c.	multicoloured	10	20
		First Day Cover		50

(Des D. B. Stevenson. Litho B.W.)

1970 (9 Dec). *Discovery of Tokelau. T **12** and similar multicoloured
designs. P* 13½.

22	5 c.	Type **12**	1·50	45
23	10 c.	H.M.S. Pandora, 1791	1·50	45
24	25 c.	General Jackson, 1835 (horiz)	3·25	80
		Set of 3	5·75	1·50
		First Day Cover		3·50

13 Fan   14 Windmill Pump

(Des Enid Hunter. Litho Harrison)

1971 (20 Oct). *Various horiz designs as T **13** showing handicrafts.
Multicoloured. P* 14.

25	1 c.	Type **13**	20	20
26	2 c.	Hand-bag	30	30
27	3 c.	Basket	40	40
28	5 c.	Hand-bag	50	65
29	10 c.	Shopping-bag	60	80
30	15 c.	Fishing box	1·00	1·50
31	20 c.	Canoe	1·25	2·00
32	25 c.	Fishing hooks	1·25	2·00
		Set of 8	5·00	7·00
		First Day Cover		8·00

(Des A. G. Mitchell. Litho Questa)

1972 (6 Sept). *25th Anniversary of South Pacific Commission. T **14** and
similar vert designs. Multicoloured. P* 14 × 13½.

33	5 c.	Type **14**	35	50
34	10 c.	Community well	45	65
35	15 c.	Pest eradication	55	90
36	20 c.	Flags of member nations	60	1·00
		Set of 4	1·75	2·75
		First Day Cover		3·25

On No. 35 "PACIFIC" is spelt "PACFIC".

MINIMUM PRICE

The minimum price quoted is 5p which represents a handling charge rather than a basis for
valuing common stamps. For further notes
about prices see introductory pages.

15 Horny Coral   16 Hump-back Cowrie

(Des Eileen Mayo. Litho B.W.)

1973 (12 Sept). *Coral. T **15** and similar vert designs. Multicoloured. P* 13.

37	3 c.	Type **15**	1·00	80
38	5 c.	Soft Coral	1·00	90
39	15 c.	Mushroom Coral	1·75	1·50
40	25 c.	Staghorn Coral	2·00	1·75
		Set of 4	5·25	4·50
		First Day Cover		6·00

(Des G. F. Fuller. Litho Questa)

1974 (13 Nov). *"Shells of the Coral Reef". T **16** and similar horiz designs.
Multicoloured. P* 14.

41	3 c.	Type **16**	1·50	1·00
42	5 c.	Tiger Cowrie	1·75	1·00
43	15 c.	Mole Cowrie	3·00	2·50
44	25 c.	Eyed Cowrie	4·00	3·00
		Set of 4	9·00	6·75
		First Day Cover		7·50

17 Moorish Idol   18 Canoe Building

(Des Eileen Mayo. Litho Questa)

1975 (19 Nov). *Fishes. T **17** and similar vert designs. Multicoloured.
P* 14.

45	5 c.	Type **17**	50	75
46	10 c.	Long-nosed Butterfly-fish	70	1·00
47	15 c.	Lined Butterfly-fish	85	1·50
48	25 c.	Red Fire-fish	1·10	1·75
		Set of 4	2·75	4·50
		First Day Cover		5·00

(Des F. Paulo. Litho Questa)

1976 (27 Oct)–**81**. *T **18** and similar multicoloured designs showing local
life. P* 14 × 13½ *(9 c. to* $1*) or* 13½ × 14 *(others).*

49	1 c.	Type **18**	15	30
		a. Perf 14½ × 15 (15.7.81)	10	15
50	2 c.	Reef fishing	20	40
51	3 c.	Weaving preparation	25	25
		a. Perf 14½ × 15 (15.7.81)	10	15
52	5 c.	Umu (kitchen)	30	45
		a. Perf 14½ × 15 (15.7.81)	10	15
53	9 c.	Carving (vert)	10	25
		a. Perf 15 × 14½ (15.7.81)	10	15
54	20 c.	Husking coconuts (vert)	15	40
		a. Perf 15 × 14½ (15.7.81)	15	20
55	50 c.	Wash day (vert)	20	70
		a. Perf 15 × 14½ (15.7.81)	20	20
56	$1	Meal time (vert)	35	1·00
		a. Perf 15 × 14½ (15.7.81)	30	30
		Set of 8	1·10	1·50
		First Day Cover		2·00

19 White Tern   **20** Westminster Abbey

(Des F. Paulo. Litho Questa)

1977 (16 Nov). *Birds of Tokelau. T* **19** *and similar horiz designs. Multicoloured. P* 14½.

57	8 c. Type **19**	30	40
58	10 c. Turnstone	35	45
59	15 c. White-capped Noddy	60	70
60	30 c. Common Noddy	90	1·25
	Set of 4	2·00	2·50
	First Day Cover		3·50

(Des Eileen Mayo. Litho Questa)

1978 (28 June). *25th Anniv of Coronation. T* **20** *and similar vert designs. Multicoloured. P* 14.

61	8 c. Type **20**	20	20
62	10 c. King Edward's Chair	20	20
63	15 c. Coronation regalia	20	35
64	30 c. Queen Elizabeth II	50	60
	Set of 4	1·10	1·25
	First Day Cover		1·60

21 Canoe Race   **22** Rugby

(Des F. Paulo. Photo Heraclio Fournier)

1978 (8 Nov). *Canoe Racing. T* **21** *and similar horiz designs showing races. P* 13½ × 14.

65	8 c. multicoloured	25	25
66	12 c. multicoloured	30	30
67	15 c. multicoloured	45	45
68	30 c. multicoloured	55	55
	Set of 4	1·40	1·40
	First Day Cover		2·00

(Des F. Paulo. Photo Heraclio Fournier)

1979 (7 Nov). *Sports. T* **22** *and similar horiz designs. Multicoloured. P* 13½.

69	10 c. Type **22**	15	15
70	15 c. Cricket	40	50
71	20 c. Rugby (*different*)	40	55
72	30 c. Cricket (*different*)	60	70
	Set of 4	1·40	1·75
	First Day Cover		2·25

23 Surfing   **24** Pole Vaulting

(Des F. Paulo. Litho J.W.)

1980 (5 Nov). *Water Sports. T* **23** *and similar horiz designs. Multicoloured. P* 13.

73	10 c. Type **23**	10	10
74	20 c. Surfing (*different*)	12	15
75	30 c. Swimming	20	25
76	50 c. Swimming (*different*)	25	35
	Set of 4	60	75
	First Day Cover		1·25

(Des F. Paulo. Photo Heraclio Fournier)

1981 (4 Nov). *Sports. T* **24** *and similar vert designs. Multicoloured. P* 14 × 13½.

77	10 c. Type **24**	10	10
78	20 c. Volleyball	20	20
79	30 c. Running	25	30
80	50 c. Volleyball (*different*)	30	35
	Set of 4	75	85
	First Day Cover		1·50

25 Wood Carving   **26** Octopus Lure

(Des R. Conly. Litho Enschedé)

1982 (5 May). *Handicrafts. T* **25** *and similar vert designs. Multicoloured. P* 14 × 13½.

81	10 s. Type **25**	10	10
82	22 s. Bow-drilling sea shell	15	25
83	34 s. Bowl finishing	20	35
84	60 s. Basket weaving	35	50
	Set of 4	70	1·10
	First Day Cover		1·60

(Des R. Conly. Litho Questa)

1982 (3 Nov). *Fishing Methods. T* **26** *and similar vert designs. Multicoloured. P* 14.

85	5 s. Type **26**	10	10
86	18 s. Multiple-hook fishing	30	20
87	23 s. Ruvettus fishing	35	25
88	34 s. Netting flying fish	40	30
89	63 s. Noose fishing	50	40
90	75 s. Bonito fishing	60	45
	Set of 6	2·00	1·50
	First Day Cover		2·25

27 Outrigger Canoe   **28** Javelin Throwing

(Des R. Conly. Litho Cambec Press, Melbourne)

1983 (4 May). *Transport. T* **27** *and similar horiz designs. Multicoloured. P* 13 × 13½.

91	5 s. Type **27**	10	10
92	18 s. Wooden whaleboat	15	15
93	23 s. Aluminium whaleboat	15	20
94	34 s. *Alia* (fishing catamaran)	25	25
95	63 s. M.V. *Frysna* (freighter)	35	40
96	75 s. McKinnon "Goose" flying boat	45	50
	Set of 6	1·25	1·40
	First Day Cover		2·00

(Des R. Conly. Litho Questa)

1983 (2 Nov). *Traditional Pastimes. T* **28** *and similar horiz designs. Multicoloured. P* 14.

97	5 s. Type **28**	10	10
98	18 s. String game	15	15
99	23 s. Fire making	15	20
100	34 s. Shell throwing	25	25
101	63 s. Hand-ball game	35	40
102	75 s. Mass wrestling	45	50
	Set of 6	1·25	1·40
	First Day Cover		2·00

29 Planting and Harvesting   **30** Convict Tang ("Manini")

(Des R. Conly. Litho J.W.)

1984 (2 May). *Copra Industry. T* **29** *and similar vert designs. Multicoloured. P* 13½ × 13.

103	48 s. Type **29**	40	45
	a. Horiz strip of 5. Nos. 103/7	1·90	
104	48 s. Husking and splitting	40	45
105	48 s. Drying	40	45
106	48 s. Bagging	40	45
107	48 s. Shipping	40	45
	Set of 5	1·90	2·00
	First Day Cover		2·50

Nos. 103/7 were printed together, *se-tenant*, in horizontal strips of 5 throughout the sheet.

(Des R. Conly. Litho B.D.T.)

1984 (5 Dec). *Fishes. T* **30** *and similar horiz designs. Multicoloured. P* 15 × 14.

108	1 s. Type **30**	5	5
109	2 s. Flying Fish ("Hahave")	5	5
110	5 s. Fire Wrasse ("Uloulo")	5	5
111	9 s. Unicorn Fish ("Ume ihu")	5	5
112	23 s. Napoleon Fish ("Lafilafi")	15	20
113	34 s. Red Snapper ("Fagamea")	20	25
114	50 s. Yellow Fin Tuna ("Kakahi")	30	35
115	75 s. Castor-oil Fish ("Palu po")	50	55
116	$1 Grey Shark ("Mokoha")	65	70
117	$2 Black Marlin ("Hakula")	1·40	1·50
	Set of 10	3·00	3·50
	First Day Cover		4·50

Examples of Nos. 108/17 are known postmarked at Nukunonu on 23 November 1984.

The 50 s., No. 114, was sold at the "STAMPEX 86" Stamp Exhibition, Adelaide, overprinted "STAMPEX 86 4–10 AUGUST 1986" in three lines. These overprinted stamps were not available from post offices in Tokelau. Used examples came from dealers' stocks subsequently sent to the islands for cancellation.

31 *Ficus tinctoria* ("Mati")   **32** Administration Centre, Atafu

(Des R. Conly. Litho Wyatt and Wilson Ltd., Christchurch, N.Z.)

1985 (26 June). *Native Trees. T* **31** *and similar vert designs. Multicoloured. P* 13.

118	5 c. Type **31**	5	5
119	18 c. *Morinda citrifolia* ("Nonu")	15	15
120	32 c. Breadfruit Tree ("Ulu")	20	25
121	48 c. *Pandanus tectorius* ("Fala")	35	40
122	60 c. *Cordia subcordata* ("Kanava")	40	45
123	75 c. Coconut Palm ("Niu")	50	55
	Set of 6	1·50	1·60
	First Day Cover		2·25

Nos. 118·23 were issued with matt, almost invisible PVA gum.

(Des R. Conly. Litho Questa)

1985 (4 Dec). *Tokelau Architecture. Public Buildings. T* **32** *and similar horiz designs. Multicoloured. P* 14.

124	5 c. Type **32**	5	5
125	18 c. Administration Centre, Nukunonu	15	15
	Ea. Black (design caption, etc.) printed double	†	—
126	32 c. Administration Centre, Fakaofo	20	25
127	48 c. Congregational Church, Atafu	35	40
128	60 c. Catholic Church, Nukunonu	40	45
129	75 c. Congregational Church, Fakaofo	50	55
	Set of 6	1·50	1·60
	First Day Cover		2·40

33 Atafu Hospital

(Des R. Conly. Litho Cambec Press, Melbourne)

1986 (7 May). *Tokelau Architecture (2nd series). Hospitals and Schools. T* **33** *and similar horiz designs. Multicoloured. P* 13½.

130	5 c. Type **33**	5	5
131	18 c. St. Joseph's Hospital, Nukunonu	10	10
132	32 c. Fenuafala Hospital, Fakaofo	20	25
133	48 c. Matauala School, Atafu	35	40
134	60 c. Matiti School, Nukunonu	40	45
135	75 c. Fenuafala School, Fakaofo	55	60
	Set of 6	1·50	1·60
	First Day Cover		2·25

34 Coconut Crab   **35** *Scaevola taccada* ("Gahu")

(Des R. Conly. Litho Questa)

1986 (3 Dec). *Agricultural Livestock. T* **34** *and similar horiz designs. Multicoloured. P* 14.

136	5 c. Type **34**	5	5
137	18 c. Pigs	15	15
138	32 c. Chickens	20	25
139	48 c. Reef Hawkesbill Turtle	35	40
140	60 c. Goats	40	45
141	75 c. Ducks	55	60
	Set of 6	1·50	1·75
	First Day Cover		2·40

(Des R. Conly. Litho Questa)

1987 (6 May). *Tokelau Flora. T* **35** *and similar horiz designs. Multicoloured. P* 14.

142	5 c. Type **35**	10	5
143	18 c. *Hernandia nymphaeifolia* ("Puka")	15	15
144	32 c. *Pandanus tectorius* ("Higano")	25	25
145	48 c. *Gardenia taitensis* ("Tialetiale")	40	40
146	60 c. *Pemphis acidula* ("Gagie")	45	45
147	75 c. *Guettarda speciosa* ("Puapua")	55	55
	Set of 6	1·75	1·60
	First Day Cover		2·40

36 Javelin-throwing

(Des F. Paulo. Litho Leigh-Mardon Ltd, Melbourne)

1987 (2 Dec). *Tokelau Olympic Sports. T* **36** *and similar horiz designs.*
Multicoloured. P 14 × 14½.

148	5 c. Type **36**	5	5
149	18 c. Shot-putting	15	15
150	32 c. Long jumping	20	25
151	48 c. Hurdling	35	40
152	60 c. Sprinting	40	45
153	75 c. Wrestling	50	55
	Set of 6	1·50	1·60
	First Day Cover		2·40

37 Small Boat Flotilla in
Sydney Harbour

38 Island Maps and
Ministerial
Representatives

(Des and litho CPE Australia Ltd, Melbourne)

1988 (30 July). *Bicentenary of Australian Settlement and "Sydpex '88"*
National Stamp Exhibition, Sydney. T **37** *and similar square designs.*
Multicoloured. P 13.

154	50 c. Type **37**	35	40
	a. Horiz strip of 5. Nos. 154/8	1·60	
155	50 c. Sailing ships and liners	35	40
156	50 c. Sydney skyline and Opera House	35	40
157	50 c. Sydney Harbour Bridge	35	40
158	50 c. Sydney waterfront	35	40
	Set of 5	1·60	1·75
	First Day Cover		2·50

Nos. 154/8 were printed together, *se-tenant*, in horizontal strips of five
throughout the sheet, forming a composite aerial view of the re-enact-
ment of First Fleet's arrival.

(Des F. Paulo. Litho Leigh-Mardon Ltd, Melbourne)

1988 (10 Aug). *Political Development. T* **38** *and similar horiz designs.*
Multicoloured. P 14½.

159	5 c. Type **38** (administration transferred to N.Z. Foreign Affairs Ministry, 1975)	5	5
160	18 c. General Fono (island assembly) meeting, 1977	15	15

161	32 c. Arms of New Zealand (first visit by New Zealand Prime Minister, 1985)	20	25
162	48 c. U.N. logo (first visit by U.N. representative, 1976)	35	40
163	60 c. Canoe and U.N. logo (first Tokelau delega-tion to U.N., 1987)	40	45
164	75 c. Secretary and N.Z. flag (first islander appoin-ted as Official Secretary, 1987)	50	55
	Set of 6	1·50	1·60
	First Day Cover		2·40

39 Three Wise Men in
Canoe and Star

(Des F. Paulo. Litho Govt Ptg Office, Wellington)

1988 (7 Dec). *Christmas. T* **39** *and similar horiz designs showing*
Christmas in Tokelau. Multicoloured. P 13½.

165	5 c. Type **39**	5	5
166	20 c. Tokelau Nativity	15	20
167	40 c. Flight to Egypt by canoe	30	35
168	60 c. Children's presents	40	45
169	70 c. Christ child in Tokelauan basket	50	55
170	$1 Christmas parade	70	75
	Set of 6	1·90	2·10
	First Day Cover		2·50

40 Launching Outrigger Canoe

(Des F. Paulo. Litho Leigh-Mardon Ltd, Melbourne)

1989 (28 June). *Food Gathering. T* **40** *and similar horiz designs. Multi-*
coloured. P 14 × 14½.

171	50 c. Type **40**	35	40
	a. Horiz strip of 3. Nos. 171/3	1·00	
172	50 c. Paddling canoe away from shore	35	40
173	50 c. Fishing punt and sailing canoe	35	40
174	50 c. Canoe on beach	35	40
	a. Horiz strip of 3. Nos. 174/6	1·00	
175	50 c. Loading coconuts into canoe	35	40
176	50 c. Tokelauans with produce	35	40
	Set of 6	1·90	2·10
	First Day Cover		2·50

Nos. 171/3 and 174/6 were each printed together, *se-tenant*, in horizontal strips of three throughout the sheets, forming composite designs.

ALBUM
LISTS

Please write for our latest lists of albums and accessories.
These will be sent free on request.

Western Samoa

12 Pence   = 1 Shilling
20 Shillings = 1 Pound

PRICES
Victoria to George V issues (1877–1937)

First column = Mounted Mint
Second column = Used

INDEPENDENT KINGDOM OF SAMOA

The first postal service in Samoa was organised by C. L. Griffiths, who had earlier run the *Fiji Times* Express post in Suva. In both instances the principal purpose of the service was the distribution of newspapers of which Griffiths was the proprietor. The first issue of the *Samoa Times* (later the *Samoa Times and South Sea Gazette*) appeared on 6 October 1877 and the newspaper continued in weekly publication until 27 August 1881.

Mail from the Samoa Express post to addresses overseas was routed via New South Wales, New Zealand or U.S.A. and received additional franking with stamps of the receiving country on landing.

Cancellations, inscribed "APIA SAMOA", did not arrive until March 1878 so that examples of Nos. 1/9 used before that date were cancelled in manuscript.

1

(Des H. H. Glover. Litho S. T. Leigh & Co, Sydney, N.S.W.)

1877 (1 Oct)-**80**.

A. *1st state: line above "X" in "EXPRESS" not broken. P 12½*
1	1	1d. ultramarine	£200	85·00
2		3d. deep scarlet	£225	85·00
3		6d. bright violet	£200	85·00
		a. *Pale lilac*	£250	85·00

B. *2nd state: line above "X" broken, and dot between top of "M" and "O" of "SAMOA". P 12½* (1878–79)
4	1	1d. ultramarine	80·00	75·00
5		3d. bright scarlet	£200	85·00
6		6d. bright violet	£130	75·00
7		1s. dull yellow	£120	75·00
		a. Line above "X" not broken	£100	80·00
		b. Perf 12 (1879)	60·00	75·00
		c. *Orange-yellow*	75·00	80·00
8		2s. red-brown	£200	£140
		a. *Chocolate*	£200	£275
9		5s. green	£700	£950

C. *3rd state: line above "X" repaired, dot merged with upper right serif of "M" (1879). (a) P 12½*
10	1	1d. ultramarine	75·00	65·00
11		3d. vermilion	85·00	80·00
12		6d. lilac	90·00	75·00
13		2s. brown	£150	£120
		a. *Chocolate*	£150	£120
14		5s. green	£400	£500
		a. Line above "X" not repaired	£450	

(b) P 12
15	1	1d. blue	20·00	30·00
		a. *Deep blue*	28·00	60·00
		b. *Ultramarine*	24·00	30·00
16		3d. vermilion	35·00	50·00
		a. *Carmine-vermilion*	35·00	60·00
17		6d. bright violet	35·00	38·00
		a. *Deep violet*	35·00	70·00
18		2s. deep brown	£100	£140
19		5s. yellow-green	£375	£500
		a. *Deep green*	£350	£450
		b. Line above "X" not repaired	£400	

D. *4th state: spot of colour under middle stroke of "M". P 12* (1880)
20	1	9d. orange-brown	40·00	80·00

Originals exist imperf, but are not known used in this state.

On sheets of the 1d., 1st state, at least eight stamps have a stop after "PENNY". In the 2nd state, three stamps have the stop, and in the 3rd state, only one.

In the 1st state, all the stamps, 1d., 3d. and 6d., were in sheets of 20 (5 × 4) and also the 1d. in the 3rd state.

All values in the 2nd state, all values except the 1d. in the 3rd state and No. 20 were in sheets of 10 (5 × 2).

As all sheets of all printings of the originals were imperf at the outer edges, the only stamps which can have perforations on all four sides are Nos. 1 to 3*a*, 10 and 15 to 15*b*, all other originals being imperf on one or two sides.

The perf 12 stamps, which gauge 11.8, are generally very rough but later the machine was repaired and the 1d., 3d. and 6d. are known with clean-cut perforations.

Remainders of the 1d., unissued 2d. rose, 6d. (in sheets of 21 (7 × 3), 3d., 9d., 1s. (in sheets of 12 (4 × 3) and of the 2s. and 5s. (sheet format unknown) were found in the Samoa post office when the service closed down in 1881. The remainders are rare in complete sheets, but of very little value as singles, compared with the originals.

Reprints of all values, in sheets of 40 (8 × 5), were made after the originals had been withdrawn from sale. These are practically worthless.

The majority of both reprints and remainders are in the 4th state as the 9d. with the spot of colour under the middle stroke of the "M", but a few stamps (both remainders and reprints) do not show this, while on some it is very faint.

There are three known types of forgery, one of which is rather dangerous, the others being crude.

The last mail despatch organised by the proprietors of the Samoa Express took place on 31 August 1881, although one cover is recorded postmarked 24 September 1881.

After the withdrawal of the Samoa Express service it would appear that the Apia municipality appointed a postmaster to continue the overseas post. Covers are known franked with U.S.A. or New Zealand stamps in Samoa, or routed via Fiji.

In December 1886 the municipal postmaster, John Davis, was appointed Postmaster of the Kingdom of Samoa by King Malietoa. Overseas mail sent via New Zealand was subsequently accepted without the addition of New Zealand stamps, although letters to the U.S.A. continued to require such franking until August 1891.

2 Palm Trees

3 King Malietoa Laupepa

(Des A. E. Cousins (T **3**). Dies eng W. R. Bock and A. E. Cousins (T **2**) or A. E. Cousins (T **3**). Typo Govt Ptg Office, Wellington)

1886–1900.   (i) *W* **12***a of New Zealand.* (*a*) *P* 12½ (Oct–Nov 1886).

21	**2**	½d. purple-brown	15·00	22·00
22		1d. yellow-green	5·50	12·00
23		2d. dull orange	7·50	7·50
24		4d. blue	14·00	8·50
25		1s. rose-carmine	45·00	7·50
		a. Bisected (2½d.) (on cover)*	†	£250
26		2s. 6d. reddish lilac	48·00	38·00

(*b*) *P* 12 × 11½ (July–Nov 1887)

27	**2**	½d. purple-brown	80·00	80·00
28		1d. yellow-green	95·00	27·00
29		2d. yellow	75·00	£140
30		4d. blue	£200	£175
31		6d. brown-lake	18·00	8·00
32		1s. rose-carmine	—	£120
33		2s. 6d. reddish lilac		£190

(ii) *W* **12***c of New Zealand. P* 12 × 11½ (May 1890)

34	**2**	½d. purple-brown	70·00	30·00
35		1d. green	40·00	27·00
36		2d. brown-orange	60·00	25·00
37		4d. blue	£100	5·00
38		6d. brown-lake	£175	11·00
39		1s. rose-carmine	—	13·00
40		2s. 6d. reddish lilac		8·50

(iii) *W* **12***b of New Zealand.* (*a*) *P* 12 × 11½ (1890–92)

41	**2**	½d. pale purple-brown	1·25	2·50
		a. Blackish purple	1·25	2·50
42		1d. myrtle-green (5.90)	8·50	1·40
		a. Green	8·50	1·40
		b. Yellow-green	8·50	1·40
43		2d. dull orange (5.90)	10·00	1·75
44	**3**	2½d. rose (11.92)	75·00	3·50
		a. Pale rose	75·00	3·50
45	**2**	4d. blue	£175	10·00
46		6d. brown-lake	£100	8·00
47		1s. rose-carmine	£175	4·00
48		2s. 6d. slate-lilac	—	5·00

(*b*) *P* 12½ (Mar 1891–92)

49	**2**	½d. purple-brown		
50		1d. green		
51		2d. orange-yellow	—	80·00
52	**3**	2½d. rose (1.92)	15·00	4·50
53	**2**	4d. blue	—	£350
54		6d. brown-purple	£1500	£600
55		1s. rose-carmine	—	£300
56		2s. 6d. slate-lilac		

(*c*) *P* 11 (May 1895–1900)

57	**2**	½d. purple-brown	75	1·75
		a. Deep purple-brown	65	1·75
		b. Blackish purple (1900)	65	35·00
58		1d. green	1·25	1·75
		a. Bluish green (1897)	1·25	1·75
		b. Deep green (1900)	1·25	22·00
59		2d. pale yellow	32·00	35·00
		a. Orange (1896)	32·00	35·00
		b. Bright yellow (1.97)	5·50	4·00
		c. Pale ochre (10.97)	4·50	1·00
		d. Dull orange (1900)	5·50	
60	**3**	2½d. rose	70	4·50
		a. Deep rose-carmine (1900)	1·10	42·00
61	**2**	4d. blue	5·75	2·00
		a. Deep blue (1900)	60	50·00
62		6d. brown-lake	5·50	4·00
		a. Brown-purple (1900)	1·75	60·00
63		1s. rose	5·50	4·50
		a. Dull rose-carmine/toned (5.98)	2·00	35·00
		b. Carmine (1900)	1·25	
64		2s. 6d. purple	55·00	9·50
		a. Reddish lilac (wmk inverted) (1897)	7·50	7·50
		b. Deep purple/toned (wmk reversed) (5.98)	4·75	9·50
		ba. Imperf between (vert pair)	£500	
		c. Slate-violet	£120	

*Following a fire on 1 April 1895 which destroyed stocks of all stamps except the 1s. value perf 12½, this was bisected diagonally and used as a 2½d. stamp for overseas letters between April and May 1895, and was cancelled in blue. Fresh supplies of the 2½d. did not arrive until July 1895, although other values were available from 23 May.

Examples of the 1s. rose perforated 11, No. 63, were subsequently bisected and supplied cancelled-to-order by the post office to collectors, often with backdated cancellations. Most of these examples were bisected vertically and all were cancelled in black (*Price* £7).

The dates given relate to the earliest dates of printing in the various watermarks and perforations and not to issue dates.

The perf 11 issues (including those later surcharged or overprinted), are very unevenly perforated owing to the large size of the pins. Evenly perforated copies are extremely hard to find.

For the 2½d. black, see Nos. 81/2 and for the ½d. green and 1d. red-brown, see Nos. 88/9.

FIVE PENCE	FIVE PENCE	5d
(5)	(6)	(7)

1893 (Nov–Dec).   *Handstamped singly, at Apia.*

(*a*) *In two operations*

65	**5**	5d. on 4d. blue (37)	40·00	38·00
		a. Bars omitted	—	£350
66		5d. on 4d. blue (45)	60·00	£100
67	**6**	5d. on 4d. blue (37)	85·00	£110
68		5d. on 4d. blue (45)	90·00	

(*b*) *In three operations* (Dec)

69	**7**	5d. on 4d. blue (37) (R.)	12·00	17·00
		a. Stop after "d"	£250	55·00
		b. Bars omitted		
70		5d. on 4d. blue (45) (R.)	12·00	40·00

In Types **5** and **6** the bars obliterating the original value vary in length from 13½ to 16½ mm and can occur with either the thick bar over the thin one or vice versa.

Double handstamps exist but we do not list them.

No. 69a came from a separate handstamp which applied the "5d." at one operation. Where the "d" was applied separately its position in relation to the "5" naturally varies.

	Surcharged	R
★ ♛ SAMOA POST FIVE **5** PENCE	1½d.	3d.
8	(9)	(10)

The "R" in Type **10** indicates use for registration fee.

(Des and die eng A. E. Cousins. Typo New Zealand Govt Ptg Office)

1894–1900.   *W* **12***b of New Zealand* (*sideways*). (*a*) *P* 11½ × 12.

71	**8**	5d. dull vermilion (3.94)	12·00	2·75
		a. Deep red	12·00	3·50

(*b*) *P* 11

72	**8**	5d. dull red (1895)	10·00	6·50
		a. Deep red (1900)	1·25	13·00

1895–1900.   *W* **12***b of New Zealand.*

(i) *Handstamped with T* **9** *or* **10.** (a) *P* 12 × 11½ (26.1.95)

73	**2**	1½d. on 2d. dull orange (B.)	5·00	5·00
74		3d. on 2d. dull orange	14·00	8·00

(*b*) *P* 11 (6.95)

75	**2**	1½d. on 2d. orange (B.)	1·50	2·50
		a. Pair, one without handstamp		
		b. On 2d. yellow	75·00	60·00
76		3d. on 2d. orange	5·00	7·50
		a. On 2d. yellow	75·00	60·00

(ii) *Surch printed*. P* 11

77	**2**	1½d. on 2d. orange-yellow (B.)	

(iii) *Handstamped as T* **9** *or* **10.†** *P* 11 (1896)

78	**2**	1½d. on 2d. orange-yellow (B.)	2·50	20·00
79		3d. on 2d. orange-yellow	3·00	45·00
		a. Imperf between (vert pair)	£400	
		b. Pair, one without handstamp		

(iv) *Surch typo as T* **10.** *P* 11 (Feb 1900)

80	**2**	3d. on 2d. deep red-orange (G.)	1·50	£130

*It is believed that this was type-set from which clichés were made and set up in a forme and then printed on a hand press. This would account for the clear indentation on the back of the stamp and the variation in the position on the stamps which probably resulted from the clichés becoming loose in the forme.

†In No. 78 the "2" has a serif and the handstamp is in pale greenish blue instead of deep blue. In No. 79 the "R" is slightly narrower. In both instances the stamp is in a different shade.

A special printing in a distinctly different colour was made for No. 80 and the surcharge is in green.

Most of the handstamps exist double.

1896 (Aug).　*Printed in the wrong colour. W* **12***b of New Zealand.*

(a) P 10 × 11

81	3	2½d. black	90	3·00

(b) P 11

82	3	2½d. black	75·00	75·00
		a. Mixed perfs 10 and 11	£350	

Surcharged

2½d.
(11)

PROVISIONAL

GOVT.
(12)

1898–99. *W* **12***b of New Zealand. P* 11. *(a) Handstamped as T* **11** (10.98).

83	2	2½d. on 1s. dull rose-carmine/*toned*	16·00	25·00

(b) Surch as T **11** (1899)

84	2	2½d. on 1d. bluish green (R.)	55	2·00
		a. Surch inverted	—	£350
85		2½d. on 1s. dull rose-carmine/*toned* (R.)	3·50	8·00
		a. Surch double	£350	
86		2½d. on 1s dull rose-carmine/*toned* (Blk.)	3·50	8·00
		a. Surch double	£350	
87		2½d. on 2s. 6d. deep purple/*toned*	4·75	11·00

The typographed surcharge was applied in a setting of nine, giving seven types differing in the angle and length of the fractional line, the type of stop, etc.

1899.　*Colours changed. W* **12***b of New Zealand. P* 11.

88	2	½d. dull blue-green	65	1·40
		a. *Deep green*	65	1·40
89		1d. deep red-brown	55	1·25

1899–1900.　*Provisional Government. New printings optd with T* **12** *(longer words and shorter letters on* 5d.*). W* **12***b of New Zealand. P* 11.

90	2	½d. dull blue-green (R.)	25	1·00
		a. Yellowish green (1900)	25	1·25
91		1d. chestnut (B.)	60	1·75
92		2d. dull orange (R.)	40	1·75
		a. *Orange-yellow* (1900)	40	2·50
93		4d. deep dull blue (R.)	45	1·50
94	8	5d. dull vermilion (B.)	90	4·50
		a. *Red* (1900)	90	4·50
95	2	6d. brown-lake (B.)	1·10	3·50
96		1s. rose-carmine (B.)	1·50	7·00
97		2s. 6d. reddish purple (R.)	4·75	16·00

The Samoan group of islands was partitioned on 1 March 1900: Western Samoa (Upolu, Savaii, Apolima and Manono) to Germany and Eastern Samoa (Tutuila, the Manu'a Is and Rose Is) to the United States.

The Samoan Kingdom post office run by John Davis was suspended in March 1900.

NEW ZEALAND OCCUPATION OF WESTERN SAMOA

The German Islands of Samoa surrendered to the New Zealand Expeditionary Force on 30 August 1914 and were administered by New Zealand until 1962.

G.R.I.
(13)

G.R.I.
(13)

1 d.

1 Shillings.
(14)

SETTINGS. Nos. 101/9 were surcharged by a vertical setting of ten, repeated ten times across the sheet. Nos. 110/14 were from a horizontal setting of four repeated five times in the sheet.

Nos. 101b, 102a and 104a occurred on position 6. The error was corrected during the printing of No. 102.

Nos. 101c, 102c, 104d and 105b are from position 10.

Nos. 101d, 102e and 104b are from position 1.

No. 108b is from position 9.

(Surch by Samoanische Zeitung, Apia)

1914 (3 Sept).　*German Colonial issue* (*ship*) (*no wmk*) *inscr* "SAMOA" *surch as T* **13** *or* **14** (*mark values*).

101		½d. on 3 pf. brown	9·50	8·50
		a. Surch double	£500	£300
		b. No fraction bar	40·00	30·00
		c. Comma after "l"	£600	£500
		d. "1" to left of "2" in "½"	35·00	23·00
102		½d. on 5 pf. green	30·00	10·00
		a. No fraction bar	70·00	40·00
		c. Comma after "l"	£350	£170
		d. Surch double	£450	£300
		e. "1" to left of "2" in "½"	45·00	40·00
103		1d. on 10 pf. carmine	95·00	40·00
		a. Surch double	£350	£300
104		2½d. on 20 pf. ultramarine	30·00	10·00
		a. No fraction bar	60·00	38·00
		b. "1" to left of "2" in "½"	60·00	40·00
		c. Surch inverted	£550	£500
		d. Comma after "l"	£450	£325
		e. Surch double	£550	£500
105		3d. on 25 pf. black and red/*yellow*	50·00	35·00
		a. Surch double	£400	£250
		b. Comma after "l"	£3500	£750
106		4d. on 30 pf. black and orange/*buff*	95·00	60·00
107		5d. on 40 pf. black and carmine	£110	70·00
108		6d. on 50 pf. black and purple/*buff*	55·00	35·00
		a. Surch double	£450	£500
		b. Inverted "9" for "6"	£120	£100
109		9d. on 80 pf. black and carmine/*rose*	£190	95·00
110		"1 shillings" on 1 m. carmine	£3000	£2750
111		"1 shilling" on 1 m. carmine	£9500	£7000
112		2s. on 2 m. blue	£3000	£2750
113		3s. on 3 m. violet-black	£1400	£1200
		a. Surch double	£6000	£6000
114		5s. on 5 m. carmine and black	£1000	£950
		a. Surch double	£9500	£10000

No. 108b is distinguishable from 108, as the "d" and the "9" are not in a line, and the upper loop of the "9" turns downwards to the left.

UNAUTHORISED SURCHARGES. Examples of the 2d. on 20 pf., 3d. on 30 pf., 3d. on 40 pf., 4d. on 40 pf., 6d. on 80 pf., 2s. on 3 m. and 2s. on Marshall Islands 2 m., together with a number of errors not listed above, were produced by the printer and supplied by local collectors. These were not authorised by the New Zealand Military Administration.

SAMOA.
(15)

1914 (29 Sept).　*Stamps of New Zealand, T* **50**, **51**, **52** *and* **27**, *optd as T* **15**, *but opt only* **14** *mm long on all except* 2½d. *Wmk* "N Z" *and Star, W* **43** *of New Zealand.*

115		½d. yellow-green (R.) (*p* 14 × 15)	25	30
116		1d. carmine (B.) (*p* 14 × 15)	25	10
117		2d. mauve (R.) (*p* 14 × 14½)	60	95
118		2½d. deep blue (R.) (*p* 14)	1·50	1·75
119		6d. carmine (B.) (*p* 14 × 14½)	1·50	1·75
		a. Perf 14 × 13½	15·00	17·00
		b. Vert pair. Nos. 119/19a	35·00	50·00
120		6d. pale carmine (B.) (*p* 14 × 14½)	10·00	9·50
121		1s. vermilion (B.) (*p* 14 × 14½)	3·50	9·00

1914–24.　*Postal Fiscal stamps as Type F* **4** *of New Zealand optd with T* **15**. *W* **43** *of New Zealand* (*sideways*). *Chalk-surfaced "De La Rue" paper.*

(a) P 14 (Nov 1914–17)

122		2s. blue (R.) (9.17)	80·00	£100
123		2s. 6d. grey-brown (B.) (9.17)	4·50	8·50
124		5s. yellow-green (R.)	9·00	12·00
125		10s. maroon (B.)	20·00	28·00
126		£1 rose-carmine (B.)	60·00	80·00

(b) P 14½ × 14, comb (1917–24)

127	2s. deep blue (R.) (3.18)	4·00	5·50
128	2s. 6d. grey-brown (B.) (10.24)	90·00	90·00
129	3s. purple (R.) (6.23)	9·00	22·00
130	5s. yellow-green (R.) (9.17)	13·00	15·00
131	10s. maroon (B.) (3.18)	40·00	40·00
132	£1 rose-carmine (B.) (3.18)	60·00	70·00

We no longer list the £2 value as it is doubtful if this was used for postal purposes.

See also Nos. 165/6d.

1916–19. *King George V stamps of New Zealand optd as* T **15**, *but 14 mm long.* (a) T **61**. *Typo. P 14 × 15.*

134	½d. yellow-green (R.)	20	25
135	1½d. slate (R.) (1917)	25	25
136	1½d. orange-brown (R.) (1919)	15	40
137	2d. yellow (B.) (14.2.18)	40	15
138	3d. chocolate (B.) (1919)	75	9·00

*(b) T **60**. Recess. P 14 × 14½, etc.*

139	2½d. blue (R.)	65	60
	a. Perf 14 × 13½	35	35
	b. Vert pair. Nos. 139/9a	10·00	14·00
140	3d. chocolate (B.) (1917)	35	90
	a. Perf 14 × 13½	45	1·60
	b. Vert pair. Nos. 140/40a	10·00	15·00
141	6d. carmine (B.) (5.5.17)	1·25	90
	a. Perf 14 × 13½	1·50	3·25
	b. Vert pair. Nos. 141/1a	11·00	16·00
142	1s. vermilion (B.)	3·50	9·00
	a. Perf 14 × 13½	1·25	1·25
	b. Vert pair. Nos. 142/2a	14·00	25·00
	Set of 9	4·50	12·00

LEAGUE OF NATIONS MANDATE

Administered by New Zealand.

1920 (July). *Victory. Nos. 453/8 of New Zealand, optd as* T **15**, *but 14 mm long.*

143	½d. green (R.)	1·25	1·75
144	1d. carmine (B.)	1·25	85
145	1½d. brown-orange (R.)	1·25	3·50
146	3d. chocolate (B.)	3·00	6·50
147	6d. violet (R.)	4·00	6·50
148	1s. orange-red (B.)	11·00	11·00
	Set of 6	20·00	27·00

SILVER JUBILEE OF KING GEORGE V 1910 - 1935.

16 Native Hut   (17)

(Eng B.W. Recess-printed at Wellington, N.Z.)

1921 (23 Dec). W **43** *of New Zealand.* (a) P 14 × 14½.

149	16	½d. green	40	2·50
150		1d. lake	35	20
151		1½d. chestnut	40	3·75
152		2d. yellow	40	1·90
		Set of 4	1·40	7·50

(b) P 14 × 13½

153	16	½d. green	65	1·75
154		1d. lake	70	20
155		1½d. chestnut	6·00	7·50
156		2d. yellow	5·50	35
157		2½d. grey-blue	70	3·00
158		3d. sepia	75	3·00
159		4d. violet	80	3·00
160		5d. light blue	75	5·00
161		6d. bright carmine	80	3·50
162		8d. red-brown	1·25	9·00
163		9d. olive-green	1·25	9·00
164		1s. vermilion	1·25	11·00
		Set of 12	18·00	50·00

1925–28. *As Nos. 127/32, but thick, opaque, white chalk-surfaced Cowan paper.*

165	2s. blue (R.) (12.25)	80·00	85·00
166	2s. 6d. deep grey-brown (B.) (10.28)	60·00	80·00
166a	3s. mauve (R.) (9.25)	45·00	50·00
166b	5s. yellow-green (R.) (11.26)	12·00	20·00
	ba. Opt at top of stamp	£650	
166c	10s. brown-red (B.) (12.25)	45·00	48·00
166d	£1 rose-pink (B.) (11.26)	50·00	75·00
	Set of 6	£250	£300

1926–27. T **72** *of New Zealand, optd with* T **15**, *in red.*

(a) Jones paper

167	2s. deep blue (11.26)	4·50	12·00
168	3s. mauve (10.26)	7·00	22·00

(b) Cowan paper

169	2s. light blue (10.11.27)	5·00	26·00
170	3s. pale mauve (10.11.27)	42·00	65·00

1932 (Aug). *Postal Fiscal stamps as Type* F **6** *of New Zealand optd with* T **15**. W **43** *of New Zealand. Thick, opaque, white chalk-surfaced Cowan paper. P 14.*

171	2s. 6d. deep brown (B.)	13·00	25·00
172	5s. green (R.)	20·00	32·00
173	10s. carmine-lake (b.)	45·00	60·00
174	£1 pink (B.)	60·00	75·00
175	£2 bright purple (R.)	£550	
176	£5 indigo-blue (R.)	£1600	

The £2 and £5 values were primarily for fiscal use.

1935 (7 May). *Silver Jubilee. Optd with* T **17**. P 14 × 13½.

177	16	1d. lake	30	30
		a. Perf 14 × 14½	75·00	£100
178		2½d. grey-blue	60	65
179		6d. bright carmine	1·75	2·50
		Set of 3	2·40	3·00
		First Day Cover		12·00

18 Samoan Girl    19 Apia

21 Chief and Wife    25 Lake Lanuto'o

(Recess D.L.R.)

1935 (7 Aug). T **18/19, 21, 25** *and similar designs.* W **43** *of New Zealand ("N Z" and Star).* (a) P 14 × 13½, (b) 13½ × 14 *or* (c) P 14.

180	½d. green (a)		10	35
181	1d. black and carmine (b)		10	10
182	2d. black and orange (c)		1·00	75
	Wi. Wmk inverted			
	a. Perf 13½ × 14		2·75	3·00
183	2½d. black and blue (a)		10	10
184	4d. slate and sepia (b)		40	15
185	6d. bright magenta (c)		30	10
186	1s. violet and brown (b)		25	10
187	2s. green and purple-brown (a)		50	50
188	3s. blue and brown-orange (a)		1·75	3·50
	Set of 9		4·00	5·00

Designs: *Horiz*—2d. River scene; 4d. Canoe and house; 6d. R. L. Stevenson's home "Vailima"; 1s. Stevenson's Tomb. *Vert (as* T **25**)—3s. Falefa Falls.

See also Nos. 200/3.

WESTERN SAMOA.

(27)

1935–42. *Postal Fiscal stamps as Type* F **6** *of New Zealand optd with* T **27**. *W* **43** *of New Zealand.* P 14.

(a) Thick, opaque chalk-surfaced Cowan paper (7.8.35)

189	2s. 6d. deep brown (B.)	6·00	13·00
190	5s. green (B.)	10·00	15·00
191	10s. carmine-lake (B.)	32·00	45·00
192	£1 pink (B.)	60·00	85·00
193	£2 bright purple (R.)	£170	£225
194	£5 indigo-blue (R.)	£450	£475

(b) Thin, hard chalk-surfaced Wiggins, Teape paper (1941–42)

194a	5s. green (B.) (6.42)	65·00	60·00
194b	10s. pale carmine-lake (B.) (6.41)	90·00	90·00
194c	£2 bright purple (R.) (2.42)	£400	£450
194d	£5 indigo-blue (R.) (2.42)	£600	£650

The £2 and £5 values were primarily for fiscal use.
See also Nos. 207/14.

PRICES
George VI issues (1937–1952)

First column = Unmounted Mint
Second column = Mounted Mint
Third column = Used

---

28 Coastal Scene   **31** Robert Louis
                                     Stevenson

(Des J. Berry (1d. and 1½d.). L. C. Mitchell (2½d. and 7d.). Recess B.W.)

1939 (29 Aug). *25th Anniv of New Zealand Control.* T **28**, **31** *and similar horiz designs.* W **98** *of New Zealand.* P 13½ × 14 *or* 14 × 13½ (7d.).

195	1d. olive-green and scarlet	30	15	10
196	1½d. light blue and red-brown	35	15	30
197	2½d. red-brown and blue	90	40	65
198	7d. violet and slate-green	2·50	1·00	1·25
	Set of 4	3·75	1·50	2·00
	First Day Cover			4·50

Designs:—1½d. Western Samoa; 2½d. Samoan dancing party.

32 Samoan Chief   **33** Apia Post Office

(Recess B.W.)

1940 (2 Sept). *W* **98** *of New Zealand (Mult "N Z" and Star).* P 14 × 13½.

199	**32** 3d. on 1½d. brown	5	5	5

T **32** was not issued without surcharge.

(T **33**. Des L. C. Mitchell. Recess B.W.)

1944–49. *As Nos. 180, 182/3 and* T **33**. *W* **98** *of New Zealand (Mult "N Z" and Star) (sideways on* 2½d.). P 14 *or* 13½ × 14 (5d.).

200	½d. green	25	15	3·00
202	2d. black and orange	1·25	60	3·75
203	2½d. black and blue (1948)	2·75	1·25	9·00
205	5d. sepia and blue (8.6.49)	20	10	50
	Set of 4	4·00	1·90	15·00

1945–48. *Postal Fiscal stamps as Type* F **6** *of New Zealand optd with* T **27**. *W* **98** *of New Zealand. Thin hard, chalk-surfaced Wiggins Teape paper.* P 14.

207	2s. 6d. deep brown (B.) (6.45)	2·00	1·00	5·50
	Wi. Wmk inverted	2·50	1·25	6·00
208	5s. green (B.) (5.45)	5·00	2·50	7·50
	Wi. Wmk inverted	6·50	3·25	8·50
209	10s. carmine-lake (B.) (4..46)	16·00	8·00	17·00
	Wi. Wmk inverted	20·00	10·00	22·00
210	£1 pink (B.) (6.48)	70·00	40·00	£140
	Wi. Wmk inverted			
211	30s. brown (8.48)	£140	80·00	£180
	Wi. Wmk inverted	£160	80·00	£200
212	£2 bright purple (R.) (11.47)	£140	80·00	£180
	Wi. Wmk inverted	£160	80·00	£200
213	£3 green (8.48)	£170	95·00	£250
	Wi. Wmk inverted	£190	95·00	£275
214	£5 indigo-blue (R.) (1946)	£250	150	£325
	Wi. Wmk inverted	£325	£160	£425
	Set of 4 (Nos. 207/10)	85·00	45·00	£140

The £2 to £5 values were mainly used for fiscal purposes.
See also Nos. 232/5.

WESTERN SAMOA

(34)

1946 (1 June). *Peace Issue. Nos. 668, 670 and 674/5 of New Zealand optd with* T **34** *(reading up and down at sides on* 2d.).

215	1d. green	10	5	5
216	2d. purple (B.)	10	5	5
217	6d. chocolate and vermilion	10	5	5
218	8d. black and carmine (B.)	10	5	10
	Set of 4	35	15	20
	First Day Cover			60

UNITED NATIONS TRUST TERRITORY

Administered by New Zealand.

PRICES
Elizabeth II issues (from 1953)

First column = Unmounted Mint
Second column = Used

---

35 Making Siapo Cloth   **42** Thatching a Native Hut

43 Preparing Copra   **44** Samoan
                                     Chieftainess

(Recess B.W.)

1952 (10 Mar). T **35**, **42/4** *and similar designs.* W **98** *of New Zealand (sideways on* 1s. *and* 3s.). P 13 (½d., 2d., 5d. *and* 1s.) *or* 13½ (others).

219	½d. claret and orange-brown	5	20
220	1d. olive-green and green	5	5

221 2d. carmine-red   5   5
222 3d. pale ultramarine and indigo   30   5
223 5d. brown and deep green ....   2·00   70
224 6d. pale ultramarine and rose-magenta   30   5
225 8d. carmine   25   30
226 1s. sepia and blue   15   5
227 2s. yellow-brown ....   1·40   60
228 3s. chocolate and brown-olive ....   3·00   1·75
       Set of 10 ....   6·50   3·50
Designs: *Horiz (as T 43)*—1d. Native houses and flags; 3d. Malifa Falls
(wrongly inscribed "Aleisa Falls"); 6d. Bonito fishing canoe; 8d. Cacao
harvesting. *Vert (as T 35)*—2d. Seal of Samoa; 5d. Tooth-billed Pigeon.

1953 (25 May). *Coronation. Designs as Nos. 715 and 717 of New
Zealand, but inscr "WESTERN SAMOA".*
229 2d. brown (as No. 715)   75   15
230 6d. slate-grey (as No. 717) ....   1·00   35
       Set of 2 ....   1·75   50
       First Day Cover ....   2·50

WESTERN

SAMOA

(45)

1955 (14 Nov). *Postal Fiscal stamps as Type F 6 of New Zealand optd
with T 45. W 98 of New Zealand. Chalk-surfaced Wiggins, Teape paper.
P 14.*
232 5s. green (B.) ....   13·00   15·00
233 10s. carmine-lake (B.) ....   16·00   22·00
234 £1 pink (B.) ....   27·00   32·00
235 £2 bright purple (R.) ....   70·00   £130
       Set of 4 ....   £110   £170
The £2 value was mainly used for fiscal purposes.

46 Native Houses and Flags   47 Seal of Samoa

(Recess B.W.)

1958 (21 Mar). *Inauguration of Samoan Parliament. T 46/7 and similar
horiz design. W 98 of New Zealand (sideways). P 13½ × 13 (6d.) or 13½
(others).*
236 4d. cerise   5   5
237 6d. deep reddish violet   10   5
238 1s. deep ultramarine   10   10
       Set of 3   20   15
       First Day Cover   60
Design:—1s. Map of Samoa, and the Mace.

Western Samoa became independent on 1 January 1962.

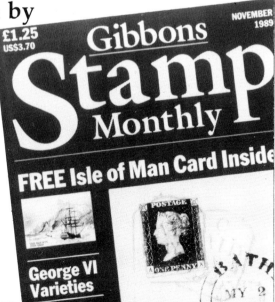

Notes

STANLEY
GIBBONS
FOR
ALBUMS
CATALOGUES
HANDBOOKS
ACCESSORIES

The following pages give details
of selected items from the
Stanley Gibbons Publications range

A complete listing with current prices
is available from your local stockist
or direct from

Stanley Gibbons Publications Limited
Unit 5 Parkside,
Christchurch Road,
Ringwood,
Hampshire BH24 3SH.
or telephone 0425 472363

Keep this Catalogue up to date month by month with

COVER ALBUMS

With cover collecting growing in popularity all the time we are proud to offer a comprehensive range of albums to meet the needs of first day cover collector and postal historian alike. All leaves have black card inserts to set off your covers to best advantage.

1. THE NEW PIONEER COVER ALBUM

A fully padded PVC Binder in a choice of black, green or red. Holds up to 40 covers in a high capacity, low priced album, ideal for the beginner.

2. THE PROTECTOR COVER ALBUM

The luxury padded binder comes in deep blue, brown or maroon with gold blocking on the spine and a secure 4-ring arch mechanism. The album contains 19 double and 1 single-pocket leaves, the former being specifically designed to house the current standard British Post Office first day covers. The leaves are made from 'Polyprotec' a material which does not crease or tear easily, will not degrade and offers considerable protection against heat and ultra violet light. Holds up to 78 covers.

3. THE MALVERN COVER ALBUM

Another great value album suitable for collectors at all levels. The 4-ring arch fitting binder contains 19 double-pocket leaves, 1 single-pocket leaves and holds up to 78 covers in all. Available in blue, green or red.

4. THE NEW CLASSIC COVER ALBUM

A compact de-luxe album with 20 crystal clear leaves offering full protection for up to 40 covers and two clear fly leaves to hold an index of notes. Available in black, red or blue and supplied in a protective slip box.

5. THE SG MAJOR COVER ALBUM

(Not illustrated)
A luxury album recommended for that really special collection. The fully padded, leather grained PVC binder has peg fittings and comes with 13 crystal clear leaves (12 double-pocket and 1 single pocket) and two clear fly leaves in which to insert notes. Available in dark red or deep blue – the top of the range.

6. THE UNIVERSAL COVER ALBUM

The cover album which allows stamps, booklets and presentation packs to be housed all together – see page 166 for details.

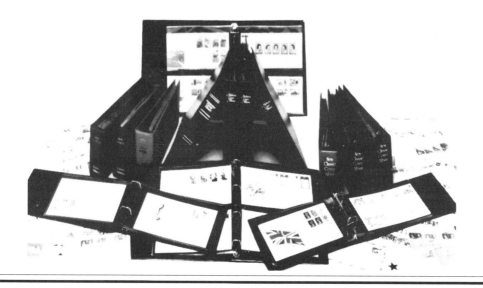

BLANK SPRINGBACK ALBUMS

These fine albums give the more advanced collector the freedom and flexibility he needs to arrange his collection exactly as he wants it.

Leaves are finely printed with a feint quadrille and most have side and centre markings to aid arrangement.

Albums and binders are now supplied with a sheet of self-adhesive, gold-blocked title panels, a selection of country titles and a run of volume numbers; allowing them to be clearly identifiable on the shelf or left blank if you prefer.

1. Tower (Item 0331) A choice of red, green, or black binder with 100 leaves of white cartridge 11⅛″ × 9⅞″. Boxed.

2. Senator Medium (Item 0384) A very popular 'first blank leaved album for many years now. 50 leaves 10⅜″ × 8¾″, a choice of three binder colours; black, green or red.

3. Senator Standard (Item 0386) As the Senator Medium but with 100 larger sized leaves (11⅛″ × 9⅞″). One of our best selling albums!

4. Simplex Medium (Item 3810) Fifty leaves of high quality cream paper with a subtle decorative border (10⅜″ × 8¾″). Binder choice of green or red.

5. Simplex Standard (Item 3812) 100 larger sized leaves (11⅛″ × 9⅞″), otherwise the same style as the Simplex Medium. Boxed. Popular with generations of stamp collectors!

6. Utile (Item 3821) 25 white cartridge special double linen-hinged transparent faced leaves (11⅛″ × 9⅞″) designed to lie flat when album is opened. Attractive binder in choice of green or red.

Transparent Interleaving Fine quality glazed transparent paper in packs of 100 sheets for Tower, Senator, Simplex or similar types of loose-leaf springback albums.

Item 3310 Standard size 11″ × 9⅝″.
Item 3311 Medium size 10″ × 8⅛″.

For further details visit your favourite stamp shop or write to:
**Stanley Gibbons Publications Ltd.,
5 Parkside, Christchurch Road,
Ringwood, Hampshire BH24 3SH
Telephone 0425 472363**

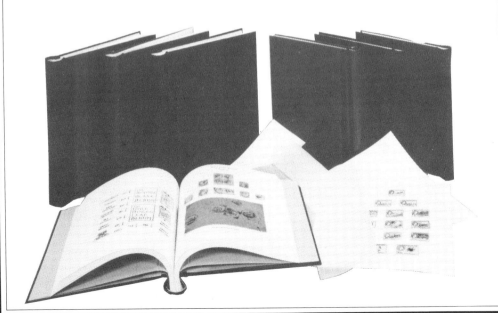

PEG-FITTING
BLANK LOOSE-LEAF ALBUMS

Stanley Gibbons blank albums give you the freedom and flexibility you need to arrange your collection exactly as you want it.

All those items which can add real interest to a collection: shades, inverted watermarks, gum variations, cylinder blocks, unusual cancellations, etc. can be easily accommodated and there is no need to be frustrated by empty spaces perpetually reminding you of the stamps you do not have.

Peg-fitting albums represent the very peak of Stanley Gibbons range – albums which have stood the test of time from the Devon, now in its 30th year of production to the Philatelic which has been housing the great collections of the world for over a century!

The Devon
A strong elegant, large-capacity binder containing 100 fine quality cartridge leaves (10⅜ × 9¾ in.). Choice of maroon, green, black or blue. Ideal for collections where that extra capacity is required. Transparent interleaving available, boxed.

The Exeter
A quality binder in a choice of red, blue or green containing 40 leaves (10¼ × 9¼ in.) of fine white cartridge. All leaves are double linen-hinged with transparent facing so that leaves lie flat when the album is opened and damaging friction is minimised.

An illustrated colour brochure giving prices of these and all other Stanley Gibbons Publications Products is available by post from

**Stanley Gibbons Publications Ltd.,
5 Parkside, Christchurch Road,
Ringwood, Hampshire BH24 3SH.
Telephone 0425 472363.**

The Plymouth
Maroon, black, green or blue, a connoisseur's album in a strong matching slip-case. Supplied with 40 double linen-hinged leaves (10⅛ × 9¾ in.) with glassine facing for additional protection.

The Philatelic
The largest album in the Stanley Gibbons range, it not only accommodates more stamps per page than other albums but also allows sheets, blocks, etc., to be arranged and mounted on its 12⅞ × 10¼ in. leaves. Bound in handsome deep green cloth with leather corners and spine, supplied with 80 double linen-hinged, transparent faced leaves and presented in a sturdy deep green slip-case.

The Oriel
Supreme among luxury blank albums, the Oriel will enhance the very finest collection. Half bound in rich red leather with gold tooling, each album contains 50 superior gilt-edged double linen-hinged leaves (10⅜ × 9⅝ in.) with transparent facings and is supplied in a luxury matching slip-case.

The most prestigious home for your stamps.

Additional binders and leaves are available for all Stanley Gibbons peg-fitting albums.

STOCKBOOKS

We are pleased to announce that Stanley Gibbons are now offering a selected range of Lighthouse stockbooks in addition to the popular S.G. branded junior style. Fastbound with stout linen-hinged leaves, all come with glassine interleaving to ensure complete protection for your stamps and will give years of use.

1. Junior Stockbooks

With a bright full-colour, stamp design cover these stockbooks have white leaves with glassine strips and interleaving – ideal for the younger collector.

	Size (ins)	No. of Pages	No. of Strips
Item 2625	7½ × 5¼	8	48
Item 2659	8½ × 6⅝	8	48
Item 2650	11 × 8¾	8	72

2. Lighthouse Stockbooks

A variety of bright single colour covers with gold blocking on the front and spine.

	Size (ins)	No. of Pages	No. of Strips
Item 2679	6¼ × 4⅝	16	64
Item 2651	9 × 7	16	96
Item 2631	9 × 7	32	192

For further details visit your favourite stamp shop or write to:

**Stanley Gibbons Publications Ltd.,
5 Parkside, Christchurch Road,
Ringwood, Hampshire BH24 3SH
Telephone 0425 472363**

The larger page size stockbooks feature a luxury leather look binding and have double glassine interleaving for even greater protection. NOTE the new 48-page stockbook (item 2662) has double linen hinged 'lay flat' leaves.

	Size (ins)	No. of Pages	No. of Strips
Item 2652	12 × 9	16	144
Item 2653	12 × 9	32	288
Item 2662	12 × 9	48	432

3. Two stylish stockbooks with binding as above but with black leaves and crystal clear acetate strips. Double glassine interleaving.

Item 2664	12 × 9	16	144
Item 2665	12 × 9	32	288

4. The 'King Size' member of the S.G. Stockbook range! Cover Specifications as above with 64 double linen-hinged leaves to ensure that the book lies absolutely flat when open. White leaves with glassine strips and double interleaving. Definitely the top of the range and a luxury stockbook any collector would be proud to own.

Item 2678	12 × 9	64	576

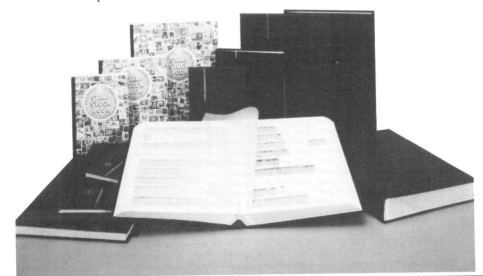

ACCESSORIES

From Stamp Hinges to Ultra Violet Lamps; from Tweezers and Magnifiers to Colour Keys and Watermark Detectors—Stanley Gibbons accessories are the answer to every collector's requirements.

The range has been completely revised with an improved selection of tweezers and the addition of a drying book and photo mounts for cover and postcard collectors.

The magnifiers have been completely revised to allow a wider variety of choice with each item having been carefully selected for its quality and value for money.

Current details of our superb range are available direct from Stanley Gibbons or your favourite supplier.

**Stanley Gibbons Publications Ltd.,
5 Parkside, Christchurch Road,
Ringwood, Hampshire BH24 3SH**

Telephone 0425 472363

IMPORTANT MESSAGE TO NEW ZEALAND COLLECTORS!

You know how important it is to have the very latest edition of the Stanley Gibbons New Zealand Concise Catalogue with its listings of all the new issues, up to date information on earlier stamps and of course prices accurately set by experts with their finger on the pulse of the current international stamp market.

If you would like us to notify you of the next edition all you have to do is complete the form below and post it to:

**The Advance Information Service,
Stanley Gibbons Publications Ltd.,
5 Parkside, Christchurch Road,
Ringwood, Hampshire BH24 3SH.**

For similar information on other catalogues in the Stanley Gibbons range, please indicate title of interest on the form.

ADVANCE INFORMATION WITHOUT OBLIGATION!

To: **The Advance Information Service,
Stanley Gibbons Publications Ltd.,
5 Parkside, Christchurch Road,
Ringwood, Hampshire BH24 3SH.**

Please notify me of publication dates of new editions

of . . . .

Name: . . . .

Address: . . . .

. . . .

. . . .